MAP
Showing Route of Marches of the Army of
GENERAL W.T. SHERMAN
From SAVANNAH, GA. to RALEIGH, N.C.
JANUARY - APRIL, 1865
Statute Miles

15th Army Corps } Right Wing
17 " " }
14 " " } Left Wing
20 " " }
Cavalry
(At Goldsboro the 10th and 23rd Corps
Joined Sherman)
From there, entire Army Indicated as:

Sherman's
March
Through
the
Carolinas

JOHN G. BARRETT

Sherman's March Through the Carolinas

The University of North Carolina Press
CHAPEL HILL – 1956

To my wife, LUTE and
my mother, "Miss Ruby"

PREFACE

GENERAL WILLIAM TECUMSEH SHERMAN always maintained that the Carolinas campaign of 1865 was his greatest military achievement. Writing after the war he said: "No one ever has and may not agree with me as to the very great importance of the march north from Savannah. The march to the sea seems to have captured everybody, whereas it was child's play compared with the other." The Georgia campaign, as Sherman suspected, has through the years caught the interest of both the public and the historian. The story of this march has been often and well told. Little has been written of Sherman's important operations in North and South Carolina. This omission has left incomplete the story of the end of the war on the Eastern front. The author has attempted both to correct the omission and to assess the validity of Sherman's personal judgment.

This book was prepared under the immediate direction of Professor Fletcher M. Green, head of the history department of the University of North Carolina. Without his advice, encouragement, and understanding this volume would not have been possible.

Sincere thanks are also due to Professors Hugh T. Lefler and James W. Patton of the University of North Carolina, and Richard E. Welch, Jr. of the Virginia Military Institute. These three historians read the manuscript in its entirety and made invaluable criticisms.

In addition I am indebted to The University of North Carolina Press, to Mrs. John B. Graham, my sister, and to Mrs. Marion Smith of Chapel Hill, North Carolina, whose careful examination of the manuscript prevented many literary errors.

Special thanks go to Mr. Jay Luvaas of Duke University who made available to me much valuable material on the battle of Bentonville.

The staffs of the Southern Historical Collection of the University of North Carolina, the Manuscript Division of Duke University Library, the North Carolina Department of Archives and History, the South Caroliniana Collection of the University of South Carolina, the Manuscript Division of the Library of Congress, and the Library of the Virginia Military Institute have all been most helpful.

Finally and especially I wish to express appreciation to my wife, Lute Buie Barrett, who not only listened and encouraged but spent many long and tiring hours at a typewriter.

Lexington, Virginia
May 1, 1956

CONTENTS

THE FOLLOWING ABBREVIATIONS HAVE BEEN USED IN THE FOOTNOTES

AHR—American Historical Review

B and L—Battles and Leaders of the Civil War

Hist. Mag.—The Historical Magazine and Notes and Queries concerning the Antiques, History and Biography of America

JSH—Journal of Southern History

L.C.—Library of Congress

M.R.—The Medical and Surgical History of the War of Rebellion, 1861-1865

M.V.H.R.—Mississippi Valley Historical Review

Mag. of Amer. Hist.—Magazine of American History, with Notes and Queries

Mass. Mil. Papers—Papers Read Before the Military Historical Society of Massachusetts

Mil. Order of the Loyal Legion, Commandery—War Papers Read Before the Commandery of the State of   , Military Order of the Loyal Legion of the United States

N.R.—Official Records of the Union and Confederate Navies in the War of Rebellion

NCC—North Carolina Collection

NCHR—North Carolina Historical Review

OR—The War of Rebellion: A Compilation of the Official Records of the Union and Confederate Armies

VQR—The Virginia Quarterly Review

SCL—South Caroliniana Library

SHC—Southern Historical Collection

Sherman's
March
Through
the
Carolinas

CHAPTER I

Tent Pins Under A Magnolia

WILLIAM TECUMSEH SHERMAN, third son and sixth child of Charles and Mary Sherman, was born February 8, 1820, in Lancaster, Ohio. The sudden death of Judge Charles Sherman of the state supreme court in 1829 left his wife with a meager income and eleven children to rear. There was no other recourse for her but to distribute some of the children among relatives, neighbors, and friends. Hence, young "Cump," as he had been nicknamed by his brothers and sisters who could not pronounce Tecumseh, went to live in the home of his father's close friend and neighbor, Thomas Ewing. The wealthy Ewing was more than glad to welcome the redheaded youngster into his family. He owed much to "Cump's" father, who had helped him get a start as a frontier lawyer.

Sherman, in turn, became indebted to his foster father for his early education and appointment to the United States Military Academy in 1836. West Point, aristocratic in manner, ideals, and religion, was an institution in which Southern ideals primarily held sway. The youth of the South, with their polished manners and easy confidence, had enrolled in proportionately larger numbers than the young men of the North and West. Thus Sherman in his sixteenth year came under the influence of an army which had from the first been largely under Southern influence.[1]

"Cump" Sherman's record at West Point was not exceptional. In later years he wrote: "I was not considered a good soldier. I was not a Sunday-school cadet. I ranked 124 in the whole student body for good behavior. My average demerits, per annum, were about 150, which reduced my final class standing from Number 4 to Number 6."[2] He was never one to place much emphasis on tidiness of dress. Unshined shoes,

1. Lewis, *Sherman*, pp. 54-55.
2. *Ibid.*, p. 56.

tarnished buttons, and soiled clothing accounted for many demerits. His yearly average of 150 black marks was perilously close to the 200 mark which meant dismissal from the Academy.

At West Point Sherman's closest friends were Stewart Van Vliet of Vermont and George Henry Thomas of Virginia. The latter he called "his best friend . . . a high-toned, brave, and peculiar Virginia gentleman."[3] The class rolls carried the names of many Southerners who were to win fame on the field of battle. Braxton Bragg, Pierre Gustave Toutant Beauregard, and Jubal Early fought gallantly for the South, whereas Edward Otho Cresap Ord, Edward Richard Sprigg Canby, and Don Carlos Buell, along with Thomas, cast their lot with the North.

After graduation in 1840 Lieutenant Sherman's first assignment was with the Third Artillery at Fort Pierce, Florida. This duty lasted eighteen months, after whch he was transferred to Fort Moultrie on Sullivans Island in Charleston harbor. Here he remained for four years. During this period Sherman traveled extensively through the South. He became acquainted with the people and the problems of the region. What he saw appealed to him. The young officer not only learned about the South but learned to like it. For the first time he came in direct contact with slavery, an institution he was soon to accept almost without reservation.

While stationed in Florida and South Carolina, Sherman actively participated in and enjoyed social life. In the South, where army life had a strong appeal, "the bright button was a passport at all times to the houses of the best."[4] On the other hand, the sporadic war waged against the Seminole Indians of Florida was boring to the young Lieutenant for he had the opportunity to fire only a few shots at the wily adversary. But the gay social life at St. Augustine more than compensated for the long hours of garrison duty.

Although he had a sweetheart back in Lancaster, Sherman's eyes were not closed to the charm of Southern womanhood. The dark Spanish beauty of the women of St. Augustine completely captivated him.[5] Never before had he witnessed anything like the ease and grace with which these ladies danced. With them it was "dancing, dancing, and nothing but dancing. . . ." This nimbleness of foot "together with the easy and

3. *Ibid.*, p. 57.
4. Howe, *Home Letters of Sherman*, p. 21.
5. *Ibid.*, p. 19.

cordial hospitality" extended to all officers won a husband for many a Latin beauty.[6] Young "Cump," naïve in the ways of love, wrote Ellen Ewing, his fiancée as well as his foster sister, that the Spanish girls had already enticed twenty officers into matrimony.[7] This brought an immediate reply from her suggesting he leave the army and go into religious work. But the field of religion was anything but appealing to the young officer. He believed in the main doctrines of Christianity, but he followed no particular creed. Satisfied with the army and completely happy in his Southern environment, Sherman was soon again extolling to Ellen the many virtues of the women of the South. From Mobile, Alabama, where he was on temporary duty in April, 1842, he wrote that it would take a volume to record the kindness, beauty, and accomplishments of the ladies of that city.[8]

Social life was to continue almost unabated for the young officer for in June, 1842, he was transferred to Fort Moultrie. Here he was at the social capital of the South. In Charleston Sherman had the acquaintance of all the prominent families. He was constantly in attendance at various social functions. These entertainments ranged from the "highly aristocratic and fashionable, with sword and epaulettes" to "horse racing, picnicing, boating, fishing, swimming, and God knows what not." To escape the boredom of camp life and get relief from these social activities, Sherman often slipped off to the plantation of some rich planter to hunt or just "ramble among the green and noble live oakes."[9]

His Southern acquaintances extended far beyond the Charleston area. In April, 1845, Sherman enjoyed the hospitality of Wilmington, North Carolina, where he attended the wedding of Governor Edward Bishop Dudley's daughter. Three days of dinner parties and balls kept the popular Lieutenant constantly on the go.[10] A short tour of duty at Augusta, Georgia, was highlighted by numerous parties given by the wealthy of that city. All the homes on the "Sand Hill," as the fashionable section of the city was called, were open to the officers of the garrison.[11]

6. Thorndike, *Sherman Letters,* p. 22.

7. Howe, *Home Letters of Sherman,* p. 18.

8. *Ibid.,* pp. 19-21.

9. Thorndike, *Sherman Letters,* pp. 23, 29; J. H. Cornish Diary, June 30, 1846, SHC, U.N.C.

10. Thorndike, *Sherman Letters,* p. 27.

11. Sherman to G. E. Leighton, Mar. 23, 1888, Sherman Papers, MS Div., Duke Univ. Lib.

With the outbreak of the Mexican War Sherman was transferred to California. He carried across the continent happy memories of his six years in the South. Left behind were many fast Southern friends. Even in California he was destined to be closely associated with numerous officers of Southern birth. After four years of service on the west coast Sherman received orders to go to Missouri. At Jefferson Barracks, outside of St. Louis, he reported for duty to his friend and fellow West Pointer, Captain Braxton Bragg. In the meantime Sherman had married Ellen Ewing, who was soon to join him at his new post. This duty in St. Louis lasted until the fall of 1852 at which time Sherman was moved to New Orleans to continue his work in the Commissary Department. Here he and his family, now consisting of Ellen and two children, took up residence on fashionable Magazine Street. As in Charleston, Sherman moved in the best of society. General Daniel Emanuel Twiggs, along with Zachary Taylor's son, Richard, and son-in-law, Colonel William Wallace Smith Bliss, saw to it that "Cump" and Ellen met the aristocratic element of the city.

Sherman was soon to leave the army, however, and try his hand in the field of business. In 1853 he resigned his commission and returned to California to become affiliated with the branch bank of the St. Louis concern, Lucas and Symonds. This venture into banking brought nothing but misfortune. In the spring of 1857 the California bank failed, and in October of the same year, the New York office to which he had been transferred closed its doors. By this time Sherman was convinced that of all earthly pursuits, banking was the worst. He wrote Ellen that it was no wonder bankers were "specially debarred all chances of heaven."[12]

Deeply humiliated over these bank closures, Sherman was more concerned over another matter. While in California, army friends, among them Braxton Bragg, had sent him large sums of money with the request that he invest it for them. It was their hope to reap profits from the booming West, but the investments did not pay dividends. By law Sherman was not obligated in any way for these losses, but a deep sense of honesty caused him to assume voluntarily these obligations, all of which were eventually paid back in full.

After a very unhappy Christmas in Lancaster, the melancholy Sherman departed for Leavenworth, Kansas. There he read law, passed the bar and went into practice with his brothers-in-law, Thomas and Hugh

12. Howe, *Home Letters of Sherman*, p. 148.

Ewing. After acting as counsel in only one case, which he lost, the new barrister was ready to leave Kansas and the legal profession. His life since leaving Fort Moultrie had been marked by frustration, failure, and reliance upon his foster father's generosity for the support of his family. "I am doomed to be a vagabond, and shall no longer struggle against my fate," he wrote Ellen from Kansas in 1859. "I look upon myself as a dead cock in the pit, not worthy of further notice and will take the chances as they come."[13]

Soon he was writing his old friend, Don Carlos Buell, now Assistant Adjutant General, inquiring about the chances of getting back in the army. Buell answered that there were no openings for officers at the time but suggested that he apply for the job of superintendent of a proposed state military academy near Alexandria, Louisiana. Happy recollections of past years in the South, as well as force of necessity, prompted Sherman to mail immediately his application. On August 3, 1859, General George Mason Graham, vice president of the Board of Supervisors, notified him that he had been elected. Two months later Sherman left Lancaster to assume his new duties as superintendent of the Louisiana Seminary of Learning and Military Academy.

At his new home the Superintendent was welcomed by several of his friends, among them Bragg, Beauregard, and the Taylors. He speedily set to work learning his fourth profession and fashioning a school out of an empty mansion and four hundred acres of land. Being a fine organizer and capable executive, Sherman, after a few weeks, had the academy in operation and on a sound footing. The new Superintendent was very popular with both the faculty and cadets. He was not aloof in the least with either group. He took great pleasure in mingling socially with the staff, and, if at all possible, he made a point to talk personally with each of the fifty-six students every day. This fatherly attention brought respect and affection from the youths. David French Boyd, the academy's professor of ancient languages, felt certain that "all [the cadets] loved him."[14]

It now looked as though Sherman's wanderings had come to an end, that he had found at last a place of peace and contentment. To Ellen, still in Lancaster, he wrote: "If Louisiana will endow this college properly, and is fool enough to give me $5,000 a year, we will drive our

13. *Ibid.*, p. 159.
14. Boyd, *Sherman*, pp. 2-3.

tent pins, and pick out a magnolia under which to sleep the long sleep."[15]

Shortly after arriving in Louisiana, Sherman had the opportunity to express publicly his views on slavery. Since most Southerners considered John Sherman, his brother in Congress, an abolitionist, some members of the Board of Supervisors feared their new superintendent might be of similar mold. At a dinner given by Governor Thomas Overton Moore, Sherman quickly dispelled their fears.[16] He had known when applying for a position in the South that his opinions on slavery would be "good enough" for the region.[17] To him the institution of slavery was not only constitutional but was also the proper place for the Negro in society. He thought that if the Negro was not subject to the white man he would have to be either amalgamated or destroyed, and, said Sherman, "all the congresses on earth can't make the Negro anything else than what he is. . . ."[18] In a letter to Thomas Ewing, Jr., he expressed views on slavery far different from those of his brother-in-law. Said he:

I would not if I could abolish or modify slavery. I don't know that I would materially change the actual political relation of master and slave. Negroes in the great numbers that exist here must of necessity be slaves. Theoretical notions of humanity and religion cannot shake the commercial fact that their labor is of great value and cannot be dispensed with.[19]

He went on to say that he wished the institution did not exist. "The mere dread of revolt, sedition or external interference makes men ordinarily calm, almost mad." At one time he seriously considered "buying niggers" for household servants. He was reluctant to make the purchase because he felt that about the house they were "dirty and of no account" even though in a cotton or sugar field they were invaluable.[20]

Sherman was pronounced in his dislike of abolition. His feelings on the matter were much akin to those of the average Southerner. He felt that the abolitionist movement would result in "disunion, civil war, and anarchy. . . ." He thought "it would be wise if northern people would confine their attention to the wants and necessities of their own towns

15. Howe, *Home Letters of Sherman*, pp. 176-77.
16. Sherman, *Memoirs*, I, 148-49.
17. Fleming, *Sherman as President*, p. 77.
18. *Ibid.*, p. 241.
19. *Ibid.*, p. 88.
20. *Ibid.*, pp. 124-25.

and property, leaving the South to manage slavery."[21] He was willing to aid the Southern states if they were forced to protect themselves against the Negroes and abolitionists, but not if they proposed to leave the union. His loyalty then would be to Ohio and the Northwest.[22]

The threat of secession and war pained Sherman greatly, but he never tried to conceal his views on the nature of the Union. The constitution, he believed, was not "a mere rope of sand, that would break with the first pressure."[23] Secession was treason and it could not succeed, he reasoned, because the government of the United States was a reality which would defend its flag, property, and servants.[24] Such use of force Sherman would approve although he knew it would result in bloodshed.[25] His theory of union he hammered into his students, faculty, and friends day after day but with little success. Although few agreed with Sherman, no one reproached him for his political views. He was respected so much that no one wanted to offend him.[26]

Sherman remained in Louisiana during the Christmas season of 1860. It was a lonely time for him. Ellen and the children were in Lancaster, and all the cadets were at home for the holidays. And his mind was troubled over the talk of war and secession. Christmas eve he spent in his private room at the school in the company of his friend and admirer, Professor Boyd. The mails of that day brought the news that South Carolina had withdrawn from the Union on the 20th. This momentous announcement brought tears to Sherman's eyes. For an hour or more he paced the floor. Now and then he would stop and address Boyd in heart-broken tones on the tragedy and folly of South Carolina's action. Said he:

You, you, the people of the South, believe there can be such a thing as peaceable secession. You don't know what you are doing. . . . If you will have it, the North must fight you for its own preservation. Yes, South Carolina has by this act precipitated war. . . . This country will be drenched in blood. God only knows how it will end. . . . Oh, it is folly, madness, a crime against civilization.

You speak so lightly of war. You don't know what you are talking about. War is a terrible thing. I know you are brave fighting people but for every day of actual fighting, there are months of marching, exposure, and suffering.

21. *Ibid.*, p. 89.
22. *Ibid.*, pp. 44-45.
23. Sherman, *Memoirs*, I, 153.
24. Thorndike, *Sherman Letters*, p. 195.
25. Fleming, *Sherman as President*, p. 212.
26. Fleming, *Sherman as Teacher*, p. 10.

More men die in war from sickness than are killed in battle. At best war is a frightful loss of life and property, and worse still is the demoralization of the people. . . .

Besides where are your men and appliances of war to contend against them? The Northern people not only greatly outnumber the whites of the South, but they are a mechanical people with manufactures of every kind, while you are only agriculturist—a sparse population covering a large extent of territory. . . . You are bound to fail. Only in your spirit and determination are you prepared for war. In all else you are totally unprepared, with a bad course to start with.[27]

Sherman now realized that events beyond his control would speedily end his teaching career. The nation was falling apart and with it fell his dream of making a home in the South.

With each passing day it became more apparent that Louisiana would not remain loyal to the federal government. Nevertheless Sherman had vowed all along to serve the state "honestly and faithfully" until the minute it quit the Union.[28] On Christmas Day, in a letter to General Graham, whom he considered a "high toned, fine gentleman," he reaffirmed this stand:

But if Louisiana secedes from the government, that instant I stop. I will do no act, breathe no word, think no thought hostile to the government of the United States. Weak as it is, it is the only semblance of strength and justice on this continent. . . .[29]

The withdrawal of South Carolina from the Union created a problem as to the disposition of the federal property within that state, in paricular Fort Sumter in Charleston harbor. President James Buchanan's irresolute policy in handling this ticklish question greatly disturbed Sherman. In command of the federal garrison in the city was his former instructor at West Point and friend of Fort Moultrie days, Major Robert Anderson. "Let them hurt a hair on his head in the execution of his duty," wrote Sherman in December, 1860, "and I say Charleston must [be] blotted from existence."[30] He felt that Fort Sumter should be reinforced "if it cost ten thousand lives" and every habitation in the area.[31] Sherman did not intend for these utterances to be taken literally.

27. Boyd, "Sherman's Early Life," *Confed. Vet.*, XVIII, 412.
28. Fleming, *Sherman as President*, p. 315.
29. *Ibid.*, pp. 317-18.   30. *Ibid.*, p. 319.
31. *Ibid.*, p. 360.

Yet, they comprise examples of a glaring weakness in his character, that of making loose and extreme statements which did not always express his true views. Sherman was not a cruel individual. His instincts were not those of a barbarian.[32]

Exaggerated as these pronouncements were, they should not be completely disregarded for they were evidence of Sherman's strong conviction that the people of South Carolina should be punished for their leadership in the secession movement. This conclusion was reached before the outbreak of hostilities and while he still resided happily in Louisiana. Sherman's love of the Union was stronger than personal ties. He was aware that if war commenced he would have to fight the people he loved best. In South Carolina he actually had more friends than in his native state of Ohio.[33]

The new year found events moving swiftly towards Louisiana's withdrawal from the Union. On January 18 Sherman officially submitted his resignation to Governor Moore, reminding the state's chief executive that when he accepted the position of superintendent of the academy "Louisiana was still a state in the Union, and . . . the motto of . . . [the] Seminary was inscribed in marble over the main door, 'By the liberty of the General Government of the United States. The Union, Esto perpetua.' "[34] In a personal letter to the Governor he said it was with the deepest regret and kindest feelings toward all that he left but that in time of great events everyone must choose one way or another.[35] Moore accepted Sherman's resignation reluctantly but assured Sherman that he would always carry with him the respect, confidence, and admiration of all who had been his associates while in Louisiana.[36] Dr. S. A. Smith, a member of the Board of Supervisors, attributed the unusual success of the academy primarily to its superintendent. He urged Sherman to become a citizen of the state of Louisiana and remain in the South.[37] From Braxton Bragg came the sincere hope that even should the worst come, they would be personal friends.[38]

By the latter part of February Sherman had turned over to the proper authorities all property, records, and money of the academy. When the

32. Fletcher, *Sherman,* p. 348.
33. Boyd, "Sherman's Early Life," p. 412.
34. Sherman to T. O. Moore, Jan. 18, 1861, Sherman Letter Bk., MS Div., L.C.
35. Sherman to T. O. Moore, Jan. 18, 1861, *ibid.*
36. T. O. Moore to Sherman, Jan. 23, 1861, *ibid.*
37. S. A. Smith to Sherman, Feb. 11, 1861, *ibid.*
38. Fleming, *Sherman as President,* p. 320.

day of his departure arrived, the battalion of cadets was formed in his honor on the parade grounds.   After passing down the line and bidding each officer and cadet farewell, Sherman attempted to say a few words but emotion choked his efforts.   Several minutes elapsed before he placed his hand over his heart and said: "You are all here."   Then turning on his heel, he quickly disappeared.[39]

Very few people who had lived in Louisiana such a short time ever commanded so thoroughly the respect, confidence, and love of the people of the state as did Sherman.[40]   Testimonial to these feelings are the resolutions drawn up by the Academic Board of the academy in appreciation of his splendid work.[41]

It was not hatred of the South that caused Sherman to leave Louisiana. It was his devotion to the constitution and the union of all the states for which it stood that made him the South's enemy.   Torn between respect for the Union and affection for the South, Sherman had no desire to take part in the strife that seemed inevitable.   He wrote: "I would prefer to hide myself, but necessity may force me to another course."[42]

39. Boyd, *Sherman,* p. 6.
40. Boyd, "Sherman's Early Life," p. 411.
41. P. Clark to Sherman, Feb. 14, 1861, Sherman Letter Bk., MS Div., L.C.
42. Fleming, *Sherman as President,* p. 339.

CHAPTER II

"War Is War"

EARLY IN MARCH Sherman went to Washington, seeking a desirable position in the government service. He was shocked by the carefree air prevailing in all circles in the capital. Disorganization in high places and a general lack of preparedness were much in evidence. Thoroughly disgusted, he railed out at his brother, John: "You politicians have got things in a hell of a fix, and you may get them out as best as you can."[1] Thereupon he set out for St. Louis to become president of a street railway company at the meager salary of $2,000 a year. From this time on Sherman had little use for politicians and never hesitated to express openly his feeling on the subject.

Sherman rejected a clerkship in the War Department and an appointment as brigadier general in the volunteer army. He was eager to serve his country but only in a capacity for which he was best trained. He thought efficiency, as well as speed, was necessary in war preparation.[2] He was also motivated by the need for personal security in steadfastly holding out for a permanent commission. A background of failure and embarrassment had created in him an incentive to make good. For the sake of individual pride and the welfare of his family, he felt compelled to find a permanent position.[3] In May, 1861 he was delighted to accept a commission as colonel of the Thirteenth Regular Infantry.

Following a short period of inspection duty, Sherman went into battle at Bull Run in July, 1861. In the fall of this same year he reported to Brigadier General Robert Anderson in Kentucky, where his friend was attempting to raise a force large enough to protect the state from an expected invasion. When ill health forced Anderson to resign from the

1. Sherman, *Memoirs*, I, 168.
2. Coulter, "Sherman and the South," *NCHR*, VIII, 46.
3. Walters, "Total War," *JSH*, XIV, 451-52.

army, his duties devolved on Sherman, much to the latter's dismay. Fearing that those in high command during the early stages of war would be sooner or later pushed into oblivion he had decided to move with caution, until he considered himself ready for a responsible assignment. Sherman thought he had President Abraham Lincoln's assurance that he would be permitted "to serve in a subordinate capacity, and in no event be left in superior command."[4]

Anderson's shoes proved too big for the new commander to fill. Sherman immediately began to bombard Washington for men and arms far in excess of his needs. His exaggerated estimates of Confederate forces in Kentucky and his prediction of an immediate Southern attack were perplexing to the authorities. Sherman was soon in such a state of nervous tension that many newspaper correspondents began to question his sanity. A reporter for the *Chicago Tribune* wrote:

I know not whether it is insanity or not but the General . . . indulged in remarks that made his loyalty doubtful. He even spoke despondingly; said the rebels could never be whipped; talked of a thirty years war.[5]

The *Cincinnati Commercial* carried the bold assertion that Sherman was stark mad and in need of deepest sympathy in his great calamity.[6] Yielding to these bitter attacks, he asked to be removed from command. Henceforth, Sherman harbored a deep-seated dislike and mistrust of all newspaper men. He never abandoned his warfare against the free press, which he believed was a detriment to the Union cause.

A twenty day leave in Lancaster and heroic action in the battle of Shiloh, April, 1862, restored Sherman's shattered pride. He was promoted to the rank of major general and earned commendations from his superiors for his work on the field of battle. Self-confidence regained, Sherman decided he might as well submit to the prominence which had come his way.

After Shiloh, Sherman was placed in command of the District of West Tennessee, with headquarters in Memphis. On July 21, 1862, the General assumed his new duties. While in Tennessee his concepts of war began to change. At the outset of hostilities his notions on the methods of conducting warfare conformed to those of most professional soldiers. He

4. Sherman, *Memoirs*, I, 193.
5. Lewis, *Sherman*, p. 197.
6. *Ibid.*, p. 201.

understood and accepted the sanction that the noncombatant population, as well as private property generally, should be free of molestation except where military necessity prevailed.[7] The pillaging of the Federal army in Northern Virginia the previous year had been most appalling to him. He said:

Each private thinks for himself. If he wants to go for water he asks leave of no one. If he thinks right, he takes the oates and corn and even burns the house of his enemy. . . .

No curse could be greater than invasion by a volunteer army. No Goths or Vandals ever had less respect for the lives and property of friends and foes, and hence forth we aught never to hope for any friends in Virginia.[8]

A few weeks in Memphis changed Sherman's ideas. Of special concern to him was the Federal government's cotton buying activities centering in this river port, the largest cotton market north of New Orleans. To encourage the loyal planters of the border states, as well as New England textile interests, Union authorities permitted open trading in cotton between the Southern farmer and Northern buyer. For their bales the planter received either gold or supplies which, in Sherman's opinion, were eventually used by the civilian population to aid the Confederate cause. This fact plus guerilla activity and unorganized civilian resistance in the region around Memphis caused Sherman to conclude that "when one nation is at war with another all the people of one are enemies of the other."[9] For his brother in Congress the General made the following observations: "It is about time the North understood the truth. The entire South, man, woman, and child are against us, armed and determined."[10]

Certain by October, 1862, that it was impossible to change the hearts of the people of the South, Sherman deduced that he could "make war so terrible" that Southerners would exhaust all peaceful remedies before commencing another conflict. He stated that while the Southern people "cannot be made to love us, [they] can be made to fear us, and dread the passage of troops through their country."[11]

7. *OR*, III, Ser. III, 148-64.

8. Howe, *Home Letters of Sherman*, p. 209.

9. Sherman, *Memoirs*, I, 267. Also disturbing to Sherman were the hit and run tactics employed by small units from the Confederate forces under Nathan Bedford Forrest and Earl Van Dorn.

10. Thorndike, *Sherman Letters*, p. 162.

11. *OR*, XVII, Pt. II, Ser. I, 260.

By this time, Sherman had determined his philosophy of total war. Considering all the people of the South as enemies of the Union, he planned to use his military forces against the civilian population as well as the armies of the enemy. He believed this plan of action would not only demoralize the noncombatants but also the men under arms. The Southern armies in the field, he felt certain, could be disheartened by attacks on the civilian population, as easily as by defeats on the battlefield. Sherman's program of total war also called for the destruction of the enemy's economic resources. By paralyzing the Confederate economy he hoped to destroy the South's ability to supply its fighting forces with war materials. In bringing war to the homefront he hoped to destroy the South's will to fight.[12]

"Collective responsibility," the theory upon which total war rests, made possible a new mode of warfare in which the accepted rules of the time were transgressed. The effect was a certain disregard for human rights and dignity. But with Sherman "war . . . [was] war and not popularity seeking."[13] He could not recall saying "war is hell," but he did state in September, 1864: "You cannot qualify war in harsher terms than I will. War is cruelty, and you cannot refine it. . . ." He thought the South, for its part in bringing on the war, deserved "all the curses and maledictions a people can pour out."[14] Nevertheless, he held out to his enemies the sincere promise of a helping hand if they would lay down their arms and rejoin the Union. It was not a sense of cruelty and barbarism that prompted Sherman to formulate his theory of total war. This conception was the outgrowth of a search for the quickest, surest, and most efficient means to win a war. Victory, he determined, could be won more easily by moving troops than by fighting. Strategy had become to him the master of tactics. The purpose of his strategy was to minimize fighting by playing on the mind of the opponent.[15]

Activities around Memphis in the fall of 1862 were only experimental. The full application of his new philosophy of war was to be applied by Sherman in campaigns through Mississippi, Georgia, and the Carolinas. In Mississippi the Federal army destroyed the state's resources and lines of communication and demonstrated to the inhabitants how cruel a matter

---

12. A thorough study of Sherman's philosophy of total war is J. B. Walters, Sherman and Total War (Ph.D. dissertation, Vanderbilt Univ., 1947).

13. *Ibid.*, p. 133; OR, XXXVIII, Pt. V, Ser. I, 794.

14. Howe, *Home Letters of Sherman*, p. 309; Sherman, *Memoirs*, II, 126.

15. Liddell Hart, *Sherman*, p. 426.

war could be. In the spring of 1864 Sherman, now a lieutenant general, was in Chattanooga, Tennessee busily preparing for a march into the heart of the Confederacy. In Georgia Sherman was to repeat the Mississippi performance but on a much grander scale.

The previous fall the Federal forces under the command of Major General Ulysses Simpson Grant had defeated Braxton Bragg at Chattanooga and driven him back to Dalton, Georgia, twenty-five miles to the southeast. Bragg was soon replaced by the able Joseph Eggleston Johnston and Grant, who was made general-in-chief of all Federal forces in March, 1864, was replaced by Sherman as commander of the Military Division of Mississippi.

Sherman was now on the threshold of greatness. He was about to commence an eleven months' movement, comprising three distinct campaigns, through Georgia and the Carolinas. These marches were to bring him fame and glory and a high place in the annals of American military history. His orders, dated April 4, were to move against Johnston's army and "break it up" and to move into the interior of the Confederacy as far as he could, inflicting all the damage possible against the war resources of the region.[16] Sherman's reply to Grant shows that he was fully aware that his primary objective was the destruction of Johnston's army and the movement into the interior was only secondary.[17]

Sherman put the Federal troops in motion for Dalton on May 5. Outnumbering his adversary almost two to one, Sherman was confident of success. He could not, however, hope to live off the land as he had done in Mississippi. North Georgia was a mountainous region almost devoid of forage and food and defended by one of the Confederacy's ablest generals. Under these conditions Sherman would not tolerate loose organization and lax discipline. Consequently, he could not possibly carry the war to the civilian population with any marked success. For supplies Sherman's 100,000 men and 35,000 animals had to depend on a connected line of railroad stretching some 500 miles between Louisville, Kentucky, and Atlanta, Georgia. For four months he made this lifeline to the rear his "indispensable ally." The protection of this long, single track was the delicate point of Sherman's game. His chief concern was the Confederate cavalry of Major General Nathan Bedford

16. Sherman, *Memoirs*, II, 26. Grant's strategy for the 1864 campaigns called for attacks on Lee's army and Richmond and several subsidiary offensives. It was one of these subsidiary operations that Sherman conducted.

17. *Ibid.*, p. 27.

Forrest. Keeping Forrest occupied in Mississippi was an essential part of Sherman's preparation for advance into Georgia.[18]

Sherman's plans also called for a flanking movement around Johnston at Dalton. While Major Generals George Henry Thomas and John McAllister Schofield, commanding the armies of the Cumberland and the Ohio respectively, pinned Johnston to his entrenchment, Major General James Birdseye McPherson, with the Army of Tennessee, was to turn his left and cut in behind him at Resaca. McPherson failed in his objective and on the night of May 12 Johnston fell back to Resaca. Three days later he retired across the Oostanaula River. From that day forward until he was relieved of his command, Johnston was flanked out of every position he held. Sherman became so efficient in this maneuver that his men were heard to boast that their commander could flank the devil out of hell, if necessary.[19] From each of these successive developments, however, Johnston ably extricated himself.

The Federal advance had reached Marietta twenty miles north of Atlanta by June 30. Here Sherman took time out from the responsibilities of conflict to answer a letter from Mrs. Annie Gilman Bower of Baltimore whom he had known as a young girl in Charleston before the war.[20] The pen of Sherman for once revealed his true self. This remarkable bit of correspondence, written when his name was fast becoming an anathema in all the South, shows clearly that he still harbored a strong affection for his former friends. He wrote:

Your welcome letter of June 18th came to me amid the sound of battle, and as you say little did I dream when I knew you . . . that I should control a vast army pointing, like a swarm of Alaric, towards the plains of the South.

Why, oh, why is this? If I know my own heart, it beats as warmly as ever toward those kind and generous families that greeted us with such warm hospitality in days long past but still present in memory; and today were . . . any or all of our cherished circle, their children, or even their children's children, to come to me as of old, the stern feeling of duty and conviction would melt as snow before the genial sun, and I believe I would strip my own children that they might be sheltered.

And yet they call me barbarian, vandal, and a monster and all the

18. Henry, *Confederacy,* pp. 376-78.

19. Boies, *33 Mass.,* p. 118. Johnston's Fabian tactics simplified Sherman's flanking movements.

20. Annie Gilman Bower was the daughter of the distinguished clergyman, Samuel Gilman.

epithets that language can invent that are significant of malignity and hate. All I pretend to say, on earth as in heaven, man must submit to an arbiter. He must not throw off his allegiance to his Government or his God without just reason and cause. The South had no cause—not even a pretext. . . . She bantered and bullied us to conflict. Had we declined battle, America would have sunk . . . meriting the contempt of all mankind. . . . I would not subjugate the South in the sense so offensively assumed, but I would make every citizen of the land obey the command, submit to the same that we do—no more, no less—our equals and not our superiors. . . . Even yet my heart bleeds when I see the carnage of battle, the desolation of homes, the bitter anguish of families, but the very moment the men of the South say that instead of appealing to war they should have appealed to reason, to our Congress, to our courts, to religion, and to the experience of history, then will I say peace, peace; go back to your point of error, and resume your places as American citizens, with all their proud heritages.

Whether I shall live to see this period is problematical, but you may, and may tell your Mother and Sisters that I never forgot one kind look or greeting, or ever wished to efface its remembrance, but putting on the armor of war I did it that our common country should not perish in infamy and disgrace. . . .

I hope when the clouds of anger and passion are dispersed, and truth emerges bright and clear, you and all who knew me in early years will not blush that we were once close friends. . . .[21]

This letter received wide publication in the press, both North and South. The response to such sentiments was varied but one letter in particular must have pleased Sherman. In it the correspondent had expressed himself as having rather been the author of the letter than victor of one of the war's battles.[22]

President Jefferson Davis, dissatisfied with Johnston's Fabian tactics removed him from command on July 17 and placed Lieutenant General John Bell Hood in charge of the Army of Tennessee. Sherman's new adversary, only thirty-three years old, was crippled of body but not of spirit. Hood's West Point classmates, McPherson and Schofield, informed their commander that the new Confederate General was both bold and reckless and would fight.

Hood did give battle and the Confederate forces fought bravely. For a retreating and discredited army, Hood's rapidly delivered blows to

21. *Columbia Phoenix,* May 2, 1865.
22. W. M. McPherson to Sherman, Feb. 28, 1865, Sherman Papers, MS Div., L.C.

Sherman before Atlanta were brilliant in conception and delivery, but heavy losses, poor staff work, and ill fortune prevented success. Hood was an "unlucky general." He never had a long run of luck against Sherman.[23] The Federal forces occupied Atlanta on September 2. The effect on the North was electrical. To most Northerners, weary of war and heavy losses of manpower, the fall of Atlanta was the most important military achievement of the year 1864. This victory also assured President Lincoln's re-election.

Sherman had no intention of permanently garrisoning Atlanta with troops. While in Missouri, early in the war, he had seen how the Confederates, when not tied down to any one base, had controlled most of the state although they had only one-fifth the number of troops of the Federals. At Memphis he had experienced the same frustration. In a speech delivered after the war to the Society of the Army of Tennessee, Sherman explained that prior to reaching Atlanta he had decided that the Federal policy of protecting cities had to be changed because it re-quired such a large number of soldiers to garrison adequately a location that the victorious forces were appreciably weakened, thereby playing into the hands of the enemy.[24] His decision was to abandon Atlanta after destroying its vital parts and lines of communication. While the city was under Federal occupancy, it was to be a "pure military garrison or depot, with no civil population to influence military measures."

As was expected, the order for the removal of the civilian population brought forth a storm of protest but the General was convinced "that time would sanction the wisdom of the order."[25] It was not an utter disregard for the people's welfare that made Sherman issue the order, but instead, his conviction that it was an essential war measure. In answer to a request from Mayor James M. Calhoun and Councilmen E. E. Rawson and S. C. Wells that he revoke his order, Sherman force-fully wrote:

But I assert that our military plans make it necessary for the inhabitants to go away, and I can only renew my offer of services to make their exodus in any direction as easy and comfortable as possible.

You cannot qualify war in harsher terms than I will. War is cruelty, and you cannot refine it; and those who brought war into our country de-

23. Burne, *Lee, Grant and Sherman*, pp. 110-13. Part of Hood's misfortune must be attributed to Sherman's quick grasp of the situation at the crisis of the battle of Atlanta.
24. *Report of the Soc. of the Army of Tenn., Nov. 13 and 14, 1867*, p. 103.
25. Sherman, *Memoirs*, II, 111.

serve all the curses and maledictions a people can pour out. I know I had
no hand in making this war, and I know I will make more sacrifices today
than any of you to secure peace. But you cannot have peace and a division of
our country. . . . Once admit the Union, once more acknowledge the authority of the national Government . . . I and this army become at once, your
protectors and supporter, shielding you from danger, let it come from what
quarter it may. You might as well appeal against the thunderstorm as against
these terrible hardships of war. They are inevitable, and the only way the
people of Atlanta can hope once more to live in peace and quiet at home, is
to stop the war. . . .

We don't want your negroes, or your horses, or your houses, or your land,
or anything you have, but we do want and will have first obedience to the
laws of the United States. That we will have, and, if it involves the destruction of your improvements, we cannot help it. I want peace, and believe it
can only be reached through union and war, and I will ever conduct war with
a view to perfect and early success.

But, my dear sirs, when peace does come, you may call on me for anything. Then will I share with you the last cracker, and watch with you to
shield your homes and families against danger from every quarter.[26]

According to the *Macon Telegraph* and the reports of Hood's officers, who received the evacuated families, Sherman's treatment of the
citizens of Atlanta was kind. For the needy who remained in the city a
series of theatrical performances was arranged. These performances,
running eighteen nights, raised $8,000.[27]

During his stay in Atlanta Sherman began to meditate on the idea of
marching into the interior of Georgia to smash things up[28] and "to make
Georgia howl."[29] As early as September 10, he was corresponding with
Grant on his future operations. The weeks passed and the notion of
marching through Georgia grew steadily in Sherman's mind. It occupied more and more of his correspondence with the general-in-chief.[30]

While Sherman's active mind was pouring out suggestions to Grant,
Hood was formulating a plan of his own. Although he had been unable
to hold Atlanta, he had no idea of remaining passive. He moved his

26. *OR,* XXXIX, Pt. II, Ser. I, 418-19.   27. Lewis, *Sherman,* p. 422.
28. *OR,* XXXIX, Pt. II, Ser. I, 202.   29. Sherman, *Memoirs,* II, 152.
30. *OR,* XXXIX, Pt. II, Ser. I, 356. J. F. C. Fuller, noted military historian, is of the
opinion that Grant originated the idea of the "march to the sea" when he sent Sherman a
map in April, 1864, showing the proposed areas of operation for the campaign of 1864.
The idea of the march might have been Grant's but its "elaboration and eventual execution"
was Sherman's. It was he who insisted on the campaign although Hood was still in the
field with a powerful army. Fuller, *Grant,* pp. 436-38.

army on September 20 from Lovejoy to Palmetto, twenty-four miles southwest of Atlanta. The next day he divulged his plan, already approved by Davis, to Bragg:

> I shall—unless Sherman moves South—as soon as I can collect supplies cross the Chattahoochee River, and form a line of battle near Powder Springs. This will prevent him [Sherman] from using the Dalton Railroad, and force him to drive me off or move South, when I will follow upon his rear. I make this move as Sherman is weaker now than he will be in the future and I as strong as I can expect to be.[31]

Hood hoped by assuming the offensive to checkmate Sherman. If the Federals gave chase to him, he planned to give battle in an advantageous location. In case Sherman moved south, he would follow. On the other hand, if Sherman split his forces, the Confederate General felt he could defeat a separate wing.

When Hood began his movement the latter part of September, Sherman was in complete cognizance of his plans. From a series of indiscreet speeches delivered in Georgia by President Davis, the General had learned of Hood's proposed operations.[32] The "full key" to the Confederate General's future designs was divulged by Davis in his address to the Army of Tennessee at Palmetto in which he said: "Be of good cheer, for within a short while your faces will be turned homeward, and your feet pressing Tennessee soil."[33] Leaving one corps to garrison Atlanta, Sherman set off in pursuit. Before commencing his march, he dispatched Thomas to Chattanooga "to meet the danger in Tennessee." Forrest had already appeared in the state and Hood was evidently "edging off in that direction."[34]

Sherman soon found that he had small chance of bringing Hood to battle; so his thoughts reverted back to his proposed march through Georgia to the sea. By September 19 he felt it almost hopeless to bring his mobile opponent to bay.[35] On this date Sherman informed Thomas that he planned to stop the chase and "make a hole in Georgia. . . ." He added: "If you can defend the line of the Tennessee in my absence of three months, it is all I ask."[36] On November 2, Grant wrote Sherman assenting to the proposed march to the coast:

31. Hood, *Advance and Retreat*, pp. 252-53.
32. Rhodes, *Hist. of the U.S.*, V, 7-8.   33. Hay, *Hood*, p. 23.
34. Sherman, *Memoirs*, II, 144.
35. Hood by this time had decided definitely to march into Tennessee.
36. *OR*, XXXIX, Pt. III, Ser. I, 365.

Hood's army, now that it had worked so far north, ought to be looked upon now as the "object." With the force, however, that you have left with General Thomas, he must be able to take care of Hood and destroy him.

I do not see that you can withdraw from where you are to follow Hood, without giving up all we have gained in territory. I say, then, go on as you propose.[37]

Sherman answered Grant immediately, assuring his commander that the results of a march through the heart of the South, even with a battle "would produce fruits more compensating for the expense, trouble, and risk." He reasoned that to act upon the Confederacy's resources, be it considered war or statesmanship, would be positive proof to sensible men in the South and abroad that the North would prevail in the contest, "leaving only open the question of its willingness to use that power."[38]

By November 12, Sherman was back in Atlanta and Hood was marching for Tennessee. Thus the two main armies in the west separated and withdrew in opposite directions, never to meet again, a phenomenon described by Professor James Garfield Randall as "one of the curiosities of the war."[39]

Hood's generalship during October had been almost flawless. He had drawn Sherman over a hundred miles from his base and had wrested the initiative from him, thereby improving the morale of his own troops. Also, by keeping his army intact, Hood had caused Sherman to fail in his major objective, that of destroying the Confederate forces.

In moving the greater part of his army from the theatre of war while the enemy troops in the region were still strong, Sherman acted boldly but in so doing he played "lady luck" to the hilt. When he departed for the sea with sixty thousand troops, Hood was left locally with a superior number of troops. Had fortune smiled upon the gallant Confederate he possibly would have advanced and overwhelmed Thomas before the latter's widely scattered forces were able to unite. Neither Grant nor Sherman had reason to count on the unforeseen adversities encountered by Hood on his march into Tennessee.[40]

The Federal army on November 15, rolled into the Georgia countryside

37. *Ibid.*, p. 594. Thomas' army totaled close to sixty thousand men but so many were detached that his immediate command numbered less than half that figure.
38. OR, XXXIX, Pt. III, Ser. I, 660.
39. Randall, *Civil War*, p. 554.
40. Ropes, "Sherman," *Mass. Mil. Papers*, X, 142. Sherman had implicit faith in Thomas' ability to handle any situation.

to begin its famous "march to the sea." On a hill outside of Atlanta, Sherman paused to look back at the city which lay "smouldering and in ruins, the black smoke rising high in the air, and hanging like a pall over the ruined city."[41]   The evening before, Colonel Orlando Metcalfe Poe of the engineers had fired the debris of the depot, roundhouse, and machine shops of the Georgia Railroad. One of these buildings, formerly used by the Confederates as an arsenal, still contained some shells.   The combination of exploding munitions and drunken soldiers fanned the flames to the heart of the city; so that over 30 per cent of Atlanta was razed before the fire was brought under control.[42]

Having destroyed the railroad to his rear, Sherman was dependent upon the countryside for supplies.[43]   The army in order to subsist was permitted to forage freely as it moved through the fertile lands of Georgia. Meeting only token resistance from Wheeler's cavalry and the Georgia militia, the troopers turned the march into a wild holiday. The weather was fine, the food was plentiful, and the order to forage freely was interpreted by some as the right to loot and burn. On a sixty mile front the army devastated the land as it moved toward the coast.

Twenty-four days after leaving Atlanta, Sherman was before Savannah, having covered a distance of more than three hundred miles. In command of the city's defense was Lieutenant General William Joseph Hardee with only eighteen thousand men. Sherman, hesitant as always to throw his entire force into battle, allowed Hardee and his small garrison to evacuate the city on the night of December 20. There is no plausible excuse for Sherman's allowing Hardee to escape. This much Sherman himself admitted in a letter to Thomas Ewing. He wrote:

I ought to have caught its garrison, but the swamp ground prevented my reaching the causeway on the South Carolina shore, but if Hardee had given me two more days I would have closed that also.[44]

On December 21, the Federal forces occupied Savannah and the following day Sherman presented the city to President Lincoln as a Christmas present.[45]

41. Sherman, *Memoirs*, II, 178.
42. Miers, *General Who Marched to Hell*, p. 221.
43. Sherman's destruction of the railroads to his rear was a most revolutionary move. It necessitated the army's living off the land but at the same time it freed Sherman from a fixed line of supply and gave him considerable mobility. Liddell Hart, *Strategy*, pp. 144-45.
44. Howe, *Home Letters of Sherman*, p. 320.
45. Sherman, *Memoirs*, II, 231.

The "march to the sea" was a brilliantly conceived move by Sherman, but it drew off no Confederate troops, and when the coast was reached, there were no Southern soldiers, to speak of, within several hundred miles. Without Thomas' resounding victory over Hood at Nashville on December 15 and 16, this successful operation "would have been worm wood."[46] With Thomas doing his fighting for him, Sherman had applied total war to Georgia and in so doing marched to fame and glory. As the Federal forces had penetrated deeper and deeper into the heart of Georgia, Sherman's star rose to great heights. His dramatic march absorbed public attention while Grant, apparently dozing in Virginia was mentioned less and less by the press. Sherman became the hero of the day. He was no longer the "crazy man" but "Tecumseh the Great."[47] Grant's critics were soon demanding that he be replaced by Sherman as general in charge of the armies. To these cries Sherman turned a deaf ear. He wrote his brother, John: "I will accept no commission that would tend to create a rivalry with Grant. . . . I have all the rank I want."[48] The two men were close personal friends. Sherman once jokingly remarked: "General Grant is a great general. I know him well. He stood by me when I was crazy and I stood by him when he was drunk; and now, sir, we stand by each other always."[49]

By all the accepted rules of strategy Sherman's sixty thousand veterans should have been immediately transferred to a theatre where they "could pull their own weight." The Federal navy had the ships to transport the army to Richmond where Grant had Lee bottled up behind fortifications.[50] Grant was very desirous of this move and had written Sherman on December 6:

My idea now is that you establish a base on the sea-coast, fortify and leave in it all your artillery and cavalry, and enough infantry to protect them. . . . With the balance of your command come here by water with all dispatch. Select yourself the officer to leave in command, but you I want in person. Unless you see objections to this plan which I cannot see, use every vessel going to you for purposes of transportation.[51]

46. Hay, *Hood*, p. 198; Palfrey, "Sherman's Plans," *Mass Mil. Papers*, VIII, 519.
47. Garland, *Grant*, pp. 294-95.
48. Thorndike, *Sherman Letters*, p. 245.
49. Brockett, *Our Great Captains*, p. 175.
50. Ballard, *Genius of Lincoln*, p. 223. Because of the heavy demands on ocean transportation it probably would have taken two months to move Sherman's entire army to Richmond. Sherman, *Memoir's*, II, 224.
51. Sherman, *Memoirs*, II, 206.

Much to Grant's dismay Sherman did have strong objections to this plan. He hoped to march on to Richmond by way of Columbia and Raleigh in the Carolinas.[52] Every step northward from Savannah, Sherman felt, was as much a direct attack on Lee as though he were operating within sound of the artillery of the Army of Northern Virginia. He was firmly convinced that an application of total war in the Carolinas would have a direct bearing on the outcome of Grant's struggle around Richmond.[53]

In addition Sherman was not adverse in the least to the idea of punishing South Carolina. To the general-in-chief he declared his belief "that the whole United States, North and South, would rejoice to have this army turned loose on South Carolina, to devastate the State in the manner we have done in Georgia. . . ."[54]

The news of Thomas' victory at Nashville reached Grant on December 18 and on the same day he penned Sherman a confidential note giving him permission to move through the Carolinas. Said he:

I did think the best thing to do was to bring the greater part of your army here and wipe out Lee. The turn affairs now seem to be taking has shaken me in that opinion. I doubt whether you may not accomplish more toward that result where you are than if brought here. . . .[55]

On Christmas eve Sherman received Grant's communication approving the Carolinas campaign. Nothing could have pleased him more. Gladdened by this news and confident of success, he wrote his chief: "In about ten days I expect to be ready to sally forth again. I feel no doubt whatever as to our future plans. I have thought them over so long and well that they appear as clear as daylight."[56]

52. *Ibid.*, p. 209.
54. *Ibid.*, p. 213.
56. *Ibid.*, p. 225.

53. *Ibid.*, pp. 213, 227.
55. *Ibid.*, pp. 223-24.

CHAPTER III

"Desire to Wreak Vengeance"

IN SAVANNAH the Federal troops generally behaved themselves with propriety and kindness. With the exception of a few minor incidents, all depredations ceased. The soldiers actually had little choice to act otherwise since there was an order in force to shoot down on the spot anyone caught "in unsoldier like deeds."[1] The days and nights were so quiet that every day seemed like a Sunday to Sherman.[2] This tranquil air was in part due to the General's order keeping in office the city officials, who in turn cooperated fully with the occupation forces. This concurrence was brought about by the judicious conduct of both the mayor, Dr. Richard Dennis Arnold, and the officer in command of the city, Major General John White Geary.[3]

The behavior of the soldiers "excited the wonder and admiration" of many of the inhabitants of Savannah.[4] Nevertheless, the ladies looked with disdain on their conquerors. Often they would cross the street rather than pass under the Union flag. Others absolutely refused to attend any social function where Federal officers were in attendance.[5] This attitude of the ladies failed to alter the Union soldiers' favorable impression of the city. Major James Austin Connolly wrote to his wife from Savannah: "I have been most courteously treated by all of its citizens with whom I have come in contact. . . . Our whole army has fallen in love with this city. . . ."[6]

1. Volwiler, "Letters of a Civil War Officer," *MVHR*, XIV, 526.
2. *OR*, XLIV, Ser. I., 841.
3. Dyer, "Northern Relief," *JSH*, XIX, 457.
4. *OR*, XLIV, Ser. I, 841; Lewis, *Sherman*, p. 473.
5. Dyer, "Northern Relief," p. 457.
6. Connolly, "Connolly's Letters," *Trans. of Ill. St. Hist. Soc.*, pub. No. 35, p. 375. An Illinois Captain wrote his sister from Savannah: "I found the sweetest girl here that ever man looked at. She is just your size and form, with large very deep brown eyes, almost black that sparkle like stars. I swear I was never so bewitched before." Wiley, "Billy Yank Down South," *VQR*, XXVI, 573.

Benevolence also characterized the occupation policy in Savannah. The pressing problem of feeding the population of the city, swollen by a flood of refugees, was immediately tackled by Sherman. He turned over to the city council all the food taken when this seaport was garrisoned. He also suggested that some fifty thousand bushels of captured rice be sold in the North and the money be used to buy other food.[7] Sherman even went so far as to allow the Episcopal churches to omit prayers for President Lincoln and substitute in their places one for Jefferson Davis.[8] But this was doubtless done with tongue in cheek, since the General felt that the President of the Confederacy needed prayers more than the President of the United States.

There was a touch of irony in the situation which called for Sherman to protect the families of Confederate officers active in the field against him. Awaiting him in Savannah were letters from Major Generals Gustavus Woodson Smith and Lafayette McLaws requesting individual care for their households. Sherman promptly visited these homes and assured the ladies of "courteous protection" as asked by their husbands. The wife of Lieutenant General Alexander Peter Stewart of Hood's army along with the brother of General William Joseph Hardee came to his headquarters and asked for special assistance which he gladly gave.[9]

The personal attention of Sherman was extended to families beyond those of high ranking Confederate officers.[10] He received many letters from persons in the North desiring consideration for friends in Savannah. From a lady in New York came a letter thanking Sherman for his "generous promise to look after" her people and his "kindness in writing so fully." She went on to say:

For yourself it is easy to see that besides the great flame of patriotism which fires your heart there is no room for revenge and that you feel Georgia and South Carolina are as much your country as Ohio, and the accompanying

7. Dyer, "Northern Relief," pp. 458-72.

8. Lewis, *Sherman*, p. 474.

9. Sherman, *Memoirs*, II, 235-36. After the war Smith asked the Federal cavalry commander, James H. Wilson, to thank "General Sherman in my name for the courtesy and kind politeness he extended to my wife in Savannah . . . assure him it is fully appreciated . . . he may rest assured I will never forget under any circumstances that he was the kind friend and protector of my wife when I and others upon whom she had claims were compelled by pressure of war to leave her in captivity." G. W. Smith to J. H. Wilson, July 6, 1865, Sherman Papers, MS Div., L.C.

10. On one occasion Sherman had a Federal army physician attend a local resident who was seriously ill. *Chicago Times Herald*, n.d., in Sherman Papers, MS Div., Duke Univ. Lib.

severities of war are as horrid to you on the one hand as they would be on the other.[11]

In a benign mood Sherman even promised to shield the dead. One W. G. Freeman wrote Sherman from Pennsylvania that he understood Federal soldiers had molested some graves around Atlanta and would he see to it that his brother-in-law's resting place in Savannah would not be bothered. Sherman answered the letter in the affirmative but he told Freeman, without mincing any words, that stories of his men violating graves were exaggerations "if not pure falsehoods."[12]

Under the leadership of Dr. Arnold, a definite movement was on foot to take Georgia out of the war. Arnold was not a Union sympathizer but rather a pragmatist who felt that it was useless to continue the struggle. Under his gavel, and with Sherman's complete approval, the city council drew up a set of resolutions requesting the governor to call a convention to give the people of Georgia an oppotunity "of voting upon the question whether they wish[ed] the war between the two sections of the country to continue." Article five was a request that Brigadier General John White Geary, who had "by his urbanity as a gentleman and his uniform kindness to . . . [the] citizens done all in his power to protect them and their property from insult and injury," be allowed to remain as the military commander of the city.[13]

As the news of the peace movement spread, letters asking about the Federal policy of reconstruction for the state began to pour into Sherman's headquarters. In a printed circular addressed to "N. W. ———— Esq. ————County, Georgia," Sherman stated that Georgia was not out of the Union, only in a state of rebellion and in view of this there could be no talk of reconstruction. He reminded the people that as long as Georgia had troops in the field the Federal army would be active. He advised the Georgians to lay down their arms and resume a normal place in the Union. Neither negotiations, commissions, conventions, "nor anything of the kind" were necessary for a peaceful return, so thought the General. It was simply a matter of the people of the state ceasing their rebellion against the government and electing members to the national Congress. When these individuals were duly seated in Washington, Georgia, according to Sherman, would "have resumed her functions

---

11. Caroline Carson to Sherman, Jan. 31, 1865, Sherman Papers, MS Div., L.C.
12. W. G. Freeman to Sherman, Dec. 31, 1864, *ibid.*
13. Dyer, "Northern Relief," pp. 460-62.

in the Union."[14] Thus the General made it quite clear that he had in mind no harsh policy of reconstruction for the South. He was fighting for the preservation of the national government not for the opportunity to punish the Southern people after the close of hostilities.

Sherman found the Negro, "inevitable Sambo" as he called him, was a major problem in Savannah.[15] He was also amused by the Negro. He wrote home that they flocked to him, young and old, praying, shouting, and mixing up his name with Moses, Simon, and other Biblical heroes, as well as "abram Linkon" and the "Great Messiah of Dis Jubilee."[16] But his attitude toward the black man had changed little since his days in Louisiana. For several months he had been at odds with the administration over the use of Negro refugees as soldiers. Sherman was strongly opposed to putting the colored man in his army. He preferred to use the Negro only as servants and laborers. The General admitted to a fellow officer that the Negro could stop a bullet as well as a white man, but he questioned the former slave's ability to "improvise roads, bridges, sorties, flank movements, etc."[17] Sherman felt that the Negro was in a state of transition and not the equal of the white man. From Atlanta he had written: "Iron is iron and steel is steel; and all the popular clamor on earth will not impart to one the qualities of the other. So a nigger is not a white man, and all the Psalm singing on earth won't make him so."[18]

General Henry Wager Halleck, in congratulating Sherman on his "march to the sea" and the capture of Atlanta, informed him that there was a powerful group in Washington disposed to make an issue of his policy toward the Negro. This group was circulating the story that Sherman "manifested an almost criminal dislike to the Negro," repulsing him with contempt and refusing to carry out the government's policy with respect to the race.[19] A few days later Sherman received a similar letter from Salmon Portland Chase, Secretary of the Treasury, pointing out that his actions towards the blacks was the one feature of his military administration that "causes worry to many."[20]

14. Sherman to "N. W.——Esq.," Jan. 8, 1865, Sherman Papers, MS Div., L.C.
15. H. W. Halleck to Sherman, Dec. 30, 1864, *ibid*.
16. Howe, *Home Letters of Sherman*, p. 319.
17. *OR*, XXXVIII, Pt. V, Ser. I., 169; Lewis, *Sherman*, pp. 393-94.
18. Sherman, "Letter," *Hist. Mag.*, XXI, 113.
19. H. W. Halleck to Sherman, Dec. 30, 1864, Sherman Papers, MS Div., L.C. Halleck, having been replaced by Grant as general-in-chief of the Federal forces, was now chief of staff.
20. S. P. Chase to Sherman, Jan. 2, 1865, *ibid*.

On January 11, Secretary of War, Edwin McMasters Stanton, one of Sherman's severest critics, arrived in Savannah. He had made the trip ostensibly for rest and recreation, but more in particular to investigate the General's handling of the Negro question.[21] He had not arrived totally ignorant of Sherman's attitude on this matter, for in October Sherman had written him:

I much prefer to keep negroes yet for some time to come in a subordinate state, for our prejudices, yours and mine, are not schooled yet for absolute equality. . . . I would use the negroes as surplus but not spare a single white man, not one.[22]

In response to a request by Stanton, Sherman summoned to his headquarters for questioning twenty-five colored Methodist and Baptist preachers. These men assertd that Sherman's treatment of the Negro was fair and courteous and that they had supreme confidence in his policies. In addition they pointed out to Secretary Stanton that colored enlistments did not strengthen the army, only left white men at home. One of Sherman's chief grievances with the Negro soldier was the fact that he was more generally enlisted by the "ravenous recruiting agent who was motivated by the profit derived from bounties than by love of the Union or the black race." Although he did not want any colored troops in his army, Sherman never denied their right of voluntary enlistment. Finding little fault with the General's policies Stanton departed on January 15.[23]

Meanwhile preparations for the march northward were being pushed. Very few changes were made in the organization of the army. It was to be substantially the same as that which had campaigned from Atlanta to the coast. As during the "March to the sea" the fighting force was divided into two wings. Major General Oliver Otis Howard commanded the right wing which was composed of the Fifteenth and Seventeenth Corps, commanded respectively by Major Generals John Alexander Logan and Francis Preston Blair, Jr. The left wing was under the charge of Major General Henry Warner Slocum. The Fourteenth Corps, under Major General Jefferson Columbus Davis and the Twentieth Corps, under Brigadier General Alpheus Starkey Williams, composed

21. Sherman, *Memoirs*, II, 252.
22. Hay, "Arming the Slaves," *MVHR*, VI, 35.
23. Sherman, *Memoirs*, II, 244-49.

this wing. The cavalry was led by Brigadier General Hugh Judson Kilpatrick.

For the most part these generals and all the officers in the upper commands were men of high character. The one notable exception was Kilpatrick. The cavalry commander, better known as "Don Juan" or "Little Kil," was notorious for his immorality and rapacity. Kilpatrick's behavior "set so demoralizing an example to his troops," thought a high ranking Federal officer, "that the best disciplinarians among his subordinates could only mitigate its influence."[24] Legends about "Little Kil's" numerous affairs with the female sex—black and white—ran through the army. The two Negro women who cooked for him were the subjects of much campfire talk.[25] In spite of Kilpatrick's unsavory reputation, Sherman had great confidence in his military ability and was apt to wink at his many escapades. Kilpatrick in return was devoted to his chief. In response to a congratulatory note from Sherman at Savannah he vowed that no task would be too difficult, "no march too long—no rebel force too formidable. . . ."[26]

Sherman was also quite fond of Davis and Howard, who with the exception of their fighting abilities, were almost complete opposites in character. Davis, a product of the midwest, upheld both his belief in the institution of slavery and his reputation as the most profane soldier in the Union army. In contrast was the very pious New England abolitionist, Oliver Otis Howard, who spent much of his time in prayer and scripture reading. Around his camp profanity was seldom heard.[27] Sherman, although he considered crackers and oats more of a necessity to his army than moral and spiritual guidance, respected Howard's convictions.[28] Henry Slocum, in the commanding general's eyes, was "one of the best soldiers and best men that ever lived. He would not hear a word against him."[29] Of all the members of his staff, Sherman cared least for Logan and Blair, his two political generals. They were oftentimes subject to his criticism but this was to be expected in view of Sherman's particular dislike for most politicians. Both men, with the

24. Cox, *March to the Sea*, p. 40.

25. Lewis, *Sherman*, p. 404.

26. H. J. Kilpatrick to Sherman, Jan. 2, 1865, Sherman Papers, MS Div., L.C.

27. Nichols, *Great March*, p. 143.

28. Some units of Sherman's army held prayer services every night, even under the most difficult circumstances. Smith, *Christian Commission*, p. 391; Shanks, "Recollections," *Harpers New Monthly Mag.*, XXX, 640-46.

29. Fletcher, *Sherman*, pp. 292-94.

exception of service in the Mexican War, were devoid of military training and had left promising political careers to enter the army. As for
the gentlemanly Williams, he was not aggressive enough for his superiors
and was eventually removed as commander of the Twentieth Corps.
Major John Chipman Gray, a Federal staff officer, writing in January,
1865, had this to say about Sherman's staff:

General Blair, who is a very common man both in appearance and language
. . . bears but an indifferent reputation as a corps commander. . . . I rather
think that Slocum is the best man Sherman has with him; Sherman's staff
except Captain Poe of the Engineers contains nothing remarkable. . . . He
has a miserably inefficient quatermaster, General Easton. . . .[30]

Surrounded by officers of mediocre ability, but strong willed and quick
to decision himself, Sherman seldom consulted his subordinates. The
minutest details of a campaign were generally attended to by him in
person. Sherman could be easily approached by any of his soldiers, but
none of them dared to be too familiar. On the march, he never failed to
acknowledge any salutation directed his way. He was greatly beloved by
the men in the ranks partly for the success they had achieved under him
and partly for his kind treatment of them.[31]

While stalemated before Savannah, Sherman was visited by Major
Gray who recorded his impressions of the meeting in an interesting letter
to his friend, John Codman Ropes:

I have just passed a whole morning in the company of the greatest
military genius of the country in the height of his success. If I were to
write a dozen pages I could not tell you a tenth part of what he said, for he
talked incessantly and more rapidly than any man I ever saw.

General Sherman is the most American looking man I ever saw, tall and
lank, not very erect, with hair like thatch, which he rubs up with his hands,
a rusty beard trimmed close, a wrinkled face, sharp prominent red nose, small
bright eyes, coarse red hands; black felt hat slouched over the eyes (he says
when he wears anything else the soldiers cry out, as he rides along, 'Hallo,
the old man has got a new hat'), dirty dickey with points wilted down, black
old-fashioned stack brown field officers coat with high collar and no shoulder
stripes, muddy trousers and one spur. He carries his hands in his pockets, is
very awkward in his gait and motions, talks continually and with immense

30. Gray, *Gray, Ropes Letters*, pp. 436-37. Gray was Judge Advocate on the staff of
Major General Quincy Adams Gillmore, commander of the Department of the South.

31. Wiley, "Billy Yank and the Brass," *Jour. of Ill. St. Hist. Soc.*, XLIII, 25; Johnson,
Sherman, pp. 509-10; Oakey, *"Marching,"* B and L, IV, 671.

rapidity. . . . It would be easier to say what he did not talk about than what he did. . . . At his departure I felt it a relief and experienced almost an exhaustion after the excitement of his vigorous presence.[32]

The most striking feature of Sherman's character was a peculiar nervous energy which knew no cessation. As a result of this characteristic he acquired the habit of decision in the most perfect degree. He jumped to conclusions with tremendous springs. On the battlefield he seldom gave a courier time to finish his message, answering as soon as he had learned enough to convey the idea. In giving instructions and orders he would take the officer by the shoulder and push him as he talked, following him to the door, all the time conversing and urging him off. One contemporary described Sherman as "bundle of nerves, all strung to the highest tension." He was never completely relaxed. His fingers were usually nervously twitching his red whiskers, or coat buttons, or playing a tattoo on a table. None of the features of Sherman's countenance, with the exception of his eyes, was indicative of his character. His eyes, though, were as restless as his mind.

The General was an inveterate smoker. He smoked, as he did everything else, with great energy. He puffed on his cigar as though under obligation to finish it as soon as possible. The puffs came fast and furiously and shot out of his mouth with great gusto. Every few minutes he would snatch the cigar from his mouth and flip the ashes. In contrast to Sherman, Grant gave every appearance of thoroughly enjoying his smokes. The Federal soldiers were sure that Sherman and Grant between themselves could smoke Lee out of Richmond if they could get him out by no other means.

Impulsiveness marked Sherman's writings as well as his speech and actions. Almost incapable of reason, he was apt to compose lines that were only thoughts of the moment. His vigorous mind leaped from one idea to another with such rapidity, that he took no account of the path in between.[33] It naturally follows that the correspondence of such a restless person cannot be depended upon to reveal the true man. If letters alone were used to determine Sherman's character, a false but damaging case of waging barbarous warfare could be built up against him.

32. Gray, *Gray, Ropes Letters,* pp. 425-29. Ropes, a native of Massachusetts, was trained for the law but is best known as a historian of the Civil War.

33. Shanks, "Recollections," pp. 640-46; Headly, *Grant and Sherman,* p. 235; Boyd, *Sherman as President,* p. 4; Howe, *Home Letters of Sherman,* p. 334.

On the march and in camp Sherman's life was marked with simplicity. He had few aides about him and had little use for clerks. He slept very little and any hour of the night his lean figure might be seen walking to and fro by the camp fire.[34]

The strength of Sherman's army was approximately 60,079 men. The trains were made up of about 2,500 wagons and 600 ambulances[35] under the charge of teamsters, who, undoubtedly, were the most profane group in the service. David P. Conyngham, a reporter for the *New York Herald,* felt certain they had a contract to do all the swearing for the army. He was not too sure they did not pray in oaths.[36] The wagons carried an ample supply of ammunition for a great battle but forage for only seven days and provision for twenty days.[37] On good roads these trains stretched out twenty-five miles. Consequently, it was necessary for each corps to move upon a separate road. To shorten further each corps' column, roads were reserved exclusively for wheels, the troops marching alongside but outside of the roads.[38]

Having previously been stationed in South Carolina, Sherman was familiar with the treacherous topography of the region he was about to enter. He was aware of the fact that heavy rainfall would make the existing roads almost impassable. The success of the campaign, he knew, would depend largely upon the efficiency of the pioneer corps whose duty it was to build and repair roads and bridges. In order that this large army might remain on the move, every division and brigade had a regularly organized pioneer corps.[39]

This corps performed a remarkable engineering feat in maintaining the roads through the swampy and sandy areas of the Carolinas. To keep the roads in a usable state, they made extensive use of the corduroy process whereby logs were laid transversely across the muddiest part of a roadway to give it foundation. The pioneer was so successful at this work that one Confederate soldier remarked: "If Sherman's army had gone to hell and wanted to march over and there was no other way, they would corduroy it and march on."[40] The *New Bern North Caro-*

34. Byers, "Recollections," *McClures Mag.,* III, 216.
35. Sherman, *Memoirs,* II, 269.
36. Conygham, *Sherman's March,* p. 316.
37. Sherman, *Memoirs,* II, 269.
38. J. G. Barrett, Sherman in N.C. (M.A. thesis, Univ. of N.C., 1949), pp. 1-2.
39. Force, "Marching," *Mil. Order of Loyal Legion, Ohio Commandery,* I, 1-2.
40. Calkins, *104 Ill.,* p. 284.

lina Times of April 25, 1865, carries a Federal soldier's interesting description of corduroying a road:

The road was imprecated a great deal which did no good; then it was corduroyed, which did a great deal of good for a time, but after the passage of a score or two of heavy laden wagons, the corduroying sank into a muddy chasm, and new layer of rails and trees had to be put down on the muddy surface through which the first had disappeared. It is detestable work felling trees and trimming them of limbs and boughs among those boggy pines, after working knee-deep in the oozy soil. After the trees are shaped they have to be dragged through morass to the pool or mud pits where they are needed and then laid down. . . . At times, as a wagon goes bumping over the road, a log flies up on end, one end piercing through the bottom of the wagon, the other sinking deep down in the mud by force of the sudden jolt. The wagon thus becomes transfixed. The driver sits in his saddle and swears. If the army in Flanders were as profane as our teamsters, then the atmosphere of Flanders must have assumed a certain hue at times. While the drivers utter their horrid and needless imprecations, the soldiers, more philosophical, get under the wagon, cut the upright log, bid the teamster pull up and repair the road for the next customers.[41]

Sherman planned to cut himself off completely from his base in Savannah; hence, he could expect no government supplies until he reached the Cape Fear River in North Carolina. His wagons could carry only limited provisions; hence, the army of sixty thousand would have to "forage liberally on the country during the march." To regulate the foraging parties, very strict orders were issued. Each brigade commander was to organize a foraging detail, "under the command of one or more discreet officers," which was to gather along the route "corn or forage of any kind, vegetables, cornmeal or whatever was needed by the command." These groups could appropriate from the inhabitants horses, mules, wagons, etc., "freely and without limit." But the soldiers were not to enter any dwelling or "commit any trespass." All parties engaged in foraging were to refrain from "abusive or threatening language" and when possible leave each family with "a reasonable portion for their maintenance." Only corps commanders were empowered "to destroy mills, houses, cotton gins, etc." In districts where the army was un-

41. *New Bern N.C. Times,* April 25, 1864. In spite of the strenuousness of his work, the pioneer managed to amuse himself by occasionally felling a tree without warning and watching the men scatter and run as it crashed to earth. Stormont, *Hight Diary,* pp. 464-65.

molested "no destruction of such property should be permitted" but where guerillas, bushwhackers, or inhabitants molested the march, the commanders were to "enforce a devastation more or less relentless, according to the measure of such hostility."[42]

These orders were in complete compliance with the accepted rules of warfare. Yet there was wide discrepancy between the orders and the actions of some of the men. In Georgia many of the foraging parties had degenerated into marauding bands of robbers which operated not under the supervision of an officer but on their own. These groups committed every sort of outrage. Most of the pillage and wanton destruction of private property in the two Carolinas was the work of the "bummer," "smoke house rangers," or "do-boys" as this peripheral minority of self-constituted foragers was called.[43] The majority of officers and men in Sherman's army neither engaged in indiscriminate looting nor condoned the actions of those who did. The foragers, who many times absented themselves from their commands for several days at a time, always returned with a peace offering in the form of the choicest spoils of the land. "Imagine" wrote Lieutenant Charles Booth of the Twenty-second Wisconsin, "a fellow with a gun and accoutrements, with a plug hat, a captured militia plume in it, a citizen's saddle, with a bed quilt or table cloth, upon an animal whose ears are the larger part of the whole. Let us take an inventory of his stock as he rides into camp at night. Poor fellow! he had rode upon that knock-kneed, shave tail, rail fence mule over 30 miles, had fought the brush and mud, and passed through untold dangers, and all for his load, which consists of, first, a bundle of fodder for his mule; second, three hams, a sack of meal, a peck of potatoes; third, a fresh bed quilt, the old mother's coffeepot, a jug of vinegar, and a bed cord. You call him an old, steady bummer. I'll give you one more picture. Here comes a squad of eighteen or nineteen, no two alike. Look at the chickens, geese, beehives; see that little fellow with a hugh hog strapped upon his nag's back. There rides the commander, a Lieutenant, completely happy for the day had been a good one, and his detail has got enough for a day's good supply for his regiment."[44]

42. Sherman, *Memoirs*, II, 175-76.
43. Force, "Marching," p. 15. On most occasions these self-constituted foragers were referred to as "bummers." The origin of the term is obscure but it was in use at the time of the "march to the sea." A member of Sherman's staff termed the "bummer" as "a raider on his own account, a man who temporarily deserts his place in the ranks and starts upon an independent foraging mission." Commager, *Blue and Gray*, II, 952.
44. Bradley, *Star Corps*, pp. 474-75.

Besides gathering forage and food from the countryside, the "bummer" secured maps, newspapers, and letters. These he brought back to camp to be carefully read by officers detailed for that purpose. Occasionally these materials furnished valuable information on Confederate military operations.[45]

Some "bummers," in search of adventure, would envelope marching columns with a widespread cloud of skirmishers through which the enemy found it difficult to push. General Joseph E. Johnston is reputed to have called Sherman's "bummers" the most efficient cavalry ever known.[46]

As commanding general, Sherman was responsible for the discipline of his troops.[47] For the abuses of the Federal army in Georgia his name already bore an odium. Prior to the Carolinas campaign the *Macon Telegraph* had tagged him a ravisher, incendiary, and thief who had a hyena's soul lurking in a "foul mass of corruption" which had shaped itself into humanity.[48] But Sherman had not one word of apology to offer for the conduct of his men. He asserted that "for the forcible hauling down of the U. S. flag which floated over that property of the historical government by the peoples of Georgia in 1861 and substituting their own, they deserved all the punishment they received and more too."[49]

South Carolina was marked for an even harsher fate. This was in part due to her leadership in the secession movement. The intense feeling in some quarters of the Federal army against South Carolina, was more of a personal hatred against the state, nurtured throughout months of fighting, than an impersonal feeling directed against the enemy.[50] Sherman doubted that even the devil himself "could restrain . . . his men."[51] A soldier from Ohio wrote the folks back home: "We will make her suffer worse than she did the time of the Revolutionary War. We will let her know that it isn't So Sweet to Secede as She thought it would

45. Slocum, "Sherman," *Mil. Order of Loyal Legion, N.Y. Commandery*, II, 62; Atkins, "Sherman's Cavalry," *Mil. Order of Loyal Legion, Ill. Commandery*, II, 389.

46. Force, "Marching," p. 15.

47. It was impossible, of course, for Sherman to have complete discipline over sixty thousand troops.

48. Lewis, *Sherman*, p. 452.

49. Sherman to G. E. Leighton, Mar. 23, 1888, Sherman Papers, MS Div., Duke Univ. Lib.

50. J. B. Walters, Sherman and Total War (Ph.D. dissertation, Vanderbilt Univ., 1947), p. 302.

51. Gray, *Gray, Ropes Letters*, p. 428.

be."[52] A Hoosier, whose sister informed him that she had named her newborn son for him, wrote in reply:

I fear you cannot get him into the service soon enough to help us in this war, but there may be other wars hereafter. Be sure you teach him to despise South Carolinians and there is no danger of his ever fighting on the wrong side.[53]

Although he envisaged his march through South Carolina as "one of the most horrible things in the history of the world . . . ," Sherman was determined to apply total war in its fullest to the region.[54] This policy of utter destruction was the keystone of his strategy and to put it aside was unthinkable. He was fighting not to prolong the conflict but to hasten its end, and total war was the most effective means at hand in securing this object. That South Carolina should experience the complete horrors of war was not a spontaneous creation of Sherman's alert mind. It should be remembered that the General had expressed such sentiments while living in Louisiana.[55] The Palmetto State was to him the "hellhole of secession" and for that reason could ask for little pity.[56]

The plan of campaign called for feints on both Augusta and Charleston and a march directly on Columbia and thence to Goldsboro, North Carolina, by way of Fayetteville on the Cape Fear. Goldsboro was chosen as the destination because that city was connected to the North Carolina coast by two rail lines running respectively from New Bern and Wilmington. By this circuit Sherman could destroy the chief railroads of the Carolinas and devastate the heart of the two states.[57]

52. Wiley, "Billy Yank Down South," p. 570.
53. Ibid.
54. Gray, Gray, Ropes Letters, p. 428.
55. See above, pp. 10-11.
56. Kilpatrick actually referred to South Carolina as the "hellhole of secession," but Sherman was of like mind. Miers, General Who Marched to Hell, p. 285.
57. OR, XLVII, Pt. II, Ser. I, 154. "The subsidiary operations which were intended to cooperate with Sherman's march northward from Savannah were two." First was the capture of Fort Fisher at the mouth of the Cape Fear River in North Carolina. Second was the transfer of General John M. Schofield with the Twenty-third Corps from Middle Tennessee to the North Carolina coast, where, with a provisional corps, comprised of detachments from the Twenty-fourth and Twenty-fifth Corps, commanded by Major General Alfred Howe Terry, and the Twenty-third Corps he was to reduce Wilmington and advance upon two lines from that city and from New Bern, which had been in Federal hands since March 14, 1862, to Goldsboro, at which place it was expected a junction with Sherman would be made. Fort Fisher fell to the Federal forces on February 15, 1865, and on the 22nd. of the same month Wilmington was captured by the Federals. Cox, The March to the Sea, p. 137.

Augusta had been left untouched by Sherman on the "march to the sea," so the Confederates would be in doubt as to his first objective on the march north. After he crossed the Savannah River, the enemy could only guess as to "whether it be Augusta or Charleston and . . . would naturally divide his forces." For strategic reasons also, Sherman planned to ignore the latter place. To Grant on December 24, he pointed out that the city was then "a mere desolated wreck . . . hardly worth the time it would take to starve it out." Only if the administration thought Charleston historically and politically important enough would he give it his attention.[58]

It must have come as a great disappointment to Halleck to learn that Sherman planned to bypass Charleston. On December 18, he had written the General that in case the city fell into Federal hands he hoped "some accident" might destroy it and a little salt sown upon the sight to prevent "the growth of future crops of nullifiers and secessionists."[59] Sherman was very tactful in answering this letter. He promised to keep in mind the hint as to Charleston, but he doubted if salt would be necessary since the Fifteenth Corps, which always did its work thoroughly, would be the command to take the city. Sherman went on to say that the whole army was "burning with an insatiable desire to wreak vengeance" not solely upon Charleston but upon the entire state of South Carolina. "I almost tremble at her fate, but feel she deserves all that seems in store for her. . . . I look upon Columbia as quite as bad as Charleston and I doubt if we shall spare her public buildings there as we did at Milledgeville."[60]

The route of march was determined by the topography of the land. The seaboard area of South Carolina and Georgia was a low, sandy region crossed by deep rivers and numerous and extensive swamps, making the Confederate defense of the region a relatively simple matter. To avoid these frequent and difficult crossings, Sherman decided to move his army into the interior of South Carolina upon the ridges between two or more of these rivers until the upper waters were reached where a crossing could be more easily accomplished It was his plan to march the left wing of the army northwest along both banks of the Savannah River as if headed for Augusta. At Sister's Ferry, about half the distance, the troops on the left bank would cross the river and join the remainder

---

58. Sherman, *Memoirs*, II, 225.   59. *Ibid.*, p. 223.
60. *Ibid.*, pp. 227-28.

of the wing at Robertsville in South Carolina. From there Slocum was to move his troops north across the Big and the Little Salkehatchie rivers until the Charleston-Augusta Railroad was reached near its crossing of the Edisto River. In the meantime, Howard was to transport the right wing from Savannah to Beaufort, South Carolina, by ship as if to threaten Charleston. From Beaufort he was to move west and take Pocotaligo and then push north until a junction with the left wing was effected on the above rail line. After destroying much of the railroad, the four corps were to move directly on Columbia with the Edisto being the only deep river between them and the banks of the Congaree at the state capital.[61]

When practical, Sherman advanced his army in a "Y" formation with the two wings well forward pointing to two different objectives, the center was held back to reinforce either wing hit by the enemy. In case the General decided to strike, the blow was usually prefaced by a previous or simultaneous feint at an alternate objective rather than the one selected. In most cases the diversionary movements were carried out by the cavalry or light infantry.[62] All marches were punctuated by frequent rests and it was the General's practice to ride with each corps successively as the army moved along.[63]

South Carolina awaited with despair and trepidation the appearance of Federal soldiers on her soil. Sherman's intemperate language in Savannah and the conduct of his troops in Georgia certainly warranted this apprehension. General Lafayette McLaws wrote his wife from Pocotaligo: "There is a great alarm all through the country and a strong disposition to give up, among the old residents even, and with the females especially. . . ."[64] Edmund Rhett of Charleston, disheartened over the morale of the troops arriving in Charleston from Savannah, hoped that Lee would come to the rescue by sending a portion of the Army of Northern Virginia to South Carolina. He wrote William Porcher Miles, a member of the Confederate Congress, that: "The officers are worse than the men. The men desert at every opportunity and run without any cause and without any shame."[65] Furthermore, he felt that the reserve and militia units were both useless and inefficient. Said he: "Indeed

61. Cox, *March to the Sea*, pp. 163-72.
62. Sheppard, *Civil War*, p. 137.
63. Adams, *Doctors in Blue*, p. 216; Oakey, "Marching," p. 671.
64. L. McLaws to wife, Jan. 13, 1865, McLaws Papers, SHC, U.N.C.
65. E. Rhett to W. P. Miles, Nov. [ ], 1865, Miles Papers, SHC, U.N.C.

they are worse than useless. They use arms (or rather they fling them away) that are needed. They will not fight and produce panic, destroying discipline in those around them and produce disorganization where they go."[66]

Yet many South Carolinians instead of preparing themselves for invasion spent their efforts in sending taunting messages into the Federal lines. In Georgia, Sherman received many notes to the effect that when South Carolina soil was invaded, he would find a people prepared to fight to the bitter end.[67] The editor of the *Charleston Daily Courier,* more aware than many persons of the imminent danger faced by his state, had for some time tried to arouse his readers from their complacency. As early as November, 1864, he had bitterly attacked the tendency of the Confederate press to create overconfidence by giving glowing reports on the achievements of Southern military commanders, when the truth should have been printed. "It is worse than idle and useless," he wrote, "it is positively mischievous and injurious in a degree almost equal to overt treason to underrate Sherman and to persistently . . . overrate Bragg and Wheeler and others. . . ."[68] When it became certain that South Carolina would feel the full weight of the Federal forces, the editor endeavored to stir up all within the state to the defense of their native soil. The columns of the *Courier* carried the plea for all South Carolinians to "look unpleasant facts in the face . . . and then resolve with solemn earnestness to do their whole duty with their whole hearts."[69]

To meet the emergency the state legislature made liable to military service "all free white men between the ages of sixteen and sixty, and not already in uniform." All those not volunteering would be drafted.[70] Governor Andrew Gordon Magrath contemplated arming the slaves but the rush of events prevented him from taking action on the matter.[71] Early in January, 1865, he issued a proclamation announcing the invasion of the state:

Let all who falter now or hesitate be henceforth marked. If any seek escape from duty or danger at this time, let him depart. There is no room

66. E. Rhett to W. P. Miles, Jan. 11, 1865, Miles Papers, SHC, U.N.C.
67. Sherman, *Memoirs,* II, 254.
68. *Charleston Daily Courier,* Nov. 29, 1864.
69. *Ibid.,* Jan. 6, 1865.
70. *Ibid.,* Dec. 30, 1864.
71. E. Rhett to W. P. Miles, Jan. 11, 1865, Miles Papers, SHC, U.N.C.; Cauthen, *S. C. Goes to War,* p. 221.

in the state but for one class of men; they are men who are willing to fight in cause. . . . Remove all your property from reach of the enemy; carry what you can to a place of safety; then quickly return to the field. What you cannot carry destroy.[72]

He then reminded the citizens of South Carolina that they had led in secession, fired the first shot, and yet had suffered less than any other people. "You have spoken words of defiance: let your acts be equally significant."[73]

72. Shanks, "Recollection," pp. 669-70.
73. *Ibid*.

CHAPTER IV

"Sherman Is Stuck Sure"

SHERMAN PLANNED to begin his march through the Carolinas about the middle of January, 1865, hoping that fair weather would prevail after that date. Preliminary movements commenced earlier. On December 30, 1864, Major General William T. Ward was ordered to move his division of the Twentieth Corps across the Savannah River into South Carolina. Because of driving rains and the occasional fire of Confederate pickets, the operation consumed over a week.[1] The few Confederates on the South Carolina side of the river could offer only minor resistance to the crossing. They retired on the first day of the new year, but left the following note tacked to a tree: "Yankees, you had better leave this country, for France and England have recognized the Confederacy and Lincoln is ordered to withdraw his troops from our soil."[2] Ignoring this bit of false propaganda, the Federal troops continued to skirmish Southern scouts for two days. On January 14 the division went into camp on the Hardee plantation, near the town of Hardeeville, where it remained until January 17.[3] Thus the first week of the new year found Federal troops safely entrenched on South Carolina soil and in spite of Southern warnings to the contrary, the earth had not opened up and swallowed this "grand army of Mudsills," as it had been tagged by the Confederate press.[4]

In accordance with orders General Blair began on January 3 the movement of the Seventeenth Corps by water from Savannah to Beaufort. In nine days the move was completed. The Fifteenth Corps under similar instructions was not able to complete the task so easily. On January 17, after only a portion of the corps had been moved, embarkation was halted and orders were issued for the remainder of the corps to

1. *OR*, XLVII, Pt. I, Ser. I, 782.
2. Bradley, *Star Corps*, p. 252; *OR*, XLVII, Pt. I, Ser. I, 1067, 1115.
3. *OR*, XLVII, Pt. I, Ser. I, 788.
4. Committee, *92 Ill.*, p. 211.

march to Beaufort. This change proved to be a mistake for a severe storm set in on January 18 and lasted until the 20th. Because of the rain, said by local inhabitants to have been the heaviest in twenty years, the roads on the north side of the Savannah River "became submerged and entirely impassable for man or train and navigable in boats."[5] Of the Fifteenth Corps troops, still in Savannah, only the Second Brigade of the Third Division was able to cross the pontoon bridge over the Savannah, and it proceeded with great effort toward Pocotaligo, to the west of Beaufort. The remainder of the Third Division was moved to the latter place by ship. The remaining division of Logan's corps was ordered to march with the left wing when it moved out for Sister's Ferry.

Beaufort, "very handsome" but small, was the first town in South Carolina entered in force by Sherman's troops.[6] It had been in Federal hands since November, 1861, and at the time was garrisoned by Negro troops. Sergeant Theodore Upson from Indiana thought the Negroes made "pretty good looking soldiers" but most of Sherman's veterans, who still considered the conflict a white man's war, did not think much of their colored comrades in arms.[7] Several affrays took place in the town between the colored and white troops and in the words of an Ohio soldier: "The darkeys . . . always got the worse of it, two or three of them having been killed and several wounded."[8]

With the town garrisoned by Negro soldiers wholesale pillage was out of the question. Many of the local citizens, however, found themselves missing much of what they had possessed prior to the arrival of the troops.

In anticipation of reaping a considerable profit the sutlers of Beaufort had on hand a large stock of "Northern delicacies" when Sherman's army arrived. These "delicacies" were "held at prices . . . only a sutler's conscience dared to impose."[9] But for men accustomed to taking much of what they wanted these sharpies, along with the Jews who owned most of the local stores, were considered "fair game for all." Consequently,

5. OR, XLVII, Pt. I, Ser. I, 221; Boies, 33 Mass., p. 109.
6. Orendorff, 103 Ill., p. 169.
7. Winther, Upson Diary, p. 149.
8. Wiley, "Billy Yank and the Black Folk," Jour. of Negro Hist., XXXVI, 49-50.
9. Arbuckle, War Experiences, p. 122; Marcy, "Sherman's Campaign," Mil. Order of Loyal Legion, Mass. Commandery, II, 333.

the shop keeper and sutler both came out on the short end of most transactions.[10]

Foraging was more to the men's liking and they were eager to resume their old ways. When the command moved out toward Pocotaligo on January 13, the soldiers were joyous at being cut loose once more from a base. On the march they acted more like school boys having a holiday than seasoned veterans.[11] By sundown of January 14, General Blair had advanced the Seventeenth Corps over "an almost impossible swamp" and was within musket range of the enemy's defense at Pocotaligo. Under cover of nightfall, the Confederate troops abandoned their fortifications and withdrew across the Salkehatchie.[12] General McLaws, in command at Pocotaligo, was later charged with being intoxicated on the night of the evacuation. He was supposedly seen by the side of the road vomiting profusely. But the charge of drunkenness was never proven and he remained at his command until the end of the war.[13]

As the right wing pulled out of Beaufort, Slocum, in Savannah, put the left wing in motion. The First Division of the Twentieth Corps crossed the flooding Savannah River above the city and after a very difficult march reached Purysburg, South Carolina, by January 19. It might have been more appropriate had the navy been in charge of this operation. The heavy rains of January 21, 22, and 23 had flooded the entire area to such an extent that it was possible to row a boat over much of the road back to the Savannah.[14] Around Purysburg the only thing "at home" were the alligators.[15] To keep comparatively dry, the men had to construct an extensive system of ditches around their camps. They used pine knots, the only wood not completely saturated, for drying their clothes. The results were smoked faces and black uniforms.[16] In the meantime, Ward's division of the Twentieth Corps, which had been at the Hardee plantation since January 4, occupied Hardeeville. Having affected several strong lodgements in South Carolina, Sherman was now ready to begin his march in strength through the Carolinas. On January

---

10. Winther, *Upson Diary*, p. 170.

11. Orendorff, *103 Ill.*, p. 148.

12. OR, XLVII, Pt. I, Ser. I, 375.

13. J. C. Farley to L. P. Gandell, Jan. 19, 1865, L. McLaws Papers, SHC, U.N.C. There are eight letters in the McLaws Papers pertaining to the condition of the General on the night of January 14, 1865.

14. Morse, *Letters*, p. 208.

15. Bradley, *Star Corps*, p. 249.

16. Calkins, *104 Ill.*, p. 285.

20, Slocum turned over the command of Savannah to Major General John Gray Foster and led the remainder of the army out of the city in the direction of Sister's Ferry. The following day Sherman embarked by steamer for Beaufort. The campaign of Carolinas was in full swing, a campaign that the General was to consider his greatest military achievement. The major objective was Lee's army around Richmond, and Sherman's Westerners intended to have the honor of taking the Confederate capital themselves.[17]

Sherman's hope that fair weather would prevail after the middle of January proved vain. Incessant rains were to plague practically every step of the march north. To attempt a movement in the dead of winter, under such conditions, seemed almost incredible to Confederate officers, including Generals Johnston and McLaws.[18] But Sherman had great faith in his army, especially the work of the pioneer corps upon whom so much depended.

General Slocum on his march to Sister's Ferry encountered such torrential rains that his command, composed of the Fourteenth Corps, John Murray Corse's division of the Fifteenth Corps, and Kilpatrick's cavalry did not reach its destination until January 29. Chaplain John J. Hight came to the conclusion that bad roads in this part of Georgia meant a very different thing from bad roads in his home state of Indiana. "In the hoosier state one could get stuck in the mud but in Georgia the bottom falls out. Nearly every mule and horse stumbled at least once, usually throwing its rider head long into the mud."[19] One entire day the Fourteenth Corps did not move at all. It was "completely swamped. For once Sherman is stuck sure," thought Captain Dexter Horton.[20] Nevertheless, most of the men were "in festive spirits ready and anxious to campaign through South Carolina."[21] A few like Charles S. Brown of the Twenty-first Michigan were not so jubilant. The prospects of fighting the adverse elements dampened somewhat their ardor for punishing South Carolinians. From Sister's Ferry, Brown wrote to "all Browns and any other man" that he was "stuck in the swamps, in the sand knee

17. Thorndike, *Sherman's Letters*, p. 260; Sherman, "Strategy," *B and L*, IV, 256-57; *N.Y. Times*, Mar. 30, 1865.

18. L. McLaws to T. B. Ray, Jan. 17, 1865, McLaws Papers, SHC, U.N.C.; *N. Y. Times*, Apr. 27, 1865.

19. Stormont, *Hight Diary*, p. 461.

20. Eaton, "Diary of an Officer," *JSH*, IX, 241.

21. Padgett, "Letters of a Federal Soldier," *Ga. Hist. Quar.*, XXXIII, 69.

deep, cold as a dog, sick as the dickens on poor rations and in the month of February. . . ."[22] Soldiers of this Michigander's mold were heard to remark that "glory was a good thing to cover oneself with but not so warm as a blanket."[23]

On January 29, the First and Third Divisions of the Twentieth Corps moved to Robertsville, three miles from Sister's Ferry on the Carolina side of the river. Slocum immediately tried to contact General Williams who was traveling with these two divisions. He was not able to contact Williams until January 30, and then only by the use of a row boat could he navigate the roads on the South Carolina side, which in some places were under twelve feet of water.[24]

The erection of a bridge over the Savannah was a doubly hazardous job because of the high water and the logs and rafts being floated downstream by the Confederate cavalry.[25] Further difficulties were encountered by the pioneers in the form of torpedoes concealed under the driftwood and in the roads on the north bank. The use of torpedoes, considered by the Federal troops as a "low and mean spirit of warfare," took several lives and in so doing intensified the soldiers' desire for vengeance upon a state they called "miserable and rebellious."[26] As the soldiers set foot on South Carolina soil, they let out long and loud cheers, keeping it up for several hours. They seemed to think the day of retribution had come and the army was to be the avenging instrument.[27]

When Sherman commenced his march in January, the Confederate forces that could possibly be brought to oppose him were scattered from Virginia to Mississippi. General William Joseph Hardee in command of the Departments of South Carolina and Georgia had Lafayette Mc-Laws' division and Ambrose R. Wright's division near the head of Port Royal Sound and William Booth Taliaferro's division at Charleston. Matthew Calbraith Butler's division of cavalry ordered to South Carolina in February was still in Virginia. At Augusta Lieutenant General Daniel Harvey Hill had General Gustavus Woodson Smith's Georgia militia and Joseph Wheeler's cavalry. Two divisions of this cavalry were

22. C. S. Brown to "All Browns," Feb. 8, 1865, Brown Papers. MS Div., Duke Univ. Lib.
23. Calkins, *104 Ill.*, p. 285.
24. *OR*, XLVII, Pt. I, Ser. I, 420.
25. J. Wheeler to C. C. Jones, Aug. 1, 1860, Jones Papers, MS Div., Duke Univ. Lib.
26. *OR*, XLVII, Pt. I, Ser. I, 420; Morse, *Letters*, p. 209.
27. Chamberlin, *81 Ohio*, p. 151.

in South Carolina and one in Georgia. The shattered remnants of the Army of Tennessee were regrouping themselves at Corinth, Mississippi, after their defeat at Nashville. This army now commanded by General Alexander Peter Stewart was under orders to move by rail from Tupelo, Mississippi, to Augusta to assist in the defense of South Carolina.

On February 2, 1865, General Pierre Gustave Toutant Beauregard, head of the Military Division of the West, met with Generals Hill and Smith at Green's Cut Station, near Augusta, to discuss a plan of defense for South Carolina. They estimated that there were 33,450 troops that could be brought to oppose Sherman. It was decided that the line of the Combahee River would be held as long as possible by Hardee, assisted by Major General Carter Littlepage Stevenson's division of the Army of Tennessee. If this position was penetrated, Hardee was to fall back on Charleston and in case this city came under heavy attack, it was to be evacuated. Hardee with his forces would then join Beauregard who was ordered to leave one division of cavalry in Augusta and with the remainder of his troopers fall back slowly on Columbia. Hill was to remain in Augusta to organize the troops of the Army of Tennessee and send them north.

From Augusta, Beauregard wrote President Davis that he did not have sufficient forces to halt Sherman. He urged that troops be sent him from Virginia and North Carolina for concentration at Columbia. Lee felt that he could spare no men other than Butler's cavalry. He had already detached Major General Robert F. Hoke's division from his Army of Northern Virginia and placed it under General Braxton Bragg, commanding the Department of North Carolina. Bragg could not deplete his forces because they were all actively engaged in the fighting around Wilmington.

To darken further the picture, Beauregard's estimate of 33,450 men was a gross exaggeration. The actual number of troops available was much smaller and there was little hope that new recruits, with the exception of the very young, could be added to this meager force. These would not even compensate for desertions on the march. Neither could Beauregard count on the Georgia militia which was not allowed to serve outside of the state.[28]

28. Fieberger, *Campaigns,* pp. 401-14; Roman, *Beauregard,* II, 337-41.

As the Confederate generals mapped defensive plans, Sherman pushed deeper into South Carolina and the opportunity for effective concentration against him passed. So swift and deceptive were Sherman's movements that Beauregard and his lieutenants did not have time to deploy properly the forces immediately available, and in spite of a great effort the Army of Tennessee did not arrive in time to be used in the defense of the interior of South Carolina.

By February 7, all the Federal army but Slocum's command was encamped along the Charleston-Augusta Railroad from its crossing of the Edisto River east of Midway to Blackville. General Slocum, accompanying Geary's division of the Twentieth Corps, reached Blackville on the 9th, where the other divisions of this corps were encamped. Geary met no Confederate opposition on the march but the crossing of the flooded Coosawhatchie Swamp turned into a job of major proportions. Only through the prodigious efforts of a six hundred man pioneer corps was the swamp passable. It was necessary to construct a three-hundred-foot bridge and to corduroy the approach to the water. Much of the corduroyed road was built under three to four feet of water and had to be pinned down to keep it from floating away.[29]

Of all the corps the Seventeenth had the most arduous undertaking to reach the railroad. Progress out of Pocotaligo was slow. The enemy had felled trees, burned bridges, and erected obstructions to impede the march. In spite of their delaying tactics, the Confederates had been pushed across the Salkehatchie at Rivers Bridge by February 2. Hurriedly retreating, they had been unable to burn the sixteen structures along the causeway leading to the main bridge, which was also left intact. The Salkehatchie at this point was a dense swamp approximately one and one-half miles wide and fed by numerous small streams. The approach to the main bridge was over a narrow causeway commanded almost its entire length by McLaws' artillery. Disregarding the strength of the enemy position, the audacious Joseph Anthony Mower, with mighty oaths ordered the Sixty-third Ohio to cross the causeway and not to stop until the other bank was reached. This foolhardy advance was easily repulsed by the Confederate artillery, which swept the men of the Sixty-third off the approach. Many of the wounded had to remain in the swamp all night and only by propping themselves against the trees did they avoid drowning. Mower, determined as ever, put his men to

29. OR, XLVII, Pt. I, Ser, I, 683.

work on the morning of February 3 cutting two roads through the swamps in an effort to turn the Confederate position. At the same time he continued his frontal attack. All day the soldiers of Mower's First Division worked in the mud and water up to their waists and by nightfall had met with success. Outflanked, the Confederates withdrew in haste and had not Wheeler's cavalry come to the assistance of an infantry brigade, it might have been cut off from retreat.[30]

Upon reaching the Charleston-Augusta line, Sherman's soldiers proved themselves as apt at destroying a railroad as they were efficient in constructing roads and bridges. The different divisions of both the wings detailed men to tear up the rails and burn the ties. After a hearty breakfast, "say of turkeys, chickens, fresh eggs, and coffee," each detail was divided into three equal groups. The bountiful repast, General Slocum thought, was a prerequisite for a hard day's labor. Each man of the first group would get behind a tie and with a "Ready-hee-ah-hee" put the ties on end. At a second signal they pushed the ties forward so they fell with rails on top. Each soldier then disconnected his tie from the rail. This done, the first group moved on and was replaced by number two, which collected the ties, usually thirty in a pile, and placed the rails over them. Before moving up the line, these men set fire to the ties. The third section performed the most important task, the effectual destruction of the rails. An efficient officer in charge was needed here because the men, if not closely watched, would merely bend the rails around a tree. Simply bent rails could be restored. To be properly treated a rail had to assume the shape of a doughnut and be twisted. The finished product was termed a "Lincoln gimlet." In order to twist the rails a special device known as "Poe's railroad hooks" was necessary. The handling of this hot metal barehanded was the only thing looking toward the destruction of property that Slocum ever knew a man in Sherman's army to decline doing.[31]

The work of demolishing the railroad was completed by February 10, and the next day orders were issued for the corps to resume their march north. The south fork of the Edisto River remained as the one deep stream between the Federal army and the Congaree at Columbia. The most difficult area was behind. The improbable had been accomplished.

---

30. Jackson, *Colonel's Diary*, p. 177; J. Wheeler to C. C. Jones, Aug. 1, 1866, Jones Papers, MS Div., Duke Univ. Lib.; *OR*, XLVII, Pt. I, Ser. I, 376, 412.

31. Slocum, "Sherman's March," *B and L*, IV, 685; Bryant, *3 Wis.*, p. 306; Underwood, *33 Mass.*, p. 262.

Sherman had a right to be proud of his army, in particular the work of the pioneer corps. "Yankee" ingenuity, strong backs, excessive profanity and a considerable amount of whiskey had done the job. Chaplain Hight entered in his diary that "not a few oaths were sworn and some bad whiskey was consumed" in the swamps of South Carolina, and much to the consternation of the Bible-reading surgeon of the Seventh Illinois, Elijah P. Burton, the regimental colonel issued regular liquor rations to the men "in view of the exposure." The weather remained inclement. Hence, a large number of these Illinoians remained intoxicated.[32]

In contrast to the splendid work of the pioneers were the actions of those men in the army who gave expression to their long harbored hatred for South Carolina through acts of vandalism. Much of the lower part of the state lay in smouldering ruins by February 11. McPhersonville, Hickory Hill, Brighton, Purysburg, Lawtonville, Hardeeville, Roberts-ville, Barnwell, and the towns along the railroad had all felt the vengeful hands of Sherman's men.

The cavalry was responsible for much of this devastation. One of the favorite tales circulating in the Federal camps was that Kilpatrick filled all of his troopers' saddle bags with matches before leaving Savannah.[33] At a dinner given for his officers on the eve of the Carolinas campaign, the cocky little commander announced to all present: "In after years when travelers passing through South Carolina shall see chimney stacks without houses, and the country desolate, and shall ask 'who did this?' some Yankee will answer 'Kilpatrick's Cavalry.' "[34] This boast was carried out to the fullest extent in lower South Carolina as numerous dwellings along Kilpatrick's line of march were burned.

In Barnwell, Kilpatrick had the effrontery, so a Federal soldier said, to hold a grand ball in his hotel headquarters as flames consumed the town.[35] He made no effort to protect private property and allowed his men to rifle the local residences at will. By the time the fires finally burned themselves out, practically all of the town's business and resi-dental sections were in ashes. So thoroughly had the soldiers fired the town that they no longer called it Barnwell but "Burnwell."[36]   The

32. Stormont, *Hight Diary*, p. 461; Eaton, "Diary of an Officer," p. 242; Burton, *Diary of E. P. Burton*, II, 53.
33. Stomont, *Hight Diary*, p. 472.
34. Committee, *92 Ill.*, p. 211.
35. *Ibid.*, p. 212.
36. Stormont, *Hight Diary*, p. 474.

Fourteenth Corps, which entered this locality a few days later, leveled most of what was left of this once prosperous town of four hundred. One of the few houses left standing, when the soldiers of Davis' command marched in, was that of Miss Clara Belle Tobin who, although a "bitter rebel," was able to save her home for the second time in a matter of days. She had the foresight to graciously open her doors to the Federal officers. Clara Belle, being a woman of beauty and charm, had little trouble keeping her house filled with soldiers of rank, whose presence, she knew, would keep the incendiaries at bay. She, no doubt, had used the same technique while the cavalry was around.[37]

In Hardeeville churches suffered along with private property. One of the town's larger and more beautiful places of worship was deliberately razed almost plank by plank by men of the Twentieth Corps. The soldiers first removed the pulpit and then tore out the seats. Next the siding and blinds were ripped off. Finally the corner posts were cut so the spire would crash to the earth, making rubble out of the rest of the building. As the walls began to crumble, the soldiers yelled out to the local citizens near by: "There goes your d—d old gospel shop."[38] The remainder of the buildings in Hardeeville were either burned or torn down to make shelters for the troops. A soldier, James T. Ayres, said the town literally disappeared.[39]

Uninhabited dwellings along the line of march served always as a license for the soldiers to apply the torch.[40] There were ample opportunities for incendiarism under these conditions because many families in the southern part of the state had deserted their homes and fled north in hopes of avoiding Sherman's path.[41] Sergeant Rufus Meade, after several days in South Carolina, had seen but one white person.[42] Occasionally a lady would be seen standing beside the road imploring protection or maybe a white flag flying from the window of a home.[43] Robertsville and McPhersonville were both practically deserted when the Federal troops entered, but in ruins when the troops departed. In country and

37. Eaton, "Diary of an Officer," p. 243.
38. Fleharty, *102 Ill.,* p. 132.
39. Franklin, *Ayers Diary,* p. 74.
40. Morse, *Letters,* p. 209; Padgett, "Letters of a Federal Soldier," p. 68.
41. J. B. Walters, Sherman and Total War (Ph.D. dissertation, Vanderbilt Univ., 1947), pp. 304-10.
42. Padgett, "Letters of a Federal Soldier," p. 68. Meade was a commissary sergeant in the Fifth Connecticut Volunteers.
43. Hurst, *73 Ohio,* p. 168.

town alike the officers always occupied the better residences which saved them, at least temporarily, from destruction. In most instances, as soon as the march was resumed the house was burned. Near Hickory Hill, Sherman spent the night in the home of a Mrs. McBride. The next morning he was scarcely out of sight of the dwelling before a straggler had set it on fire.[44]

All the unoccupied houses and barns on the Langdon Cheves plantation near Hardeeville were demolished by Ward's division of the Twentieth Corps. So noisy was the clattering of hammers, the ripping loose of siding and the crashing of timbers that some of the men actually thought the enemy was launching an attack. The buildings were not burned since the materials were needed by the soldiers as shelters against the bitter cold.[45]

It took only a few days on the march to deplete the stores in the wagons. As the army pushed deeper into South Carolina, foraging became more of a vital necessity to the success of the campaign. In compliance with Sherman's orders, officers commanded the authorized foraging parties. Nevertheless, scores of foragers roamed about under no supervision, intent only on plunder "and in their nefarious work threw off all restraint—fearing neither God nor man nor his mythical majesty, the devil."[46] This rabble, the fringe group of the Federal army, visited the rich, the poor, the young, the old, the white, and the black alike. Their attitude toward foraging is expressed in the following jingle:

> My boys can live on chicken and ham
> For everything that we do find
> Belongs to Uncle Sam.[47]

Along with his search for personal loot, the "bummer" usually managed to gather enough necessary supplies to make his appearance in camp welcome. To the officers this was proof enough that something besides "hell" could be raised in South Carolina, but the numerous fires along the way made one Illinois soldier wonder if that much talked of place did not have its location in the state.[48]

With Sherman's "bummers" on the loose in South Carolina, every sort of scene was possible. If the house being seized had a piano the "bummers" liked to pound the keys with their hatchets to see who could

44. Padgett, "Letters of a Federal Soldier," p. 68; Gage, *12 Ind.*, p. 275.
45. Fleharty, *102 Ill.*, p. 130.   46. *Ibid.*, p. 135.
47. Boies, *33 Mass.*, p. 111.   48. Calkins, *104 Ill.*, p. 287.

make the most noise. Sometimes the lady of the house would be forced to play for the men to dance, and in case the music was not to their liking, the soldiers would slash their hatchets through the top of the piano to improve the tune. Ultimately the piano wires went for bails for the coffee kettles and the wood for a fire to heat the coffee. Another favorite pastime of the pillagers was to stack all the dishes they could find in one pile and "order arms" to see who could break the most. Others took delight in dressing themselves in the finest women's clothes. It was not an uncommon practice for the "bummer," in answer to a lady's plea for food and protection, either to turn from her with oaths and take the last morsel of food in the house or politely answer, "Certainly, madame: God knows I'm disgusted with all this," and then proceed to the next room and begin filling his pockets.[49]

Chaplain Hight, interestingly enough, did not attribute the demoralization of the army to any particular desire on the part of the soldiers for vengeance or to the work of the unorganized forager but to draftees and whiskey rations. The Chaplain was very unhappy to learn of the large number of "wild young men amongst drafted people." He entered in his diary that his regiment was then composed of:

deserters from the Confederate Army, refugees from the South, bounty jumpers, men who have been in the army before and played out of service, shirks, butternuts and substitutes, many of whom are the scrapings of society. The three hundred added to this Regiment, together with the whiskey rations, have demoralized this command to a shameful extent. . . . There is more profanity and card playing in the Regiment than ever before.[50]

The major perpetrators of these lawless acts, the "bummers," were seldom punished. General Davis, though, upon catching two soldiers stealing women's clothes, ordered them dressed in the stolen apparel and tied behind a wagon for six days. General Geary also roped a plunderer to a wagon. With a considerable number guilty of outrageous deeds and still others feeling South Carolina warranted any punishment inflicted on her, there were few informers.[51] For this condoning group, burning houses, barns, and cotton gins served to relieve the long nights of their dreariness, if nothing else.[52]

49. C. S. Brown to Etta [Brown?], Apr. 26, 1865, Brown Papers, MS Div., Duke Univ. Lib.; Underwood, *33 Mass.*, p. 264; *Augusta Southern Presbyterian*, Mar. 9, 1865.
50. Stormont, *Hight Diary*, p. 467.
51. Conyngham, *Sherman's March*, p. 467.
52. Bradley, *Star Corps*, p. 260.

The soldier who was innocent of any wrongdoing himself but did not condemn barbarous behavior on the part of others, naturally felt little sympathy for the people of South Carolina in their frightful condition. Lieutenant Colonel Charles Fessenden Morse of the Second Massachusetts expressed the sentiments of this group when he said:

Pity for these inhabitants I have none. . . . I might pity individual cases brought before me, but I believe that this terrible example is needed in this country as a warning to those men in all time to come who may cherish rebellious thoughts; I believe it is necessary in order to show the strength of this Government and thoroughly to subdue these people.[53]

In constrast to this line of thought was that of Charles S. Brown, a sympathetic lieutenant from Michigan, who wrote the folks back home:

I have been thankful ever since I have been in the army that this war was South. You never can imagine a pillaged house, never—unless an army passes through your town and if this thing had been North I would Bushwhack untill every man was either dead or I was. If such scenes should be enacted through Michigan I would never live as long as one of the invading army did. I do not blame the South and shall not if they go to Guerrilla warfare. . . .[54]

The Federal army, with the exception of the cavalry division, resumed its march north on February 11 as ordered. Kilpatrick, on the morning of this date, was approaching Aiken, South Carolina, to the west, where he had been ordered to make a strong demonstration to keep up the delusion that Sherman's objective was Augusta. Wheeler had learned of Kilpatrick's plans in time to concentrate a large body of his cavalry in this South Carolina town.[55] He concealed his troopers in the rear of the town and awaited the enemy which he hoped would ride in unaware of the trap that had been set for them. His plan was to strike the Federals when they broke ranks to enter the town. One column was to hit the Federal flank and the other, broken into squads, was to advance down the different streets striking the enemy at regular intervals.[56]

By daylight of February 11, Kilpatrick's advance brigade was within eight miles of Aiken. A short distance from the town a woman informed

53. Morse, *Letters,* p. 209.
54. C. S. Brown to Etta [Brown?], Apr. 26, 1865, Brown Papers, MS Div., Duke Univ. Lib.
55. J. Wheeler to C. C. Jones, Aug. 1, 1866, Jones Papers, MS Div., Duke Univ. Lib.
56. Dyer, *Wheeler,* pp. 217-18; *Dodson, Wheeler,* p. 322.

the General that Wheeler had just left her home. Also Federal scouts by this time were reporting many Confederates in the area. Completely disregarding these alarming reports, Kilpatrick continued his leisurely advance. When the Ninety-second Illinois, in the lead, met no resistance, Kilpatrick himself went forward. As the Federals rode unconcernedly into Aiken, Wheeler's men suddenly charged them from both flanks.[57] A hand to hand skirmish resulted which, in the eyes of a Federal sergeant, was typical of most cavalry engagements. There was a clash of horses, flashing of sabres, a few minutes of blind confusion, and then those who had not been knocked out of their saddles by their neighbor's knees or had not cut off their horse's head instead of the enemy's, found themselves either running away or being run from.[58] In this case, the Federals were doing the running. For four miles they galloped as fast as their horses would go. An elderly lady living on the outskirts of Aiken said the blue clad cavalrymen came by her house "as fast as old scratch would carry them."[59] Leading the parade was "Little Kil." As he came within sight of the Federal pickets, forty or fifty of Wheeler's men were in hot pursuit, three or four of them were actually grabbing for the hatless General.[60]

Wheeler's victory might have been more complete had not some trigger-happy Alabama troopers fired a volley prematurely, thus springing the trap too soon.[61] Just the same, this engagement was widely acclaimed throughout victory-starved South Carolina. Governor Andrew Gordon Magrath wired Wheeler in behalf of the state his thanks "for the defense of the town . . . , and the protection given in that defense to the population of that town."[62]

The Confederate defense of Aiken saved the town from Kilpatrick's incendiaries, but in the eyes of Henry William Ravenel, it suffered treatment from Wheeler's men almost as bad as could have been expected had the Federals occupied the place. Ravenel, who had been away from his plantation, Hampton Hill, since January, returned after the battle to find that it had been completely sacked by the Confederate cavalry, which had encamped on and around the grounds. Wheeler's men in their

57. Committee, *92 Ill.,* pp. 213-18.
58. Hinman, *Sherman Brigade,* p. 911.
59. O. P. Hargis Reminiscences, 1861-1865, Hargis Papers, SHC, U.N.C.
60. Committee, *92 Ill.,* p. 218.
61. Morgan, "Fighting at Aiken," *Confed. Vet.,* XXXII, 300.
62. Dodson, *Wheeler,* p. 324. Kilpatrick did not admit defeat. *OR,* XLVII, Pt. II, Ser. I, 450.

short stay took all the "corn . . . fodder, some salt, rifled the house, broke open all locks, and took away what they wanted, carpets, blankets, clothes, . . . etc., etc." Ravenel's desk was broken open and all of his papers scattered about. Much to the owner's dismay, twenty-two gallons of year old wine were also missing. The disheartened Ravenel felt that his only blessing was an upright house. Knowing the fate of Barnwell and other neighboring towns, he should have been deeply appreciative of this single ray of sunshine.[63]

In some areas of the South, Wheeler's appearance was dreaded as much as Sherman's.[64] This apprehension was not without foundation, as shown by Ravenel's experience at Hampton Hill, but in judging Wheeler, it should be kept in mind that he was under orders to destroy all supplies within his reach to keep them from falling into Sherman's hands. In addition his instructions were to forage off the land and to impress the supplies he needed. Wheeler not once denied that he had men in his command who carried the above orders to an extreme, but he attributed most of the pillage to a large band of marauders who falsely claimed to belong to his corps.[65] So concerned was Wheeler over the charges leveled against him that he published in several South Carolina newspapers the offer either to return, or to pay for, any goods stolen by his men. There was very little response to this pledge as was also the case in regard to his circular requesting all those with complaints against his command to state them.[66]

As Kilpatrick beat a hasty retreat from Aiken, the greater part of Sherman's army was in the midst of a rather difficult crossing of the south fork of the Edisto River. The Seventeenth Corps which had managed a crossing on the night of February 9, was now only three and a half miles south of Orangeburg, which it occupied on the morning of February 12. The local citizens and a small detachment of Confederate troops had thrown up slight breastworks around the town, but these were easily broken through by the Federal advance. The token resistance put up by the few soldiers was solely for the purpose of gaining time for those citizens of Orangeburg who desired to flee north.[67] The first

63. Childs, *Ravenel Journal*, p. 224.

64. E. Rhett to W. P. Miles, Jan. 11, 1865, Miles Papers, SHC, U.N.C.; *Charleston Courier*, Jan. 13, 1865.

65. J. Wheeler to C. C. Jones, Aug. 1, 1866, Jones Papers, MS Div., Duke Univ. Lib.

66. *Charleston News and Courier*, Mar. 14, 1898, U. R. Brooks Papers, MS Div., Duke Univ. Lib.

67. *Augusta Southern Presbyterian*, Mar. 30, 1865.

Federals to enter the town set fire to a large store, standing at the head of the main street. High prevailing winds plus a general inclination on the part of the Federal soldiers to assist rather than extinguish the fires resulted in a general conflagration.[68] By the time the flames were finally brought under control, approximately half the town lay in ruins.[69] Fortunately, the local orphanage escaped destruction. To assure its safety, Sherman ordered guards stationed there and provisions given the children.[70] Both Howard and Sherman attribute the fire to a Jewish merchant, who in anger over the Confederate authorities' burning his cotton, fired his store and left town.[71]

Before order was restored in Orangeburg, the "bummer" had a free hand. The scenes around town were a combination of tragedy and comedy. The first onslaught was on the chickens, turkeys, geese, fowls, and pigs which disappeared in the twinkling of an eye. Stores were rifled just as promptly and every article of value or no value was dragged out into the street. The objects dumped on the ground ranged from postage stamps to peacock feathers. But in the face of all this there was not a single instance of an outrage being committed against any lady of Orangeburg, although several were threatened.[72] Eventually the guards, who were stationed at all homes desiring them, brought this chaos to an end. Once quiet was restored, the Federal officers and men generally treated the inhabitants "with real kindness and consideration." Sherman was no exception. He treated with extreme consideration a lady whom he had formerly known at Fort Moultrie although she came to his headquarters to complain not to recall bygone days.[73]

The afternoon of February 13 was spent in the demolition of the railroad depot, cotton bales, and two miles of track south of town.[74] The next morning the command moved out in the direction of Columbia, destroying the railroad as it went. By February 15, the corps was encamped along Harrells Branch some eight and one-half miles south of the state capital.

The Fifteenth Corps operating near by on this date encountered some

68. Jackson, *Colonel's Diary*, p. 180.

69. Childs, *Ravenel Journal*, p. 225; *Augusta Southern Presbyterian*, Mar. 30, 1865.

70. Sherman, *Memoirs*, II, 276; Calkins, *104 Ill.*, p. 28.

71. Sherman, *Memoirs*, II, 276; *OR*, XLVII, Pt. I, Ser. I, 196. General Blair attributed the fire to the retreating Confederate cavalry. *OR*, XLVII, Pt. I, Ser. I, 378.

72. *Augusta Southern Presbyterian*, Mar. 30, 1865; Hood, "Sherman in Orangeburg," *Our Women in the War*, pp. 153-60.

73. Howard, *Autobiography*, II, 111-12.

74. Sherman, *Memoirs*, II, 276; *OR*, XLVII, Pt. I, Ser. I, 196.

Confederate opposition at a crossing of Congaree Creek, one of the numerous tributaries emptying into the Congaree River, south of Columbia. By 2:30 P.M. Logan's men had flanked the Confederate position by pontoons above the bridge. The enemy cavalry attempted unsuccessfully to ignite the wet timbers of the structure.[75] Federal casualties of the day were six killed and seventeen wounded. The known Confederate loss was one drunken colonel.[76]

After nightfall the Confederates were heard from again. Throughout the evening their batteries shelled General William Babcock Hazen's camp. Apparently oblivious to the outlandish deeds of his own "bummers," Sherman called the bombardment the "basest act he ever heard of. . . ." In his eyes there was no possible object involved other than to kill "a few miserable devils rolled in their blankets." He was especially incensed because he considered it the work of Wade Hampton whom he thought the embodiment of all that was distasteful in Southern aristocracy. Sherman was momentarily so infuriated that he contemplated total destruction for Columbia, publicly avowing this, but after some reflection he abandoned the idea.[77]

By the evening of February 15, both corps of the left wing were bivouaced in the immediate neighborhood of the town of Lexington, twenty miles west of Columbia. General Geary, in charge of the occupying forces, reported that private property was strictly protected and no houses burned while his troops were there.[78] This could very well be true, but Kilpatrick, encamped nine miles north of the town, had left it in flames when he passed through.[79] The noted Southern scientist, Joseph LeConte, stopped in Lexington two weeks later and recorded in his journal that the town no longer existed. "A blackened ruin only remained in its place."[80] In addition to destroying property, the soldiers stripped the countryside of all forage. What the wagons could not carry away was burned. To the delight of the local citizens, no doubt, smoke from one tremendous heap of corn almost stifled some of the enemy.[81]

In the course of the morning of February 16, Sherman's entire army

75. J. Wheeler to C. C. Jones, Jones Papers, MS Div., Duke Univ. Lib.; Dodson, "Broad River Bridge," *Confed. Vet.*, XVII, 463.

76. Wills, *Wills Diary*, p. 350.

77. *Mixed Commission on Claims*, pp. 100-3; Sherman, *Memoirs*, II, 279; Arbuckle, *War Experiences*, p. 126.

78. *OR*, XLVII, Pt. I, Ser. I, 686.

79. Committee, 92 *Ill.*, p. 219.

80. LeConte, *Ware Sherman*, p. 81.

81. Stormont, *Hight Diary*, pp. 480-81.

concentrated itself on the left bank of the Congaree River. Directly east across this body of water and in plain view was the "famed city of Columbia—the cradle of secession."[82] Rising high above the surrounding buildings was the unfinished structure of the new state Capitol, the soft rays of the morning sun reflecting off its granite blocks.[83] West of the river a series of low hills rose in the distance. The plain in between was covered with moving columns of blue-clad soldiers, their bayonets glistening in the sun. Martial music added to the splendor of the occasion. Surgeon E. P. Burton thought this impressive spectacle of might was as if a grand exhibition was being put on for the people of Columbia who could be seen walking the streets of their beloved city.[84]

Within such easy range of Columbia, Captain Francis De Gress, a European member of the army, could not resist the temptation to un-limber some of his twenty-pound Parrots and fire at the Confederate cavalry clearly visible at the intersections of the streets. Sherman ordered this shelling of the heart of the city to cease, but he gave De Gress permission to burst a few shells near the depot of the South Carolina Railroad and the new statehouse before securing his guns. At the depot Negroes were seen making away with bags of meal and corn which Sherman wanted.[85] The shelling of the uninhabited Capitol was merely a show of strength; yet today the accuracy of De Gress' artillerist can be seen in six scars on the façade of the building.

Sherman did not intend to cross the Congaree at this point and enter Columbia from the west. The bridge had been destroyed by the Confederates, and he feared the stream was too broad and swift for a safe crossing. He decided the most feasible approach was from the north. The Fifteenth Corps, assigned the task of occupying Columbia, was ordered to move north across the less treacherous Saluda and Broad rivers, which meet a short distance above the city to form the Congaree. Once these crossings were accomplished, the corps was to turn south and march the short distance into Columbia. These instructions, plus orders for the government of the troops while occupying Columbia, were em-bodied in Sherman's General Field Orders No. 26, dated February 16, 1865. Once in the city, Howard was to destroy "the public buildings, railroad property, manufacturing and machine shops," but to "spare

82. Fleharty, *102 Ill.*, p. 142.   83. Gage, *12 Ind.*, p. 282.
84. Burton, *Diary of E. P. Burton*, pp. 62-63.
85. Sherman, *Memoirs*, II, 278.

libraries, asylums, and private property." These orders certainly imply that Sherman placed no special significance on the conquest of Columbia, simply considering it as one point on his general march.[86]

Logan easily bridged the Saluda, but as he pushed into the triangular area between this stream and the Broad River, he met stiff resistance from Wheeler's rearguard, holding a strong position on a hill. Braced by generous swags of gin, which a private in the line called "fear tonic," these few held their position until flames were noticed gushing skyward from the rosin covered Broad River bridge to the rear. Hats pulled down over their faces, the cavalrymen made a dash across the burning structure, many receiving severe burns. So sudden and consuming were the flames that all the troopers were not able to cross. In thirty minutes the structure fell into the river. The speedy and total destruction of the bridge cost Wheeler a few men, but it also halted the Federal advance.[87]

Nightfall of February 16, found the Fifteenth Corps busily at work on a pontoon bridge across the river. The Seventeenth Corps was still along the Congaree opposite Columbia. The left wing and cavalry had turned north toward Alston.

The day's march had taken Sherman's men past Saluda Factory and an abandoned prison bivouac known to them as "Camp Sorghum." Here, as one Federal captain put it, thirteen hundred of their soldiers had recently been placed in an area intended for five hundred. The pathetic appearance of the women and children employees at the mill provoked derisive remarks from the soldiers, but the wretched conditions at "Camp Sorgum" brought forth threats of violence. The mud hovels and holes in the ground, with which the Federal prisoners had tried to protect themselves against the weather, helped seal the fate of Columbia.[88]

The march from Savannah had been a difficult one for Sherman's army. But in the chill darkness of the night of February 16, the men forgot the hardships of the march. After nearly four years of war Columbia was doomed to fall. This satisfying thought, more than any other, dominated the thinking of the Federal soldier as he bivouaced for the night.

86. Ibid., p. 277; General Field Order No. 26, Feb. 16, 1865, Sherman Papers, MS Div., L.C.

87. OR, XLVII, Pt. I, Ser. I, 198, Fletcher, Rebel Private, pp. 142-43; Dodson, "Broad River Bridge," pp. 464-65.

88. Sherlock, 100 Ind., p. 197; Conyngham, Shermans March, p. 326; Nichols, Great March, p. 157.

CHAPTER V

"All Is Confusion and Turmoil"

IN 1863, Columbia became a haven for refugees fleeing before the Federal armies. Many of them came from the neighboring states of Georgia and Tennessee.[1] When Sherman's invasion of South Carolina became imminent, large numbers of people from the lower part of the state fled to Columbia.[2] During January and February, 1865, every train brought refugees into the city which was by this time "crowded to suffocation." In two years the population of Columbia had swelled from eight to twenty thousand.[3] Not a house could be found for rent. With flour selling at $100 per barrel and scarce at that, there was danger of starvation in some quarters.[4]

Each refugee brought as many of the family treasures as could possibly be transported. Alcoholic beverages always qualified as valuable property. The vaults of the city's banks were filled with silver plate, jewels, and other costly possessions. Columbia, which ordinarily had three banks, had by 1865 fourteen or fifteen, including all those of Charleston and most of those of the interior. The bankers, as well as the refugees, looked upon Columbia as a safe place.[5] Many felt that Sherman's chief objective in South Carolina would be Charleston on the coast, not the capital in the heart of the state.[6]

Those refugees, less certain that Columbia would be bypassed, felt security in the assumption that the city would be stoutly defended because of the large number of government manufactures and the mint lo-

1. Wright, *Memories*, p. 201.
2. Milling, "Ilium," *Confed. Vet.*, XXXVI, 135.
3. Hill, "Burning of Columbia," *So. Atl. Quar.*, XXV, 269; *Raleigh N.C. Standard*, Jan. 11, 1865.
4. Hamilton, *Ruffin Papers*, III, 493.
5. Gibbes, *Who Burnt Columbia?* p. 4.
6. Sherman's occupation of Beaufort had done much to stimulate the belief that Columbia would not be in the Federal line of march.

cated within its limits.[7] As late as February 9, the editor of the *South Carolinian* could "see no real tangible cause for despondency."[8] Scarcely two weeks prior, a monster bazaar had been held in the state house to raise money for Confederate hospitals.[9] However, seventeen-year-old Emma LeConte, daughter of Professor Joseph LeConte of South Carolina College in Columbia, could not help but wonder if the money raised that evening might not end up in Sherman's pockets rather than in Confederate hands.[10] Dissipation and frivolity marked the occasion to such an extent that one local lady, Lizzie P. Smith, was for several days thereafter rending her hair over the "sinfulness of people" in the midst of such critical times.[11]

For that element of the population that thought Columbia would be strongly defended, each day brought a repeated hope that either Hardee or some portion of the Army of Tennessee would shortly arrive in the city. They did not know that General Beauregard, much to the dismay of Governor Magrath, had ordered Hardee on February 11, to evacuate Charleston immediately and march northwest to Chester, near the North Carolina line.[12] Neither were they aware of the transportation difficulties being encountered by the Army of Tennessee as it moved by rail from Tupelo, Mississippi, to Augusta, Georgia. From the time the first troops left Tupelo until their arrival in the latter place, all was marked by delay and confusion. The railroads of lower South Carolina having been demolished by Sherman, before the troops reached their Georgia destination, the soldiers could only clamber from their boxcars in Augusta and start trudging in individual groups across the countryside. They were not certain of their destination. Columbia for the majority of the force was out of the question by the second week in February because Sherman was fast closing in on the city.[13] Beauregard first chose Chester, South Carolina as an assembly point and then successively Charlotte, Greensboro, and Salisbury in North Carolina. But the fall of Wilmington on

7. Salley, *Sack of Columbia, By Simms,* p. 31.
8. *Wilmington Herald of the Union,* Mar. 3, 1865, quoting the *Columbia South Carolinian,* Feb. 9, 1865.
9. Carroll, "Recollections," *Stories of the Confederacy,* p. 24.
10. Emma LeConte Diary, Jan. 18, 1865, in SHC, U.N.C.
11. Smith, *Smith Letters,* p. 163.
12. Cauthen, *S.C. Goes to War,* p. 224; A. G. Magrath to W. P. Miles, Feb. 6, 1865, Miles Papers, SHC, U.N.C.
13. Only a detachment under Major General Carter Littlepage Stevenson arrived in Columbia prior to the Federal entry.

February 22, brought him back to his original designation, Chester.[14]

Time and time again Governor Magrath called with little avail on the people of South Carolina to rally to the colors. Magrath's continuous appeals led one Confederate officer to remark that he had two brigades and five proclamations with which to oppose Sherman.[15] The Columbia papers of January 21 carried a pronouncement by the governor which threatened arrest for those men of the Twenty-third Militia Regiment who failed to assemble at the court house on the 26th. Within twenty-four hours Colonel Alexander R. Taylor of the South Carolina militia, received the following anonymous letter:

We noticed in yesterday's paper an order which threatened to arrest those men of the 23rd. Regt. S. C. M. who fail to assemble at the Court House on Thursday 26th inst prepared to go to camp. No tyrant has ever dared to issue such an infernal order as that of Lawyer A. B. Magrath. It will be a perpetual disgrace to Carolina that "she" forced old men for the hardships of wars . . . and children 16 years of age to be butchered in opposing strong and well disciplined Veteran troops under command of such an experienced General as Sherman, and for what? To save the life of a few aristocrats, who deserve to be hung. We did not expect such a man as you in whom we have had perfect confidence that you would be a shameful tool to tyrannical rulers. All we have to say is that if you execute that order, know that a bullet is prepared for you and your house will be razed to the ground.[16]

This letter expresses the sentiments of that segment of the local population which felt that it was hopeless to continue the fight. But Governor Magrath's urgent appeals for help from sources outside South Carolina did not fall completely on deaf ears. General Lee released from the Army of Northern Virginia, M. C. Butler's division of Hampton's cavalry for duty in its native state.[17] Lee also allowed Hampton, who had publicly avowed more than once to fight as long as he could wield a sabre, to accompany the division south. As his troops prepared to embark by train for Columbia, the proud Hampton wrote Senator William P. Miles at Richmond that he was willing to "fight anywhere in defense of our state" but he did not fancy the possibility of being placed under the command of General Wheeler who was his junior in service but now outranked him. In fact, the aristocratic South Carolinian thought if this

14. Black, *Railroads*, pp. 274-76.
15. Putney "Incidents," *Mil. Order of Loyal Legion, Wis. Commandry*, III, 383.
16. [Anonymous] to A. R. Taylor, Jan. 22, 1865, Taylor Papers, SCL, U.S.C.
17. R. E. Lee to W. P. Miles, Jan. 19, 1865, Miles Papers, SHC, U.N.C.

situation could not be changed, he preferred to be transferred to the infantry.[18]

Columbia was arrayed in all its glory when Butler's division disembarked in late January from the long trains that had brought it from Virginia. Flags and bunting were flying from all the establishments on the main street as well as most of the homes of the city. A huge Confederate flag floated from the dome of the Capitol. After stepping off the train, the troops mounted horses, for the most part furnished by the people of South Carolina, and rode down the street to the cheers of the crowd, many of whom were confident that the city was now safe.[19]

Emma LeConte was nearer the truth when she entered in her journal that the presence of Butler's cavalry merely meant that "Columbia couldn't be taken by raid."[20] Since the new year she had become reconciled to the fact that eventually Columbia would fall to the Federal forces. The "horrible picture" was constantly before her mind.[21] She was fully cognizant that Sherman's soldiers had promised to show no mercy to the city.[22] Others, who had followed Sherman's path through Georgia and lower South Carolina, were convinced that Columbia was a doomed city.[23] But the mayor, no later than February 14, attempted to ease these fears by announcing that the highest military officials had assured him that Columbia was safe. This effort at reassurance did little good. Rumors were already in circulation that Sherman was less than eight miles from the city. A member of Beauregard's staff, arriving in the capital on this date, straightway got the impression that the people were under the grip of complete demoralization.[24]

On February 15, strength was given the rumors of Sherman's proximity when the booming of cannons could be heard in the distance and wagons and ambulances bearing the wounded from the skirmish at Congaree Creek began to rumble down the muddy streets. "All is confusion and turmoil," wrote Emma LeConte.[25] "Terrible was the press,

---

18. W. Hampton to W. P. Miles, Jan 21, 1865, Miles Papers, SHC, U.N.C.
19. J. D. Morgan to U. R. Brooks, Oct. 30, 1908, Brooks Papers, MS Div., Duke Univ. Lib.; *Report of S.C. Banks*, newspaper clipping, SCL, U.S.C.
20. LeConte Diary, Feb. 14, 1865, SHC, U.N.C.
21. *Ibid.*, Jan. 4, 1865.
22. *Ibid.*, Dec. 31, 1864.
23. J. B. Walters, Sherman and Total War (Ph.D. dissertation, Vanderbilt Univ., 1947), p. 319.
24. "Jno. W. G." to sister, Mar. 1, 1865, Sherman Papers, MS Div., L.C.
25. LeConte Diary, Feb. 15, 1865, SHC, U.N.C.

the shock, the rush, the hurry" in Columbia from Tuesday, February 15, through Friday, February 17.[26] Hundreds of women and children were attempting to flee the city, and at the same time the Confederate authorities were moving off stores. Pandemonium reigned at the station of the Charlotte and South Carolina railroad as swarms of people with baggage of all sorts struggled to get aboard the Charlotte-bound trains. Shouting, pushing, cursing, and swearing characterized the scene.[27] Only those who arrived early had a chance for a seat. Lizzie P. Smith, who left Columbia before the big rush, had to go to the station at 5:00 A.M. in order to get a seat on the 7:30 train.[28] One of the last trains to leave for Charlotte carried in the neighborhood of one thousand persons. The passengers who could not get inside hung on to whatever they could. The aisles and platforms resembled "bees swarming around the doors of a hive."[29]

The unfortunate ones, unable to get out by rail, left by foot or by whatever means was available. Joseph LeConte in an effort to save some family treasures and the stores of the Nitre Bureau left Columbia by wagon on February 16. North of the city he "met one of the Rhetts with an immense train of wagons, his man servant, and his maid servant, his ox and his ass and everything that was his, including a drove of about 40 hogs and a flock of at least 50 turkeys . . . [and] with all his family. . . ." Rhett carried with him more than most refugees but, as all the rest on the road, he was fleeing before Sherman.[30]

A member of Beauregard's staff was of the opinion that the Confederate authorities bungled badly their efforts to remove supplies from Columbia. He wrote his sister that the loss of property was tremendous and that seldom had he witnessed so much confusion and mismanagement. The Treasury Department lost its "papers and stock, with five *million dollars*. Ordnance stores and machinery, medical and naval stores, commissary, Qr. Master, Nitre and Mining Bureau and all the departments lost." This same staff officer thought that all the property of the Transport Department would have been saved had he been listened to. The railroad cars he begged for Tuesday were burned Friday morning.[31]

26. Trowbridge, *The South*, p. 554.   27. Taylor, *S.C. Women*, p. 219.
28. Smith, *Smith Letters*, p. 168.
29. Massey, "Southern Refugees," *NCHR*, XX, 12.
30. LeConte, *Ware Sherman*, p. 90.
31. "Jno. W. G." to Sister, Mar. 1, 1865, Sherman Papers, MS Div., L.C.

Major N. R. Chambliss, sent to Columbia on February 14 to "take charge of all ordnance stores, establishments, and other stores, except the armory," found the task confronting him insuperable. Rail transportation of any type could not be had, and offers of $500 each brought no wagons. On the night of February 16, in a city overcome by the "wildest terror," he managed to get one carload of ammunition out of Columbia. This feat was accomplished by forcibly dislodging a group of treasury employees from a freight car in the yard and then getting it attached to one of the trains about to leave. In Chambliss' words "the loss of ordnance, especially in machinery, was very great." Nevertheless, the Major felt, "God knows," that he had done his job with as much zeal as had the property been his own.[32]

Captain C. C. McPhail, in charge of the Columbia arsenal, met with even less success than Chambliss. With deep mortification and chagrin he reported on February 25, that his entire establishment was lost. He was unable to "save an article of any kind."[33]

Acting under orders from Richmond, Professor LeConte put the college chemical laboratory aboard a train bound for Charlotte.[34] Professor William J. Rivers of the faculty of South Carolina College in Columbia, "made a valiant effort" to save the school library but he was unable to secure transportation. This was a disguised blessing in that the Federal troops destroyed very few of the books during their occupation of Columbia, whereas the chemical equipment was lost in transit and never recovered by the college.[35]

Columbia had been placed under martial law on February 15, but this did not prevent acts of robbery and pillage. That same night several stores in the city were entered.[36] According to a correspondent of the Richmond *Whig*, Wheeler's cavalry rode into town the next day and as as if bred to the practice of plunder "proceeded to break into the stores along main street and rob them of their contents."[37] Major Chambliss as he labored late into the night of February 16 noticed that "the straggling cavalry and rabble were stripping the warehouse and depots."[38]

32. *OR*, LIII, Ser. I, 1049-50.
33. *Ibid.*, p. 1053.
34. LeConte, *Ware Sherman*, p. 81.
35. Hollis, *Univ. of S.C.*, I, 227.
36. Salley, *Sack of Columbia, By Simms*, p. 33; Fletcher, *Rebel Private*, p. 142; Scott, *Recollections*, p. 175; LeConte Diary, Feb. 16, 1865, SHC, U.N.C.
37. Rhodes, "Who Burned Columbia?" *AHR*, VII, 490-91.
38. *OR*, LIII, Ser. I., 1049-50.

The sacking of the South Carolina Railroad depot resulted in an accidental explosion of the powder stored there.[39] This terrific blast, occurring around 6:00 A.M., shattered window panes throughout the city and brought most of the dozing people upright in their beds, paralyzed with mute terror.[40] Although the cause of the explosion was soon ascertained, troubled minds were not put at ease. Captain J. D. Witherspoon, chief commissary officer in Columbia, had in the early hours of the morning ordered all Confederate storehouses thrown open to the public.[41] This could mean only one thing. The authorities considered the city doomed.

During the night of February 16, Hampton, who was now a lieutenant general in charge of all cavalry in South Carolina, had notified Mayor T. J. Goodwyn that the city would be evacuated the following morning. The mayor was also informed that he would be left in charge of the city and that he was to surrender it peacefully to the Federal forces.[42]

This same night Hampton went to the hotel headquarters of General Beauregard to discuss the disposition of the large quantities of cotton in the city. This was a very pressing matter because two days earlier Hampton had ordered Major Allen Green, post commander in Columbia, to transport all of the cotton from the warehouses to the outskirts of town and prepare to burn it. In order to facilitate its movement to the open fields, Green moved the cotton from the warehouses into the street, but because of the absence of transportation facilities, he was able to move it no further.[43] Thus a fire hazard was now involved in burning the cotton. Present at the conference between Hampton and Beauregard on the night of February 16, was the latter's aide, A. R. Chisolm. He gives the following account of the meeting:

Late in the evening Hampton called . . . at the hotel, and after stating the condition of affairs on his front . . . the matter of disposing of the large quantity of cotton piled in the streets was discussed. General Beauregard immediately said that it should on no account be burnt, for by doing so it would endanger the city . . . whereas, if saved, it would be of much value

39. Salley, *Sack of Columbia, By Simms,* p. 34.
40. LeConte Diary, Feb. 17, 1865, SHC, U.N.C.
41. Gibbes, *Who Burnt Columbia?* p. 5.
42. Roman, *Beauregard,* II, 649. Beauregard was still in command at Columbia. He authorized all orders issued by Hampton.
43. A. Green to [D. H. Trezevant?], n.d., Trezevant Papers, SCL, U.S.C.; Copy of Hampton's Order Feb. 14, 1865, Trezevant Papers, SCL, U.S.C.

to the citizens. It was then determined that orders should be issued by General Hampton that none of the cotton should be burnt. . . .[44]
Soon after leaving the hotel Hampton had Captain Rawlins Lowndes of his staff draw up the appropriate orders. These instructions were passed on to Major Green immediately.[45]

Around daybreak of February 17, Mayor Goodwyn was summoned to the town hall where, in conference with several aldermen, it was decided to fly a white flag over the market place. While preparations were being made to raise this symbol of capitulation, Hampton sent word not to act until he gave the command. Between eight and nine o'clock the General, in person, advised Goodwyn to leave at once to meet the advance Federal columns moving rapidly upon the city from the north. The cotton in the street caught Hampton's eye. Before turning away he recommended that a guard be placed over this highly inflammable substance so no one might carelessly set it on fire. Shortly thereafter the Mayor, in company with Aldermen McKenzie, Bates, and Stork, set out in a carriage flying a white flag to surrender the city.[46]

By this time Columbia was a scene of disorder and chaos. The first rays of morning light, after filtering the mucky, smoke-filled air, made visible large numbers of Negroes, soldiers, and citizens either vying with one another for government provisions or turning their attention to the looting of shops and stores. A few of the city's private concerns had thrown their doors open to the public.[47] All the while Hampton's troops were slowly withdrawing from Columbia along the Winnsboro and Camden roads. Young Julia Lee, as she listened to the hoof beats of the cavalry mounts, sadly realized that with Hampton's departure went the last hope of protection from the Federal hordes.[48]

Undefended and deranged, Columbia was at the complete mercy of Sherman. For a few like Emma LeConte, the "confusion and turmoil" of the past days had held something exciting and sublime, but for most Columbians there was the "horrible uncertainty" of what lay ahead.[49]

44. Chisolm, "Chisolm Letter," *So. Hist. Soc. Papers*, VII, 249.
45. Davidson, "Who Burned Columbia?" *So. Hist. Soc. Papers*, VII, 190; Roman, *Beauregard*, II, 649; Green to [D. H. Trezevant?] n.d., Trezevant Papers, SCL, U.S.C.; Overly, "Union Prisoners," *Confed. Vet.*, XIV, 513; R. Lowndes to W. Hampton, Aug. 15, 1866, Trezevant Papers, SCL, U.S.C.
46. *The Burning of Columbia*, p. 7.
47. LeConte Diary, Feb. 17, 1865, SHC, U.N.C.
48. Julia Lee to Mrs. J. H. Lee, n.d., J. H. Lee Papers, SHC, U.N.C.
49. LeConte Diary, Feb. 15, 1865, SHC, U.N.C.

CHAPTER VI

"Night Turned into Noonday"

GENERAL SHERMAN spent the night of February 16 on the west bank of the Congaree near "Camp Sorghum." At daybreak he rode to the head of Howard's column and there learned that George A. Stone's brigade of Major General Charles R. Woods' division had been ferried across the Broad River without mishap during the night. Confederate picket fires clearly visible in the distance had not slowed the operation, although several anxious moments were experienced when two rafts lashed together and carrying sixty men became lodged on a rock several yards from the opposite bank.[1] When Sherman arrived, Stone's brigade was being deployed as cover for the construction of a pontoon bridge across the river. The General sat down on a log with Howard to watch the engineers at work, but such peaceful repose was not for Sherman. Soon he was walking to and fro along the bank with the everpresent and, in this instance, unlit, cigar in his mouth. Between 9:00 and 10:00 A.M. a messenger from Colonel Stone halted the General's pacing with word that Mayor Goodwyn of Columbia was on the opposite bank and prepared to surrender the city to the Federal forces. Sherman, by this carrier, ordered Stone to accept the surrender and enter the city with haste. He also informed the Colonel that the remainder of the corps would be along as soon as the bridge was completed.[2]

In accordance with these orders, Stone's brigade began the short march on Columbia. In the advance was the Colonel's former regiment, the Thirty-first Iowa, and from the mayor's carriage the Thirty-first regimental banner waved.[3] A short distance from the city the sound of rifle fire brought the party to a halt. The mayor was unable to explain

1. Farwell, "Letter of Major Farwell," *Annals of Ia.,* XV, 62.
2. Conyngham, *Sherman's March,* p. 327; Sherman, *Memoirs,* II, 279.
3. Farwell, "Letter of Major Farwell," p. 63.

the firing, and Colonel Stone threatened strong reprisals on the city in case his troops were fired upon. Unknown to the Colonel, Columbia was already under partial occupation by a small detachment from the Seventeenth Corps, and the men were celebrating their conquest by taking pot shots at the retiring Confederate cavalry.

The previous day, General Sherman, while viewing Columbia from the west bank of the Congaree, had casually mentioned to Brigadier General William W. Belknap, a brigade commander of the Seventeenth Corps, that he "would appreciate the men who first made a lodgement in Columbia." Taking this as a hint, Belknap authorized Lieutenant Colonel Justin C. Kennedy of the Thirteenth Iowa to attempt a crossing of the Congaree before Columbia with a small squad of his men. The next morning a detachment of approximately thirty men and three officers managed to ferry themselves across the river in a leaky river boat. Reaching the east bank, the officers impressed a buggy, and, with a color bearer, took off at a fast gallop for the heart of the city. They were soon joined by the remainder of their party and a detachment of the Thirty-second Illinois which had also crossed the river that morning.[4] When Stone's Iowans entered the city forty-five minutes later they were much chargined to find regimental flags from the Seventeenth Corps flying from the old and new statehouses as well as the city hall. Stone's men were able to replace the flags on the statehouses with their own banners but not that of the Thirty-second Illinois on the city hall. The men of this regiment had had the foresight to lock the trapdoor leading to the bell tower of this building. This assured the safety of the flag but it also meant the color guard, much against its wishes, was to be locked inside the tower.[5]

Columbia in February, 1865, was virtually one vast warehouse filled with spiritous liquors. Not only had the refugees, who had been flocking to the city for several months, brought a large amount of alcoholic liquors with them, but the whiskey merchants of Charleston had also shipped large quantities of their merchandise to Columbia for safe keeping. Mayor Goodwyn was well aware of the danger of having so much whiskey about and had brought the matter to the attention of

4. Hedley, *Marching Through Ga.,* pp. 367-70; McArthur, *Destruction of Columbia,* pp. 3-5; Nourse, "Burning of Columbia," *Mass. Mil. Papers,* IX, 428; Jackson, *Colonel's Diary,* p. 183; *OR, XLVII,* Pt. I, Ser. I, 21.
5. Hedley, *Marching Through Ga.,* p. 367.

Generals Hampton and Beauregard who replied that they had no authority to destroy or tranship the whiskey because it was private property.[6] The confusion of the days preceding Columbia's fall had enabled the Negroes to get their hands on large quantities of these various beverages and they, wishing to make the city as hospitable as possible, passed out whiskey in every sort of container to the men in blue as they approached the capital from the north and west. After the war, Colonel Stone wrote the editor of the *Chicago Tribune* that as his troops "entered one of the principal streets, the sidewalks were lined with negroes of every age, sex, and condition, holding in their arms vessels of every conceivable size and shape, filled with almost every conceivable kind of liquor. Here was an old white-wooled man, who, with 'Lord bless you, Massa; Try some dis,' offered brandy from a gourd that had been filled from the bucket held in his hand. Others were offering wines, champagnes, etc. from original packages, tin cups, crocks, etc."[7]

Shortly after halting in the heart of the city, the troops stacked arms, broke ranks, and began to plunder the shops, stores, and public buildings. Reverend A. Toomer Porter, refugee Episcopal minister from Charleston, was witness to a perfect orgy which occurred in the old state house where drunken soldiers took great delight in destroying "the many trophies and mementoes" of South Carolina's "not inglorious past."[8] A large number of the group amused themselves by taking shots at a picture of Jefferson Davis hanging on the wall,[9] whereas those outside unlimbered their throwing arms by tossing stones at a statue of George Washington.[10]

One of the first shops broken into by the pillagers was a liquor store, but pickings were much better in the cellars of other downtown stores where barrels of whiskey had been placed for storage.[11] These they rolled out into the streets where the heads were knocked in so that all

6. *Mixed Commission on Claims*, p. 106.

7. *The Burning of Columbia*, p. 16; Arbuckle, *Civil War Experiences*, p. 131; Hedley, *Marching Through Ga.*, p. 376; OR, XLVII, Pt. I, Ser. I, 243.

8. *Destruction of Property in Columbia, Speech by C. L. Blease*, p. 21.

9. LeConte Diary, Feb. 18, 1865, SHC, U.N.C.

10. The statue of George Washington before the Capitol in Columbia bears the following inscription: "During the Occupation Of Columbia By Sherman's Army February 17-19, 1865, Soldiers Brickbatted This Statue and Broke Off The Lower Part Of The Walking Cane."

11. Scott, *Random Recollections*, p. 176.

so desiring could drink their fill.[12] In one vault on main street, seven-teen casks of wine were uncovered. Yet, practically every drop of this wine was consumed by the thirsty soldiers in less than an hour.[13] One unfortunate citizen was discovered attempting to destroy forty barrels of whiskey. Suspecting him of poisoning the liquid, the soldiers forced him to take a drink from each of the barrels with the "consequence that he was drunk for a week."[14]

With alcohol flowing like water in the streets of Columbia, the color guard of the Thirty-second Illinois, locked in the bell tower of the town hall, was extremely unhappy. Not wanting to miss all the fun, the members of the guard cut the bell rope and let it down from the outside with the request that a jug be sent up. The request was promptly granted. Boosted by their haul, the occupants of the tower enlivened things below by firing wildly into the milling crowd.[15]

The superabundance of intoxicating spirits, plus the fact that many of Stone's men had had little sleep or food for twenty-four hours, re-sulted in 30 per cent of the command getting dead drunk in short order. In an effort to curb the disorders, a number of the drunks, in-cluding the color detail of the Thirty-second Illinois, were put under guard.[16] The remainder of the command was given specific instructions "to preserve order, to protect the people in their homes and places of business, [to] prevent all rowdyism and destruction of property."[17] But Stone's depleted regiment was unable to maintain order. Convicts re-leased from the city jail and escaped Federal prisoners, who in the course of the morning joined the unruly group of Negroes and soldiers, added to the disciplinary problems. How the convicts gained their freedom is unknown. They certainly had no business being out even with Federal troops in town. General Charles R. Woods referred to them as "villains improperly freed from jail."[18] On the other hand the presence of the escaped Federal prisoners is easily explained. Up to a few days prior to Columbia's fall twelve hundred officers had been imprisoned in the city, but a few had managed to escape before being moved by rail out of the

12. Wright, 6 Ia., p. 411.
13. Columbia Phoenix, Mar. 24, 1865.
14. Salley, Sack of Columbia, By Simms, p. 45.
15. Hedley, Marching Through Ga., p. 376.
16. The Burning of Columbia, p. 16.
17. Arbuckle, Civil War Experiences, p. 133.
18. C. R. Woods to Major [W. Atwood?], Feb. 21, 1865, Sherman Papers, MS Div., L.C.

city. They had found hiding places in Negro cabins, surrounding woods, and some cases, in the better homes of Columbia.[19] Although the number of escapees was relatively small, some of them retained bitter memories of their imprisonment and welcomed the opportunity to vent their wrath on the city of their captivity.

Sometime before noon, Sherman in company with Generals Howard and Logan rode into Columbia at the head of the Fifteenth Corps. The soldiers in column were singing a profane doggerel which prophesied what was in store for the "mother of secession":

> Hail Columbia, happy land
> If I don't burn you, I'll be damned.[20]

Once inside the city the bands struck up "Hail Columbia" and other national airs. For the first time in four years the tune, "Yankee Doodle" wafted along on the morning breezes.[21] Probably many Columbians reacted as did the Reverend A. Toomer Porter when he realized the nature of the music. This ecclesiastic at the time would rather have heard the awakening notes of Gabriel's trumpet than these "Yankee" melodies.[22] To young Emma LeConte the sight of the stars and stripes within the city was as disheartening as the sound of "Yankee Doodle." From her upstairs window, she viewed the raising of the United States flag over the statehouse. This spectacle brought from her the exclamation: "Oh, what a horror! What a degradation. After four long bitter years of bloodshed and hatred, now to float there at last! That hateful symbol of despotism!"[23]

Sherman's reception by the crowds in the streets was tumultuous but General Howard correctly observed that the enthusiasm for the conquering hero was largely due to the inebriated condition of those present.[24] In front of the Capitol a drunk attired in a long figured dressing gown and plug hat, staggered up to the General and, tipping his hat, said: "I have the honor (hic) General, to present (hic) you with (hic) the freedom of the (hic) city."[25] Thus for the second time in a matter of

19. Byers, *Fire and Sword*, p. 166; Nichols, *Great March*, pp. 208-9; *OR*, VII, Ser. II, 213, 443.
20. Pepper, *Recollections*, p. 311.
21. Conyngham, *Sherman's March*, p. 328.
22. Porter, *Work of Faith*, p. 112.
23. LeConte Diary, Feb. 17, 1865, SHC, U.N.C.
24. Howard testimony, *Mixed Commission on Claims*, pp. 26-27.
25. Winter, *Upson Diary*, p. 152.

hours Columbia had been surrendered to Federal authorities. Through the swarms of Negroes about him, many of whom were shouting, "Glory! Glory! The year of jubilee has come,"[26] the General noticed several white men edging their way toward him. Finally reaching Sherman, these men identified themselves as Federal officers who had been imprisoned in Columbia but had managed to escape. After talking with these soldiers a few minutes, Sherman rode off in the direction of the "Charleston depot" and then to a large foundry three or four hundred yards down the track.[27] There he was told it would be unwise to go any further because Confederate cavalry was still visible on a hill to the east. Still in company with Howard, Sherman turned back toward the market square. On this ride Sherman noticed several soldiers that were under the heavy influence of whiskey. He called Howard's attention to this fact, and warned him of the grave consequences that might result from drunken men on the loose.[28] This was Sherman's first reference to the inebriated condition of the occupation forces. Evidently the enthusiasm of his reception had previously blinded him to this fact.

On his trip about the city, Sherman had the unusual experience of observing large quantities of loose cotton being scattered about by prevailing high winds. The stately trees of Columbia were made white with this inflammable material, actually giving the semblance of a "northern snowstorm."[29] The loose cotton came from the numerous bales lining the streets, a large number of which had been cut open.[30] In the course of the morning some of the cotton bales caught on fire. At the market square, Sherman, in order to avoid "a long pile of burning cotton bales," had to ride his horse on the sidewalk.[31] The General always maintained that the cotton was burning in the streets when he entered the city, and he is supported in this contention by Howard.[32] Generals Logan and C. R. Woods who rode in soon afterwards, however, do not mention burning cotton in their reports.[33] Colonel Michael C. Garber, chief quartermaster of the Army of Tennessee, who most likely would have noticed burning contraband, did not make note of any such in writing his

---

26. Farwell, "Letter of Major Farwell," p. 63.
27. Sherman, *Memoirs*, II, 280-81. This was the depot of the South Carolina Railroad.
28. Sherman, *Memoirs*, II, 281.
29. *Ibid.*, p. 280.
30. Wright, *6 Ia.*, p. 412.
31. Sherman, *Memoirs*, II, 280.
32. *OR*, XLVII, Pt. I, Ser. I, 21.
33. *Ibid.*, pp. 227, 243.

official account.[34] There is the possibility that these men did not think it significant. Nevertheless, had enough cotton been burning to constitute a real menace to the city, one of them surely would have mentioned it, especially since a high wind was blowing.[35]

There is conclusive evidence, however, that at least some cotton was fired before Sherman entered Columbia. Henry Clay McArthur who entered the city with a small detachment of the Seventeenth Corps forty-five minutes prior to Stone's arrival passed smouldering cotton along the way.[36] An escaped Federal prisoner, from his place of refuge in a Negro cabin, saw the Confederate cavalry firing cotton before departing the city.[37] William Gilmore Simms, a well-known Southern literary figure, in recording a fire at the city jail noted that this fire "had been preceded by that of some cotton piled in the streets."[38] Major Chambliss, the Confederate ordnance officer, in his official report stated that at 3:00 A.M. on February 17 the city was actually "illuminated by burning cotton."[39]

The origin of the early fires is still a matter of dispute. Sherman in his official report, dated April 4, 1865, placed the responsibility for these acts of incendiarism squarely on the shoulders of Wade Hampton.[40] Hampton did not let Sherman's charges go unanswered. In a letter to the editor of the *New York Day Book,* he angrily exploded that thousands of witnesses could testify that "not one bale of cotton was on fire" when Sherman entered Columbia.[41] Hampton urged Reverdy Johnson, in the United States Senate, to set up an "honest, tribunal" before which he pledged himself to prove that he "gave a positive order, by direction of General Beauregard, that no cotton should be burned; that not one bale was on fire when Sherman's troops took possession of the city. . . ." Not only did Hampton emphatically deny "that any cotton was burned in Columbia "by his order but he also completely discounted Sherman's charge "that the citizens set fire to thousands of bales rolled out in to the streets."[42]

34. *Ibid.,* pp. 264-65. Garber's fourteen year old son, accompanying his father on the march, noticed cotton fires when he entered Columbia. Garber, "Reminiscences of the Burning of Columbia," *Ind. Mag. of Hist.,* XI, 288.
35. Hill, "Burning of Columbia," *So. Atl. Quar.,* XXV, 275.
36. McArthur, *Destruction of Columbia,* p. 9.
37. Byers, *Fire and Sword,* p. 166.   38. Salley, *Sack of Columbia, By Simms,* p. 37.
39. *OR,* LIII, 1050.   40. *Ibid.,* XLVII, Pt. I, Ser. I, 21-22.
41. Miers, *General Who Marched to Hell,* pp. 314-16.
42. Hampton, "Hampton Letter," *So. Hist. Soc. Papers,* VII, 156-57.

General Butler substantiates Hampton's denial of Sherman's accusations. Butler, who had brought up the cavalry rear guard as it evacuated Columbia, remained on a hill outside the city for two hours watching the Federal occupation. He vouches that prior to the enemy's appearance in the capital, he saw no evidence of fire.[43] Private Edward L. Wells, before taking position on the crest, received permission to return to Columbia in search of twelve bottles of madeira wine and to warn a lady refugee friend of his. On this trip into town and later from his location on the hill, he "saw no Confederate cavalrymen or stragglers and no fires. . . ."[44] A lieutenant from Kentucky who rode back into Columbia after the Confederate cavalry had departed did not observe any cotton burning.[45]

Contrary to the above assertions of Hampton, Butler, and others, the confusion in Columbia on the morning of February 17 made it impossible to enforce strictly Beauregard's orders. No doubt, in the press and hurry of evacuating the city, the burning cotton failed to register with these men.

The firing of cotton continued after Sherman's appearance in the city. Around 1:00 P.M. James Guignard Gibbes, prominent Columbia citizen, counted sixty bales on fire and later in the afternoon he saw thirty more ignited.[46] Alderman James McKenzie and the Reverend Peter J. Shand were witnesses to this burning cotton.[47]

For these fires any number of persons, including local Negroes, escaped Federal prisoners, released convicts, and drunken soldiers, stand as possible culprits. The most likely incendiaries in this group were the drunken soldiers who on more than one occasion were seen to light a cigar and then throw the match into some loose cotton.[48]

In the final analysis the origin of these morning and afternoon fires is of little significance because they had all been completely extinguished by mid-afternoon.[49] In some cases the soldiers helped the citizens fight the fires,[50] but more often they either stood idly by or cut the hose with

43. Butler, "Curtain Falls," *Butler and His Cavalry*, p. 466.
44. Wells, "Who Burnt Columbia," *So. Hist. Soc. Papers*, X, 113.
45. Overly, "Burning of Columbia," *Confed. Vet.*, XI, 550.
46. Gibbes, *Who Burnt Columbia?* p. 6.
47. "Sherman's Story Examined," *So. Hist. Soc. Papers*, XII, 449-50. Shand was an Episcopal minister.
48. *Ibid.*
49. *Ibid.*, p. 450; Winther, *Upson Diary*, p. 152; *The Burning of Columbia*, p. 16.
50. Sherman, *Memoirs*, II, 280.

their bayonets.[51] This destruction of hose eventually put all the fire engines in Columbia out of commission. On occasions the men went so far as to destroy the engines themselves.[52] The unruly conduct of the occupying forces was not responsible, however, for the flames getting out of control. In the opinion of Major General William B. Hazen, Fifteenth Corps, the cotton fires were so completely extinguished by the middle of the afternoon that "a dozen men with tin cups could have managed it."[53]

When the smoke from the smoldering cotton began to clear away, other columns of smoke were seen to the east of the city, two to five miles off. Sherman's incendiaries were at work. The residences of General Hampton, Dr. John Wallace, George A. Trenholm, Confederate Secretary of the Treasury, and many others, were going up in flames.[54]

For Sherman, the afternoon passed pleasantly. He settled himself comfortably at his headquarters in the Blanton Duncan home.[55] The command of the city had been turned over to Howard. Alone in his private room Sherman opened a piece of paper that one of the escaped prisoners had handed him at the market square that morning. It contained a song entitled "Sherman's March to the Sea" written by Adjutant Samuel Hawkins Marshall Byers of the Fifth Iowa infantry. The stirring lines of this song so impressed the General that he made its author a member of his staff.[56]

The General's rest was interrupted from time to time by the visits of women, importuning guards for their homes. One of these callers, Mrs. Campbell Bryce, found Sherman "respectful and kindly" and quite willing to write out an order assigning a guard to her home.[57] Mayor Goodwyn, anxious about the fate of Columbia, called late in the afternoon. He was much impressed by the polite and courteous manner with which Sherman received him and his anxiety was allayed when Sherman promised protection for the city.

The two men took a walk together. The Mayor introduced Sherman

51. Gibbes testimony, *Mixed Commission of Claims*, p. 17.
52. Sill, "Who Is Responsible," *Land We Love*, IV, 363.
53. *The Burning of Columbia*, p. 18.
54. Gibbes, *Who Burnt Columbia?* p. 7.
55. Blanton Duncan, who held the contract for making Confederate money, had fled the city.
56. Sherman, *Memoirs*, II, 282; Byers, *Fire and Sword*, pp. 174-76.
57. Bryce, *Personal Experiences*, p. 25.

to "new and old acquaintances."[58]   In answer to a note of invitation
Sherman requested they go first to the daughter of the Poyas family,
whom he had known twenty years earlier at Charleston. Happy memories of his duty at Fort Moultrie had been rekindled. The General was
pleased to find that the large frame house, located near the Charlotte
depot, had not been pillaged and that "a general air of peace and
comfort" prevailed. Much to his surprise Sherman learned that he was
responsible for the "perfect safety of . . . [the] house and property."
Upon entering the yard earlier in the day, the Federal soldiers had been
confronted by the Poyas girl who held in her hand a book in which
Lieutenant Sherman had written his name years earlier. Fortunately
for the girl, one of the group verified the signature on the fly leaf. This
so impressed the others that a guard was immediately stationed at the
house and a young boy from Iowa was assigned the job of helping with
the baby of the home. Sherman, clearly flattered by this story, paid a long
social call. From here Goodwyn took the General to the home of
Harris Simons, whose brother, James, had been Sherman's friend in
Charleston. Sherman had also known Mrs. Simons in her maiden days
as Miss Wragg.[59]

At sundown the Mayor and the General returned to the Duncan
house. Before going inside, Sherman again made it clear to his companion that Columbia was secure: "Go home and rest assured that your
city will be as safe in my hands as if you had controlled it." He did,
however, acquaint Goodwyn with his plan to burn several public buildings
and inquired about the condition of the city's fire engines and water
works. But he went on to say that this undertaking would have to be
delayed until a succeeding day when the winds were not so strong. Sherman feared the present gale-like gusts might spread the flames to private
property, not "one particle" of which did he wish to destroy.[60]

Having walked over much of Columbia during the afternoon, Sherman was tired when he lay down on his bed for a nap. Scarcely had he
closed his eyes when he was awakened by a bright light flickering back
and forth on the walls of his room. Fearful that the high winds had
fanned the smoldering cotton fires, he sent his aide, Major George Ward
Nichols, to inquire into the cause of these fire shadows. The Major re-

58. *The Burning of Columbia*, p. 7.
59. Sherman, *Memoirs*, II, 284-85.
60. *The Burning of Columbia*, p. 7.

turned and divulged the worst, a block of buildings in the heart of the city was on fire. But he hastened to add that General Woods "with plenty of men" was working tirelessly to bring the fires under control. Thereafter, periodic word came from Logan and Woods that the maximum effort was being exerted to curb the blazes. But man in this instance was no match for nature. The high winds were turning Columbia into a raging inferno. Around eleven o'clock, with the entire heavens lurid from the glow of dancing flames, Sherman went out himself to aid in stemming the conflagration.[61]

Shortly after nightfall, red, white, and blue rockets had been visible in the sky above the new state house. The sight of these flares had caused the guard at Mayor Goodwyn's to jump up and exclaim: "My God, is it coming to this" and then rush off without explanation.[62] A minister, standing in his front yard when the first rocket went up, heard Federal soldiers near by remark: "Now you will catch hell—that is the signal for a general setting of fire to the city."[63] If there was an organized plot on foot to burn Columbia, it is likely that the conspirators awaited these signals to begin their work since it was the general practice of the signal corps to send up rockets each night to give troop locations.[64] Planned or not, numerous fires broke out almost simultaneously in several areas of Columbia directly after the rockets were seen in the heavens.

Among the first fires of the evening were those which broke out in the low wooden houses on Gervais Street, used mostly as places of prostitution.[65] Presently alarms were sounded in "Cotton Town," the northwest corner of Columbia, and along the river front and to the west. In a few minutes twenty or more fires were raging in different sections of Columbia, including the very heart of the city.[66] There can be little doubt that the capital city of South Carolina was deliberately fired by the soldiers in blue, in General Hazen's belief, "in more than a hundred places."[67]

At dusk the hitherto deserted streets of Columbia had begun to fill up with shadowy figures carrying fire brands, cotton balls saturated in

61. Sherman, *Memoirs*, II, 286. 62. *The Burning of Columbia*, p. 7.
63. "Sherman's Story Examined," pp. 450-51.
64. Howard testimony, *Mixed Commission on Claims*, p. 32.
65. Salley, *Sack of Columbia, By Simms*, p. 41.
66. *The Burning of Columbia*, p. 16. 67. *Ibid.*, p. 18.

combustible material, cans of turpentine, and pockets full of matches.[68] Prepared for the job at hand, emboldened by whiskey, and ever increasing in members, "the drunken devils roamed about setting fire to every house in every direction. . . ." The local citizens gave up all thought of sleep and watched by the red glare of burning buildings the "wretches" in blue as they walked the streets shouting, hurrahing, cursing South Carolina, swearing, blaspheming, and singing ribald songs. The horror of this scene implanted itself in the mind of young Emma LeConte, who wrote:

Imagine night turned into noonday, only with a blazing, scorching glare that was terrible—a copper-colored sky across which swept columns of black rolling smoke glittering with sparks and flying embers, while all around us were falling thickly showers of burning flakes. Everywhere the palpitating blaze walled the streets as far the eye could reach—filling the air with its terrible roar. On every side the crackling and devouring fire, while every instant came the crashing of timbers and the thunder of falling buildings. A quivering molten ocean seemed to fill the air and sky.[69]

Heart-rending cries of those in distress, the terrified lowing of cattle, and the frenzied flight of pigeons added to the pathos of the occasion.[70]

The college library next to the LeConte home "seemed framed by the gushing flames and smoke, while through the windows gleamed the liquid fire. . . ."[71] The other buildings on the campus, filled with three hundred sick and wounded soldiers, were soon on fire. Only through the valiant efforts of the few doctors and nurses present were those buildings saved. From the rooftops they fought the flames, while the patients as best they could, dragged themselves out into the yard. Sometime before daybreak drunken soldiers tried to storm the campus gate although a yellow hospital flag was flying and the wounded inside were both Confederate and Federal soldiers. Three of the college professors and Dr. Thompson of the hospital staff stationed themselves at the main entrance to the grounds, which were encompassed by a high wall, and warded off the intruders until a strong guard arrived.[72]

68. Stanley testimony, *Mixed Commission on Claims,* p. 5.
69. LeConte Diary, Feb. 18, 1865, SHC, U.N.C.
70. Mme. Sosnowski, "Burning of Columbia," MS, SCL, U.S.C., p. 10; Crittenden, "Sack of Columbia," *S. C. Women,* p. 331; Gibbes, *Who Burnt Columbia?* p. 117.
71. LeConte Diary, Feb. 18, 1865, SHC, U.N.C.
72. Salley, *Sack of Columbia, By Simms,* pp. 70-71; Hollis, *Univ. of S.C.,* I, 227; W. J. Rivers to D. L. Swain, Jan. 23, 1868, Swain Papers, SHC, U.N.C.

The soldiers, foiled in their attempt to raze the college buildings, were intent upon leveling the Baptist church where the South Carolina secession convention first met. The detail sent to burn this edifice did not know its location and had to inquire of a colored man which of the many places of worship in Columbia it was. This Negro, who it is said was the sexton of the desired church, purposely directed the detail to the Washington Street Methodist Church less than a block away. Thus a faithful Negro, saved from certain destruction this symbol of South Carolina's leadership in the secession movement.[73] Three times the Methodist Church was set on fire. The pastor, the Reverend Mr. Connor, twice put out the flames, but when the parsonage next door was fired, he had to tend his sick child whom he carried out of the house in his arms. So incensed was one soldier by this time that he tore off the child's blanket and threw it into the flames, saying: "D—n you, if you say a word I'll throw the child after it."[74]

The Ursuline Convent suffered the same fate as the Methodist Church, even though Sherman had penciled a note to the Mother Superior promising protection for the school. His concern for the institution was based on the knowledge that this lady had once been a teacher in a convent in Ohio at the time his daughter, Minnie, was there.[75] During the night, as the soldiers milled around the convent and sparks began to fall on the building, the Mother Superior decided to evacuate the premises. Foolishly the nuns removed none of their possessions or church valuables. Consequently, no sooner had the teachers and pupils departed than the guards, joined by drunken soldiers, began to ransack the school. A thorough job of pillage was enacted before flames destroyed the building.[76]

A great historical and scientific loss was the home of Dr. Robert Wilson Gibbes. Soldiers fired the house of this noted man of letters and science by piling furniture in the drawing room and igniting it. The lone guard, befriended by Gibbes, tried without success to halt this lawlessness. Lost in the blaze was a large library, many portfolios of fine engravings, more than a hundred paintings, "a remarkable cabinet of

73. *Destruction of Property in Columbia, Speech by C. L. Blease*, p. 4; Baum, "An Incident," *Mag. of Amer. Hist.*, XIV, 619.
74. *Destruction of Property in Columbia, Speech by C. L. Blease*, p. 5.
75. Sherman, *Memoirs*, II, 279-80.
76. "Burning of Columbia," extract from a circular letter to "Congregation de Paris," *S.C. Women*, pp. 289-97.

southern fossiles," one of the finest collections of shark's teeth in the world, American and Mexican Indian relics, and an extensive collection of historical documents, including much original correspondence on the Revolution.[77]

The uncontrollable fires which engulfed the city did not curb the cupidity of the soldiers. Their search for spoil continued. The men, plied with whiskey, rushed from house to house, first emptying them of their valuables, and then applying the torch.[78] Jewelry and plate were found in abundance. Drunks staggered under the accumulation of sterling trays, vases, candelabra, cups, and goblets. Clothes and shoes, when new, were usually appropriated, the rest left to burn. Fraternal orders were not overlooked. Men absurdly attired in Masonic and Odd Fellow regalias strolled about the streets.[79]

Many guards followed the example of those at the convent by deserting their posts and entering into the rowdyism of the night. At the Agnes Law residence the four guards conducted themselves admirably for a while. Here they were fed supper, after which one lay down on the sofa. The others walked about the yard. But when the city began to burn and Agnes wanted to remove her furniture, the guards objected on the grounds that the house was in no immediate danger. Before long these same men took lighted candles upstairs and set the curtains on fire.[80]

More than once superhuman strength enabled an individual to salvage a heavy piece of furniture or other cumbersome possessions from a burning home. Alice Boatwright managed to get a fully packed trunk from her upstairs to her front yard, only to have the soldiers break the lock and take what they wanted.[81]

The Federal camps, where a few of the homeless sought refuge, were not free from theft either. The soldiers attempted to steal what little these families had salvaged.[82]

The Negroes, urged by the ruffians to get in on the fun, were told they were receiving their wages for years of unpaid labor. It was not

77. Rhodes, "Who Burned Columbia," *AHR*, VII, 493; Gibbes, *Who Burnt Columbia?* p. 19.

78. Conyngham, *Sherman's March*, p. 331.

79. Salley, *Sack of Columbia, By Simms;* Trowbridge, *The South*, p. 559.

80. Gibbes, *Who Burnt Columbia?* p. 136.

81. Julia Lee to Mrs. J. H. Lee, J. H. Lee Papers, SHC, U.N.C.; Williams, *Old and New Columbia*, p. 122.

82. Leaphart, "Experiences," *S.C. Women.*, pp. 248-49.

unusual, though, for the servants, after they had filled their pails, or gunny sacks with loot, to put this haul at their master's disposal. A fair number, having been disillusioned by the conduct of their "friends" from the North, remained loyal to their owners.[83]   An exception was "Old Peter," a servant in one of the Mordecai homes, who betrayed the hiding place of the family silver.[84]

There were very few cases of rape against the white women of Columbia.[85]   In fact, Harriot Ravenel observed that the Federal soldiers, on most occasions, addressed white females as "lady" and seldom swore directly at them.[86]   In some quarters relations between the men under arms and the young beauties of Columbia were so amiable that romance resulted.   In the ranks of the Sixth Iowa alone two such courtships occurred.[87]   Even so, a large number of the women suffered indignities at the hands of the intruder.   An extreme practice followed by a few of the soldiers in looking for valuables hidden on a woman's person was to catch her by the throat and feel in her bosom for a watch or pull up her dress in search of a purse hidden in her girdle or petticoat.   Those not so brazen did not hesitate to point a pistol at a woman's head to learn the location of the family heirlooms.[88]

Negro women were for the most part the victims of the soldiers' lust. A number of them were woefully mistreated and ravished.   The disorders of the night had caused many to flee their huts and seek a place of refuge. But in the "shadows and out of the way places" more than one fell victim to the soldiers' desires.   The next morning their unclothed bodies, bearing the marks of detestable sex crimes, were found about the city.[89]   An old Negro woman belonging to the Reverend Mr. Shand was subjected to several brutal assaults.   Then at the proposition of one of the attackers, "to finish the old Bitch," she was "put into the ditch and her head held under the water until life was extinct."[90]

This detestable treatment of the colored women did nothing to

83. Milling, "Ilium," p. 180.
84. Gibbes, *Who Burnt Columbia?* p. 13.
85. Salley, *Sack of Columbia, By Simms,* p. 54.
86. Ravenel, "When Columbia Burned," *S.C. Women,* p. 325.
87. Wright, *6 Ia.,* p. 416.
88. Trezevant, *Burning of Columbia,* p. 10.
89. Walters, Sherman and Total War (Ph.D. dissertation, Vanderbilt Univ., 1947), p. 325.
90. Comments by D. H. Trezevant on Federal treatment of Women in Columbia, Trezevant Papers, SCL, U.S.C.

strengthen friendship between the Northern soldier and the Negro. Neither did the open hostility of the western troops for the black man help matters.[91] One Westerner made a stump speech to a large gathering of whites and blacks in which he expressed the desire that all Negroes be placed on an immense platform under which was enough powder to blow the congregation "to atoms."[92]

Disregarding the animosity exhibited toward their race, a few Negro women publicly associated with the soldiers. On the streets of Columbia, men in blue were seen hugging and kissing mulattoes. A member of General Blair's staff is reputed to have slept with his Negro companion in the home of a white family. Adding further insult to the occasion he allowed his copper-colored companion to take from the house what she wanted.[93]

The night of February 17, although characterized by horror and terror, was not void of acts of kindness on the part of the Federal soldiers. To the more kind hearted, the distress of the citizens touched their deepest sympathies. This element of the army rendered assistance to those in need, especially women and children.[94] Their deeds ranged from forcibly holding off the incendiaries to building a coffin for a child's dog.[95] While many guards deserted their posts in order to pillage, others remained staunchly loyal to their duty throughout the night. Madame S. Sosnowski, Mrs. Campbell Bryce, Mrs. W. K. Bachman, to name a few, were fortunate enough to secure guards who were conscientious about their orders. Mrs. Bachman was so thankful for the work of a young Iowan, Private William Davis, that she gave him a small silver cup stating that she never thought she could feel toward an enemy as she did toward him.[96]

One of the most fascinating stories to come out of the Federal occupation of Columbia was that of the Episcopal minister, A. Toomer Porter, and his relationship with Lieutenant John A. McQueen of the Fifteenth Illinois. This Illinois officer profoundly deplored the wanton destruction of property and the insults visited upon the defenseless

91. Milling, "Ilium," p. 180.
92. Andrews, *Women of the South*, p. 268.
93. Trezevant, *Burning of Columbia*, p. 10.
94. Wright, *6 Ia.*, p. 415; Winther, *Upson Diary*, p. 153.
95. Gibbes, *Who Burnt Columbia?* p. 13.
96. Mrs. W. K. Bachman to Kate Bachman, Mar. 27, 1865, W. K. Bachman Papers, SCL, U.S.C.; Bryce, *Personal Experiences*, p. 44; Andrews, *Women of the South*, pp. 274-75.

women and children of the city. The Dr. William Reynolds house in Columbia, where Porter and his family had lodgings, was saved from destruction through the efforts of McQueen. At pistol point, the Lieutenant drove out the pillagers and secured a strong guard and bucket brigade for the night. When Porter was accosted on the street by a drunken sergeant, McQueen brought the soldier back at the point of a bayonet to apologize to the minister. He did what he could to bring order out of this chaos. In the Reverend Mr. Porter's words, McQueen was one of the finest gentlemen he had ever known, "a brave soldier, a chivalrous enemy, a devoted friend, and a most devout and honest Christian gentleman."

When McQueen prepared to depart with the army as it moved north, Porter wished to give him a piece of his wife's jewelry as a token of appreciation for his kindness. The Lieutenant refused on the grounds that some one might think he stole it. Instead the Minister wrote two similar letters, one addressed to Wade Hampton and the other to Confederate soldiers relating what this Illinoian had done for him and urging every consideration in case he fell into Confederate hands.[97]

Sherman himself on the night of February 17, stopped by the Simons' home and advised the ladies to move to his headquarters where they would be safe. He ordered his own headquarter's wagon hitched up to move their personal effects.[98]

On main street Sherman found Generals Howard, Logan, Woods, and Hazen barking orders to the men and toiling themselves in a fruitless effort to halt the flames.[99] Guards watched over furniture piled in the middle of the street. Sherman saw Stone's disorderly troops removed from the city and Brigadier General W. B. Woods' brigade brought in.[100] Woods immediately began a roundup of all drunken and lawless soldiers. Three hundred and seventy were placed under arrest, two were killed, and thirty wounded.[101] Sherman in person ordered the arrest of a drunken private and saw Colonel L. M. Dayton, his aide, shoot the man down when he resisted arrest.[102] Woods' brigade, in spite

97. *Charleston News and Courier*, Apr. 4, 1884, U. R. Brooks Papers, MS Div., Duke Univ. Lib.

98. Sherman, *Memoirs*, II, 286.

99. Sherman testimony in the case of *A. Barclay v. U.S.*, Mar. 26, 1872. Penciled copy in Sherman Papers, MS Div. L.C.

100. Howard testimony, *Mixed Commission Claims*, pp. 27-28.

101. *OR*, XLVII, Pt. I, Ser. I, 309.

102. Sherman testimony, *Mixed Commission on Claims*, p. 77.

of its hard work, fared little better than its predecessor in bringing order to the city and stemming the fires. Eventually all of Hazen's division was ordered into Columbia[103] but only a shift of wind around 4:00 A.M. saved the city from total annihilation.

General Sherman spent the greater part of the night battling the flames but at no time did he take immediate personal charge of the fire-fighting activities. No general orders were issued by him that night because, in his opinion, his subordinates were doing all that was possible to bring the situation under control.[104]

Many Federal soldiers, including high ranking officers, labored diligently into the early morning hours to curb the conflagration. The aging William Gilmore Simms admitted that this is true.[105] Just the same, the fact stands that the small force on duty in Columbia could offer only meager efforts at stemming the raging fires. Either Sherman or one of his lieutenants should have ordered a large body of troops into the capital early in the evening. With a high wind blowing and the city full of those who did not wish to see the scene closed, "the viriest scum of the army," a force much larger than four brigades was necessary for effective action.[106]

It seemed to the inhabitants of Columbia that dawn would never come. To them it was as though "the gates of hell had been opened...."[107] A drunken trooper "with a musket in one hand and a match in the other is not a pleasant visitor to have about the house on a dark, windy night...." In the minds of the local citizenry such an individual surely must have crossed the river Styx on his journey to Columbia.[108] When the sun rose at last, dim and red through the murky atmosphere, it shone upon a smouldering ruins that was once a beautiful and proud city. With the first light of dawn and the sound of reveille the "drunken devils" disappeared like ghosts at the cock crowing.[109] Their work was finished. The greater part of Columbia was in ashes. From the center of town as far as the eye could reach, nothing was to be seen "but heaps

103. OR, XLVII, Pt. I, Ser. I, 228, 272.

104. Sherman testimony, A. Barclay v. U.S.

105. Salley, Sack of Columbia, By Simms, p. 17.

106. C. R. Woods to Major (W. Atwood?), Feb. 21, 1865, Sherman Papers, MS Div., L.C.

107. Porter, Work of Faith, p. 114.

108. Slocum, "Sherman's March," p. 686.

109. LeConte Diary, Feb. 18, 1865, SHC, U.N.C.; Ravenel, "When Columbia Burned," p. 327.

of rubbish, tall dreary chimneys, and shattered brick walls. . . ."[110] The fires had ranged over 84 of the city's 124 blocks, containing 500 edifices.[111]

The homeless, gathered in the open spaces and parks of the city and huddled around their few belongings, were a pitiful sight. From her porch Emma LeConte looked across the street to the common which "was crowded with homeless women and children, a few wrapped in blankets and many shivering in the night air."[112] Some were crying and despondent. A few were patient, submissive, and quiet. Others complained terribly about the "Yankees." This pathetic sight was too much for even the war hardened heart of an Illinois surgeon who entered in his diary: "I talked with some but it made me feel too bad to be endured."[113]

Whitelaw Reid, the Ohio politician, called the burning of Columbia the "most monstrous barbarity of the barbarous march."[114] The people of Columbia, in full agreement with Reid, were also positive that one day the Devil "with a wild sardonic grin will point exultant to a crime which won the prize from SIN."[115] For them Sherman had out-Heroded Herod and "Beast" Butler was a gentleman in comparison.[116]

It was the drunken soldier who was primarily responsible for the holocaust of February 17, but he was not acting under orders from his commanding general. Sherman's orders for the campaign of the Carolinas contain no instructions for the molestation of private property in Columbia.[117] In 1872, when called to testify in a lawsuit regarding the fire, he swore: "I gave no order at anytime to burn any private home or dwelling. . . . Nor did I give permission to anyone to set fire to any private dwelling. . . ."[118] The question of who was responsible for the burning of Columbia was investigated by a mixed commission on American and British claims under the Treaty of Washington in 1873. The plaintiffs asked compensation for privately owned cotton on the grounds that Columbia had been "wantonly fired by the army of General Sherman either under his orders or with his consent and permission."

110. LeConte Diary, Feb. 22, 1865, SHC, U.N.C.
111. Snowden, *Hist. of S.C.*, II, 810.
112. LeConte Diary, Feb. 18, 1865, SHC, U.N.C.
113. Burton, *Diary of E. P. Burton*, II, 63.
114. Reid, *Ohio in the War*, I, 475.
115. Love, *Burning of Columbia*, p. 4.
116. Andrews, *South Since the War*, p. 31.
117. *OR*, XLVII, Pt. II, Ser. I, 1 ff.
118. Sherman testimony, *A. Barclay v. U. S.*

This commission cleared Sherman's name when it found that the destruction of property in the capital was due to neither "the intention or default of either the Federal or Confederate officers."[119]

On the night of the fire Sherman was inclined to attribute the conflagration to whiskey. In conversation with Mayor Goodwyn that evening he complained: "Who could command drunken soldiers?" The blame for what happened on February 17 was the mayor's, said Sherman, because the large stores of liquor in the city had not been removed by him.[120] A few days reflection changed his mind. He then concluded that Hampton and cotton should bear the guilt, not whiskey. On the witness stand in one of the cotton cases he asserted:

The fire was originated with the imprudent act of Wade Hampton in ripping open bales of cotton, piling it in the streets, burning it and then going away. . . . If I had made up my mind to burn Columbia I would have burnt it with no more feeling than I would a common prairie village; but I did not do it. . . . God Almighty started wind sufficient to carry that cotton wherever He would, and in some way or other that burning cotton was the origin of the fire. . . .[121]

Three years later in 1875, with the publication of his *Memoirs*, Sherman admitted that his charges against Hampton were designed to shake the faith of the people of South Carolina in their cavalry commander. He considered Hampton a braggart and the self-appointed champion of his people.[122] But Sherman never wavered in his conviction that cotton fired on the morning of February 17 played the major role in commencing the fires of that evening. He did concede that some soldiers after the fire originated may have been concerned in spreading it, but not concerned in starting it.[123]

The findings of the Mixed Claims Commission did not silence those who contended that the devastation on Columbia was carried out with Sherman's tacit consent. This group likes to quote out of context from the General's letter to Halleck, December 24, 1864, in which he used his usual intemperate language to speculate on the fate of South Carolina at the hands of his troops.[124] By omitting the line, "I doubt if we will spare the public buildings as we did in Milledgeville" Sherman's loose

119. Sherman, *Memoirs*, II, 287; Lewis, *Sherman*, p. 507.
120. *The Burning of Columbia*, p. 8.
121. Sherman testimony, *Mixed Commission on Claims*, pp. 96-97.
122. Sherman, *Memoirs*, II, 287.   123. *OR*, XLVII, Pt. I, Ser. I, 22.
124. See above p. 40.

words condemn him. At Milledgeville the Federal officers did amuse themselves by holding a mock session of the Georgia legislature, but they spared the Capitol as they did most of the public buildings in the town. Private homes and property were also respected.[125] In view of this conduct, Sherman's statement that in Columbia he would probably destroy public buildings shows more clearly that he anticipated only the destruction of public property than it shows he reflected on a policy of general devastation for the city.[126]

In the long run Sherman felt that the burning of private homes, though not designed by him, was a trifling matter when compared with the manifold results which soon followed. "Though I never ordered it and never wished it, I have never shed any tears over the event, because I believe that it hastened what we all fought for, the end of the war."[127] This laconic statement pretty well sums up Sherman's sentiments on the burning of Columbia.

The army remained in Columbia for two days, destroying public and railroad property as ordered by Sherman.[128] General Howard's men tore up the railroad track toward the Wateree as well as demolishing all railroad property in the city.[129] A detail under Colonel O. M. Poe of the engineers leveled what remained of the public buildings with the exception of the unfinished state house.[130] As one native of Columbia expressed it: "They destroyed everything which the most infernal Yankee ingenuity could devise means to destroy."[131] The Confederate arsenal, several foundries, the gas works, and a printing establishment for Confederate money all fell before the wrecking crews.[132] Large amounts of currency, in various stages of manufacture, fell into the hands of the soldiers who "spent and gambled with it in the most lavish manner."[133]

A terrific explosion rocked the city on February 18 when the Federal ordnance crew became careless in dumping wagon loads of captured ammunition in the Saluda River. The accident took the lives of sixteen

125. Sherman, *Memoirs,* II, 190.
126. Hill, "Burning of Columbia," pp. 273-74.
127. Sherman testimony, *A. Barclay v. U.S.*
128. *OR,* XLVII, Pt. I, Ser. I, 22.
129. *Ibid.,* p. 199.
130. *Ibid.,* p. 171. The old state house had been burned on the night of Feb. 17.
131. Andrews, *South Since the War,* p. 33.
132. Sherman testimony, *A. Barclay v. U.S.*
133. Sherlock, *100 Ind.,* p. 199.

Federal soldiers much to the delight of Emma LeConte who rejoiced "to think of any of them being killed."[134]

After February 17, wholesale pillage and plunder stopped, but much petty theft and rummaging in the ruins for more booty continued. The soldiers made no pretense of hiding their loot. Stolen jewelry and coin were very much in evidence on their persons as they strolled the streets boasting of having burned Columbia.[135]

Sherman was not indifferent to the suffering of the people. From his own stores he gave rice and ham to the Poyas and Simons families.[136] Harris Simons' hesitancy to accept the stores from an enemy, kindled the General's temper. Eyes flashing, Sherman denounced him as a damn fool and added that he did not care if Simons starved but that the rice and ham were for his wife and children. Sherman had considerable admiration for many of the upper class. He termed the aristocracy of South Carolina men "of great honor and integrity" but for one of them to raise a point of honor at such a time was utterly ridiculous to him.[137]

To the Mother Superior and the children of the Ursuline Convent, Sherman turned over the mansion of General John S. Preston, Wade Hampton's brother-in-law. Its occupant, General Logan, was preparing to ignite the barrels of pitch in the cellar when the white clad children arrived. Logan let out mighty oaths when handed Sherman's order but he had the barrels of pitch removed.[138] Inside the nuns found that the evacuating personnel had left their mark. The many fine paintings and pieces of statuary which adorned the halls had been mutilated. Dignified portraits carried penciled mustaches and nude statues bore clothing.[139]

Sunday, February 19, a delegation of local citizens went to Sherman seeking food for the city and firearms for police protection. He received them courteously but on this particular Sabbath he seemed "to be on particularly good terms with himself."[140] He alone of the Federal officers present at the conference "appeared flushed with victory and made no effort to conceal his exultation."[141] After hearing the purpose of the

134. LeConte Diary, Feb. 19, 1865, SHC, U.N.C.
135. Pepper, *Recollections*, p. 313.
136. Sherman, *Memoirs*, II, 285.
137. Sherman testimony, *Mixed Commission on Claims*, p. 105.
138. Martin and Avary, *Diary from Dixie*, p. 358.
139. Milling, "Ilium," p. 180.
140. Scott, *Random Recollections*, p. 183.
141. Walters, Sherman and Total War (Ph.D. dissertation, Vanderbilt Univ., 1947), p. 328.

visit and expounding on the folly of war, he consented to leave behind five hundred head of cattle, one hundred muskets, ammunition, all the salt at the Charleston depot, wire enough to work a flat across the river, and medicine for the sick.[142] The beef was poor, the arms, old, and the drugs, small in quantity, but they were better than nothing. In Sherman's eyes, an enemy under arms deserved little quarter. He saw no reason to shed tears over Columbia's plight as long as South Carolina was at war with the Union.

On February 20, to the accompaniment of hisses and boos from the people along the streets, the troops resumed their march north toward Winnsboro. As the columns in blue filed by the scattered groups of men, women, and children they were spat upon and "not a few of the women undertook to lay violent hands upon . . ." them.[143] Moving with the army were a large number of inhabitants, both white and black, of Columbia and neighboring areas who wished to go north.[144] The reasons for departure varied. Mrs. George Crafts, her three children, and white nurse, left in one of the baggage wagons because she felt to remain behind meant starvation.[145] Among the refugees were several families who claimed they had harbored escaped Federal prisoners. Conspicuous in this number was the indecorous Mary Boozer, described by General John S. Preston as the "most beautiful piece of flesh and blood" his eyes had ever beheld.[146] Mary, because of her interest in the Federal prisoners lodged in the Asylum, had been socially ostracized in Columbia and placed under military surveillance during the latter stages of the war.[147] Thus she and her mother, Mrs. Feaster by a fourth marriage, were delighted at the opportunity to leave with the occupation forces. As befitting her great beauty, Mary, on the outskirts of the city, "exchanged" her old dilapidated carriage for a more elegant one owned by Mrs. Elmore.[148]

Only after the soldiers had departed and the fear and excitement of the past days had begun to ebb did the citizens of Columbia really feel

142. Gibbes, *Who Burnt Columbia?* p. 48.

143. Arbuckle, *Civil War Experiences,* p. 135.

144. *OR,* XLVII, Pt. I, Ser. I, 228. Each division of the Fifteenth Corps was assigned an equal number of the refugees. Wright, *6 Ia.,* p. 419.

145. Smith, *Smith Letters,* p. 181. Mrs. Craft was a northern woman who had married a Charlestonian. *N.Y. Herald,* Mar. 12, 1865.

146. *Checkered Life of Marie Boozer,* pp. 27-28.

147. Mary helped a young officer from Ohio to escape and kept him concealed at her house until the arrival of the Federal army at Columbia. Simkins and Patton, *Women of the Confederacy,* p. 63.

148. Gibbes, *Who Burnt Columbia?* p. 21

the full impact of the destruction and devastation around them. For young Emma LeConte the "very air . . . [was] frought with sadness and silence." The few noises that broke the stillness seemed melancholy to her.[149] In Emma's mind the word "Yankee" was synonymous for all that was *"mean,* despicable and abhorrent."[150]

149. LeConte Diary, Feb. 21, 1865, SHC, U.N.C.
150. *Ibid.,* Feb. 23, 1865.

CHAPTER VII

"Death to All Foragers"

By FEBRUARY 20, most South Carolinians had learned of the doom that befell Columbia. The reaction to this news was varied. General Lafayette McLaws, writing from St. Stephens Depot on February 22, concluded that although the people of the state had suffered much, they did not, in general, appear too downcast.[1] On the other hand, Dr. Samuel McGill, a distinguished citizen of the Williamsburg District, was overcome with despondency. On February 28, he entered in his diary:

All is gloom and uncertainty, and preparations are being made for the worst. Furniture and provisions are hidden against pending raids. . . . It is feared famine will possess the land; our army is demoralized and the people panic stricken. All is gloom, despondency, and inactivity. The power to do has left us. . . . To fight longer seems to be madness; to submit tamely is dishonor.[2]

The next day the news was worse and he observed: "The whole country is in the wildest commotion and many are fleeing to the woods with their wives and daughters, while a few have gone to meet the advance and to give battle."[3]

At Newberry, a short distance northwest of Columbia, Captain F. N. Walker, a Confederate enrolling officer, managed to rally one hundred men to protect the city. Pickets were posted and scouts sent out but to no purpose. Sherman moved his army to the east in the direction of Winnsboro.[4]

As the Federal troops approached the historic and old town of Winnsboro, several of its few remaining male citizens "took to the

1. L. McLaws to wife, Feb. 22, 1865, McLaws Papers, SHC, U.N.C.
2. Boddie, *Hist. of Williamsburg*, p. 427.
3. *Ibid.*, p. 428.
4. O'Neal and Chapman, *Annals of Newberry*, Pt. I, 455.

woods." At least one of those departing in great haste was returning to "hiding places of which he had become familiar during his frequent flights to escape conscription."[5] Soon Winnsboro was left with an adult male population of two, the Reverend W. W. Lord, rector of Christ Episcopal Church, and his four-hundred-pound vestryman, the village doctor. These two men visited the Federal camp in hope of securing a promise of protection for their village. Their efforts proved futile. Winnsboro was destined to be visited by the notorious "bummers" before the main army entered the town.

It was the lowing of driven cattle, the squawking of poultry, and the squealing of pigs that heralded the approach of Sherman's army early on the morning of the 21st—not the drum and bugle. The "bummer" had already visited the fertile countryside and with his haul was on the outskirts of the village. Laughing, shouting, and cursing, these self-appointed foragers rode into Winnsboro. Dismounting, they immediately turned to pillaging and burning. "Like truants out of school," said the Reverend Mr. Lord's son, "these overgrown 'Boys in Blue' played snowball along the fire-lit streets with precious flour; made bonfires of hams and sides of bacon; set boxes and barrels of crackers afloat on streams of molasses and vinegar; fed horses from hats full of sugar." All in all, they destroyed enough food to have fed the town for a year.[6]

While this high carnival was being held amid burning stores downtown, the residential sections were not neglected. Many private homes were sacked and then burned. Chaplain John McCrae, Thirty-third Indiana, who had once lived near Winnsboro, did not have the heart to visit old acquaintances with "soldiers . . . everywhere pillaging, burning."[7]

The Episcopal Church, in the northwest corner of the town and away from the general conflagration, fell prey to the vindictive spirit of this group. It was alleged that before firing the building the men removed the organ so they might play "the devil's tunes" on it.[8] Calling upon the dead to view their fiendish deed, a coffin was exhumed from an adjacent grave, split open with an axe and stood on end so that its recently dead occupant might witness the spectacle.[9]

General John W. Geary, leading the advance of the left wing, saw the heavy smoke rising from these fires and ordered his two most advanced regiments to move at "double-quick" in hope they would reach Winns-

5. Lord, "Path of Sherman," *Harpers Mag.*, CXX, 422.
6. *Ibid.*, pp. 443-44.   7. Stormont, *Hight Diary*, p. 485.
8. Trowbridge, *The South*, p. 577.   9. Cook, *Sherman's March*, p. 9.

boro in time to arrest the flames. These two regiments, along with the remainder of the Second Division of the Twentieth Corps, performed the part of firemen with great efficiency and soon had the fires under control. Learning that the "bummers" were not his men, Geary ordered the men back to their respective commands. He put Brigadier General N. Pardee in charge of the town with orders to protect private property.[10] Guards whose "conversation . . . was generally kind and indicated respect" were stationed throughout Winnsboro.[11] But the possession of these qualities was not enough to curb all the disorders.[12]

In all probability, between twenty and thirty buildings, including homes, stores, and public edifices, were destroyed in the town.[13] The *Winnsboro News* estimated that between eight and ten stores were burned the first day and that the torch was applied to ten or twelve private homes on the second.[14] General Geary in his official report stated that "one square was burned before the fire could be arrested."[15]

Pardee's brigade remained on duty in Winnsboro on February 22 until all of the troops in the vicinity, comprising the Seventeenth, Twentieth, and Fourteenth Corps, had passed through the town.

Local persons gathered on the sidewalks to watch the army march by with bands playing and flags flying. Their joy at the departure of the enemy was dampened somewhat by the sight of former friends traveling in the refugee train. Particularly incensed were they when Mary Boozer and her mother rode by in a carriage, the daughter in lively conversation with a young officer.[16] In the short distance between Columbia and Winnsboro, the golden-haired Mary had acquired a retinue of admirers and was ruling as a veritable Cleopatra within the army.[17]

At the urgent request of local citizens, General Geary left behind two mounted troopers from his provost guard to protect the town from stragglers. He was correct in assuming that Hampton would keep his word that any Federal soldiers left behind as safeguards after the departure of the main forces would be protected from arrest or injury if

---

10. *OR*, XLVII, Pt. I, Ser. I, 687; Bryant, *3 Wis.*, p. 308.

11. *Raleigh Conservative*, Mar. 10, 1865, quoting the *Winnsboro News*, n.d.

12. Jackson, *Colonel's Diary*, p. 186.

13. *Winnsboro Courier*, n.d., Emma Mordecai Diary, SHC, U.N.C.

14. *Raleigh Conservative*, Mar. 10, 1865, quoting the *Winnsboro News*, n.d.

15. *OR*, XLVII, Pt. I, 687.

16. Poppenheim, "Sherman at Liberty Hill," *S.C. Women*, p. 259.

17. Simkins and Patton, *Women of the Confederacy*, p. 63, quoting *Augusta Chronicle*, Sept. 18, 1927.

they fell into Confederate hands. The two guards organized the citizens of Winnsboro and drove out of town several stragglers, including six who had hidden in the court house tower, hoping to remain and loot the town after the army was out of sight. The next morning a detachment of Confederate cavalry rode into town, relieving the two guards of their duty. The men in gray showed the two Federal soldiers "every courtesy in their power," and the people of the town openly expressed their gratitude to these two. The guards rejoined their command safely.[18]

At Winnsboro the army was ordered to march east on the road to Cheraw. The right wing was to cross the Wateree River at Peay's Ferry and the left wing, further north at Rocky Mount. The cavalry, previously instructed to make a strong demonstration on Chester, was then to turn east and cross the Wateree with the left wing.

Kilpatrick on his feint toward Chester halted at Monticello on the afternoon of February 20. The General learned, much to his delight, that this small place northwest of Columbia contained a "female institution," but little did he dream that he would have to compete with two equally "Don Juanish" officers of the Fourteenth Corps for the attention of the young ladies. Two miles outside of Monticello was the camp of the Third Division of the Fourteenth Corps, among whose officers were Captain Dexter Horton and Colonel George Este. These two had decided that the surest way to get a visit with the fairer sex was to see that a regiment was sent to guard the seminary. They approached General Baird on the matter, but before they could get an answer, Kilpatrick rode up and announced to all that since his camp was in town he would take it upon himself to see that the young ladies were protected. Horton and Este were not to be outdone. They somehow secured an ambulance, filled it with food stuffs, and went to the seminary themselves where they were received "very kindly." That night, these two young officers attended a "gay and festive dance," with music furnished by the cavalry band.[19] The next morning the outwitted Kilpatrick resumed the practice of war and moved along the railroad to within a short distance of Chester, destroying the track, as well as telegraph lines, as he went. This put the town "truely in a dark corner," thought Charles Holst, a resident of Chester, but he was thankful to have a shelter over his head.[20]

18. *OR*, XLVII, Pt. I, Ser. I, 687; Lord, "Sherman Path," p. 444.
19. Eaton, "Diary of an Officer," p. 245.
20. C. F. A. Holst to Mrs. Pinkind, Mar. 19, 1865, Isabella A. Woodruff Papers, MS Div., Duke Univ. Lib.

By February 23, the entire army had reached the Wateree and some divisions had crossed. Heavy rains set in on this date and lasted three days, causing the river to flood. At Rocky Mount the left wing encountered great difficulty in effecting a crossing. The bridge, heaving like a ship in a storm, held up under the crossing of the Twentieth Corps and the cavalry.[21] Before Davis' Fourteenth Corps could be put in motion, however, it gave way to the logs and driftwood swept downstream by the swift current. The frail canvas boats used in the construction of the pontoon bridge were torn to pieces by this refuse, and rapidly rising waters and lack of proper materials rendered impossible an immediate reconstruction of the bridge. With the pioneers temporarily defeated, General Davis gave the order to attempt nothing further. The Fourteenth Corps, stranded on the west bank of the Wateree, could only await the recession of the waters.[22]

Although the soldiers of the Twentieth Corps had crossed this treacherous body without mishap, difficulties befell them on the eastern bank where the heavy rains had made a steep hill on the approach to the river almost impassable. It took the supreme effort of man and beast to keep the wagons rolling through the sea of mud, in places three feet deep.[23] By nightfall of February 23 the corps had covered a mere five miles in the direction of Hanging Rock. Three succeeding days of continuous rainfall slowed the progress to a snail's pace.[24] The men, "slipping, stumbling, swearing, singing, and yelling," finally arrived at Hanging Rock on February 26. They had marched only twenty miles in four days.[25]

At Hanging Rock General Slocum, learning of Davis' predicament, ordered the advance to halt while he himself rode back to the Wateree to expedite, if possible, the crossing of his other command.[26] Sherman by this time had become exceedingly annoyed at the general delay caused by the Fourteenth Corps. He was ready to destroy the wagons, spike the cannons, shoot the mules belonging to Davis, and then ferry the men across if it was necessary to get the entire army on the move.[27]

The Federal army temporarily halted, Southern newspaper men began to editorialize optimistically on the possibilities of the situation. From the

21. OR, XLVII, Pt. I, Ser. I, 421; Stormont, Hight Diary, p. 489.
22. OR, XLVII, Pt. I, Ser. I, 421; Nichols, Great March, p. 187.
23. Nichols, Great March, p. 182.   24. OR, XLVII, Pt. I, Ser. I, 583.
25. Boies, 33 Mass., p. 274.   26. OR, XLVII, Pt. I, Ser. I, 421.
27. N.Y. Herald, Mar. 15, 1865.

day the enemy force left Savannah, the people of the Carolinas had hoped it would flounder in the swamps and mires of South Carolina and be annihilated. The editor of the *Richmond Dispatch* saw Sherman as hopelessly "stuck in the mud." He deducted that if it had rained only half as much in South Carolina as it had in the vicinity of Richmond, the army could not possibly move.[28] *The Southern Presbyterian* pointed out that in view of the recent heavy rains Sherman's route north from Columbia was almost impracticable.

From Camden . . . to Cheraw the country is flat and swampy, and Sherman must construct his road as he progresses. It is confidently believed in military circles that if our forces in the two Carolinas can have time given them for concentration in front of this half-swamped army its destruction may be easily accomplished.[29]

The elements were not to detain Sherman's army long. On February 26, the sun finally broke through the overcast and the rains ceased. It shone upon "bedraggled mules, toiling soldiers, and seas of mud," but the warmth of its rays did considerable toward ebbing the tension of the men, much on edge after three days of steady rain.[30] The next day the Wateree began to fall. Brigadier General George P. Buell, amid the sneers of the more skeptical, began work immediately on a pontoon structure to be anchored by forks of trees and weighted down by hugh stones. By midnight, this bridge was in position and the troops and trains of the Fourteenth Corps were rolling again.[31]

In the meantime, Kilpatrick had been ordered by Sherman to move on Lancaster to the north, keeping up a general illusion of a movement on Charlotte, North Carolina, to which point Sherman understood Beauregard was directing all Confederate detachments.[32] The Federal occupation of Lancaster was accompanied by some disorder, but in comparison to Winnsboro the town suffered very little. Brigadier General Smith D. Atkins, one of Kilpatrick's brigade commanders, was especially considerate of those with whom he came in contact. Upon learning that a wounded Citadel cadet, recuperating in his father's home, had been roughly treated by some soldiers, the General apologized to the boy's father. He assured the father that it would not happen again.[33] On the

28. *Raleigh N.C. Standard*, Mar. 7, 1865, quoting the *Richmond Dispatch*, Mar. 1, 1865.
29. *Augusta Southern Presbyterian*, Mar. 9, 1865.
30. Nichols, *Great March*, p. 184.   31. Stormont, *Hight Diary*, p. 492.
32. *OR*, XLVII, Pt. I, Ser. I, 22.
33. Old Dominion, "Fair Women," *Our Women in the War*, p. 329.

other hand, General Kilpatrick was too well situated at his headquarters in the home of W. D. Brown to be concerned with military duties, much less acts of kindness. A "tall, handsome, well-dressed" woman had accompanied him to Lancaster and was occupying a room at his headquarters opposite his own. "Little Kil" paid full court to his female companion and the morning the cavalry left Lancaster, he turned over to her the family carriage, with all of Mrs. Brown's "beautiful white blankets" piled on the front seat.[34]

The right wing experienced relatively little difficulty in crossing the Wateree at Peay's Ferry on February 23. The Fifteenth Corps was fortunate to bivouac that night at Liberty Hill, an attractive village situated on a plateau not too distant from the river. A "spacious church," a "splendid academy," and "handsome women" made a very favorable impression on the men.[35] Here General Logan decided to divide his command into two columns and to send a detachment from one in a raid on Camden to the south. On February 24, Colonel R. N. Adams, a brigade commander in the Fourth Division, was given a small force and instructed "to move through Camden, driving out any force of the enemy he might encounter. . . ." His orders also called for the destruction of all "Government property, stores, and cotton in the city."[36]

The impression prevailed among the citizens of Camden that Sherman would follow the railroad toward Charlotte and in so doing would bypass their town.[37] When Adams unexpectedly approached Camden from the north, he met many people fleeing, among them Thomas Puryear, who had with him valuable racing stock, including the thoroughbreds "Censor" and "Albion." These two horses were enviable prizes for the cavalrymen.[38] Around 2:00 P.M. the main body of troops reached Camden. The day's ride had brought only minor skirmishing with the enemy and a few shots of greeting from the local citizenry. The troops proceeded immediately down Broad Street to the heart of the town. The remainder of the force had lagged behind to rob the homes along the way.[39]

"Camden was a beautiful town . . ." but this made Surgeon E. P. Burton more wary of its survival. He knew "the soldiers went in for

34. Foster, "Sherman Passed Through Lancaster," *S.C. Women*, p. 349.
35. Pepper, *Recollections*, p. 320.   36. *OR*, XLVII, Pt. I, Ser. I, 339.
37. Kirkland and Kennedy, *Historic Camden*, Pt. II, 165.
38. *Raleigh Conservative*, Mar. 21, 1865.
39. Kirkland and Kennedy, *Historic Camden*, Pt. II, 164.

plunder."[40]   The raiders first released fourteen Federal prisoners.   Then they began the work of destroying government stores and demolishing public buildings.   First to be fired were the freight and passenger depots and engine-house of the South Carolina Railroad.   Next went up the "Old Cornwallis" house, at the time containing a large supply of government meat, and a large commissary warehouse on the corner of Broad and DeKolb Streets.   Lost to the Confederacy were three hundred boxes of soap, two hundred barrels of meat, two thousand sacks of flour and corn meal, twenty hogsheads of rice, and three hundred horse collars. Also destroyed during the afternoon were two thousand bales of cotton and a large flour mill with several thousand bushels of wheat and corn in its bins.   The fires from the large commissary structure spread south, consuming several nearby buildings.   Separately fired were the Masonic Hall and adjacent edifices.   The heavy rains of the past days which had thoroughly saturated everything saved other structures from the torch.[41]

In the heart of town, stores were broken into and gutted.   What the men could not carry away, they either threw into the streets or gave to the Negroes.   The news of this "generosity" spread fast and the streets soon became crowded with those hoping to receive a portion of the spoils.[42]   Private homes were also plundered.   The *Camden Journal and Confederate* estimated that nearly every private residence in the town was visited by these spoilers.   Nevertheless, the reporter admitted that in some rare instances the soldiers "behaved with courtesy."[43]   Lieutenant McQueen, as he had done in Columbia, did his best to protect local citizens from the abusive soldiers.   According to Mrs. E. S. Davis, a niece of Dr. William Reynolds of Columbia, McQueen was directly responsible for protecting several homes in Camden.[44]

Late in the afternoon, Adams withdrew his command and by nightfall had rejoined the Fourth Division, encamped six miles northeast of the town.   The Federal occupation of Camden had been short, but as one local inhabitant observed, in those few hours hair turned gray and bodies aged.[45]

40. Burton, *Diary of E. P. Burton,* II, 64-65.
41. *OR,* XLVII, Pt. I, Ser. I, 353-54; Kirkland and Kennedy, *Historic Camden,* Pt. II, 164.
42. Kirkland and Kennedy, *Historic Camden,* Pt. I, 164-68.
43. *Ibid.,* p. 164, quoting the *Camden Journal and Confed.,* Mar. 10, 1865.
44. *Charleston News and Courier,* Apr. 4, 1884, U. R. Brooks Papers, MS Div., Duke Univ. Lib.; Kirkland and Kennedy, *Historic Camden,* Pt. II, 170-73.
45. Kirkland and Kennedy, *Historic Camden,* Pt. II, 170.

The shameful acts of robbery and destruction committed by the Federal "bummers" were not restricted to the hamlets and towns along the army's main routes of march. Scarcely a rural home escaped a call from at least one of this lawless fringe group. Homes were not only robbed but often burned. From the house of James Stewart in Winnsboro sixteen distinct fires could be counted in the surrounding country.[46] Stock and cattle were slaughtered with great abandon, seemingly for the sport of it. The stench became almost unbearable as scores of dead animals were left in the field to decompose.[47] The ruination of Columbia had only served to whet the rapacious appetite of the "bummer."

General Howard, who had blamed the destruction of Columbia on Hampton, not on drunken soldiers, now became very much concerned over the behavior of the Federal army. During the first day's march a soldier of his command was caught stealing and put under arrest but was freed by his armed companions who threatened the guard. This incident plus tales of pillage brought to his attention, inclined Howard to think there was a regularly organized "banditti" who committed these outrages and shared the spoils. That night he addressed similar letters to his two corps commanders. Said he:

I desire to call your attention to the fact that some of our soldiers have been committing the most outrageous robberies. . . . A case has come to my notice where a watch and several articles of jewelry were stolen by a foraging party under the eye of a commissioned officer in charge. Another, where a brute had violently assaulted a lady by striking her, and then robbed her of a valuable gold watch. In one instance money was stolen to the amount of one hundred and fifty dollars, and another, where an officer with a foraging party had allowed his men to take rings off the fingers of ladies in his presence. These outrages must be stopped at all hazards, and the thieves and robbers who commit them be dealt with severely and summarily.[48]

Howard's concern did very little to check these outrages. The "bummer" continued to roam almost completely undisciplined. The severe and summary punishment Howard wished for these "thieves and robbers" was in most instances left to the Confederate cavalry, at the time the only force opposing the Federal advance.[49] Hampton's South Carolinians,

46. Maclean, "Return of a Refugee," *So. Hist. Soc. Papers,* XIII, 502-15.
47. Pringle, *Chicora Wood,* p. 241.   48. *OR,* XLVII, Ser. I, 505-6.
49. As Sherman's army moved north from Columbia daily skirmishes took place between the Federal advance and the Confederate cavalry but there were no major engagements until North Carolina was reached.

distressed and outraged at the plight of their native state, took "intense pleasure" in "chasing and killing" the forager, "taken often in the act of committing" some dastardly deed.[50] Since the days of Sherman's "march to the sea" Wheeler's men had dealt with the "bummer" in their own particular way. As Captain Daniel Oakey of the Second Massachusetts expressed it: "The 'coffee-coolers' of the Army of the Potomac were archangels compared to our 'bummers,' who often fell to the tender mercies of Wheeler's Cavalry, and were never heard of again."[51] It was no longer an uncommon sight to see the dead body of a Federal forager along the road side.[52]

When it was reported to Kilpatrick on February 22 that the bodies of eighteen Federal soldiers, two with their throats cut from ear to ear, had been found, he immediately charged Wheeler with murder. In a communication to the Confederate General, Kilpatrick threatened with execution eighteen of Wheeler's men, then his prisoners, unless a satisfactory explanation was forthcoming by sundown of the next day. Wheeler answered immediately. He was satisfied that Kilpatrick was mistaken in his accusation of murder. He pointed out that he had no Texas regiments armed with Spencer rifles and none commanded by a lieutenant colonel. Kilpatrick had attributed the death of nine of his men to a regiment identified in that manner. Wheeler assured his adversary that the matter would be investigated thoroughly and if any parties were found guilty as charged, he would see that prompt justice was carried out. Kilpatrick was satisfied with the answer. He promised to take no action on the matter for the present. In closing his rejoinder on February 23, Kilpatrick tacitly admitted that the eighteen might have been caught in the act of pillage. He informed Wheeler that his men had orders to shoot on the spot any stragglers "found in the houses of citizens committing any outrages whatever. . . ;" and furthermore he expected the officers and men of the Confederate cavalry to do the same.[53]

This verbal duel did not go unnoticed by Sherman. On February 24, he wrote directly to Hampton that it had been brought to his attention that foraging parties were being murdered after capture and labeled "Death to all foragers." He continued:

50. Smith, *Smith Letters*, p. 201.
51. Oakey, *"Marching,"* p. 678.
52. Jackson, *Colonels Diary*, p. 189; *OR*, XLVII, Pt. II, Ser. I, 566, 567-68.
53. *OR*, XLVII, Pt. I, Ser. I, 860-61.

I have ordered a similar number of prisoners in our hands to be disposed of in like manner. I hold about one thousand prisoners . . . and can stand it as long as you; but I hardly think these murders are committed with your knowledge, and would suggest that you give notice to the people at large that every life taken by them simply results in the death of one of your Confederates.

In addition Sherman took this opportunity to defend the practice of foraging on the grounds that it was "a war right as old as history." He admitted that foraging was the occasion for "much misbehavior" on the part of his men but declared that he would not permit "an enemy to judge or punish with wholesale murder." In closing, he reminded Hampton "that those who struck the first blow and made war inevitable ought not, in fairness, reproach . . . [him] for the natural consequences."[54] The next day, in spite of the aggressive tone of his correspondence, Sherman issued orders that foragers "were to be kept within reasonable bounds" and that they were not to be protected "when they enter dwellings and commit wanton waste. . . ."[55] He wrote Kilpatrick that foragers were "to be regulated and systematized, so as not to degenerate into common robbers. . . ."[56]

Hampton, vowing to shoot two Federal prisoners, officers receiving preference, for every one of his men executed, answered Sherman as follows:

In reference to the statement you make regarding death of your foragers, I have only to say that I know nothing of it; that no orders given by me authorize the killing of prisoners after capture, and that I do not believe my men killed any of yours, except under circumstances in which it was perfectly legitimate and proper that they should kill them. It is a part of the system of the thieves whom you designate as your foragers to fire the dwellings of those citizens whom they have robbed. To check this inhuman system . . . I have directed my men to shoot down all of your men who are caught burning houses. This order shall remain in force so long as you disgrace the profession of arms by allowing your men to destroy private dwellings.[57]

While this battle of words was in progress, the right wing was experiencing great difficulty at Lynch's Creek. Although the bridges had not been destroyed, the previous rains had so swollen the stream that the water for several hundred yards on each side was deep enough to swim

54. *Ibid.*, XLVII, Pt. II, Ser. I, 546.   55. *Ibid.*, p. 568.
56. *Ibid.*, p. 544.   57. *Ibid.*, p. 596.

a horse. Beyond the water was what appeared to be an endless gulf of mud. With the creek too wide to be bridged and too deep to be forded by the trains, Howard had no option but to wait until the water subsided.[58] This "deuced creek" so termed by an Illinois colonel, delayed the right wing "four days, more than any three rivers did before."[59]

By March 1, Sherman was in communication with all parts of his army for the first time since the crossing of the Wateree. The next day, after a brief skirmish with Butler's cavalry, he entered Chesterfield with the Twentieth Corps. Sherman remained overnight in this "dirty little town" of about twenty houses, one hotel, and a court house.[60] There he received word from Howard that the Seventeenth Corps was encamped near Cheraw, ready to occupy the town the following day, and that the Fifteenth Corps was close by. Sherman therefore ordered the left wing and cavalry to Sneedsboro, North Carolina, about ten miles north of Cheraw and there to cross the Pee Dee River. The General himself proposed to join Howard in Cheraw on March 3.[61]

General Hardee, who had been ordered on February 11 to abandon Charleston and move on Chester, had delayed evacuation until the 18th. By this time it was impossible to cross in front of Sherman and reach Chester. So he put his command in motion for Cheraw. He availed himself of the only remaining railroad, that through Florence, to move a portion of his men and supplies. The available trains were always loaded far beyond their normal capacity. General McLaws, starting for Cheraw with part of James Conner's brigade, had to put many of his men on top of the cars, even though a driving rain was falling.[62] The dilapidated condition of the road, plus mismanagement on the part of those in charge of the line, resulted in much delay and confusion in the movement of the army. As late as February 28, Hardee was awaiting men and supplies by rail.[63]

In the meantime, those troops of Hardee's command not moved by train trudged slowly north. Beside the line of march the women of South Carolina left peanuts, sweet potatoes, and other food stuffs, but these offerings did little to raise the morale of soldiers whose ranks were being

58. *Ibid.*, XLVII, Pt. I, Ser. I, 228, 230.
59. Wills, *Wills Diary*, p. 355.
60. Padgett, "Letters of a Federal Soldier," p. 73.
61. Sherman, *Memoirs*, II, 290.
62. L. McLaws Order Bk., 1865, SHC, U.N.C, p. 8.   General Hardee was sick on Feb. 18 and McLaws led the troops out of Charleston.
63. *OR*, XLVII, Pt. II, Ser. I, 1290.

constantly depleted by desertions.[64] The news of the devastation wrought by Sherman caused many to slip away home. Arthur P. Ford tells the story of a sergeant who on this march both justified and advised the desertion of his men. Upon being reproved by a lieutenant for these actions, he drew his pistol and tried to shoot the officer. This fit of anger cost him his life. A drumhead court-martial sentenced him to be shot. The sergeant died without the prayers of the chaplain, saying: "Preacher, I never listened to you at Fort Sumter and I won't listen to you now."[65]

In contrast to this demoralized element was a detachment of "Kid" soldiers, average age sixteen, who had been called to the colors a few months before. Anxious to defend their native state, these young boys had been assigned to Hardee's command at Charleston and had moved north with him. These youths were thrilled by martial music and flashy uniforms. They were completely captivated by the grand review of all the Confederate troops in Cheraw. To one youngster General McLaws, in his elegant attire and seated upon a fine charger, was every inch his idea of a soldier.[66]

The ailing Beauregard had been in a complete quandary as to the Federal objective after Sherman turned east across the Wateree. On February 26, he wrote Hardee that Sherman would "move thence upon this place [Charlotte] or upon Fayetteville, North Carolina, via Cheraw. . . ."[67] It was not until March 1 that he gave up his assumption that the Federal army was moving on Charlotte, though he earlier had information to this effect.[68] General Butler had learned from a soldier of the Twentieth Corps, captured near Winnsboro, that Slocum was to cross the Wateree at Rocky Mount and then march on Cheraw. This information was immediately passed on to both Hampton and Beauregard, but it was evidently disregarded.[69] Further confusion was added to the Confederate picture when the first set of orders directing Hardee to turn toward Fayetteville were, for some reason, never delivered.[70]

Closely pressed by the Federal advance Hardee evacuated Cheraw

64. C. S. Powell Reminiscences, 1864-1865, MS., N.C. Coll., U.N.C.
65. Ford and Ford, *Confed. Army*, pp. 43-44.
66. *Kid Soldiers*, pp. 10-11, Confed. States Pamphlets, Duke Univ. Lib.
67. *OR*, XLVII, Pt. II, Ser. I, 1281.
68. *Ibid.*, p. 1298.
69. M. C. Butler to U. R. Brooks, Mar. 16, 1906, Brooks Papers, MS Div., Duke Univ. Lib.
70. *OR*, XLVII, Pt. II, Ser. I, 1320.

on March 3.[71] After crossing the Pee Dee, he directed his columns toward Greensboro which was in accordance with his latest orders from Beauregard, dated February 24.[72]

Butler's cavalry division was acting as the Confederate rear guard. Butler hoped to check the Federal advance west of town but having no artillery, he had to abandon, after a very brief skirmish, Hardee's "remarkably strong bridge-head for artillery and infantry . . ." at Thompson's Creek.[73] The Confederate cavalry then fell back on Cheraw. As the advance of the Seventeenth Corps entered the town from the west, Pierce M. B. Young's brigade, which brought up the Confederate rear, passed out the east end. At the bridge over the Pee Dee, Butler ordered his men to dismount, sending the horses behind the abutment for safety. Horses were very scarce in the Confederate army. The dismounted cavalrymen held off the Federals long enough to fire the piles of rosin on the bridge. Then they managed to escape across the burning structure.[74]

On March 4 Hardee reached Rockingham, North Carolina, a few miles across the state line. Here orders for the Confederate army to turn toward Fayetteville finally reached him and were immediately observed.

General Sherman rode into Cheraw during the morning of March 3.[75] For a short period, while awaiting the arrival of his headquarters wagons, he stayed with General Blair who had his headquarters in one of the town's fine, old homes. Since it was cold and rainy outside General Blair asked Sherman, as well as other staff officers, to have lunch with him. On the table were twelve bottles of the finest madeira wine the General had ever tasted.[76] Relaxed by these beverages, the officers enjoyed themselves greatly. Logan, playing his own violin accompaniment, sang for the group, and nothing would do except for Adjutant Byers to recite his own work, "Sherman's March to the Sea."[77]

Upon inquiry Sherman learned that the Seventeenth Corps commander had captured eight wagon loads of this wine, which had been sent to Cheraw from Charleston for safe keeping, and had distributed it among the different headquarters "in very fair proportions."[78] The result, said Adjutant Byers, was that "some of said headquarters were

71. Not all of Hardee's troops were allowed to leave the state. W. G. De Saussure Diary, Mar. 3, 1865, MS Div., Duke Univ. Lib.

72. *OR*, XLVII, Pt. II, Ser. I, 1320.   73. *Ibid.*, p. 202.
74. Butler, "Curtain Falls," p. 473.   75. *OR*, XLVII, Pt. II, Ser. I, 1320.
76. Sherman, *Memoirs*, II, 291.   77. Byers, *Fire and Sword*, p. 182.
78. Sherman, *Memoirs*, II, 291.

pretty nearly drunk" before the day was over.[79] After the meal was finished Blair presented his commander with a large pile of fine carpets to be used as tent rugs and saddle blankets. These, too, had been shipped to Cheraw for safety.[80]

This beautiful, old town turned out to be quite a military prize for the Federal army. Its warehouses were filled with both military and civil stores sent up from Charleston prior to the Confederate evacuation of that city.[81] Because of the lack of adequate transportation facilities, most of these supplies had not been removed from Cheraw. There was no railroad north. The Cheraw and Darlington line terminated here. Neither was the Pee Dee navigable beyond the town. Hardee, although he filled his wagon trains to capacity, had not appreciably dented the vast stores. An effort had been made by him to destroy the commissary supplies and cotton. Tons of meal, rice, and flour were poured into the street, and cotton was fired.

Little concern was paid by the retiring Confederates to the few pieces of rolling stock in the railroad yard. An exception was a single locomotive standing some distance from the track, evidence of the engineer's unsuccessful attempt to run it into the Pee Dee.[82] In all, one usable engine and twelve to fifteen cars were captured.

An immense amount of ordnance, consisting of twenty-four guns, two thousand muskets, thirty-six hundred barrels of gunpowder, five thousand rounds of artillery ammunition, and twenty thousand rounds of infantry ammunition was taken by Blair.[83] One of the most valued prizes was a piece of artillery inscribed as follows: "Presented to the sovereign State of South Carolina by one of her sons abroad in memory of the 20th of December, 1860."[84] Some of this ordnance was used by the Federal army. The majority of it was destroyed, but not before being fired in celebration of Lincoln's second inauguration.[85]

At Cheraw, the carelessness of one man around an immense pile of powder cost the lives of several soldiers. The powder exploded and in a flash the whole sky seemed to burst into flame. Mule teams stampeded and general pandemonium reigned for a short while. As the debris began to fall in every direction, not a few soldiers found themselves "going up street at no very dignified pace." Suspecting sabotage, Sherman was

79. Byers, *Fire and Sword*, p. 182.
80. Sherman, *Memoirs*, II, 291.
81. Jackson, *Colonel's Diary*, pp. 189-90.
82. *Kid Soldiers*, p. 10.
83. *OR*, XLVII, Pt. I, Ser. I, 381.
84. Jackson, *Colonel's Diary*, p. 190.
85. Hedley, *Marching Through Ga.*, p. 398.

on the verge of ordering the town burned to the ground when he learned that his own men were responsible for the explosion.[86]

Orders to burn the town were not necessary. In three days of occupancy the soldiers managed to sack and then burn most of the business establishments in Cheraw. Guards at first were able to protect property. In fact, Sunday morning, March 5, was so peaceful and quiet that surgeon Burton felt "it really seemed like [the] Sabbath. No noisy brawling about town." In a reverent state of mind, he went to the Baptist Church with a friend who played for him a tune on the melodeon. Time put an end to this atmosphere of serenity. In town again that evening Burton was almost stifled by "vast clouds of dense smoke . . . arising from burning buildings and ruins of turpentine works. . . ."[87]

The disreputable conduct of the Federal soldiers brought Sherman his usual quota of visits from ladies requesting protection for their homes. One of his callers was Mrs. Hiram Gray who handed him the following note from General Hardee:

The bearer of this letter, Mrs. Gray, is a lady of high respectability and character who came from the North during our present trouble to look after her children and some property which she owned in the South. I ask that she may receive at your hands the kindly protection to which she is entitled.

Taking a pencil from his pocket, Sherman wrote at the bottom of the letter: "Certainly all officers and men will see that this family is in no manner molested or troubled."[88]

Around Cheraw, foraging activities were greatly intensified.[89] The army had plenty of meat, but was running low on foodstuffs, thus foraging parties went out daily.[90] They found the country rich enough to furnish abundant provisions for both men and horses.[91] On occasions, however, seemingly prosperous farms were discovered to be almost empty of supplies. Many residents around Cheraw, having been terrified by the activities of the forager, decided they themselves might as well eat what had been preciously hoarded for the time the men of the family

86. Arbuckle, *Civil War Experiences*, p. 137; Chamberlain, *81 Ohio*, p. 161. Shortly after the above explosion another one took place at a warehouse containing Confederate ordnance supplies. Arbuckle, *Civil War Experiences*, p. 138.

87. Burton, *Diary of E. P. Burton*, p. 67. Sergeant Rufus Meade wrote: "[Cheraw] has been quite a business place, I judge, but now all the stores, shops, etc. are in ashes while the houses on another street still remain." Padgett, "Letters of a Federal Soldier," p. 73.

88. W. J. Hardee to Sherman, Feb. 28, 1865, H. Gray Papers, MS Div., Duke Univ. Lib.

89. Osborn, *58 Ohio*, p. 194.   90. Orendorff, *103 Ill.*, pp. 191-92.

91. *OR*, XLVII, Pt. I, Ser. I, 201.

would come home. As a consequence, every meal at some plantations resembled a Christmas dinner. All turkeys and hams were consumed. Stories that Sherman's men would take everything except the clothes on one's back, started the ladies to wearing as many as three dresses at a time. Underneath these clothes and tied around their waist were bags of rice, flour, sugar, and coffee. Following this fashion a normally tall, thin woman might take on considerable size overnight.[92]

There was no uniformity of behavior among the foragers as they roamed the country side. Mrs. Allston Pringle, writing from Society Hill on March 30, 1865, said:

We are situated three miles from the village, on a by-road, and I flattered myself, our house would not be discovered. But they found us out and paid us two visits of about half hour each. However, they were not insolent to us. . . . Most everyone suffered some, but no violence [was] offered to the ladies. . . .[93]

In contrast were the "barbarities" witnessed by Dr. John Bachman, a refugee at Cash's Depot, six miles from Cheraw. He saw acts of brutality "inflicted on an aged widow, and young and delicate females." A personal friend of his, "a lady of refinement," was compelled to undress before a group of foragers so they might search her clothing for hidden valuables.[94]

The lone rail line running to Cheraw was not overlooked by Sherman. He ordered it destroyed as far south as Darlington. He also sent a mounted infantry force to Florence to level the depots, trestle-work, bridges, and "if possible . . . the public buildings and stores." Much to the General's surprise this detachment encountered both Confederate cavalry and infantry and returned with mission unaccomplished.[95]

At Cheraw Sherman saw a copy of the *New York Tribune* that betrayed the secret of his supply rendezvous at New Bern. This, he knew, would inform the Confederates that he was striking at Goldsboro. No longer was it possible for him to feint to the left and make a show of power toward Charlotte.[96] Also, while there, Sherman learned that his former adversary, Joseph E. Johnston, had replaced General Beauregard as commander of the Confederate forces in North Carolina and South Carolina. General Robert E. Lee, recently appointed commander-in-chief

92. Pringle, *Chicora Wood*, pp. 224-29.
93. Smith, *Smith Letters*, pp. 184-85.
94. Cook, *Sherman's March*, p. 18.
95. *OR*, XLVII, Pt. I, Ser. I, 23, 43.
96. Sherman, *Memoirs*, II, 292.

of all Confederate forces, had ordered Johnston on February 22 to assume command of the Army of Tennessee and of all troops in the Department of South Carolina, Georgia, and Florida, and to "concentrate all available forces and drive Sherman back."[97] Beauregard showed no bitterness at being relieved of his command. To Lee's orders he replied: "In the defense of our common country I will at all times be happy to serve with or under so gallant and patriotic an officer as Johnston."[98]

Sherman now concluded that he must be ready for a concentration in his front of all the forces subject to Johnston's orders. The battle he had wished to avoid now seemed unavoidable.

Johnston's restoration to command was favorably received in most military and civilian circles of the South.[99] An army inspector who actually feared for his life "in contending with . . . [the] troops" was much relieved to get this word. "Thank God he has been reinstated," the inspector wrote, "and I hope will be able to organize the army again, it is now a complete mob. I never have witnessed so much demoralization in my life. . . ."[100]

On assuming command Johnston's first problem was to unite his widely dispersed troops. This was a difficult task not only because Sherman was between the small Confederate forces and, by rapid marching, could keep them separated but also because of the scarcity of food in General Lee's camps. The officers of the commissariat in North Carolina, upon whom the Army of Northern Virginia depended in part for subsistence, were instructed to permit none of the provisions they collected in that state to be issued to or retained for Johnston's army. Johnston was to subsist on the country likely to be overrun by Sherman.[101] In a thinly peopled countryside such a mode of supplying an army made rapid movements almost an impossibility.

The forces available to General Johnston were approximately 16,000 infantry and artillery and 4,000 cavalry. Wheeler's division of cavalry contained around 3,000 effectives and Butler's, about 1,000. Two thousand troops of the Army of Tennessee, commanded by Major General C. L. Stevenson, were near Charlotte. A thousand under Lieutenant General

97. OR, XLVII, Pt. II, Ser. I, 1247.
98. P. G. T. Beauregard to R. E. Lee, Feb. 22, 1865, W. P. Palmer Papers, Micrf., SHC, U.N.C.
99. Raleigh Conservative, Mar. 17, 1865.
100. "Jno. W. G." to sister, Mar. 1, 1865, Sherman Papers, MS Div., L.C.
101. OR, XLVII, Pt. II, Ser. I, 1248.

A. P. Stewart were near Newberry, South Carolina, approaching Charlotte. Two thousand under the command of Major General B. F. Cheatham were between Augusta, Georgia, and Newberry, also marching toward Charlotte. The remaining troops of the Army of Tennessee were coming through Georgia in small parties or individually.[102]

On the evening of March 3, Johnston received information that Stewart's troops had reached Chester, that Cheatham's were nearby, and that Hardee had crossed the Pee Dee. Johnston now felt that it was possible for him to unite all of his available forces at a place of his choosing and strike one of Sherman's columns on the move. The Federal order of march, by wings, gave support to this idea. Giving battle to Sherman's entire army was out of the question because of the great disparity in the size of the two fighting forces. It was Johnston's ultimate aim to join Lee when and if he should abandon Richmond so that their combined forces might fall upon Sherman.[103]

Aware that the first serious opposition to Sherman's progress was to be in North Carolina, Johnston suggested to General Lee that the troops of that department be turned over to him. These troops were under General Bragg's command near Goldsboro. The suggestion was adopted and the necessary orders were given without loss of time. This added about ten thousand men to Johnston's command.[104]

While Sherman, in Cheraw, contemplated his next move, Kilpatrick, across the state line, commenced operations. The cavalry commander was not close enough to Cheraw on March 3 to harass the retreating Hardee but the next day at Phillips Cross-Roads, North Carolina, a portion of his own command was more than harassed by Wheeler. In an all day skirmish the Confederates took fifty prisoners and were on the verge of complete victory when Federal artillery was brought into play.[105]

Before this engagement started a scouting party of one hundred men from the Ninth Michigan cavalry, under the command of Major J. G. McBride, had been sent to Wadesboro with instructions to "clean out the town." The Major carried out his orders by destroying a gristmill, saw-

102. Johnston, *Narrative*, p. 372.
103. *Ibid.*, pp. 227, 378.
104. *OR*, XLVII, Pt. II, Ser. I, 1257.
105. For description of skirmish at Phillips Cross-Roads, N.C., on March 4, 1865, see reports of G. S. Acker, S. D. Atkins, C. Blanford, L. J. Jordon, D. H. Kimmel, R. H. King, T. W. Sanderson, O. Star, M. Van Buskirk, W. B. Way and J. Wheeler on campaign of the Carolinas in *OR*, XLVII, Pt. I, Ser. I.

mill, tannery, large government stables, and other public property.[106]

Wadesboro, however, had already been pillaged the previous day by detachments of Kilpatrick's scouts under Captain T. F. Northrop.[107] Thomas Atkinson, Episcopal Bishop of North Carolina, wrote of how, at the point of a gun, he was robbed of watch, clothes, jewelry, and horse. He said every house in the town where there seemed to be anything worth taking was robbed. The soldiers broke open the storehouses and took what they wanted. Atkinson went on to state that in some instances defenseless men were killed for plunder: "A Mr. James C. Bennett, one of the oldest and wealthiest men in Anson County, was shot at the door of his own house because he did not give up his watch and money, which had been previously taken from him by another party."[108]

Monroe, twenty-five miles to the west, had been visited even earlier, probably on March 1, either by Kilpatrick's men or foragers from one of the other corps. Buildings were not leveled as in Wadesboro. Yet the usual looting took place. The most lucrative prize was ten fully loaded wagons belonging to an unfortunate party of refugees from Chester, South Carolina, who arrived in Monroe almost simultaneously with the Federals.[109]

Following the skirmish at Phillips Cross-Roads both Wheeler and Kilpatrick moved their troops across the Pee Dee. At Wadesboro on March 5, Wheeler learned that the only place he could ford the river was at Grassy Island, twelve miles above Sneedsboro.[110] When Wheeler reached the river the next day, he found it at flood stage. It was imperative that he should cross and communicate with Hardee and learn the position of Sherman's army. Nevertheless, ferrymen refused to assist in the crossing. They were unanimous in asserting that any attempt to cross with the river at such a high level would prove fatal. Hence Wheeler decided to swim the Pee Dee. Twenty Texans volunteered to follow him but only the General and two privates succeeded in reaching the opposite bank. The other eighteen were swept downstream.[111] It was not until March 8 that his entire command was able to cross and proceed toward Fayetteville.

106. *Ibid.,* p. 885.
107. Pike, *Scout and Ranger,* p. 382.
108. T. Atkinson to Cornelia P. Spencer, Jan. 30, 1866, D. L. Swain Papers, SHC, U.N.C.
109. *Raleigh Conservation,* Mar. 21, 1865, quoting *Charlotte Democrat,* Mar. 7, 1865.
110. *OR,* XLVII, Pt. II, Ser. I, 1327.
111. Dodson, *Wheeler,* pp. 342-44.

Kilpatrick managed a crossing in the vicinity of Morven Post Office on March 6. The Federals, too, found the river greatly swollen. The pontoon boats were insufficient to bridge the river, so forty-two army wagon boxes were covered under the bottom and on the sides with cotton cloth covers and used.[112]

After swimming the Pee Dee, Wheeler managed to contact Captain Shannon, commander of his scouts, who, with a few men, had crossed the river above Grassy Island.[113] The next morning, March 7, Wheeler took twenty of these scouts almost to Rockingham where he "attacked and killed or captured thirty-five" of the Federals, most of whom were foragers from Sherman's Fourteenth and Twentieth Corps.[114] Another skirmish was going on in Rockingham at this time between foragers and a brigade of Butler's cavalry which had been ordered to remain in the town to act as Hardee's rear guard. When Kilpatrick's advance guard appeared on the scene, the fighting developed into a considerable skirmish, but by 11:00 A.M. the Confederates had been driven out of town.

Kilpatrick was pleased to learn that there was pro-Union sentiment in the vicinity of Rockingham. He learned that the Confederates had three local citizens under arrest for burning bridges over the Lumber River. He was quite distressed by a report that some eight hundred Federal prisoners of war, who had taken the oath of allegiance to the Confederate government, were being used by Hardee to work upon the roads. Unable to confirm either rumor, he dismissed the matter from his consideration.[115]

On March 6, Sherman crossed the Pee Dee at Cheraw and all the army marched for Fayetteville. The Seventeenth Corps kept well to the right while the Fifteenth marched by a direct road. The Fourteenth Corps followed the most direct route from Sneedsboro, where it crossed the Pee Dee. The Twentieth Corps came to Cheraw for the convenience of the pontoon bridge. It diverged to the left, so as to enter Fayetteville next after the Fourteenth which was appointed to lead the army into the North Carolina city. Still further to the left was the cavalry, operating as cover for the wagon trains.[116]

In two days South Carolina would be free of this army which had

112. Committee, 92 Ill, p. 223.
113. Du Bose, "Road Fight," Confed. Vet. XX, 84.
114. OR, XLVII, Pt. I, Ser. I, 1130, 690.
115. Ibid., XLVII, Pt. II, Ser. I, 1329, 720-21.
116. Ibid., p. 704.

applied total war in its severest terms within her borders. The notorious "bummers," who were primarily responsible for the extremes of pillage and destruction, would be gone. Lieutenant Charles S. Brown never spoke truer words than when he said: "South Carolina may have been the cause of the whole thing, but she has had an awful punishment."[117]

117. C. S. Brown to Etta (Brown ?), Apr. 26, 1865, Brown Papers, MS Div., Duke Univ. Lib.

CHAPTER VIII

A Morning Call on Kilpatrick

WHILE THE Federal army was crossing the Pee Dee on March 6, Captain William Duncan, General Howard's chief scout, with a small body of men dressed in Confederate uniforms, scouted as far as Laurel Hill, North Carolina. He found nothing more than a small squad of Confederate militia on picket duty. Duncan also learned that the civilian population in that region was still expecting Sherman to strike at Charlotte. Had the Federals scouted as far as Fayetteville, approximately fifty miles north, they would have encountered practically the same expectation.[1] Edward J. Hale, editor of the *Fayetteville Observer,* admitted that he had no reliable information on Sherman and could only renew his faith in Lee's statement that Sherman could be defeated.[2]

On January 21, 1865, however, the *Raleigh Progress* had begun to prepare North Carolinians for invasion. It said South Carolina was whipped and would not check Sherman.[3] With the fall of Fort Fisher and occupation of Wilmington on February 15 and 22 respectively, the people of North Carolina had almost surrendered themselves to a wave of despondency. In an effort to revive patriotic sentiment, a series of public meetings were held throughout the state. Some were locally called, while for others the initiative came from Governor Zebulon Baird Vance.[4] The meeting at Fayetteville where a large gathering pledged "to each other, life, fortunes, and sacred honor in this holy purpose" was hailed as a great success.[5] The Governor, though, eventually took a dim view of all these meetings, stating: "the near and triumphant approach of the enemy has so alarmed the timid and so en-

1. *OR,* XLVII, Pt. II, Ser. I, 704.
2. *Fayetteville Observer,* Mar. 6, 1865.
3. Lewis, *Sherman,* p. 499, quoting *Raleigh Progress,* Jan. 21, 1865.
4. *Raleigh Conservative,* Mar. 10, 1865.
5. *Fayetteville Observer,* Feb. 20, 1865.

grossed the loyal in preparation for his coming that I fear they will hardly have their proper effect."[6]

William Woods Holden, unsuccessful gubernatorial candidate in 1864 on a platform of peace, referred to the Fayetteville meeting as one called by certain public officials who will give advice all day and enlighten everybody, but when it comes to fighting, that turns out not to be their line. "They want the roasted chestnuts but the hand of someone else must be thrust in the fire to pull them out."[7]

Late in February General Lee declared that the despair of the North Carolinians was destroying his army. He wrote Governor Vance: "Desertings are becoming very frequent and there is reason to believe that they are occasioned to a considerable extent by letters written to the soldiers by their friends at home."[8] The diaries and letters of the men in the line around Richmond show that Lee had reason to be concerned. "Deserters increase . . . we had three more last night" is the February 21 entry in the diary of Samuel Hoey Walkup of the Forty-eighth North Carolina regiment.[9] On March 6 Walkup expressed the sentiments of those soldiers whose homes were in Sherman's path: "I am in agony of suspense to hear from home. It has been nearly a month since I left them and have received no letter since. The Yankees were there. Between them and our forces I can only look Heavenward for comfort."[10]

It was not those soldiers who looked to heaven for comfort but those who took off for home themselves that occasioned six North Carolina regimental commanders to write Senator William Alexander Graham of the Confederate Congress:

Numerous desertions are now occurring among the troops from our state. . . . We believe that the spirit of discontent among our soldiers owes its birth and growth to the influences of those of our citizens at home, who by evil councils and by fears have been made to despair of the success of our cause and are constantly, while the soldiers are home on furlough and through the mails, instilling into them opinions which too often culminate in desertion. We are led to this conclusion by intercepted letters, addressed to those who deserted.

6. Z. B. Vance to R. E. Lee, Mar. 2, 1865, Vance Letter Bk., MS Div., N.C. Dept. of Arch. and Hist.

7. *Raleigh N.C. Standard,* Feb. 17, 1865.

8. R. E. Lee to Z. B. Vance, Feb. 24, 1865, Vance Letter Bk., MS Div., N. C. Dept. of Arch. and Hist.

9. S. H. Walkup Diary, Feb. 21, 1865, SHC, U.N.C.

10. *Ibid.,* Mar. 6, 1865.

The letter closes with an appeal to the Senator and members of Congress to go immediately among the people "with words of cheer, encouraging the timid, satisfying the discontented, and suppressing party discord."[11]

Earlier Governor Vance had received a communication from a North Carolina soldier in Lee's army who wished to inform His Excellency "of what a majority of the soldiers from our State says they are going to do." The writer stated that it was openly talked by a large majority of soldiers that unless something was done by the authorities to stop the bloodshed "betwixt this and spring" they would refuse to go into another campaign.[12]

One phase of Sherman's plan of total war called for a demoralization of the Confederate armies in the field by attacks on the home front. He wrote: "The simple fact that a man's home has been visited by the enemy makes a soldier in Lee's or Johnston's army very, very anxious to get home to look after his family and property."[13] As if to verify Sherman's statements, several North Carolinians in the Army of Northern Virginia wrote Vance:

It is not in the power of the Yankee Armies to cause us to wish ourselves at home. We can face them, and can hear their shot and shell without being moved; but, Sir, we cannot hear the cries of our little ones and stand.

But it is not ourselves that we should complain, it is our wives and little ones at home who are necessities. . . . Do something for them and there will be less desertion, and men will go into battles with heartier good will. But it is impossible for us to bear up under our many troubles, the greatest of which is the suffering of our wives and little ones at home.[14]

It is very evident that General Sherman entered North Carolina with the confident expectation of receiving a welcome from its supposedly large number of pro-Union citizens. Major George W. Nichols of Sherman's staff wrote: "Our men seem to understand that they are entering a state which has suffered for its Union sentiment, and whose inhabitants would gladly embrace the old flag again if they can have the opportunity. . . ."[15]

11. N.C. officers to W. A. Graham, Feb. 27, 1865, Graham Papers, SHC, U.N.C.

12. N.C. soldier to Z. B. Vance, Jan. 1865, Vance Papers, MS Div., N.C. Dept. of Arch. and Hist.

13. OR, XLVII, Pt. II, Ser. I, 857.

14. N.C. soldier to Z. B. Vance, Jan. 24, 1865, Vance Papers, MS Div., N.C. Dept. of Arch. and Hist.

15. Nichols, Great March, p. 222.

Sherman had his generals issue orders for gentler treatment of North Carolinians. General Slocum's orders read:

All officers and soldiers of this command are reminded that the State of North Carolina was one of the last states that passed the ordinance of secession, and from the commencement of the war there has been in this state a strong Union party. Her action on the question of secession was undoubtedly brought about by the traitorous acts of other States, and by intrigue and dishonesty on the part of her own citizens. The act never even met the approval of the great mass of her people. It should not be assumed that the inhabitants are enemies to our Government, and it is to be hoped that every effort will be made to prevent any wanton destruction of property, or any unkind treatment of citizens.[16]

General Blair's orders read in part; "The State of North Carolina is to a great extent loyal, and as such, a marked difference should be made in the manner in which we treat the people and the manner in which those of South Carolina were treated. Nothing should be taken from them except what is absolutely necessary for the use of the army. . . ."[17]

Sherman's instructions to Kilpatrick were: "In conversation with people evince a determination to maintain the Union, but treat all other matters as beneath a soldier's notice. . . . Deal as moderately and fairly by the North Carolinians as possible, and fan the flame of discord already subsisting between them and their proud cousins of South Carolina. . . . Touch upon the chivalry of running away, always leaving their families for us to feed and protect, and then on purpose accusing us of all sorts of rudeness."[18]

When the state line was crossed, new orders were also issued regulating foraging. This practice was not stopped, however, even though Sherman had originally planned to issue a non-foraging order when the army reached North Carolina.[19] Faced with the prospect of battle and having many new mouths to feed in the refugee train, Sherman still found foraging a necessity. He could expect no Federal supplies until he met provision ships at the crossings of the Cape Fear and the Neuse rivers ahead. Neither could he expect much success from foraging operations between the Pee Dee River and Fayetteville. In the first place, the line of march of his troops led partially through a sandy, rolling, barren country.

16. OR, XLVII, Pt. II, Ser. I, 719.   17. Ibid., p. 760.
18. Ibid., p. 721.   19. Ibid., p. 714.

Secondly, the retreating Confederates were also having to subsist on this thinly populated countryside.

General Blair, after witnessing the "bummer's" work in South Carolina, thought the foraging system was "vicious and utterly deplorable" and wanted it changed, especially since the army was about to enter North Carolina.[20] Upon Blair's insistence, General Howard issued the following orders:

Hereafter but one mounted foraging party, to consist of sixty men with the proper number of commissioned officers, will be allowed for each division. The division commanders will be careful to select reliable officers for the command of these parties, who shall be held strictly accountable for the conduct of their men; whenever it may be necessary to send a party from the main body, a commissioned officer will be sent in charge, but in no case will it be allowed to go in advance of the advance guard of the leading division, or more than five miles from either flank of the column. All surplus animals will be disposed of by the corps quartermasters for the benefit of the artillery, bridge train, etc.[21]

General Blair made his orders on foraging stricter still. No one was to be permitted to enter dwelling houses under any circumstances. The parties were allowed to take only animals, food for the command, and forage for the stock. The provost-marshal was to arrest all men other than authorized foragers found away from their commands.[22] Blair thought the desire to be mounted would cause a strict compliance with the order. For any disobedience the offender could be sent to his place in the line.[23]

But no orders were issued prohibiting the burning of the great pine forests within North Carolina. So, "as the flames from buildings grew less frequent, smoke from burning forests grew heavier." The state's turpentine forests blazed in fantastic "splendor as 'bummers' touched matches to congealed sap in notches on tree trunks." The territory between the Pee Dee and Cape Fear rivers was one, vast, extensive pine forest, and on nearly every stream there was a factory for the making of turpentine, rosin, and tar. Seldom did the soldiers pass up an opportunity to fire these factories for burning rosin and tar created a spectacle of flame and smoke that surpassed in grandeur anything they had ever

20. *Ibid.*, pp. 714-17.   21. *Ibid.*, p. 728.
22. *Ibid.*, pp. 760-61.   23. *Ibid.*, p. 783.

seen before.[24]   J. R. Kinnear wrote: "Among the curiosities of our march the burning of these factories was the most curious."[25]   Colonel W. D. Hamilton of Kilpatrick's command remarked that oftentimes the smoke could hardly escape through the green canopy above, and being like a pall, it created a feeling of awe as though one were within the precincts of a grand old cathedral.[26]

By March 7, Sherman's entire command had not crossed the state line into North Carolina.   However, by noon of that day advance units of the Twentieth Corps reached Marks Station on the Wilmington, Charlotte, and Rutherfordton Railroad.   Here Major General J. W. Geary's division destroyed three-quarters of a mile of track and a large quantity of new iron rails.[27]   Sherman had ordered the railroad destroyed.   To Slocum he wrote: "En route break the railroad which is known as the Wilmington and Charlotte. . . . It is of little importance, but being on it, we might as well use up some of its iron."[28]

This same date the depot and temporary[29] railroad shops at Laurinburg were burned.[30] This was probably done by Captain Duncan's scouts whom General Howard reported on March 7 as having reached the railroad and destroyed some trestlework.[31]

On March 8, North Carolina for the first time felt the full weight of Sherman's army, the right wing having crossed the state line on that date.   The two columns of the Fifteenth Corps united at Laurel Hill, five miles west of Laurinburg, and went into camp.   The remainder of the wing went into camp along the banks of the treacherous Lumber River, called Drowning Creek in its upper reaches.

General Sherman, traveling with the Fifteenth Corps, made his headquarters near Laurel Hill Presbyterian Church, a region his soldiers

24. Lewis, *Sherman*, p. 509.   The Confederate soldiers also fired these great pine forests.   Fletcher, *Rebel Private*, p. 140.

25. Kinnear, *86 Ill.*, p. 101.   26. Hamilton, *Recollection*, pp. 195-96.

27. *OR*, XLVII, Pt. I, Ser. I, 690.   28. *Ibid.*, XLVII, Pt. II, Ser. I, 704.

29. The railroad shops had been moved to Laurinburg in hopes they would be safe from the Federal forces beseiging Fort Fisher.   *Raleigh News and Observer*, Mar. 12, 1933.   When it was seen that Fort Fisher was going to fall, a number of private citizens fled from Wilmington to Laurinburg and neighboring towns.   Undated newspaper clipping, N.C. Coll., U.N.C.

30. Lt. Colonel J. G. M. Montgomery, Fifth Tennessee Confederate cavalry, mentions that railroad property was burned in Laurinburg.   *OR*, XLVII, Pt. II, Ser. I, 1345, 1352. The reports of Federal officers do not mention the destruction of any property in Laurinburg.   It is known, however, that a new railroad machine shop was built in Laurinburg soon after the war was over and that it was built on the site of the old shop.   *Proceedings of the W. C. and R. Railroad Co.*, p. 24.

31. *OR*, XLVII, Pt. II, Ser. I, 713.

thought looked "real Northern like. Small farms and nice white, tidy dwellings."[32] Satisfied that Federal troops were at Wilmington, the General decided to send the following message to the commanding officer at that place:

We are marching for Fayetteville, will be there Saturday, Sunday, and Monday, and then march for Goldsboro. If possible, send a boat up Cape Fear River, and have word conveyed to General Schofield that I expect to meet him about Goldsboro. We are all well and have done finely. The rains have made our roads difficult, and may delay us about Fayetteville, in which case I would like to have some bread, sugar, and coffee. We have abundance of all else. I expect to reach Goldsboro by the 20th instant.[33]

Corporal James Pike of Fourth Ohio cavalry and two men of Howard's command, Sergeant Amick and Private Quimby, were selected to carry the dispatch. Their instructions were to cross the Lumber River at Campbell's Bridge and proceed as directly as possible to Wilmington, avoiding Lumberton and Elizabethtown.[34]

The torrential rains which set in on the 8th, and made that day one of ". . . the most disagreeable . . . of the whole campaign" for the Illinois Surgeon, E. P. Burton, continued the following day.[35] The roads soon became a sea of mud and water, and almost impassable for troops and trains. The most formidable obstacle in the path of the army was the dark swirling water of Lumber River and its adjacent swamps.[36] This region brought from Sherman the remark: "It was the damnest marching I ever saw."[37] The wagons and artillery could only be dragged along by the mules with the assistance of soldiers who either tugged at ropes out ahead of the teams or put their hands to the wheels.[38] The teamsters, reins in one hand, constantly punctuated the air with a dexterous whip lash to remind the poor mules of their "black military heart" and endless faults. Every sentence was ordained with an oath.[39] "Such a wild scene of splashing and yelling and swearing and braying has rarely greeted mortal eyes and ears" wrote one Ohioan of Sherman's army. After darkness the work was carried on in the eerie light of thousands of torches and blazing pine trees.[40]

32. Wills, *Wills Diary*, p. 357.   33. *OR*, XLVII, Pt. II, Ser. I, 713.
34. *Ibid.*, XLVII, Pt. I, Ser. I, 203; Pike, *Scout and Ranger*, p. 382.
35. Burton, *Diary of E. P. Burton*, II, 68.   36. Jackson, *Colonel's Dairy*, p. 194.
37. Calkins, *104 Ill.*, p. 294.   38. Henman, *Sherman Brigade*, p. 918.
39. Oakey, "Marching," p. 677.   40. Henman, *Sherman Brigade*, p. 918.

General Sherman, still traveling with the Fifteenth Corps, took refuge on the night of March 9 from a "terrible storm of rain" in a little Presbyterian church called Bethel.[41] Refusing the bit of carpet one of his staff had improvised into a bed on the pulpit platform, the General stretched himself out on one of the wooden pews for the night.[42] Outside in the cold and rain were the men of the Fifteenth Corps, many of them without shoes or blankets. Those fortunate enough still to have their rubber ponchos used them primarily to shield their pine-knot fires from the rain.[43] Someone left a memento of Sherman's visit to Bethel in the form of a few suggestions for the preacher. Pencilled in the church Bible are the following lines:

Mr. McNeil will please preach a sermon on the illusions of pleasure and hope—Mr. McNeil will please prove the absurdity of the universalist doctrine—Mr. McNeil will please preach a sermon from the First Epistle of John 4 chapter—Mr. McNeil will please pray for Old Abe—By Order—W. T. Sherman—Major General Commander— U.S. Forces.[44]

Before General Blair ordered the Seventeenth Corps to move from Campbell's Bridge on March 9, he sent a mounted infantry regiment to Lumberton, some thirty miles east, with orders to burn all bridges and railroad property in the area. Since late February the people of Lumberton had been in a dilemma as to Sherman's destination. The Methodist minister in town, Washington S. Chaffin, said that each day brought a different rumor as to Sherman's whereabouts.[45] It so happened that Chaffin had just entered in his diary on March 9: "The Yankees are said to be in two different places near here. I am incredulous. . . ." when shouts that "The Yankees are coming, the Yankees are coming" were heard in the distance. Dropping his pen, the minister rushed to the window where he saw the streets instantaneously fill up with troops. In front of his very door Chaffin saw a neighbor of his twice fired upon when he tried to run. Before the minister fully realized what was happening, a cavalryman had robbed him of Mrs. Chaffin's watch and stolen his horse, Kate.[46] In this raid the Federals destroyed the wagon and railroad bridges over the Lumber River, the rail depot, six box cars, and about one mile of track.[47] Following their usual custom the soldiers

41. Sherman, *Memoirs*, II, 293-94.   42. Byers, *Fire and Sword*, p. 181.
43. Sherlock, *100 Ind.*, p. 206.   44. Oates, *Fayetteville*, p. 719.
45. W. S. Chaffin Diary, Feb. 25, 1865, MS Div., Duke Univ. Lib.
46. *Ibid.*, Mar. 9, 1865.   47. *OR*, XLVII, Pt. I, Ser. I, 382.

"entered many houses and committed many depredations." After the troops departed, the clergyman completed the entry in his diary which had been so rudely interrupted. His chief concern seemed not to be for his wife "who was greatly excited" but for Kate whom he had owned for "five years, 11 months, 17 days—she had never been sick—I traveled with her on horseback, etc., 17,102 miles."[48]

Nightfall of this same day found the Seventeenth, Fourteenth, and Twentieth Corps encamped respectively at Raft Swamp between the fifteen- and twenty-mile posts on the Fayetteville plank road and near McFarland's Bridge over the Lumber River. The day's march, because of heavy rains, had been extremely difficult for all. Practically every foot of the way had to be corduroyed with fence rails and split sapplings.

The Federal cavalry under General Kilpatrick had crossed the Lumber River on March 8 and at Solomon's Grove, a crossroads around ten miles north of Love's Bridge, had struck the rear of Hardee's column, capturing a number of prisoners.[49] From these prisoners Kilpatrick learned that General Hampton's cavalry was a few miles in the rear and marching rapidly for Fayetteville. An examination of his map showed Kilpatrick that Hampton could be moving on any one or more of three different roads. Hoping to intercept the Confederate cavalry, Kilpatrick assigned each of his brigades the corner of a triangle which not only crossed the possible enemy lines of march, but also made it feasible for the brigades to protect one another.[50] The excitement and graveness of an expectant clash with Hampton caused the Federal commander to spend much of the afternoon passing from one of his detachments to another. For consolation in such troubled times "Little Kil" shared the carriage of a beautiful young lady accompanying the army north. Made to walk behind the carriage was a Confederate prisoner, Lieutenant H. Clay Reynolds, who was able to view from close range the entertaining spectacle of the General lying with his head in his lady friend's lap.[51] That night Kilpatrick made his camp with Colonel George E. Spencer's brigade north of Solomon's Grove.

About dusk the Confederate cavalry approached the vicinity of Sol-

48. Chaffin Diary, Mar. 9, 1865, MS Div., Duke Univ. Lib.
49. OR, XLVII, Pt. I, Ser. I, 861.
50. Ibid., XLVII, Pt. II, Ser. I, 786; Cox, March to the Sea, p. 179.
51. DuBose, "Road Fight," p. 85.

omon's Grove; General Butler's division was in front. Captain M. B. Humphrey's squadron, Sixth South Carolina cavalry, was the advance guard of the column. Wheeler's division brought up the rear. At the intersection of one of the Fayetteville roads, Humphrey noticed that a heavily mounted column had just passed. He reported the fact to Butler, and while they were discussing the situation, a squad of thirty Federal cavalrymen of the Fifth Kentucky appeared on the road. By a bit of trickery, Butler was able to capture all thirty without firing a shot.[52] General Kilpatrick himself was with the detachment at the moment but managed to escape with his staff.[53]

Hampton, upon learning that Kilpatrick was near, decided to turn the trick on his adversary by attacking his camp at daylight the next morning, March 10. During the early part of the evening one of Kilpatrick's officers mistakenly rode into the Confederate lines and was brought immediately to General Butler for questioning. Butler was able to learn from this officer the location of Kilpatrick's headquarters, which were in the Charles Monroe dwelling. Around midnight Butler reconnoitered the Federal position and learned that Kilpatrick had posted no pickets to protect his rear. This enabled Butler and his men to ride almost up to the camp fires without being noticed. Kilpatrick had moved around the head of a swamp and pitched his camp in front of it. His rear and right were protected by the swamp, but his left was entirely exposed.

With this information Generals Hampton, Wheeler, and Butler formed their plan of battle. The attack, which was to commence at daylight, was to be led by Butler. He was to move when the head of Wheeler's column appeared in the rear. He was to follow the road taken by Kilpatrick, move around the head of the swamp and fall suddenly upon the Federal camp from the west. Wheeler had instructions to move through the woods to the right and attack from the rear. Captain Bostick of Young's brigade was given the task of capturing General Kilpatrick. He was instructed upon entering the Federal camp at daylight to rush straight for the house in which Kilpatrick had his headquarters. He was to surround the house and hold his position until assistance came.[54]

52. Butler, "Kilpatrick's Escape," *Butler and His Cavalry*, p. 443.
53. *OR*, XLVII, Pt. II, Ser. I, 786.
54. Butler, "Kilpatricks Escape," p. 444; Oates, *Fayetteville*, p. 405.

By nine o'clock on the evening of March 9, Generals Thomas J. Jordon and Smith D. Atkins, commanding Kilpatrick's First and Second brigades respectively, discovered that while Hampton had been amusing them in front, he was passing with his main force on a road to his right. These officers at once made every effort to reach Kilpatrick before dawn but failed to do so, owing to bad roads and almost incessant skirmishing with the Confederates who were marching on a parallel road at some points not a mile distant.[55] The Confederate and Federal columns were so close that some of the time they became mixed together. One of Wheeler's men said that on this particular night he happened to glance up one time and discovered, much to his surprise, that a number of Federal cavalrymen were riding by his side, and that by the time he had reported this to his captain at the head of the column, the Federals had disappeared, taking with them as prisoners the Confederate rear guard.[56]

The night hours dragged by for Butler's men who halted in the woods near the enemy camp. The period was passed in complete silence and darkness. All conversation was prohibited. No fires were allowed. Each man sat on the ground holding the bridle-rein of his saddled mount and wondering what the morning held for him.[57] Occasionally passing through the mind of a trooper was the intriguing thought that he might get a close look at Kilpatrick's fair lady.[58] Just before the break of dawn Colonel "Gid" Wright of Butler's division gave the long awaited command to mount up, and with the first rays of daylight he struck Kilpatrick's camp, which was found to be without a picket or camp guard. Following immediately in his rear was General Butler with the other brigades. Riding into a sleeping camp, the Confederate cavalrymen were able to put the entire Federal command, including the General himself, to flight in less than a minute. For a moment it looked like a cyclone had struck the camp. Blankets were flying in the air and men in their night clothes were running in every direction. A stampede on foot was underway.[59] Kilpatrick called this attack "the most formidable cavalry charge I have ever witnessed."[60] Although his headquarters were taken, the General managed to avoid capture and reached his camp a few hundred yards to

55. OR, XLVII, Pt. II, Ser. I, 786.
56. Watkins, "Another Account," Confed. Vet., XX, 84.
57. Wells, Hampton and Reconstruction, p. 63.
58. Wells, Hampton and His Cavalry, p. 461.
59. Hamilton, "Effort to Capture Kilpatrick," Confed. Vet., XXIX, 329.
60. OR, XLVII, Pt. II, Ser. I, 786.

the rear where a fight was going on between his men and the Confederates for possession of the camp and animals.[61]

To make his escape "Little Kil" had to spring from the warm bed of his lovely lady.[62] The first thought to jump into his mind at the sound of piercing "Rebel" yells was not the embarrassment of having such a delightful nocturnal slumber abruptly interrupted, but that his four years of hard fighting for a major general's commission were going up with a surprise. The initial shock of this unexpected visit did not completely separate the cavalry commander from his wits. While standing in front of his headquarters, a Confederate rider dashed up to Kilpatrick and asked him if he had seen the General, to which he replied, "There he goes on that black horse," pointing to a man making off on such a mount. Thereupon the soldier pursued the figure pointed out to him. Kilpatrick, embarrassingly clad only in his night clothes, then jumped upon the nearest horse and made a hasty departure.[63]

By this time chance bullets were fast perforating the weather boards of the headquarters house. This was sufficient to bring the General's forsaken damsel to the doorway. For a moment she looked disconsolately at her carriage as if the vague idea were dawning that it was time for her to be leaving. This was followed by a short period of mute despair when it broke upon her that the carriage would not move without horses. The strange apparition of a lovely young woman in scanty night dress on the field of battle brought one Confederate captain's horse to a fast halt. Southern chivalry rose to the occasion. Dismounting, the cavalryman led the distressed one to the safety of a nearby ditch.[64]

Shortly Kilpatrick and his cavalrymen were driven back some five hundred yards to the swamp. The Confederates, however, did not follow up this initial success. General Kilpatrick said they stopped to plunder and this gave him time to rally his men.[65] General Butler explained this loss of initiative by the fact that Wheeler was unable to cross

61. A detail of twenty men had been picked from Hampton's ranks and given instructions to slip into the Federal camp before the general charge started and to capture Kilpatrick. This group was within twenty yards of the General's headquarters when the fighting commenced. Hamilton, "Effort to Capture Kilpatrick," p. 329.

62. *New Bern N.C. Times*, Mar. 28, 1865, quoting *N.Y. Tribune*, n.d. The true identity of Kilpatrick's companion was never determined. In all probability it was the beautiful Mary Boozer who was still traveling with the Federal army at the time.

63. Butler, "Kilpatrick's Escape," pp. 446-47. In his official report Kilpatrick states that he made his escape on foot. *OR*, XLVII, Pt. II, Ser. I, 786.

64. Wells, "Morning Call," *So. Hist. Soc. Papers*, XII, 128; DuBose, *Wheeler*, p. 499.

65. *OR*, XLVII, Pt. II, Ser. I, 787.

the swamp and attack from the rear,[66] and that Brigadier General E. M. Law's brigade, which he ordered to move up and take possession of the camp after Wright's command had been scattered, had been, without his knowledge, ordered to some other point by General Hampton.[67] No matter what the cause, the fact remains that the Confederate cavalry did not follow up their surprise attack. This enabled the Federals to rally and with the aid of rapid-firing Spencer carbines to retake their camp and artillery. The artillery they turned on the disorganized Confederates, driving them out of the camp.[68]

About eight o'clock Brigadier General J. G. Mitchell's brigade of the Fourteenth Corps came to Kilpatrick's assistance. Although the fighting was over, this infantry brigade moved into position and remained with Kilpatrick until 1:30 P.M.

The casualty reports for this skirmish are both confusing and contradictory. Kilpatrick reported that he lost four officers killed and seven wounded, fifteen men killed and sixty-one severely and several slightly wounded, and one hundred and three officers and men taken prisoners. He further stated that over eighty Confederate dead and a great number of wounded were left in his camp and that thirty prisoners and one hundred and fifty horses were captured. The horses had been abandoned in the swamp.[69]

Wheeler said he took over three hundred and fifty prisoners.[70] General Johnston put the figure at five hundred plus one hundred and seventy-three Confederate prisoners that were freed.[71]

Kilpatrick's escape on the morning of the surprise attack is as controversial a subject as the number of casualties suffered on each side. General Kilpatrick told Butler after the war that on this particular morning he walked out of his headquarters in his slippers about day-

---

66. Butler, "Curtain Falls," p. 475. General Butler is mistaken in his statement that Wheeler's command was not engaged in the fighting at Solomon's Grove. See articles by W. G. Allen, Joseph A. Jones and Sam Bennett in *Confed. Vet.*, XIX, 433-34. General Kilpatrick in his official report mentions two of Wheeler's divisions as being engaged in the action, *OR*, XLVII, Pt. I, Ser. I, 787. Wheeler himself in reporting the engagements lists the wounded in his command, *OR*, XLVII, Pt. I, Ser. I, 1130.

67. Butler, "Kilpatrick's Escape," p. 445.

68. Lieutenant Colonel Joseph F. Waring of Hampton's cavalry thought it was to the enemy's credit that they rallied so "promptly after the first surprise." J. F. Waring Diary, Mar. 10, 1865, SHC, U.N.C.

69. *OR*, XLVII, Pt. II, Ser. I, 787; *Ibid.*, Pt. I, Ser. I, 862.

70. *Ibid.*, XLVII, Pt. I, Ser. I, 1130.

71. Johnson, *Narrative*, p. 381.

light, as was his usual custom, to see that his horses were fed.[72] Such a habit was certainly the exception rather than the rule for most high ranking officers. A Confederate soldier in on this surprise attack presumed Kilpatrick to be the only example from Joshua to the nineteenth century of a major general who would walk out of a warm room in cold weather only partially dressed to see horses fed one hundred yards away.[73]

Captain T. F. Northrop, Kilpatrick's chief scout, said he saw General Kilpatrick before he had a chance to change his clothes, and that the General had on shirt, vest, trousers, and slippers or shoes, but was without hat, coat, and probably boots. He states emphatically that no nightshirt was in evidence.[74] However, J. W. DuBose in his article, "The Fayetteville (N.C.) Road Fight," quotes Sergeant A. F. Hardee, one of Shannon's scouts, as follows: "General Kilpatrick left his hat, coat, pants, sword, and pistols, etc."[75]

The General did lose around thirty valuable horses from his headquarters.[76] Among them were his two fine stallions—one a little spotted horse and the other a large black.[77]

There will always be disagreement as to who actually got the better of the fighting at Monroe's Cross-Roads, contemptuously tagged by the Federal infantry as "Kilpatrick's Shirt-tail Skedaddle."[78] Yet the fact stands that by engaging Kilpatrick in battle Hampton was able to open the road to Fayetteville which the Federal camp blocked. The Confederate cavalry joined Hardee near Fayetteville that night.

March 10 was as trying a day for the four corps of the Federal army as the one before. The different commands spent most of the day repairing roads and closing up. Only General Blair's Seventeenth Corps deviated from the major objective of covering as many miles as possible in the direction of Fayetteville. Having orders to destroy Rockfish factory, off to the right of his line of march, Blair sent the Ninth Illinois to do the job. These mounted infantrymen levelled this 318 loom textile plant.[79]

72. Butler, "Kilpatrick's Escape," pp. 446-47.

73. J. W. DuBose to M. C. Butler, Feb. 12, 1908, U. R. Brooks Papers, MS Div., Duke Univ. Lib.

74. Northrup, "Other Side of the Road Fight," *Confed, Vet.,* XX, 423.

75. DuBose, "Road Fight," p. 85.   76. *OR,* XLVII, Pt. II, Ser. I, 787.

77. DuBose, "Road Fight," p. 85.   78. Hamilton, *Recollection,* p. 199.

79. *OR,* XLVII, Pt. II, Ser. I, 382. On Mar. 17 the Great Falls Cotton Mill at Rockingham had been burned by the Federal army. Robertson, *Mich. in the War,*

Sherman had hoped that the Fourteenth Corps would occupy Fayette-ville on March 10. Three days before he had instructed Davis to make all possible speed toward the city and try to reach there in time to save the bridge across the Cape Fear.[80] Yet on the 10th not more than five miles were covered by the corps. The official reports of Generals Slocum, Davis, Carlin, and Morgan[81] give no reason for this slow progress. The weather, as bad as it was, ordinarily would not have held the advance to a mere five miles, for all three divisions were on March 9 encamped on the plank road leading directly to Fayetteville.[82] This should have facilitated the marching considerably. The explanation lies in the fascina-tion of the "bummer" for the awesome show of burning rosin. Albion Winegar Tourgée, an Ohioan in Sherman's army, tells the following story:

The morning of the 10th [of March] we foragers from the One Hundred and Fifth Ohio started at daylight; two miles from camp was a wide, swampy ravine, traversed by a winding creek. . . . Just on the bluff, across the ravine were probably 2,000 barrels of rosin, piled along the road on a grade to the creek, which someone thoughtlessly set on fire. Twenty rods further on was a bypath into which we filed.[83]

These foragers then moved to within two miles of Fayetteville without meeting any resistance. After foraging for a good part of the day, they began to look for their command, but it could not be found. Concluding that their brigade was lost, they returned to where the rosin pile had been in the morning. The situation was then explained.

It [rosin] had melted and run into the creek floating and blazing, burning all the bridges. The heat was so intense that it was hours before it could be subdued and the bridges rebuilt. Going into camp we were greeted with cheers, having been reported captured. . . . The rosin fire was frequently commented upon as causing us to lose a favorable opportunity to capture or scatter Hardee's forces. We were discreetly silent as to its cause.[84]

---

p. 500. Also destroyed by Sherman soon after his entry into North Carolina was the gun factory of Murdock Morrison near Laurel Hill. *Raleigh News and Observer*, July 26, 1953.

80. *OR*, XLVII, Pt. II, Ser. I, 721.

81. *OR*, XLVII, Pt. I, Ser. I, 422. Brigadier Generals J. D. Morgan and William P. Carlin were both members of the Fourteenth Corps.

82. *OR*, XLVII, Pt. I, Ser. I, 422.

83. Tourgee, *105 Ohio*, pp. 352-64.

84. *Ibid.*

Early on the morning of March 11, General Howard ordered Captain Duncan to take all the available mounted men at his headquarters and scout toward Fayetteville.[85] Finding a by-road not picketed by the Confederates, Duncan entered the city and surprised General Hampton. Had it not been for one of Hampton's best scouts, Hugh Scott, the General might have been captured. Scott was able to warn Hampton in time for the General to rally seven followers—two members of his staff, three privates from Company K of the Fourth South Carolina cavalry, Scott, and one man said to have been from Wheeler's command, whose name is unknown—and charge Duncan who had drawn up his command of sixty-eight in a nearby street.[86] Confused by the suddenness of the attack, the Federals wheeled about and ran; but less than one hundred yards down the street was a turn at right angles to the left into the by-road by which they had entered the city, and by which they must escape. Here they became jammed together and in the confusion all organization was lost. Eleven Federals were killed and twelve captured. Among those taken prisoner were Captain Duncan and a Federal spy, David Day, who was dressed in a Confederate uniform.[87] Two of these casualities were reported as having been inflicted by General Hampton himself but this failed to impress the Confederate General, Lafayette McLaws, who by this time was fed up with tales of South Carolina heroism. In his order book he wrote:

Report says he killed two with his own hand, but the chivalry have fallen so deep into the pit of 'want of chivalry' that they are constantly inventing Munchausen as to the prowess of those from that state, of defaming others in order that thereby they appear elevated by the contrast.[88]

Had McLaws known it he could have ridiculed another South Carolinian, E. L. Wells, who boasted of having cleaved in one fellow's head with his sabre, besides using his pistol freely.[89] So far as is known, the only Confederate casualty was a handsome, well-bred mare ridden by one of the privates.[90]

After this street fight General Butler could sympathize with Kilpatrick

85. OR, XLVII, Pt. I, Ser. I, 203.
86. W. Hampton to Lieutenant Harleston, Mar. 19, 1865, *Butler and His Cavalry*, pp. 428-29.
87. Wells, *Hampton and His Cavalry*, pp. 30-35.
88. McLaws Order Bk., 1865, SHC, U.N.C., p. 27.
89. Smith, *Smith Letters*, p. 201.
90. Wells, *Hampton and His Cavalry*, p. 35.

over the embarrassment of fleeing, not fully clothed, before the enemy. Captain Duncan's surprise visit to Fayetteville caught Butler and his aide, Lieutenant H. C. Reynolds, sound asleep in a private home while out back a Negro woman scrubbed the only uniforms and underclothes they possessed. They were awakened when a carrier burst into their room, shouting, "The Yankees, the Yankees." The two officers then had no option but to spring into the three pieces of wearing apparel available for each, which were boots, overcoats, and hats. Butler and Reynolds galloped off at a fast clip but not in the direction of the firing.[91]

Major General G. A. Smith, commanding the Fourth Division of the Seventeenth Corps, sent two hundred mounted men to the assistance of Duncan's scouts, but they arrived too late to help the captain.[92] Aided by General Howard's escort, also ordered forward, this detachment got possession of Arsenal Hill and undertook to save the bridge over the Cape Fear. While they were engaged in this, General Smith's leading brigade entered the city.

By this time the Confederate cavalry had, for the most part, withdrawn across the river and placed in position a section of a battery of artillery and opened fire on the Federal skirmish line. Even in the face of this fire the Federals were able to get within two hundred yards of the bridge before it was fired.[93] This was in part due to the high mettle of a captured horse General Smith's adjutant was riding. With the sudden blast of a brass band the adjutant's horse ran away and headed straight for the bridge. The Federal skirmishers, thinking this a bold attempt to save the crossing, followed the run-away horse and its scared rider in the direction of the river,[94] but the Confederates had piled large quantities of rosin upon the bridge, and it was already in flames and burning "beautifully" when the squad reached it.[95]

Mayor Archibald McLean made a formal surrender of the city to Lieutenant Colonel William E. Strong of Howard's staff, then to General Slocum, who came up shortly afterwards. Next the United States flag was raised over the market place.[96]

91. J. W. DuBose to U. R. Brooks, Aug. 19, 1911, Brooks Papers, MS Div., Duke Univ. Lib.
92. OR, XLVII, Pt. I, Ser. I, 413.
93. Ibid., pp. 203-4; Oates, Fayetteville, p. 408.
94. Hedley, Marching Through Ga., pp. 399-400.
95. Waring Diary, Mar. 11, 1865, SHC, U.N.C.
96. Conyngham, Sherman's March, p. 357.

In compliance with General Howard's orders, the Fourth Division of the Seventeenth Corps was withdrawn from Fayetteville to allow the Fourteenth Corps to occupy the city. Baird's division was assigned this duty.[97] All three divisions of the Seventeenth Corps encamped near the city on the night of March 11. The remainder of the Fourteenth Corps went into camp about two miles west of the city on the plank road. Only General Logan's Fifteenth Corps failed to reach the city on this date. The following day it moved into position along with the other corps.

97. *OR,* XLVII, Pt. I, Ser. I, 551.

CHAPTER IX

Sugar and Oats but No Shoes

GENERAL SHERMAN reached Fayetteville on March 11, and set up headquarters in the old United States arsenal, whose cream colored buildings comprised the handsomest structures in town and whose well kept grounds served as a municipal park.[1] This same date immediate preparations were made to lay two pontoon bridges across the Cape Fear, one near the burned bridge, and another about four miles down the river.[2]

Sunday, March 12, was a day of Sabbath stillness in Fayetteville until shortly after noon when the stillness was broken by the shrill whistle of a steam boat, which meant only one thing to the General and his men—the couriers had gotten through safely from Laurel Hill, and this was the prompt reply from Major General A. H. Terry at Wilmington.[3] Sherman states: "The effect was electric, and no one can realize the feeling unless, like us, he had been for months cut off from all communications with friends. . . ."[4]

The passage up the river of this steamboat, the army tug, *Davidson,* was unopposed until it was ten or fifteen miles from Fayetteville, where some small detachments of Confederate cavalry opened fire on it from the river banks. But Acting Ensign Charles Ainsworth of the *Davidson*

1. Mrs. J. H. Anderson, "Sherman's Army Entered Fayetteville." Undated newspaper clipping, NCC, U.N.C. Elizabeth B. Stinson, "Arsenal," *Our Women in the War,* p. 22.

2. Lieutenant Colonel Joseph Waring of Hampton's cavalry had correctly observed on March 11, while watching the bridge over the Cape Fear burn: "Mr. Sherman will find use for his pontoons." Waring Diary, Mar. 11, 1865, SHC, U.N.C.

3. Corporal Pike got lost the first night away from Laurel Hill but finally reached Wilmington by "going down the Cape Fear." The other two scouts, disguised as Confederate officers, reached Wilmington without any trouble. Pike, *Scout and Ranger,* pp. 382-83. General Schofield left Wilmington on March 6 and joined Major General J. D. Cox beyond New Bern on March 8. Cox, commander of the Third Division, Twenty-third Corps, had been sent to New Bern to organize a provisional corps to move via Kinston to Goldsboro. With Schofield gone, Terry was the commanding general at Wilmington. *OR,* XLVII, Pt. I, Ser. I, 911-12.

4. Sherman, *Memoirs,* II, 295.

had taken the precaution to cover his craft securely with cotton bales, and no damage was done.[5]

After a few minutes' conference with Ensign Ainsworth about the capacity of his boat and the state of affairs along the river, Sherman instructed him to be ready to start back at 6:00 P.M. and ordered Captain Byers of his staff to get ready to carry dispatches to Washington. He also authorized General Howard to send to Wilmington on the *Davidson* some of the refugees who had traveled with his army all the way from Columbia. Among those receiving this special consideration was Mary Boozer, whose beauty had caught Sherman's eye.[6]

Carrying Captain Byers and the refugees, the tug departed Fayetteville with a huge pile of mail cluttering its deck.[7] Ensign Ainsworth's offer to take personal correspondence back to Wilmington brought a tremendous and immediate response from the news hungry soldiers who at the time were offering outrageous prices just to read old copies of New York newspapers.[8] The announcement that mail would leave the Twentieth Corps headquarters at 4:00 P.M. was as astonishing to Colonel Charles F. Morse as if his mother had stepped into his tent and asked him to sit down to dinner at home.[9]

On March 14, the tug *Davidson* again arrived from Wilmington. Brigadier General George S. Dodge of the Quartermaster Corps was on board. He reported that the badly needed clothing was not to be had at Wilmington but that he had brought some sugar, coffee, and a bountiful supply of oats.[10]

Evidently the quartermasters in Wilmington were not familiar with the successful foraging tactics of the Federal "bummers." If they had been, they would not have wasted ship's space on forage for the animals. Forty thousand pairs of shoes, not a cargo of oats, were needed at Fayetteville.[11] One of Sherman's quartermasters, peeved at the sight of

5. *Wilmington Herald of the Union*, Mar. 14, 1865. Several efforts had been made to contact Sherman prior to dispatching the *Davidson* up the Cape Fear. General Schofield on March 4, sent a naval party from Wilmington in search of Sherman. It was not until the afternoon of March 11, in the vicinity of Lumberton, that Acting Master H. W. Grinnell in command of the party learned the definite whereabouts of Sherman's forces. The next day around 1:00 P.M. he delivered Schofield's dispatch to Sherman but being of an older date it was superseded by Terry's message which Ensign Ainsworth had delivered only a short while before. *NR*, XII, Ser. I, 90. On March 13, a portion of the Thirteenth Pennsylvania cavalry reached Sherman at Fayetteville and delivered to him cipher dispatches from General Terry. *OR*, XLVII, Pt. II, Ser. I, 813.

6. Sherman, *Memoirs*, II, 295.   7. Wright, *6 Ia.*, p. 425.
8. Sherlock, *100 Ind.*, p. 207.   9. Morse, *Letters*, pp. 212-13.
10. Sherman, *Memoirs*, II, 299.   11. Wills, *Wills Diary*, p. 362.

several boatloads of forage, asked one vessel's captain if he would like to return to Wilmington with a load of corn.[12]

The *Davidson* had been followed up the Cape Fear by two gunboats under the command of Lieutenant Commander George W. Young, United States Navy.[13] These boats joined the gunboat, *Eolus,* which had been in Fayetteville since the evening of March 12, in patrolling the river.[14] General Sherman wanted the river patrolled as long as the stage of water would permit.[15]

While at Fayetteville Sherman took the opportunity to replace all rejected animals of his trains with those taken from the local citizens and to clear his columns of the vast crowd of white refugees and Negroes that followed the Federal army.[16] He called these followers "twenty to thirty thousand useless mouths."[17] To General Terry he wrote: "They are dead weight to me and consume our supplies."[18] March 12 Sherman wrote Grant that he could leave Fayetteville the next day were it not for the large crowd of refugees that encumbered his army.[19]

Major John A. Winsor, One Hundred and Sixteenth Illinois, was detained to conduct this refugee train to Wilmington. A guard of one hundred men from each wing of the army was sent along as escort for the train.[20] Fenwick Y. Hedley in his book, *Marching Through Georgia,*

12. *N.Y. Herald,* Mar. 30, 1865.   13. *OR,* XLVII, Pt. II, Ser. I, 812.

14. *NR,* XII, Ser. I, 70.   15. *OR,* XLVII, Pt. I, Ser. I, 845.

16. The *N.Y. Herald* stated that great numbers of Negroes flocked to Sherman's army with the assistance of their masters under the promise that they would return and work for wages as soon as it was safe for them to do so. *N.Y. Herald,* Mar. 11, 1865. On the other hand, David P. Conyngham, war correspondent, reported that twenty-five slaves around Laurinburg were hanged by the Richmond County home guard for organizing a party with intentions of running away to Sherman's army. Conyngham, *Sherman's March,* p. 355.

17. *OR,* XLVII, Pt. II, Ser. I, 803.   18. *Ibid.,* p. 817.

19. *Ibid.,* p. 795.

20. *Ibid.,* p. 807. As many as possible went down the Cape Fear by steamboat. At the time Sherman's troops arrived in Fayetteville there were only eight light draft steamers lying at the wharves. The others had been sent upstream for safety. Six of the eight—the *Dawson, Chatham, Flora, Kate, Caswell,* and *Clarendon* had been partially destroyed, by the withdrawing Confederate soldiers, who had in addition burned much of the cotton stored along the waterfront. The *North Carolina,* a poor, rickety, old craft, and the *Hurt,* a fine river steamer, were saved. *Wilmington Herald of the Union,* Mar. 17, 1865; McLaws Order Bk., 1865, SHC, U.N.C. Robinson, "Recollections of the Arsenal," Undated newspaper clipping, NCC, U.N.C. In all probability, it was the *Hurt* that foragers from the Thirtieth Illinois captured, since Sherman ordered the Confederate boat reported in General Howard's hands to be filled with refugees and dispatched to Wilmington. *OR,* XLVII, Pt. II, Ser. I, 784, 817.

gives an interesting description of this refugee train as it left Fayetteville for the coast:

The white refugees and freedmen traveled together in the column, and made a comical procession. They had the worst possible horses and mules, and every kind of vehicle, while their costuming was something beyond description. Here was a cumbersome, old-fashioned family carriage, very dilapidated, yet bearing traces of gilt and filagree, suggesting that it had been a very stylish affair fifty years before. On the driver's seat was perched an aged patriarch in coarse plantation breeches, with sky-blue, brass-buttoned coat very much out of repair and his gray grizzled wool topped off with an old fashioned silk hat. By his side rode mater-familias, wearing a scoop-shovel bonnet resplendent with faded ribbons and flowers of every color of the rainbow; a silk or satin dress of great antiquity, and coarse brogans on her feet. The top of the carriage was loaded with featherbed, two or three skillets, and other "plunder." From the glassless windows of the clumsy vehicle peered half a score of pickaninnies of all sizes, their eyes big with wonder. Elsewhere in the column a pair of "coons" rode in a light spring wagon, one urging the decrepit horse to keep up with the procession, while the other picked a banjo, and made serious attempts to sing a plantation song, which was almost invariably of a semi-religious character. Those who traveled on foot, men and women, of all colors from light mulatto to coal black, loaded down with bedding, clothing and provisions, were legion. Occasionally, a wagon was occupied by white refugees, who, being unionist, had been despoiled by the Confederates. These were sad and hopeless. The colored people, on the contrary, were invariably gay hearted, regarding their exodus as a pleasure trip, and evidently strong in the faith of their lot, on "gittin to freedom," was to be one of bliss.[21]

Overlooked by Hedley in his descriptive paragraph was what General Slocum called the "best way of transporting pickaninnies." This unique procedure came to the attention of the refugees one day when a large family of slaves came through the fields to join the trains of the left wing. Mounted on a mule was the head of the family and safely stored away behind him in bags attached to a blanket covering the animal were two small Negro children, one on each side. The next day more than one mule appeared in column covered by a blanket which in some instances had as many as ten or fifteen bags tacked to it. Nothing was visible of the mule except head, tail, and feet, all else being covered by the black, wooly heads and bright shining eyes of little children. Occasionally a

21. Hedley, *Marching Through Ga.,* pp. 402-5.

cow was substituted for the mule. This was a decided improvement as the cow furnished rations as well as transportation.[22]

During the occupation of Fayetteville several skirmishes took place between Federal reconnaissance units operating across the Cape Fear River and the Confederate rear guard. These engagements were strictly minor in nature, but in each affair the Confederates gave ground very grudgingly.

Perhaps few towns in the South surpassed Fayetteville in the ardor and liberality with which she supported the war, after secession became a law of the state. The leading men of the city had been union men not secessionists; but they were Confederates, and when war started they rallied to the Southern cause. For four years the columns of the city's newspapers carried lists of donations that would have done credit to wealthier communities. As elsewhere in the South the ladies were especially active.[23] The *Fayetteville Observer*, practically up to the day of the city's capitulation, insisted that Southern independence could still be won. The paper voiced the forlorn hope that France and England would recognize the independence of the Confederacy.[24]

The *Fayetteville Observer*, ably edited by Edward Jones Hale, was certainly one of the most influential journals in the state. The editor was an old-line Whig in politics and, being opposed to secession, resisted its movements as long as it was possible to do so. His opposition to the United States government was aroused when President Lincoln called for troops, and when North Carolina seceded from the Union, Hale supported her act. He followed this with an all out effort of support of the war. He devoted his paper to the benefit of the army and to the upholding of the state and Confederate governments. Although no great admirer of Jefferson Davis, Hale gave him generous support after Davis became President of the Confederacy.[25]

Since Hale was such an ardent supporter of the Southern cause, it is easy to see why there was strong feeling among the soldiers of Sherman's army against the man and his newspaper. "It was remarked that so great was the feeling among the soldiers against this person that even a chicken coop was unsafe if it had his name upon it."[26]

22. Slocum, "Sherman's March," pp. 689-90.
23. Cornelia P. Spencer, *Ninety Days*, pp. 48-50.
24. Yates, "Vance and the End of the War," *NCHR*, XVIII, 320.
25. Spencer, *Ninety Days*, pp. 245-46.
26. *Wilmington Herald of the Union*, Mar. 26, 1865.

Fayetteville received harsh treatment at the hands of Sherman's army, not only because it was a North Carolina stronghold of Confederate loyalty, but also because of certain events that took place in the city. To Slocum, Sherman wrote: "On approaching Fayetteville you may give out that if the bridge is destroyed, we will deal harshly by the town, but if there is no positive resistance and if the enemy spare the bridge I wish the town to be dealt with generously."[27]   Practically the same instructions were sent to Kilpatrick: "If the people will spare the bridge, I want all to be easy on the citizens, but if they burn bridges or bother us we must go the whole figure."[28]   As has already been pointed out, the bridge across the Cape Fear was destroyed. The street fight between Kilpatrick and Hampton was probably considered by many as a defense of the city, and certainly the shooting from windows as Sherman's troops passed along the street was more than a "bother" to the Federals.[29]

Major Nichols goes so far as to say that instances of Confederate inhumanity were not rare in Fayetteville. He understood that a member of Hampton's cavalry shot a Federal prisoner just because he wanted to kill "another d—— Yankee."[30]

General Sherman especially wanted to reach Fayetteville so that he could retake the arsenal located there. He wrote the Secretary of War that he took it for granted the United States government would never again trust North Carolina with an arsenal to appropriate at her pleasure.[31] At the outbreak of the war the Confederates had taken over this United States arsenal without a fight and for four years this valuable government property served the South.

Most of the personnel employed at the arsenal had fled the city prior to the arrival of the Federal army. One of the few remaining behind was Edward Monagan, a former army friend of Sherman's, who now lived in Fayetteville.[32]   In hopes the General would protect his property, Monagan visited Sherman at his headquarters. A staff member, present at this meeting, saw a "ray of pleasure illuminating Sherman's face" upon seeing his old friend but this expression was soon replaced by a scowl when the realization struck that the man before him had discarded the

---

27. OR, XLVII, Pt. II, Ser. I, 708.   28. Ibid., p. 721.
29. Byers, Fire and Sword, p. 186.   30. Nichols, Great March, p. 239.
31. OR, XLVII, Pt. II, Ser. I, 794.
32. Edward Monagan had joined the United States army when Sherman was a young officer. The two became very close friends. Fayetteville Observer, May 14, 1928.

uniform of the United States army he had once worn. Turning to his friend, Sherman stated:

You have betrayed . . . me, your friend, your country, that educated you for its defense. You are here a traitor, and you ask me to be again your friend, to protect your property. . . . Turn your back to me forever. I will not punish you; only go your way.[33]

General Sherman issued specific orders as to what property was to be destroyed in Fayetteville. Having ordered the left wing to enter the city first, he instructed General Slocum to destroy nothing until he arrived.[34] Upon his arrival Sherman issued Special Field Orders, No. 28, which instructed the left wing to hold the city and lay pontoons for crossing the river. In the meantime all railroad property, all shops, factories, tanneries, etc., were to be destroyed. All grist mills, except one water-mill of sufficient capacity to grind meal for the people of Fayetteville, were to be demolished. The cavalry was charged with destroying railroad trestles, depots, mills, and factories as far up as the lower Little River. Colonel Orlando M. Poe was given the duty of utterly demolishing the arsenal building and everything pertaining to it. Lieutenant Colonel Thomas G. Baylor, chief ordnance officer, was charged with the destruction of powder and arms.[35] All of the above property was destroyed and much more. It is difficult to determine just how much real estate was actually razed within the city itself. It is known, however, that of the four cotton mills in Fayetteville all were leveled by General Baird.[36] The State Bank building was also destroyed and probably as many as eleven large warehouses were fired.[37] The sparks caught Mrs. M. Bank's home on fire. A reporter for the Wilmington newspaper, *Herald of the Union,* states that every effort was made to save the house, but all endeavors were in vain.[38]

In their work of destruction Sherman's soldiers did not overlook the city's newspapers. The offices of the *Fayetteville Observer* and the *North Carolina Presbyterian* were both burned.[39] The third printing office destroyed by Baird was probably that of the *Daily Telegraph,* which had its press in operation through March 9.[40]

33. Byers, *Fire and Sword,* pp. 184-85. 34. *OR,* XLVII, Pt. II, Ser. I, 763.
35. *Ibid.,* p. 779. 36. *OR,* XLVII, Pt. I, Ser. I, 551.
37. Johnson, *Memoir of Johnston,* p. 188.
38. *Wilmington Herald of the Union,* Mar. 16, 1865.
39. Spencer, *Ninety Days,* p. 246.
40. Greogray, *Amer. Newspapers,* 1821-1936, p. 501.

E. J. Hale, Jr., son of the editor of the *Fayetteville Observer,* wrote an interesting letter, July 31, 1865, to James H. Lane, his commanding officer during the war, discussing the destruction of his father's property in Fayetteville. He said:

My father's property, before the war, was easily convertible into $85 to $100,000 in specie. He has not now a particle of property which will bring him a dollar of income. His office, with everything in it, was burned and by Sherman's order. Slocum, who executed the order, with a number of other Generals, sat on the verandah of a hotel opposite watching the progress of the flames, while they hobnobbed over wines stolen from our cellar. A fine brick building adjacent, also belonging to my father, was burned at the same time. The cotton factory, of which he was a large shareholder, was burned; while his bank, railroad, and other stocks are worse than worthless. . . . In fact, he has nothing left, besides the ruins of his town buildings and a few town lots which promise to be of little value hereafter, in this desolated town, and are of no value at present, save his residence, which (with brother's house) Sherman made a great parade of saving from a mob. . . .[41]

The First Regiment of Michigan engineers, under the immediate supervision of Colonel Poe, did a very thorough job of demolishing the arsenal and its machinery, much of which had formerly belonged to the United States arsenal at Harper's Ferry.[42] Early on the morning of March 11, however, the Confederates shipped out of Fayetteville by rail some of the machinery and stores from the arsenal. The machinery was hidden at the Egypt Coal Mines in Chatham County, but many of the stores were carried on to Greensboro by wagon.[43] Also escaping Sherman's destructive order were a few Enfield rifles passed out to Hardee's troops during their short stay in Fayetteville.[44]

Colonel Poe and his engineers devised a plan by which bars of railroad iron, suspended by chains from timbers set up in the shape of an "X," were used to knock down the different buildings which formed a hollow rectangle with a citadel in the center. Several such rams would work simultaneously around the same building. When the walls were sufficiently weakened, the roof would fall in with a loud crash. Then the

---

41. Hale, "Sherman's Bummers," *So. Hist. Soc. Papers,* XII, 427-28.
42. *OR,* XLVII, Pt. I, Ser. I, 23.
43. Mrs. J. H. Anderson, "Confed. Arsenal," *Confed. Vet.,* XXXVI, 223.
44. Ford, *Life in the Confederate Army,* p. 47.

band would strike up and the men would cheer.[45] Finally the ruins were burned, but special care was taken to protect private property in the neighborhood. The only property loss of any consequence was the W. B. Wright residence.[46] To start the fires the soldiers used the ornamental wood work which surrounded the buildings. As the heat from the numerous piles of flaming debris became very great, Confederate shells stored underground began to explode, creating the impression of a heavy artillery engagement.[47]

Besides the actual firing of property, there was considerable pillaging, but this plundering of private property was done, for the most part, before Baird took command of the city and garrisoned it with his three brigades. After guards were posted at public buildings and at nearly every private house, good order was established and maintained.[48] Baird stated in his report that upon his arrival in the city, he found stragglers from all portions of the army who had pushed in with the advance guard and committed "many disorders" before he could clear them out.[49] These "bummers" did a very thorough job of pillaging during their short stay in Fayetteville. An eye witness to this chaotic scene was certain that every house and store in town, except where guards were promptly obtained, was entered and robbed "of everything valuable or fit to eat. . . ."[50]

For over a week the "bummers" had been happily anticipating the spoils awaiting them in Fayetteville. Many of them had not reported to their commands since leaving Cheraw, preferring to camp each night with the extreme advance. Five of this number became so bold as to venture into town the day before it was taken. Such foolhardiness cost one life and brought no plunder. The morning of March 11, though, found scores of "bummers" hovering around the outskirts of Fayetteville, impatiently watching for the lead columns which they planned to join as skirmishers. But once inside the limits it was plunder, not the enemy,

45. Josephine B. Worth, "Sherman's Raid," *War Days in Fayetteville,* pp. 51-52.
46. Oates, *Fayetteville,* p. 412. Five residences near the arsenal did catch on fire but three of these were probably the former residences for officials of the arsenal when it was United States property. Johnson, *Memoir of Johnston,* p. 188; Stinson, "Taking of the Arsenal," *War Days in Fayetteville,* p. 8.
47. Anderson, "Confed. Arsenal," p. 238.
48. *OR,* XLVII, Pt. I, Ser. I, 551; Spencer, *Ninety Days,* p. 68; Worth, "Sherman's Raid," p. 51.
49. *OR,* XLVII, Pt. I, Ser. I, 551.
50. C. P. Mallet to Cornelia P. Spencer, Mar. 22, 1865, Spencer Papers, SHC, U.N.C.

that these men "went for."[51]   A happy group they were to greet the occupying forces of General Baird's division.   On one corner stood a big strapping soldier beside a barrel of whiskey.   With gourd in hand he made a valiant effort to treat the entire Fourteenth Corps as it marched by.   On another corner stood a "bummer" who, from a large box of tobacco, would throw a plug to anyone asking for a chew.   Upon some columns it "literally rained tobacco. . . ."   Meeting with less success than his two companions, but still enjoying himself tremendously, was a third soldier who gave away books from a large stack by his side.[52]

Despite all this lawlessness, very little personal violence was inflicted upon the people of Fayetteville.   The exceptions occurred when two or three of the local gentlemen were forcibly divested of their pants, boots, and watches.[53]

Houses in the suburbs and vicinity suffered more severely than those in town.   The nights were illuminated by the glare of blazing houses all through the pine groves for several miles around Fayetteville.[54]

A lady living near Fayetteville told the following story of a visit from Sherman's "bummers":

There was no place, no chamber, truck, drawer, desk, garret, closet, or cellar that was private to their unholy eyes.   Their rude hands spared nothing but our lives. . . .   Squad after squad unceasingly came and went and tramped through halls and rooms of our house day and night. . . .   At our house they killed every chicken, goose, turkey, cow, calf, and every living thing, even to our pet dog.   They carried off wagons, carriage, and horses, and broke our buggy, wheelbarrow, garden implements, axes, hatchets, hammers, saws, etc., and burned the fences.   Our smoke house and pantry, that a few days ago were well stored with bacon, lard, flour, dried fruit, meat, pickles, preserves, etc., now contain nothing whatever except a few pounds of meal and flour and five pounds of bacon.   They took from old men, women, and children alike, every garment of wearing apparel save what we had on, not even sparing the napkins of infants, blankets, sheets, quilts, etc., such as it did not suit them to take away they tore to pieces before our eyes.[55]

Charles B. Mallet and John M. Rose, neighbors and prominent Cumberland County citizens, had similar experiences at the hands of Federal

51. Wills, *Wills Diary*, p. 360.
52. C. S. Brown to Etta (Brown?), Apr. 26, 1865, Brown Papers, MS Div., Duke Univ. Lib.
53. C. P. Mallet to Cornelia P. Spencer, Mar. 22, 1865, Spencer Papers, SHC, U.N.C.
54. Spencer, *Ninety Days*, p. 40.
55. Unidentified newspaper clipping, Mordecai Diary, SHC, U.N.C.

soldiers. In the neighborhood of these two men alone nine dwellings were burned to the ground. Several of the outstanding citizens of the vicinity—J. P. McLean, W. T. Horne, Jesse Hawley, and Alexander McArthur—were hung up by the neck until nearly dead to make them disclose hidden valuables.[56] Rose estimated that property taken from a neighboring family in the form of jewelry, plate, money, etc., to have been worth not less than $25,000.[57]

Mrs. Josephine B. Worth, resident of Fayetteville at the time of Sherman's occupation, said even the family Bible at her uncle's place, four miles outside of town, was not spared. One of the soldiers opened the Holy Book and spread it over a mule's back for a saddle and rode off on it.[58] Such men were not likely to respond to a reading of the 109th Psalm which a Miss Tillinghast attempted while her home was being ransacked. The Psalmist in this poem commends the thought that the day of the unmerciful "be few" and that their names "be blotted out."[59]

A few of the residents in the county, fearing what was in store for them, fled their homes before the Federals arrived. This was generally a mistake because the "bummers," as they had done in South Carolina, took this as a license to burn and loot.

R. K. Bryan, a boy of twelve at this time, remembered in later years how he and his father loaded a wagon with bacon, corn, and other supplies and tried unsuccessfully to get across the Cape Fear. They were overtaken by Kilpatrick's cavalry and sent home under pass, only to find the barn burned and the home plundered. Fortunately, Mrs. Bryan, who had been left behind was unharmed.[60]

Occasionally an individual would desert his premises in the face of the barbarous behavior of the "bummers." A Cumberland County doctor, returning to his home and finding his wife almost insane from fright, put her and his children in a carriage and abandoned his home and everything he possessed to the intruders.[61]

The food situation became acute for the citizens of Fayetteville soon after Sherman's troops arrived in the city. The invading army found much flour and corn and immediately proceeded to take most of it, as well

56. C. P. Mallet to Cornelia P. Spencer, Mar. 22, 1965, Spencer Papers, SHC, U.N.C.
57. Spencer, *Ninety Days*, pp. 67-68.
58. Worth, "Sherman's Raid," p. 52.
59. Andrews, *Women of the South*, p. 229.
60. Bryan, "Sherman's Army," Undated newspaper clipping, NCC, U.N.C.
61. Hamilton, *Correspondence of J. Worth*, I, 254.

as making a clean sweep of all pantries and smoke-houses which they had time to plunder. Cornelia P. Spencer, author of the *Last Ninety Days of the War in North Carolina,* doubted if all of Fayetteville, the day after the entrance of the Federal troops, could have contributed a bushel of meal to the relief of the Confederate army, so completely had every house in town been visited.[62] A well-known gentleman of the city wrote on March 14: "There will not be left more than fifty head of four-footed beasts in the country and not enough provisions to last ten days. Many, very many families have not a mouthful to eat. We have meal and meat to last two weeks, by eating two meals a day."[63] Captain Dexter Horton, the observant young Federal officer of the Fourteenth Corps, entered in his diary on March 13 that all of the residents were out of "grub." The next day he wrote that he saw many sad sights, such as weeping mothers with babies in their arms begging for meal.[64] The hungry had to apply to the Federal commissary for meal and then go to one of the mills and get it. Not only the civilians, but also Confederate officers on parole, had to beg sustenance.[65] The city's grist mills were operated as long as the Federal troops occupied the city, but when they left, all but one were destroyed.[66]

After a week in North Carolina the invading army had found booty and destroyed property, but they had found little evidence of the supposedly strong Union sentiment among the people.[67] Major Nichols wrote: "Thus far we have been painfully disappointed in looking for the Union sentiment in North Carolina about which so much has been said. Our experience is decidedly in favor of its sister state; for we found more persons in Columbia who had proved their fealty to the Union cause by their friendliness to our prisoners than all this state put together. The city of Fayetteville was offensively rebellious. . . ."[68]

62. Spencer, *Ninety Days,* p. 50. Spencer acquired much of the material for her book from correspondence with persons visited by Sherman's troops. Among the Fayetteville correspondents were C. P. Mallet and E. J. Hale.

63. *Hillsborough Recorder,* Mar. 22, 1865. Some of the citizens were without subsistence because they had given much of their food to Hardee's troops a few days before. Anne K. Kyle, "Hospital Life," *War Days in Fayetteville,* p. 43.

64. Eaton, "Diary of Officer," p. 248.

65. Worth, "Sherman's Raid," pp. 53-54.

66. *OR,* XLVII, Pt. II, Ser. I, 779.

67. For evidences of Union sentiment in North Carolina see: *N.Y. Herald,* Mar. 11, 1865; Underwood, *33 Mass.;* p. 277; Pepper, *Recollections,* p. 375; *NR,* XII, Ser. I, 9; Bradley, *Star Corps,* p. 266; Tatum, *Disloyalty,* pp. 107-35; Savage, "Loyal Element," *Mil. Order of Loyal Legion, Neb. Commandery,* I, 1-15.

68. Nichols, *Great March,* pp. 252-53.

Theodore Upson, One Hundredth Indiana, agreed with Major Nichols. He wrote in his diary that he heard a good sermon in Fayetteville on the subject of loving one's enemies but that he thought the South had a long way to go in this respect.[69]

Captain Horton, to the contrary, thought that there was a considerable amount of affable social intercourse between the Federal army and the civilian population of the invaded city. Extracts from his diary bear out this fact.

Capt. White and myself took rooms at Mrs. Ockletra's and shall have nice beds to sleep on. Seems to be a nice lady. . . . Make [made] the acquaintance of several ladies. Certainly we are enjoying ourselves hugely. . . . Went in evening with Charlie Jones and called on Misses Lily. Spent the evening very pleasantly. Pretty girls and very talkative. . . . Had heaps of fun all day. . . . Called with Charlie Jones at Mr. Lily's. Carried them some tea, coffee, and meal. How thankful they were. The girls were very interesting and shook our hands heartily when we left. . . . Received a written order to move at about one o'clock. I had gone to bed at Mrs. Ockletra's. Guard woke me up. I bid them goodbye. They really felt bad to see me go. The old lady shed tears and said let us part as friends and hoped I would reach my family in safety.[70]

Brigadier General Manning F. Force of the Seventeenth Corps said the army gave the people more than it took from them. He pointed out that a surprise inspection of the camp of the Seventeenth Corps produced in stolen articles only a little clothing and tobacco.[71]

By March 15, Sherman had his entire army across the Cape Fear, and the march on Goldsboro had begun. The Seventeenth Corps, followed by the Fifteenth, continued to march on the right. The Fourteenth and Twentieth Corps were on the extreme left with the cavalry acting in close concert. Sherman was in a happy frame of mind as he watched his troops move out. The campaign was running like clockwork. Goldsboro, he felt sure, would be his in a few days.

69. Winther, *Upson Diary,* p. 156.
70. Eaton, "Diary of an Officer," pp. 248-49.
71. Force, "Marching," p. 15.

CHAPTER X

Resistance at Averasboro

UNTIL HE REACHED Fayetteville Sherman had succeeded in interposing his army between the scattered Confederate forces and had prevented any concentrated action by Johnston. After crossing the Cape Fear, however, he was faced with the fact that most of these Confederate troops had reached North Carolina, and, under the command of the skillful and experienced "Joe" Johnston, made up an army superior to his in cavalry and formidable in artillery and infantry. Hence he must use caution on his march to Goldsboro.[1] He planned to keep his columns as compact as possible.[2]

The bad weather which had plagued Sherman's movements on the road to Fayetteville still prevailed when the Federal troops moved out from the Cape Fear and started their march on Goldsboro. The roads, resembling quagmires, slowed the advance considerably.[3] This was particularly annoying to Sherman because he was marching against time. He wanted to avoid battle if possible and to accomplish this he must prevent Johnston from concentrating his forces. To Terry he wrote: "We must not lose time for Joe Johnston to concentrate at Goldsborough. We cannot prevent his concentrating at Raleigh, but he shall have no rest."[4] With this object in mind Sherman changed his order of march, directing certain divisions of each corps to march light and the remainder to accompany the trains. By this arrangement he reckoned upon having a strong unencumbered force ready for battle on either flank.

1. Sherman greatly overestimated the Confederate forces opposing him at 37,000 infantry and 8,000 cavalry. This was one reason he felt that it would be unwise to leave behind a small detachment to garrison the arsenal and save this Federal property. He thought all available forces should be at hand to cope with Johnston. *OR*, XLVII, Pt. II, Ser. I, 794, 800.
2. *Ibid.*, p. 803.
3. Force, "Marching," p. 8.
4. *OR*, XLVII, Pt. II, Ser. I, 803.

General Kilpatrick was ordered to move up the plank road to and beyond the small village of Averasboro on the east bank of the Cape Fear. He was to be followed by four divisions of the left wing, with as few wagons as possible. The rest of the train, under escort of the two remaining divisions of that wing, was to take a shorter and more direct road to Goldsboro. In like manner General Howard was instructed to send his trains, under good escort, well to the right toward Faison's Depot and Goldsboro, and to hold four divisions light, ready to go to the aid of the left wing if it were attacked while in motion.[5]

Before leaving Fayetteville, Sherman had sent orders to General Schofield at New Bern and to General Terry at Wilmington to move with their effective forces direct to Goldsboro where he expected to meet them by March 20. He also ordered Schofield and Terry to continue their work of repairing the railroads from New Bern and Wilmington.[6]

The immediate object of Johnston's operations in North Carolina was, as before mentioned, to isolate and strike one of Sherman's columns on the move. To do this Johnston first had to unite his forces which, on March 15, were still widely scattered. Uncertain as to whether Sherman's destination, after leaving Fayetteville, was Raleigh or Goldsboro, the Confederate General selected Smithfield, a small town about midway between the two places, as the concentration point for his different commands.[7] General Bragg's troops along with those of the Army of Tennessee were ordered to Smithfield. Hardee was instructed to follow the road from Fayetteville to Raleigh, which for thirty miles was also that to Smithfield. Since March 11, Hardee had kept scouts on the west side of the Cape Fear in order to keep Johnston informed of any Federal troop movements. It was Johnston's plan to have Hardee's movements conform to those of Sherman, so a force would always be at hand to delay the Federal advance if possible. If Sherman moved on Raleigh, Bragg's troops were to be brought up and combined with Hardee's. If Sherman, on the other hand, decided to move on Goldsboro, Hardee was to join Bragg.[8] Hampton placed Wheeler's cavalry division on the Raleigh road and Butler's on that to Goldsboro.

5. *Ibid.*, Pt. I, Ser. I, 24.   6. *Ibid.*, p. 23.

7. Sherman intended to feint strongly on Raleigh but swing rapidly on Goldsboro when his wagons were well toward Faison's Depot. Johnston was not sure of Sherman's intended movements even though Beauregard had written him on March 14, that Sherman was moving "doubtless to form a junction with Schofield's forces around Goldsboro." *Ibid.*, Pt. II, Ser. I, 834-35, 1392.

8. *Ibid.*, Pt. 1375.

On March 15 Kilpatrick's cavalry, preceding the left wing on the Raleigh road, slowly pushed back Wheeler's command, which was acting as a rear guard for Hardee's Corps.[9] General Hardee, encamped at the time in the vicinity of Smith's Mill about six miles south of Averasboro, abandoned his original intention of resting a day and began to deploy for battle. He made this decision in spite of the fact that his small force had been reduced both by desertions and the withdrawal of the brigade of South Carolina militia by Governor Magrath. By doing this he hoped to ascertain whether he was followed by the whole of Sherman's army or a part of it and what was its destination.[10]

General Hardee ordered Colonel Alfred Moore Rhett's brigade of Brigadier General William B. Taliaferro's division into position in the rear of an open field on the right of the Raleigh road. Breastworks were erected, a few hundred yards in front of which a strong infantry skirmish line was established.

Hardee intended for Rhett's brigade to check only temporarily the advance of the Federals. It was his design to hold them until he was reasonably sure Taliaferro's trains were out of danger, at which time Colonel Rhett was to retire his brigade a half a mile in the rear and join the brigade of Brigadier General Stephen Elliott, Jr.[11]

Around three o'clock in the afternoon Kilpatrick's column, with the Ninth Michigan in advance, struck the Confederate skirmish line. General Atkins, commanding Kilpatrick's First Brigade, deployed the Ninth Michigan on foot and succeeded in driving the Confederate skirmishers back into their works, but in so doing he drew Confederate artillery fire. While the Ninth Michigan continued to skirmish, Kilpatrick ordered Atkins to put the remainder of his brigade and the other brigades, as they came up, into position and to build barricades. When the barricades were finished, the Ninth Michigan was withdrawn. Taliaferro's troops felt the Federal position strongly during the afternoon, but the Federal artillery kept them at a good distance most of the time.[12]

At General Kilpatrick's request, Slocum sent forward Colonel William Hawley's brigade to assist in holding the barricades. During the

9. *Ibid.*, Pt. I, Ser. I, 1130.
10. *Ibid.*, p. 1361; Johnston, *Narrative*, p. 582; A. R. Wright's division never left the state of South Carolina.
11. *OR*, XLVII, Pt. I, Ser. I, 1084.
12. *Ibid.*, p. 880.

night Hawley took position in the center of the cavalry command with his left resting on the main road.[13]

The day's skirmishing cost Taliaferro the services of one of his brigade commanders. Colonel Rhett was captured when he mistook a party of Federal cavalry for his own. The Federals called on Rhett to surrender and ordered him, "in language more forcible than polite," to turn and ride back. He first supposed these men to be of Hampton's cavalry, and threatened to report them to General Hampton for disrespectful language.[14]

The capture of Colonel Rhett caused quite a stir within the Federal lines. Besides owning the handsomest boots in the Confederate army, he was a South Carolina aristocrat. His father was the noted Robert Barnwell Rhett, a first family name of which South Carolina was quite proud.[15] The fact that Colonel Rhett had for some time been in command at Fort Sumter also contributed to the strong feeling among the Federal troops against him.[16]

Major Nichols wrote: "From the conversation of this Rebel Colonel, I judge him to be quite as impracticable a person as any of his class."[17] Major Henry Hitchcock called Rhett incarnate, selfish, and a "devil in human shape, who is but a type of his class and whose polished manners and easy assurance made him only more hideous to me [Hitchcock] and utterly heartless and selfish ambition and pride of class which gave tone to his whole discourse." Hitchcock admitted, however, that all "Southern Gentlemen" and all Confederate officers were not like Rhett.[18] General Sherman in his *Memoirs* presents Rhett in a somewhat different light. The General described Rhett as a tall, slender, handsome young man, dressed in the most approved Confederate uniform with high jackboots beautifully stitched, but mortified to find himself a prisoner in Federal hands. Sherman was very much amused at Rhett's outspoken disgust at having been captured without a fight.[19]

There was no skirmishing on the night of March 15 between Kil-

13. *Ibid.*, p. 637.   14. Sherman, *Memoirs*, II, 301.

15. Prior to the war Colonel Rhett's father had served in the United States Congress and in the South Carolina state legislature. In the legislative halls and in writing R. B. Rhett expressed violent secessionist views.

16. According to Major Henry Hitchcock of Sherman's staff, Rhett was not very popular with his own troops. Howe, *Marching With Sherman*, p. 290.

17. Nichols, *Sherman's March*, p. 254.

18. Howe, *Marching With Sherman*, pp. 289-90.

19. Sherman, *Memoirs*, II, 301.

patrick and Taliaferro. The Confederate general had been directed that in the event the Federals moved forward on March 16, he was to have Rhett's brigade, then commanded by Colonel William Butler, First South Carolina infantry, to hold its present position until it was no longer tenable. Then the brigade was to fall back upon the position occupied by Elliott's brigade, which had been brought forward to occupy an entrenched line behind a narrow swamp some two hundred yards in the rear of the front line. This second line was to be held by Taliaferro's division as long as practicable. Then it was to fall back upon an extended line six hundred yards to the rear and in part occupied by General Lafayette McLaws' division.[20]

Upon an inspection of his map it was manifest to Sherman, who was traveling with the left wing, that Hardee in retreating from Fayetteville had halted in the narrow, swampy neck between the Cape Fear and Black rivers, making it necessary to dislodge the enemy in order that he might have use of the Raleigh road and also keep up his feint on the capital city as long as possible. Again Sherman overestimated the strength of his adversary, putting Hardee's troops at twenty thousand. General Slocum was therefore ordered forward to press and carry the position. But because of bad roads the troops of the left wing did not reach Kilpatrick until around ten o'clock in the morning, four hours after skirmishing had started.[21]

At 6:00 A.M. on March 16, Lieutenant Colonel F. A. Jones' Eighth Indiana cavalry moved on Taliaferro. Colonel Jones succeeded in driving the Confederate skirmish line, under the command of Captain T. A. Huguenin, First South Carolina infantry, back into the works. The Colonel thought that had the Federal infantry then pushed forward, the first line of Confederate works, artillery, and many prisoners could have been taken without firing a shot. He even speculated that if the ground had been solid, he would have taken the line with his cavalry alone, but he explained that the rains of the previous night had made the region one vast mire.[22]

Finding further operations on horseback impossible, Jones dismounted his command and sent his lead horses to the rear. He ordered his lines to reconnect with the infantry brigade of Hawley. At this time Talia-

---

20. *OR*, XLVII, Pt. I, Ser. I, 1084-85.   21. *Ibid.*, p. 422.

22. *Ibid.*, p. 871. The possibility of taking the Confederate works, artillery, and many prisoners without firing a shot seems entirely out of reason.

ferro attacked in force and soon the entire Federal line was under heavy fire.

By ten o'clock Kilpatrick's dismounted cavalrymen, running dangerously low on ammunition, were close to having their right flank turned. Disaster was averted when portions of the Twentieth Corps arrived on the field just in time to stem the Confederate attack.

Three batteries of artillery were immediately placed in a commanding position by Major J. A. Reynolds, chief of artillery, Twentieth Corps.[23] While these guns vigorously shelled the Confederate line, the Federals took the offensive. Two brigades pressed Taliaferro's front while a third under the command of Colonel Henry Case moved in a diagonal direction toward the right of the Confederate works. Case advanced until he thought his column faced the Confederate right flank. The Colonel soon discovered from the sound of the Confederate artillery that he had not moved far enough to the rear. Hence he moved his command by the left flank about five hundred yards still farther to the left and resumed his advance toward the Confederate line. After moving a short distance, Case encountered a swamp tangled with thick undergrowth, which greatly impeded his progress. As the Federals drove forward, they met a Confederate skirmish line which they easily drove back. After passing through the swamp, Case found himself in a ravine. Upon advancing to reconnoiter, he discovered that his brigade was exactly on the enemy right flank, which was only three hundred yards away. Colonel Case ordered the One Hundred and Fifth Illinois to deploy rapidly and throw itself into line on the left of the Seventy-ninth Ohio. The Colonel then ordered a charge "at the double quick." Emerging from the thickets about 150 yards from the Confederates, the Federals opened a very destructive fire on the first line of the Confederate defenses. This sudden change routed Rhett's brigade, and it was necessary for it to withdraw to the second line of works.[24]

The Confederate losses were considerable during the morning's fighting. Rhett's brigade, which had lost its leader the day before, suffered especially heavy casualties when it was routed by Case. It must be remembered, however, that Rhett's troops had previously done only garrison and artillery duty at Charleston, and this was their first experience

23. *Ibid.,* p. 586.

24. *Ibid.,* p. 789. U. H. Farr, *Seventieth Indiana,* stated that General Hardee came very near being captured when Rhett's brigade was flanked by Case. Merrill, *70 Ind.,* p. 257.

in infantry fighting in the open. Nevertheless, they held their ground with much tenacity. General Taliaferro said they "behaved as well as troops could have done."[25]

The First and Third Divisions of the Twentieth Corps followed up Case's success by advancing upon the second line of Confederate defenses. General Mitchell's brigade of the Fourteenth Corps joined them, forming to the left. At the same time Kilpatrick was ordered to draw back his cavalry and mass it on the extreme right and to feel forward for the Goldsboro road.[26]

The cavalry moved forward under the immediate direction of General Kilpatrick whose scouts soon reported to him that a road, leading off to the right, circled around to the rear of the Confederate position. Accordingly, the General ordered the Ninth Ohio cavalry to move out upon that road. After advancing a short distance, the Ninth Ohio was attacked by Colonel G. P. Harrison's brigade of McLaws' division, which was moving through underbrush so dense that the Federal cavalry did not notice it until the brigade was within a few yards of their column. The Ninth Ohio was driven back two hundred yards to high ground. There it reformed its lines and held Harrison in check until relieved by a brigade of infantry, at which time the Confederates withdrew.[27]

In danger of being flanked and hard pressed on his front, Taliaferro withdrew his division to the main line of defense. He took position "to the right and left of the main road." McLaws' division was on his left and Wheeler's dismounted cavalry on his right. Most of Rhett's brigade, which had been so severely engaged all day, was held in reserve a few hundred yards in the rear of the line of works.[28]

The Federals pressed Hardee hard all afternoon and up into the early part of the evening, but they were unable to carry the Confederate works. Around 8:00 P.M. Hardee started withdrawing his troops and artillery on

25. OR, XLVII, Pt. I, Ser. I, 24, 1086. When Rhett's brigade had to give up its line, two pieces of light artillery were abandoned. It was impossible for the Confederates to withdraw these guns. They had practically no horses left, and the ground was very soft from the heavy rains. Besides, nearly all the cannoneers of both guns were either killed or wounded. However, all of the ammunition, to the last shot, had been expended upon the Federals. A third piece of artillery captured by the Federals in the morning's fighting was turned on the retreating Confederates. Ibid., pp. 847, 1084.

26. Ibid., pp. 24-25.

27. Ibid., pp. 889-90.

28. Ibid., pp. 1085-86.

the Smithfield road, as General Johnston had ordered.[29] Wheeler's dismounted cavalry was left behind to cover the retreat.

Generals Slocum and Kilpatrick reported their casualties for the day's fighting, called the battle of Averasboro, at 682 killed, wounded, captured, or missing. Of the casualties, 533 were wounded.[30] This was a serious loss because none of the wounded could be left behind. Every injured man had to be carried in an ambulance.[31]

Major Henry Hitchcock of Sherman's staff was one of the few soldiers on the field who never once had occasion to think he himself might be listed as a casualty at the day's end. The Major had spent his time with Sherman, "lying around in the woods . . . while the fight . . . was going on." Much to Hitchcock's disgust, the General never ventured very near the front line. On one occasion some canister shot did splash "the mud not far off," and on another "a bullet pattered among the branches overhead." But newspaper accounts of "Tecumseh directing the battle under a warm fire," the Major knew to be "just so much poetry."[32]

The battle of Averasboro was actually fought in a section of Harnett County called Smithville, so named after a prominent family of Smiths living in that rural neighborhood. The Smith homesteads survived the battle primarily because they were utilized in some capacity by both armies. The Farquhar Smith home served as General Slocum's headquarters. The William Smith residence was turned into a Federal hospital, whereas the John Smith house was used to care for the Confederate wounded.[33]

Janie Smith, a seventeen-year-old daughter of Farquhar Smith, wrote her friend Janie Robeson on April 12, 1865, a lengthy and rather fiery letter giving her impressions of the Federal soldiers and her reaction to the sight of battle. In discussing the carnage of the battlefield this young girl declared that, "the scene beggars description. The blood lay in puddles in the grove, the groans of the dying and the complaints of those undergoing amputation was horrible. I can never forget it. . . ." But

29. *Ibid.,* XLVII, Pt. II, Ser. I, 1400-1. Johnston countermanded the movement to Smithfield upon certain conditions, but Hardee did not receive the dispatch until 11:00 P.M., too late to arrest his movements. *Ibid.,* pp. 1401, 1409.

30. *Ibid.,* Pt. I, Ser. I, 66.

31. Sherman, *Memoirs,* II, 302. Leaving no occupation forces behind at Averasboro, Sherman had to take care of his wounded.

32. Howe, *Marching With Sherman,* p. 283.

33. Oates, *Fayetteville,* pp. 391-96; Smith, "Averasboro," *Confed. Vet.,* XXXIV, 48-49.

to her the battlefield did not compare in point of stench with "such fiends incarnate as fill the ranks of Sherman's army." She also told her friend how the Federal soldiers "left no living thing in Smithville but people, and one old hen, who played sick, thus saving her neck but losing her biddies." Having lost all of her personal effects to the pillagers, Janie further declared:

If I ever see a Yankeewoman I intend to whip her and take the clothes off her very back. . . . When our army invades the North, I want them to carry the torch in one hand and the sword in the other. I want desolation carried to the heart of their country; the widows and orphans left naked and starving, just as ours were left.[34]

Over fifty Confederate wounded were moved to the Farquhar Smith home after the battle, the John Smith place being filled.[35]   Before departing Federal surgeons performed all necessary operations, but little in the way of supplies was left behind for their care. Sherman, in person, visited one of the makeshift hospitals while the surgeons were at work. To get inside he had to step over arms and legs left lying in the yard and on the porch. In one of the rooms was a handsome young captain named McBeth who, upon seeing the General, identified himself as having been a boy when Sherman visited in his father's home in Charleston. After inquiring of the young officer's family, Sherman enabled him to write a note to his mother which was afterwards mailed to her from Goldsboro.[36]

General Howard still moving on the extreme right on March 16, continued his march on Goldsboro. This separated the two wings of Sherman's army considerably and played into Johnston's hands.

General Wheeler, covering Hardee's retreat, withdrew his troops on the morning of March 17 to Averasboro in the face of General W. T. Ward's division, which Sherman had ordered to keep up a show of pursuit. Hardee had instructed Wheeler not to leave Averasboro until the Federals made their appearance and to try to ascertain whether they were moving on Raleigh or Goldsboro. At 6:40 A.M. Wheeler reported: "The prisoner captured this morning states that their Army are [is] going to

34. *Raleigh News and Observer*, May 10, 1954.
35. *Ibid.*   General Hardee in his brief report by telegraph stated that his loss was between four hundred and five hundred. *OR*, XLVII, Pt. II, Ser. I, 1409. A great many of the Confederate wounded were left behind at Averasboro. The few houses in this tiny village were all filled with Hardee's wounded. Underwood, *33 Mass.*, p. 49.
36. Sherman, *Memoirs*, II, 302.

Goldsboro and not to Raleigh."[37] At 11:10 A.M. he informed Hardee as follows: "The enemy marched a short distance up the Raleigh road, skirmishing with the Eighth Texas but have advanced farther on this [Goldsboro] road. The indications are that the advance will be upon this road."[38]

Around noon General Hardee halted his troops at Elevation on the Smithfield road. Early in the morning of March 17, Johnston had sent Hardee a dispatch, instructing him to halt at Elevation until he learned definitely of Sherman's movements. At 1:00 P.M. Hardee sent a dispatch to Johnston stating that his map was incorrect, and that the intersection of the roads was not at Elevation but two miles nearer Smithfield to which place he was going to move. He also stated that he did not believe Sherman was moving on Raleigh.[39] At 2:50 P.M. Hardee sent Johnston another dispatch in which he enclosed notes from Hampton and Wheeler. Both cavalry leaders believed Sherman's movements were on Goldsboro.[40] Colonel G. G. Dibrell, Confederate cavalry division commander, also thought Sherman was moving on Goldsboro. One of his scouts had been inside the Federal line the night before to recover the body of a friend.[41] The scout reported that he saw two large camps, both on the Goldsboro road, and that all the local citizens said the Federals had told them they were moving on Goldsboro.[42]

Hardee's 2:50 P.M. dispatch reached Johnston around 7:00 P.M. Johnston thereupon decided something should be done the next morning but he still had no precise intelligence as to Sherman's movments other than the fact that he was moving on Goldsboro.[43] Oddly enough, General Sherman knew even less about Johnston's intentions or the location of his scattered troops. He had no suspicion that the delay of the left wing at Averasboro had provided Johnston with an opportunity to give battle before the Federal army could make junction at Goldsboro with the forces of Schofield and Terry. About all Sherman knew of the whereabouts of the Confederate forces was a bit of information Captain Duncan had given him. The Captain, captured at Fayetteville by

37. *OR*, XLVII, Pt. II, Ser. I, 1416.   38. *Ibid.*, p. 1417.
39. *Ibid.*, p. 1410.   40. *Ibid.*, p. 1411.
41. To get inside the Federal line Dibrell's scout may have put on a Federal uniform. General Howard reported that there were four or five Confederate scouts, dressed in complete Federal uniforms, operating behind the Federal lines at that time. He said these scouts made it their business to capture small parties of Federals. *Ibid.*, p. 873.
42. *Ibid.*, p. 1418.   43. *Ibid.*, p. 1411.

Hampton, had escaped McLaws' guard about twelve miles out on the Smithfield road. He reported that Hardee was retreating on this town.[44]

On the morning of March 17, Kilpatrick crossed Black River and moved out upon the Smithfield road to the left and front of the Fourteenth and Twentieth Corps, which were moving upon the direct road from Averasboro to Goldsboro. The distance marched by the Fourteenth Corps on March 17 was not more than six or eight miles because of the bogs and swampy creeks which lay across the way. A soldier, after patiently wading waist deep in a seemingly shoreless stream, was heard to remark: "I guess Uncle Billy has struck this stream endwise."[45] The Twentieth following the Fourteenth Corps moved up to Black River on the afternoon of March 17 and encamped on the west side.[46] General Howard, uncertain as to the result of the battle of Averasboro the day before, moved the right wing only six miles on March 17. This closed somewhat the distance between it and the left wing.[47]

The battle of Averasboro was little more than a skirmish. It is significant because the stout resistance put up by Hardee in this engagement stopped the advance of the Twentieth Corps. As a result the columns of the left wing became strung out and the distance between the two wings of the army increased. These developments made it possible for Johnston to start preparations for battle. His plan was to isolate and crush one of the Federal columns before Sherman could get his army back in compact form.

44. *Ibid.*, p. 870.   45. Aten, *85 Ill.*, p. 297.

46. *OR*, XLVII, Pt. I, Ser. I, 586. The trains of the left wing made little progress on the 17th.

47. *Ibid.*, p. 234. The Seventeenth Corps moved out on the Clinton road. When it was within six miles of Clinton the Ninth Illinois was sent forward to cover the refugee train, moving from Fayetteville to Wilmington by way of Clinton. The Ninth Illinois was also instructed to open communication, if possible, with General Terry's forces, which were moving up from Wilmington. *Ibid.*, p. 383.

CHAPTER XI

Battle of Bentonville

It was almost daybreak on March 18, when information came to Johnston from General Hampton that the Federal army was definitely marching toward Goldsboro.[1] According to Confederate cavalry reports, Sherman's right wing was approximately half a day's march in advance of the left wing. With this information in mind Johnston calculated that probably the heads of the two columns were about a day's march from each other.

To be prepared to attack the head of the left Federal column the next morning, the troops at Smithfield and Elevation were ordered to march immediately to Bentonville, a small town approximately twenty miles west of Goldsboro, and to bivouac that night between the town and the road on which Slocum's column was marching.[2] At Smithfield General Bragg had Major General Robert F. Hoke's division of North Carolinians, and General Stewart had a portion of the Army of Tennessee.

Hardee had intended to give his troops several days of badly needed rest at Elevation, as many of his men had had nothing to eat since the night of March 15 and were exhausted after the hard fight at Averasboro.[3] Nevertheless, at 8:50 A.M. on March 18, Hardee sent Johnston a dispatch stating that he was putting his command in motion for Bentonville, but that he was ignorant of the road Johnston had designated for him to take.[4]

By General Johnston's map the distance from Elevation to Bentonville was but twelve miles. This assured Johnston of the arrival of

1. *OR*, XLVII, Pt. II, Ser. I, 1429.
2. *Ibid.*, 1427-28, 1431, 1435.
3. Ford and Ford, *Life in the Confederate Army*, p. 53.
4. *OR*, XLVII, Pt. II, Ser. I, 1427. Johnston had ordered Hardee to move from Elevation to Bentonville upon a road not shown on the map. He had learned of the road from the sheriff of Johnston County.

Hardee's command on the night of March 18. The map proved to be incorrect, however, and deceived Johnston greatly in relation to the distance between the two roads on which the Federal columns were marching.[5] It exaggerated considerably the distance between Howard and Slocum, and it reduced almost as much the distance between Elevation and Bentonville.[6] General Hardee found the distance too great for a day's march. He was still six miles from Bentonville by nightfall of March 18.[7] Bragg and Stewart reached Bentonville during the night.

Johnston wrote General Lee on March 18 that his effective totals, infantry and artillery, were: Bragg, 6,500; Hardee, 7,500; Army of Tennessee, 4,000.[8] These totals plus Hampton's cavalry made up an army considerably less than the forty thousand troops Sherman thought opposed him.

Johnston was in part compensated for this paucity of manpower by the large number of able captains present at Bentonville. Besides Johnston and Bragg, who were both full generals, four officers—Hampton, Wheeler, Hardee and Stewart—carried the rank of lieutenant general.

Sherman continued to travel with the head of Slocum's column on March 18. At 2:00 P.M. he sent General Howard a dispatch stating: "I think the enemy is concentrated about Smithland [Smithfield], and I cannot make out whether Goldsborough is held in force or not. I think it probable that Joe Johnston will try to prevent our getting Goldsborough."[9] Later in the day he sent Howard a contradictory dispatch in which he expressed the belief that Johnston was near Raleigh. He wrote:

> The firing you heard was Kilpatrick, who found parties picketing roads to the north. He reports Hardee retreating on Smithfield, and Joe Johnston collecting his old Georgia army this side of Raleigh. I know that he will call in all minor posts, which embraces Goldsborough. . . . Make a break into Goldsborough from the South, and let your scouts strike out for Schofield at Kinston, though I hope to meet him at Goldsborough.[10]

Kilpatrick's poor reconnaissance work completely misled Sherman. He disregarded other information which should have led him to be-

5. General Sherman's maps were also incorrect. *Ibid.*, p. 885. Major Nichols said all of the Federal maps were of no later date than 1854. Nichols, *Great March*, p. 262.
6. Johnston, *Narrative*, p. 385. 7. *OR*, XLVII, Pt. II, Ser. I, 1428.
8. *Ibid.*, p. 1426. 9. *Ibid.*, p. 885.
10. *Ibid.*, p. 886.

lieve that Johnston was concentrating on his immediate front.[11] On March 18 Brigadier General W. P. Carlin and other Federal officers had stopped at a farmhouse for dinner. Here Carlin through conversation with the head of the household, one Cox, learned that his host was very much frightened at the idea of a battle being fought on his farm. Carlin stated his suspicions to General Davis who repeated them to General Sherman.[12] Sherman replied: "No Jeff, there is nothing there but Dibrells Cavalry. Brush them out of the way. Good Morning. I'll meet you tomorrow morning at Car's Bridge."[13] Major C. E. Belknap, one of Carlin's foragers, also gained information from citizens of the countryside and Confederate wounded that Johnston planned to make a stand near Bentonville. This information was sent to General Sherman, but he did not credit it.[14]

March 18 the Fourteenth Corps moved early with Brigadier General James D. Morgan's division in the lead. The Confederate cavalry put up a series of running fights from one patch of woods to another. In these woods were many turpentine stills which the Federals invariably fired, sending up dense black columns of smoke. This smoke served as signal flags to indicate Davis' advance.[15] The Confederate cavalry retreated to and across Bushy Swamp where it took up a strong position and opened fire with artillery. The stout resistance encountered from the Confederates and Sherman's order to halt until the rear could close up put Morgan's division into camp for the night near this swamp.[16]

For the Twentieth Corps the crossing of Black River was exceedingly difficult. The bridge repeatedly broke. The roads beyond the bridge were so cut up that almost every foot required corduroying. The two divisions of the corps managed to move twelve miles toward Bentonville and encamped during the afternoon of March 18 at Lee's plantation, nearly eight miles to the rear of the Fourteenth Corps.[17]

The right wing continued to move on somewhat parallel roads to the

11. Major Nichols thought Johnston led Sherman to believe that he was falling back on Raleigh by moving upon a road to Bentonville which was not shown on the map, and when the Federal reconnaissance units had failed to discover. Nichols, *Great March*, p. 262.

12. Carlin, "Bentonville," *Mil. Order of Loyal Legion, Ohio Commandery*, III, 235.

13. Slocum, *Slocum*, p. 274.

14. Belknap, "Bentonville," *Mil. Order of Loyal Legion, D. C. Commandery*, War Paper No. 12, p. 6.

15. *Ibid.*, p. 5.

16. *OR*, XLVII, Pt. I, Ser. I, 434, 484-85.

17. *Ibid.*, p. 586.

south. The light divisions, which were the four of Logan's Fifteenth Corps, were only six miles south of Slocum on the night of March 18. The Seventeenth Corps was to the southeast in the vicinity of Trouble-field's Store.

Kilpatrick having followed Hardee toward Smithfield was to the left and rear of the Twentieth Corps. The wagon trains of both wings toiled along as best they could, a good ways back of the light columns. Thus Sherman, despite his intentions to march in compact form from Fayette-ville to Goldsboro, had allowed his columns to be greatly drawn out with long intervals separating the divisions.

On the night of March 18 Hampton gave General Johnston all the necessary information on the position of the Federal troops. He also described the ground near the Goldsboro road, about two miles south of Bentonville, as favorable for the surprise attack. Slocum's column was moving upon this single road. The ground suggested for the battle was the eastern edge of an old plantation which extended a mile and a half to the west and lay principally on the north side of the road. It was sur-rounded east, south, and north by dense thickets of "blackjack." In the thickets were many marshes from which streams ran in all directions.[18] The Federal camp on this night was several miles nearer that ground than Hardee's bivouac, and it was only because of Hampton's vigorous efforts that the head of the Federal left wing was not past Bentonville.

It was Hampton's cavalry that skirmished continuously with Sher-man's advance, Morgan's division, on this date, gaining time for the Confederate troops to move up from Smithfield and Elevation. By the middle of the afternoon Hampton had been pushed back almost to the spot that he had selected for the battle the next day. Since it was vitally important that this position be held during the night, Hampton dis-mounted all of his men and placed them along the edge of the woods and, at the risk of losing his guns, put his artillery to the right of the road where it had a commanding position. It was late afternoon when the Federals moved on this position, but after a feeble demonstration they withdrew.[19] Unknown to Hampton, of course, was Sherman's order to Morgan to halt his advance.[20] This left Hampton in possession of the ground chosen for the fight.

18. Johnston, *Narrative*, pp. 385-86.
19. Hampton, "Bentonville," B and L, IV, 701-2; *OR*, XLVII, Pt. II, Ser. I, 1430; Orendorff, *103 Ill.*, p. 199.
20. See above p. 161.

Since General Johnston had not been able to examine the ground, Hampton suggested to him such disposition of the forces as he thought "would be most advantageous." The proposed plan called for the cavalry to move out at daylight and to occupy "the position held by it the previous evening." The infantry was then to be deployed "with one corps across the main road and the other two . . . to the right of the first." As soon as these positions were occupied, Hampton was to fall back and pass to the rear of the infantry line and take position on the extreme right. All offensive movements were to be delayed until Hardee should reach his position.[21]

Sunday morning, March 19, dawned clear and beautiful. For the unsuspecting Federal soldiers everything seemed to forecast a Sunday of peace and quiet.[22] Unknown to them, Hampton had moved out with his cavalry in the early morning hours to his position of the previous evening and had posted pickets within a mile of the Federal advance. Almost immediately his pickets became engaged with foragers of the Fourteenth Corps, who were greatly surprised to find Confederate cavalry giving ground grudgingly and even being inclined to fight.[23] So an expression of the Atlanta campaign, "They don't drive worth a damn," was brought into use again.[24] One group of foragers, under command of Major Belknap, did somehow manage to advance far enough to ascertain that a large Confederate force was entrenching itself on Slocum's front. Belknap dispatched one of his best men with this information to General Carlin, but the messenger never reached the General.[25]

The movements of the Federal left wing on March 19 began at 7:00 A.M. The First Division, Fourteenth Corps, General Carlin commanding, was in the lead. The numerous indications on the 18th that a battle was in prospect prompted Carlin to prepare for the occasion. All wagons and pack mules marched in the rear of the troops. The General even put on his newest uniform so there would not be any doubt as to his rank in the case of his capture or death.[26] Carlin advanced his troops up the road until he overtook his foragers, still skirmishing with the Confederate cavalry. At this point he was joined by General Slocum.

21. Hampton, "Bentonville," pp. 702-3.
22. Dougall, "Bentonville," *Mil. Order of Loyal Legion, Ind. Commandery*, I, 214.
23. The foragers always left camp several hours before the troops moved.
24. McClurg, "Last Chance," *Atlantic Monthly*, L, 390.
25. Belknap, "Bentonville," p. 7.
26. Carlin, "Bentonville," pp. 236-37.

Although his foragers had never before been checked so near their camp, Slocum still did not suspect that Johnston had concentrated his entire army only a few miles up the road. Slocum seemed to have overlooked this indication of battle and put his faith in the report of an escaped Federal cavalry officer. This officer had reported to him that Johnston was concentrated at or near Raleigh. Consequently, Slocum believed the force in his front to consist only of cavalry with a few pieces of artillery. He sent a dispatch to this effect to General Sherman, who had left his column during the morning to join Howard.[27]

Kilpatrick also sent a dispatch to Sherman on the morning of March 19 stating that Johnston was concentrating near Raleigh. He based his information on the number of pickets he encountered on the Raleigh and Smithfield roads and the report of Lieutenant W. M. Potter of his staff. Kilpatrick had found all the roads leading to Smithfield and Raleigh strongly picketed. Lieutenant Potter, who had escaped from the Confederates the night before, told Kilpatrick that Johnston was expected in the direction of Raleigh, and that every preparation was being made to meet Sherman about ten miles east of the city near Squire Johnson's.[28]

It took very little to convince Sherman that Johnston would not contest his advance on Goldsboro. He could not see how the Confederate General would risk a fight with the Neuse to his back.[29] In his official report Sherman states: "All signs induced me to believe that the enemy would make no further opposition to our progress, and would not attempt to strike us in flank while in motion."[30]

The deployment of the Confederate forces was a slow process. Their march was confined to a single road through the dense "blackjack" lying between Bentonville and the battlefield.[31] Hoke's division was the first on the ground. It was formed across the Goldsboro road almost at right angles. In this line was the North Carolina Junior Brigade composed entirely of youths eighteen years of age and younger—"the seed corn of the Confederacy."[32] The Army of Tennessee, commanded by General A. P. Stewart, was formed to the right of Hoke, its right strongly

27. *OR*, XLVII, Pt. I, Ser. I, 423.
28. *Ibid.*, XLVII, Pt. II, Ser. I, 908. Later in the day Kilpatrick sent Sherman another dispatch in which he attempted to explain the reasons for his misinformation concerning the location of Johnston's troops. *Ibid.*, p. 909.
29. *Ibid.*, pp. 908-9.   30. *Ibid.*, XLVII, Pt. I, Ser. I, 25.
31. Johnston, *Narrative*, p. 386.
32. Brooks and Lefler, *Clark Papers*, I, 136: Olds, "Last Battle," *Confed. Vet.* XXXVII, 51.

thrown forward, conforming to the edge of the open field.[33] The center of Johnston's position, therefore, was not on the Goldsboro road but at the corner of the plantation, a quarter of a mile north.[34] The two wings went forward from this point, the left crossing diagonally the road on which Davis' corps was advancing; and the right, hidden in a thicket reached ready to envelop any force that might attempt to move west.[35] General Hardee who was to hold the position between Hoke and Stewart had not reached the field when these two corps went into position. His absence left a gap in the center of the Confederate line which had to be filled by two batteries of horse artillery.

In the meantime, Carlin's skirmishers were pushing Hampton back, but as their progress was slow, Brigadier General H. C. Hobart, commanding Carlin's First Brigade, was directed to deploy half of his force and move in line against the Confederates until something was developed. Just before Hobart advanced, Brigadier General G. P. Buell's Second Brigade, at the suggestion of Slocum, was sent to the left of the road to attack the Confederate right flank. The advance of Hobart had reached the Cole house in a large open field when the Confederates opened with a heavy fire of artillery and musketry. The open field had to be abandoned by Hobart; so he moved three regiments to the left and front of the field into a pine thicket where light entrenchments were thrown up. The other three regiments of Hobart's First Brigade, under command of Lieutenant Colonel M. H. Fitch, were placed in position on the right of the road, supporting a battery of artillery,[36] which had been ordered up and placed in position 350 yards in the rear of the Cole house. Carlin's Third Brigade, Lieutenant Colonel D. Miles commanding, was

33. The remnants of this once proud Confederate army, as it marched into position, was divided into three corps—Stewart's, Lee's and Cheatham's—commanded respectively by Major Generals W. W. Loring, D. H. Hill, and W. B. Bate. Neither General S. D. Lee nor B. F. Cheatham were on the field this day. Lee, severely wounded at the battle of Nashville, had been unable to lead his corps northward from Augusta. General Stevenson had done this for him. Cheatham and his division did not arrive at Bentonville until after the battle was over. The delay was at Salisbury, North Carolina, where, by March 11, men and supplies clogged the rail yard to such an extent that Cheatham's departure was delayed until March 19. Black, *Railroads,* pp. 274-78. The troops under Bate's command belonged to R. R. Cleburne's and his own divisions, constituting the only part of Cheatham's corps present on March 19.

34. See above p. 162. With Johnston were four very able engineers to assist in the construction of breastworks. Mrs. J. Anderson, "Memorial on the Battlefield of Bentonville," *Confed. Vet.,* XXXV, 367.

35. The ground on Johnston's front, north of the road, was clear; that south of the road was covered with thickets. *OR,* XLVII, Pt. I, Ser. I, 1056.

36. *Ibid.,* pp. 178, 449. The left of Fitch's line rested on the road. *Ibid.,* p. 463.

placed on the right of Colonel Fitch's three regiments. At the same time General Buell was ordered to return and form on Hobart's left. This order was issued because Buell had diverged too far to the left of the main road.[37]

It was General Slocum's plan to make repeated assaults at different points along the Confederate front. As soon as Buell reached his assigned position, General Davis ordered him to attack again the enemy's right. In order to multiply the chances of success, Carlin ordered Colonel Miles to hit the Confederate left. Carlin also ordered that part of the brigade on the left of the road to join Buell in his advance. The heaviest fighting centered on Hoke's position which was charged "again and again." The attack here was so vigorous that General Bragg, never the most steadfast of battlers, thought that Hoke, slightly entrenched, would be driven from his position. He therefore urgently applied for strong reinforcements. General Hardee, the head of whose column was just appearing on the battlefield, was directed by Johnston "most injudiciously," to send his leading division, McLaws', to Hoke's assistance.[38] The other division, Taliaferro's, moved on to its position in the line on the extreme right. McLaws moved up very slowly, having to pass through a dense thicket or swamp. The officers sent to him as guides lost their way several times, and the division did not reach the ground to which it was ordered until after Hoke had decisively repulsed the Federal attack.[39]

General Hampton considered this initial Federal attack as one of those incidents that so often change the fate of battles. This one interrupted the Confederate battle plan just at the crisis of the engagement. Hampton thought the Federals struck Hoke's division at the moment when Johnston, in accordance with the plan agreed upon, should have thrown his forces on the disorganized Federals.[40]

Hampton was of the opinion that Johnston made only one mistake at Bentonville, and that was ordering McLaws to Hoke's assistance. He believed that had Hardee been in the position originally assigned him at the time Hoke repulsed Miles, Hardee's and Stewart's commands could have been thrown on the flanks of the retreating Federals, probably driving the Fourteenth Corps back in disorder.[41]

37. Ibid., pp. 449, 453, 467-68, 473, 476.   38. Johnston, Narrative, p. 386.
39. McLaws Order Bk., 1865, SHC, U.N.C., p. 39.
40. Hampton, "Bentonville," p. 703.   41. Ibid., pp. 703-4.

It was shortly after the firing had ceased on Hoke's front, that the Federals hit Johnston's right, the assault falling mostly on Stewart's own corps. This attack was repelled as firmly as that on the left.[42]

As Carlin's troops fell back to their former positions, three soldiers left the Confederate lines and came over to the Federals. The one who acted as spokesman requested to be taken immediately to the officer commanding and was brought to General Carlin. The soldier stated that he and his companions had been Federal soldiers before their capture, but had preferred entering the Confederate army to being put in a Confederate prison. This decision was made with the intention of deserting at the first opportunity.[43] He said he was originally from Syracuse, New York, and the reason he wished to see the General was to tell him that Johnston, with his entire army, was in front and expected to crush the scattered Fourteenth and Twentieth Corps. This news was so confirmatory of General Carlin's suspicions acquired the day before and so important that he sent the spokesman for the group directly to General Slocum.[44] The General was at first inclined to doubt the truth of the man's story, considering him a double deserter, but one of his staff, Major W. G. Tracy, rode up and recognized the soldier as a fellow townsman and vouched for his character. Up to this moment Slocum was certain that he faced no more than a division of cavalry, but the statement of this man changed his mind. He at once decided to take a defensive position and communicate with Sherman. Slocum entrusted this important message to the youngest member of his staff, Joseph Foraker. With instructions to ride far to the right and not to spare the horse, the young officer dashed off in the direction of Howard's columns. Slocum also sent word for the two light divisions of the Twentieth Corps to hasten forward.[45]

By this time the Second Division, Fourteenth Corps, under the command of General Morgan, had gone into position on Carlin's right, south of the Goldsboro road. John G. Mitchell's and W. Vandever's brigades formed in front and B. D. Fearing's Third Brigade to the rear.[46] Both Mitchell and Vandever deployed their respective

42. *OR*, XLVII, Pt. I, Ser. I, 453, 468.
43. Confederates called these men "galvanized yankees."
44. Carlin turned over his own horse to the soldier. Carlin, "Bentonville," pp. 239-40; *OR*, XLVII, Pt. I, Ser. I, 449.
45. Slocum, "Sherman's March," pp. 692-93; *OR*, XLVII, Pt. I, Ser. I, 423.
46. These three officers carried the rank of brigadier general.

brigades in two lines. Sturdy log works rapidly thrown up in front of these four lines had a great deal to do with the success of Morgan's command later in the day.[47]   General Carlin went so far as to say that these fortifications probably saved Sherman's reputation.[48]

In response to Slocum's urgent message that the light divisions of the Twentieth Corps move forward, General Williams, dispatched his advance, the First Division, at double quick toward the noise of battle. It was shortly after two o'clock when the Second and Third Brigades of this division, commanded respectively by Colonel William Hawley and Brigadier General J. S. Robinson, appeared on the field. Robinson was ordered to fill the gap in Carlin's line between Hobart and Miles with three of his regiments. He complied with these instructions but three regiments were not enough to close the breach.[49]

Robinson's three remaining regiments and Hawley's command dug in to the left and rear of the Fourteenth Corps line with instructions to protect the Federal left flank.[50]   Later in the afternoon they were joined by Colonel J. L. Selfridge and his First Brigade of the First Division.[51]

Between two-thirty and a quarter of three, Johnston was ready to take the initiative. General Hardee was directed to charge with the right wing, composed of Stewart's troops and Taliaferro's division,[52] and General Bragg was to join in the movements with the troops of Hoke and McLaws. Johnston had already lost much valuable time when he had not immediately followed up the successes of Hoke and Stewart in their repulse of Miles, Hobart, and Buell. Nevertheless, the advance was postponed another thirty minutes. General W. B. Bate, after a personal reconnaissance, reported that the left of the Federal line did not extend connectedly beyond his right. He urged that Taliaferro's division, lying in reserve in his immediate rear, make a detour so as to fall upon the Federal left flank. This suggestion was adopted and the division was given half an hour to get into position.[53]

Although Taliaferro had not completed his flanking movement, the Army of Tennessee moved forward in two lines at 3:15 P.M.[54]   Rebel

---

47. OR, XLVII, Pt. I, Ser. I, 485.   The encumbered division of the Fourteenth Corps did not engage in the fighting on the 19th but the next morning two of its brigades arrived on the scene of battle.

48. Carlin, "Bentonville," p. 27.   49. OR, XLVII, Pt. I, Ser. I, 666.

50. Ibid., pp. 637, 671.   51. Ibid., p. 612.

52. During the early part of the afternoon, Johnston had put Hardee in temporary command of the Army of Tennessee.

53. OR, XLVII, Pt. I, Ser. I, 1106.   54. Ibid., pp. 1090, 1094.

yells once more pierced the air from these tattered veterans of the disaster at Nashville. They were determined to redeem their reputation on the field of battle this day.[55] It was the renewal of "acquaintance with . . . [their] old antagonist of the Dalton and Atlanta Campaign."[56] Several of the officers "led the charge on horseback . . . with colors flying and line of battle in such perfect order . . . it looked like a picture. . . ." But for the men in Bragg's trenches, who for some reason had not been ordered forward by their commander, "it was a painful sight to see how close their battle flags were together, regiments being scarcely larger than companies and a division not much larger than a regiment should be."[57]

Passing "over the bodies of the enemy who had been killed in the [initial Federal] assault, and whose faces, from exposure to the sun, had turned black," the gray line kept advancing until it received Buell's first volley.[58]

The Thirteenth and Twenty-first Michigan repulsed the Confederate attack on Buell's front for a few minutes, but when the skirmish lines to the right and left were turned, the entire brigade began to fall back rapidly and in disorder.[59] Buell's men were soon scurrying to the rear "like the duce"[60] showing "to the Rebs as well as the outside some of the best running ever did . . ." according to Lieutenant Charles Brown.[61] The Lieutenant thought that this run which ended up in security behind the lines of the Twentieth Corps "was the best thing we done that whole day."[62]

General Carlin felt that Buell had, without orders or authority, ordered his troops to fall back.[63] Buell explained the reasons for his action as follows:

At the time the enemy drove the troops on my immediate right, General Carlin was first at the right of my line, but was evidently not aware of

55. Eisenchiml and Newman, *Amer. Iliad*, p. 664.
56. Clark, *Stars and Bars*, p. 192.
57. Hampton, "Bentonville," p. 704; Broadfoot, "70 Regiment," *N.C. Regiments*, IV, 21.
58. Clark, *Stars and Bars*, p. 194.
59. *OR*, XLVII, Pt. I, Ser. I, 449.
60. C. S. Brown to Etta (Brown?), Apr. 26, 1865, Brown Papers, MS Div., Duke Univ. Lib.
61. C. S. Brown to "his folks and anyone else," n.d., Brown Papers, MS Div., Duke Univ. Lib.
62. C. S. Brown to Etta (Brown?), Apr. 26, 1865, Brown Papers, MS Div., Duke Univ. Lib.
63. Carlin, "Bentonville," p. 245.

the condition of things to his right, for he was at that time looking intently to the front at the enemy as he faltered before the fire of my men. At first I waited for him to order, but seeing that too much delay would cause our certain capture, and there being no time for consultation, I ordered the retreat. Half a minute's delay, and General Carlin, myself and most my brigade would have been captured."[64]

Buell also knew that he was being flanked by Taliaferro.

On this occasion Carlin very narrowly escaped capture. When Buell retreated, Carlin had the choice of surrendering or running for his life. Although he had no horse at his disposal, and disliking the idea of surrendering, Carlin took off on foot in the direction of the Federal lines. As he ran for cover of some bushes, his conspicuous dress brought him into full view of the advancing enemy line. Fortunately the Confederate marksmanship on this occasion was poor, and Carlin reached the bushes without being hit. Here he found seven or eight Federal soldiers who had been picking off Confederate officers and color bearers. Carlin and the soldiers tried to check the Confederate progress by a form of deception and noise, but this did not work and they took off on the run. Carlin, being very fatigued, was delighted when he found two fully harnessed artillery horses tied to a tree. However, the picture of a brigadier general, in uniform, riding a harnessed horse without saddle, came vividly into his mind, and he debated for a moment the idea of mounting. Resolving to brave the laughter, he began to untie the horses. This proved to be such a difficult task that after a minute or two Carlin gave up the idea of riding and resumed his walk along the road which soon led him to the Federal line.[65]

Hardee's moving columns not only routed Buell but also the remainder of Carlin's command. Hobart, Miles, and Robinson's three brigades along with Buell were all pushed back on the line of the Twentieth Corps. A Federal soldier making his way to the front was met by "masses of men slowly and doggedly falling back along the Goldsboro road and through the fields and open woods. . . ." With minnie balls whizzing in every direction, he checked his horse. Shortly the soldier "saw the rebel regiments in front in full view, stretching through the fields to the left as far as the eye could reach, advancing rapidly, and firing as they came. . . ."[66] When Miles was driven from his

---

64. *OR*, XLVII, Pt. I, Ser. I, 468.   65. Carlin, "Bentonville," pp. 242-47.
66. McClurg, "Last Chance," p. 393.

position, all connection between Carlin and Morgan, on the Federal right, was broken. Luckily for the Federals Morgan was not hit in this initial advance. Bragg's slowness in getting underway spared this division. Of the Fourteenth Corps, Morgan's command alone remained intact after the Confederate charge.[67]

After having advanced three-quarters of a mile or more, Hardee halted to reform his lines. It was impossible for him to keep an organized line in passing through the thick underbrush. Two divisions were moved several hundred yards by the right flank, after which the whole line moved forward again.[68]

In order to check Johnston's advance, Davis ordered Morgan on the right to move Fearing's brigade, which was being held in reserve, directly to the Goldsboro road and place his lines beyond the road and parallel with it, and to strike the Confederate flank as it followed up Carlin's route.[69] Fearing moved to within thirty paces of the road before he struck the left of Lee's corps.[70] He succeeded in temporarily checking the Confederate advance, but this was due chiefly to the confusion existing at that time in Lee's corps.[71] Order was soon restored to the Confederate ranks, and a heavy concentration was brought to bear on Fearing. This Confederate counter attack doubled up the right side of the Federal line forcing it to retire three hundred yards to the rear. Here Fearing reformed his line with his left resting over the Goldsboro road and at right angles to it; at this point Lieutenant Colonel J. W. Langley assumed command of the brigade, Fearing having been wounded.[72]

In the meantime Robinson's three regiments had fallen back before Hardee in more or less good order under cover of the thick woods. His withdrawal was caused more by the retreat of Buell than by a direct attack upon his line. Robinson's new position rested in an open field and had no connection with any other command, but approximately four hundred yards to his left was the right of the Twentieth Corps line.[73] Robinson's line had hardly been formed when it was attacked by Cheat-

67. OR, XLVII, Pt. I, Ser. I, 435. 68. Ibid., p. 1102.
69. Ibid., p. 435. 70. Ibid., p. 534.
71. Brigadier General J. B. Palmer, before halting, had crossed part of his command to the left of the Goldsboro road, but General D. H. Hill had immediately directed him to return to the right of the road. About half of his command had done so when Brigadier General J. S. Baker, coming up hurriedly, threw his brigade across Palmer's, cutting it in half. It was at the time of this juncture that Fearing struck with some success. OR, XLVII, Pt. I, Ser. I, 1100.
72. Ibid., p. 535. 73. Ibid., pp. 637, 666.

ham's corps under General Bate, which was following up its route of Buell. Even though the Confederates managed to obtain a cross-fire on Robinson's regiments, the Federals did not yield ground.[74] Bate's right flank had become exposed when the left of Taliaferro's division had been driven back while attempting its turning movement. This enabled two regiments from the Twentieth Corps to pour a devastating fire into the Confederate column. Fearing a flanking movement to the right, Bate retired his own right. The Federals, seeing this withdrawal, immediately advanced. At this time General Bate asked for reinforcements.[75] Not only were the Confederates unable to dislodge Robinson, but they were also unable to pass through the gap between his line and that of the Twentieth Corps which was covered by Federal artillery.[76] "The raging leaden hailstorm of grape and canister literally barked the trees, cutting off the limbs as if cut by hand."[77] A North Carolina sergeant was certain that there was no place "in the battle of Gettysburg as hot as that place."[78]

While the Federal left was being pushed back, the First and Second Brigades of Morgan's division of the Fourteenth Corps were having a terrific struggle in their isolated position to the right. Bragg had finally moved forward. Upon the outcome of this fight the tide of battle, to a large extent, depended. The division was posted, as stated before, with General Mitchell's First and Vandever's Second Brigades each in two lines. The Third Brigade of Fearing was held in reserve a few hundred yards in the rear. Both lines of the deployed brigades had thrown up slight but vitally important entrenchments of logs.[79]

Around 2:30 P.M. General Morgan had received orders to move his division to the left and relieve Colonel Miles.[80] Before this order could be executed, the Federal left gave way under Hardee's attack, and Miles and part of Hobart's brigade began their rapid and disorganized retreat which carried them through General Mitchell's lines. Since these men were at the time operating without instructions, Mitchell assumed command of such as still possessed an organization. He also ordered his second line forward to form on and support his left by refusing the line. Thus Mitchell's brigade was formed in a single line with its left re-

---

74. *Ibid.*, p. 667.
75. *Ibid.*, p. 1107.
76. *Ibid.*, p. 667.
77. Ravenel, "Ask the Survivors," *Confed. Vet.*, XVIII, 124.
78. *Ibid.*
79. See above p. 168.
80. *OR*, XLVII, Pt. I, Ser. I, 485.

fused[81] which actually put it in a square with two sides fortified. Every axman in the brigade was ordered to assist in building entrenchments along this new line.[82]

At this point General Davis ordered Fearing to the left, as previously described.[83] Since Fearing's advance was nearly perpendicular to Mitchell's line, the gap between his right and the left of the Second Brigade increased with every step. Morgan ordered Vandever's second line to form on Mitchell's left so as to keep up contact, if possible, but this movement does not appear to have been carried out. On account of the direction of Fearing's march and his subsequent repulse, all communication with him was lost, and the First and Second Brigades of the Second Division, Fourteenth Corps, were left to themselves for the remainder of the day.

About 4:00 o'clock Bragg finally made a heavy and general attack along the whole of Mitchell's and Vandever's line. The two fronts of Mitchell's lines were hit hard. The most vigorous attack came at the angle formed by the main line with the refused line. The Confederate position at this point gave them an enfilading fire down both of Mitchell's positions. Nevertheless, the Confederates were driven back except along that portion of the line occupied by the two regiments of Carlin's division which Morgan had halted in their retreat through his position. These two regiments gave way, compelling another regiment, which was on the left of the refused line, to retreat to the First Brigade. Through the opening thus formed, that part of the Confederate force not repulsed swung. The Confederates, who a few minutes before were on Mitchell's front, were now directly to his back. To cope with this situation, Mitchell's troops immediately jumped over the log works, firing into what had been their rear, and compelled the men in gray, who had gained that part of the field, to withdraw. The Confederates suffered heavy casualties, especially in the number of men captured.[84]

In the meantime Vandever had to sustain two frontal attacks.[85] He repulsed the first attack by allowing the enemy to approach within thirty

81. Refused is used here in the military sense, meaning to bend or keep back.
82. *OR*, XLVII, Pt. I, Ser. I, 511.
83. See above p. 171.
84. *OR*, XLVII, Pt. I, Ser. I, 511.
85. The *Official Records* do not state clearly which Confederate forces attacked Mitchell, but it is clear that Hoke's division struck Vandever's First Brigade. Vandever claims that Hoke himself was captured but managed to escape. *Ibid.*, p. 497. The colors of the Fortieth North Carolina, one of Hoke's regiments, were also captured. *Ibid.*, 496.

paces of his fortifications before pouring a destructive fire into them.[86] Even under this withering fire Hoke's men rallied, but they were again driven back.[87] About this time, in consequence of the attack on Mitchell, Vandever's left flank became exposed, but again the attack was repelled. A few moments later another Confederate column was discovered approaching on Vandever's flank. Covered by the underbrush, this column reached the Federal rear and gained possession of the unoccupied line of logworks constructed earlier in the day by the second line of Mitchell's brigade.[88] For a brief period Vandever was in doubt as to whether the occupants of the works were friend or foe. By this time a combination of rifle smoke and fog had settled "heavy and dense" over the battlefield, making visibility very limited.[89] But a Confederate demand for surrender dispelled all doubts. The Federals answered with a "go to hell" and charged out of their works.[90] As Mitchell had done only a few minutes before, Vandever's men held their position by firing into what had been their rear.

General Davis, although unable to reach Morgan, was fully aware of the importance of this isolated struggle. Twice he turned to a companion and said: "If Morgan's troops can stand this, all is right; if not the day is lost. There is no reserve—not a regiment to move—They must fight it out."

This encounter between Morgan and Bragg was among the severest tests Sherman's troops had faced since leaving Chattanooga, so thought Colonel A. C. McClurg, an actor on the scene. "Seldom have I heard such continuous and remorseless roar of musketry," he wrote. "It seemed more than the men could bear. . . . Soldiers in the command who have passed through scores of battles will tell you they never saw anything like the fighting at Bentonville."[91] Veterans of the army of Northern Virginia said "it was the hottest infantry fight they had ever been in except Cold Harbor."[92]

In the midst of this hot affray Brigadier General William Cogswell

86. Lieutenant Colonel G. W. Grummond, commanding the Fourteenth Michigan, called this "the most terrific fire I ever listened to; nothing could withstand it." *Ibid.,* 504.

87. *Ibid.,* pp. 496, 504.

88. *Ibid.,* p. 497.

89. McLaws Order Bk., 1865, SHC, U.N.C., p. 241.

90. C. S. Brown to Etta (Brown?), Apr. 18, 1865, Brown Papers, MS Div., Duke Univ. Lib.

91. Lossing, *Pictorial History,* III, 501.

92. Lamb, "36 Regiment," *N.C. Regiments,* II, 651.

of the Twentieth Corps reported to General Slocum with his brigade and was ordered to proceed to the front and right to fill, if possible, the gap between Fearing and Mitchell.[93] The other two brigades of the Third Division arrived later in the afternoon but saw no fighting. Half an hour before sundown Cogswell moved in past Fearing and went into position approximately 150 yards in front of Fearing's center which was on the right of the Goldsboro road but to the left and rear of Mitchell. Here Cogswell became hotly engaged with the troops of the Army of Tennessee.[94] After dark James Conner's brigade of McLaws' division, under the command of Brigadier General J. D. Kennedy, was brought up to assist the troops opposed to Cogswell but in the darkness and confusion could effect nothing.[95]

The remainder of McLaws' division was sent to reinforce Bate on the extreme Confederate right. These troops did not reach Bate until sundown. They immediately attacked, but after half an hour's sharp conflict, they retired.[96] General Bate believed that if these fresh troops had been thrown in an hour earlier when he called for them[97] a Confederate victory might have been assured.[98]

The troops on both sides maintained the positions which they had at sunset, some hours without change. During these early hours of darkness Mitchell had once more to contend with a Confederate force to his back, but this time it was no surprise attack. He had the unique experience of being informed of the forthcoming attack by a Confederate staff officer who had lost his way in the darkness and mistook Mitchell's camp for one of his own. The weary General was aroused from his rest when out of the darkness stepped a young Confederate officer who, after saluting, said: "Sir, Colonel Hardee presents his compliments and says he is about to charge the enemy in your front; please be governed accordingly." Governing his actions accordingly Mitchell drew in his pickets and gave orders that at the tap of the drum his entire line would fire one volley. This broke up the attack and left among the dead a line of rifles and knapsacks as straight as if laid out for Sunday inspection.[99]

Spasmodic firing continued all along Johnston's and Slocum's lines

93. OR, XLVII, Pt. I, Ser. I, 424.
94. Ibid., pp. 1091, 1095, 1102. The Second Division of the Twentieth Corps was not engaged in the fighting on the 19th. It arrived at Bentonville on the 20th.
95. Ibid., pp. 1109-10.   96. Ibid., p. 601.
97. See above p. 172.   98. OR, XLVII, Pt. I, Ser. I, 1170.
99. Osborn, 55 Ohio, p. 202; McClurg, "Last Chance," p. 397.

until eight or half past. About 11:00 P.M. the Confederates withdrew to their works of the morning.

While the heavy fighting of March 19th was in progress, the right wing of Sherman's army marched steadily away from the battlefield. The Fifteenth Corps, with its columns badly stretched out, moved along the New Road which ran by way of Falling Creek Church to Goldsboro. Not far from the church and a school house by the same name, this road intersected the one upon which Slocum was traveling. Approximately three miles north of the crossroads was Cox's Bridge over the Neuse. The head of Logan's column reached the intersection of the Cox's Bridge road before noon.[100]

In the middle of the afternoon some Confederate cavalry appeared on the road leading to Cox's Bridge; so the Tenth Iowa, under command of Lieutenant Colonel W. E. Strong of Howard's staff, was immediately pushed out in that direction. His orders were to drive the Confederate cavalry from the vicinity.[101]

Logan considered the crossroads of great importance. He ordered Colonel C. R. Wever's entire brigade to that position, and after visiting that ground personally he decided to move his First and Fourth Divisions to that point with instructions to make an entrenched line. The Third Division was encamped nearby. Hazen, several miles to the rear of the crossroads, was actually closer to the left wing than the advance units.[102]

The Seventeenth Corps continued its march and halted for the night at Smith's Chapel, seven miles from Mount Olive. This put Blair approximately a six-hour march from Logan's advance at Falling Creek Church.[103]

All afternoon long the men of the right wing had listened anxiously to the distant sound of battle. The "heavy and continuous roar of artillery" was indicative to most of them of a major struggle between Slocum and Johnston, but Sherman declined to turn the head of any column in that direction.[104] The only change he made in the disposition of his troops was an order for Kilpatrick to remain with the Slocum instead of crossing over to the right flank, as had been intended. He supposed the noise to indicate about the same measure of opposition by Hardee's troops and Hampton's cavalry as before experienced.[105] He was strengthened

100. OR, XLVII, Pt. I, Ser. I, 234.   101. Ibid., pp. 206, 234.
102. Ibid., pp. 234, 321.   103. Ibid., p. 383.
104. McClurg, "Last Chance," p. 398.   105. Sherman, Memoirs, II, 303.

in this belief by Slocum's first message stating that nothing but cavalry was in his front.[106]

It was evening before Sherman learned of Johnston's bold gamble. When the courier arrived with the news, the General was resting in Howard's tent at Falling Creek Church. In his excitement Sherman rushed out to a camp fire without waiting to put on his pants. He presented a ludicrous appearance standing in ashes up to his ankles, hands clasped behind him, and with nothing on but a red flannel undershirt and a pair of drawers. Nevertheless, as he barked his orders there was immediate "hurrying to and fro and mounting in hot haste."[107]

The General's instructions for Slocum were to fight a defensive action until the remainder of the army could be rushed to his aid. All of the Fifteenth Corps except Hazen's division was ordered to move on the battlefield directly from the Cox's Bridge crossroads. This would put Logan on the Confederate rear, provided Slocum kept Johnston facing west. Since Hazen's position on the night of March 19 was closer to the scene of action than Logan's other division, he was ordered to retrace his steps to Lee's Store and there take a direct road leading to Slocum's flank.[108] The Seventeenth Corps was also ordered to move during the night to Falling Creek Church and from there to follow the Fifteenth Corps to Bentonville.[109]

Early in the morning of March 20, General Logan started his march on Bentonville. Before moving, Logan ordered Colonel Wever's brigade to advance on Cox's Bridge. Wever succeeded in pushing the Confederates across the bridge, compelling them to destroy it.[110]

General C. R. Woods' First Division led Logan's column as it moved along the Neuse River road toward Bentonville. After moving nearly four miles, Woods struck some Confederate outposts, and from that time forward his advance had to be made under cover of a good line of skirmishers. Soon Woods struck the main line of Confederate works and went into position.[111]

Woods' advance was directly upon Hoke's rear, but the skirmishing had well heralded his coming. Consequently, Johnston had time to

106. *OR*, XLVII, Pt. I, Ser. I, 423. 107. McClurg, "Last Chance," p. 399.
108. *OR*, XLVII, Pt. I, Ser. I, 234-35. 109. *Ibid.*, p. 383.
110. *Ibid.*, p. 235. Johnston wanted the bridge burned "at all hazards" if the defending forces were driven away. Had the structure not been destroyed, it would have left the way open for a Federal entry into Goldsboro and also a possible flanking movement around the Confederate forces at Bentonville. *Ibid.*, XLVII, Pt. II, Ser. I, 1436.
111. *Ibid.*, XLVII, Pt. I, Ser. I, 246.

change his position. He bent back his left so as to form a bridgehead with the Mill Creek and a single bridge in his rear. Thus Johnston's line had the form of a "V." Hampton had prolonged Hoke's left to Mill Creek with Butler's and Wheeler's divisions. The latter had come up from the direction of Averasboro.[112]

By noon nearly all of the Fifteenth Corps was on the ground.[113] The Seventeenth Corps, which was following the Fifteenth, arrived during the afternoon.[114] Both of these corps went into position facing Johnston's left. Slocum's wing was across from the right line of the Confederate "V". Sherman ordered General Howard to proceed with due caution, using skirmishers alone, until he made his junction with General Slocum.

As Sherman deployed his troops, Johnston ascertained that his left was very far overlapped by the Federal right. Therefore McLaws' division was ordered to Hoke's left. Johnston was so outnumbered that much of his cavalry was deployed as skirmishers on McLaws' left in order to show a front equal to that of the Federals.[115]

Sherman did not feel disposed to invite a general battle on March 20. He was still uncertain of Johnston's strength, his foodstuffs were low, and during the day he had received messages from General Schofield at Kinston[116] and General Terry at Faison's Depot. Both generals had assured him in their reports that they would be in Goldsboro by March 21.[117] To Slocum, Sherman wrote: "Johnston hoped to overcome your wing before I could come to your relief. Having failed in that I cannot see why he remains and still think he will avail himself of night to get back to Smithfield. I would rather avoid a general battle but if he insists on it, we must accommodate him."[118] Johnston remained on

---

112. *Ibid.*, p. 1056; Johnston, *Narrative.* pp. 389-90; Sherman, *Memoirs*, II, 304.

113. General W. B. Woods in charge of the train of the Fifteenth Corps, encamped on the night of March 20, at Buck Creek, eight miles from Dudley Station. He arrived on the field the next morning, having left his train with a division of the Seventeenth Corps. *OR.* XLVII, Pt. I, 253.

114. *Ibid.*, p. 121.

115. Johnston, *Narrative.*, p. 390.

116. The Confederate forces under General Bragg abandoned Kinston on March 10, having been defeated in the battle of Kinston or Wise's Forks, March 8-10, by the Federals under the command of Generals Schofield and Cox. Schofield, however, had no pontoon train, and as a result was unable to cross the Neuse, which flows east of Kinston, until the bridge could be repaired or pontoons could be brought by rail from Morehead City. The crossing and occupation of the town was not effected until March 19.

117. *OR*, XLVII, Pt. II, Ser. I, 912-13, 922.

118. *Ibid.*, p. 919.

Sherman's front after March 19 only to cover the removal of his wounded. Bad roads and poor means of transportation compelled him to devote two days to the operation.[119] Captain J. M. Robinson, engineer in charge of railroads, was ordered to dispatch as many trains as possible to Smithfield to carry off the wounded. A medical officer of field experience was sent to Smithfield to take charge of matters as Johnston had received several complaints of the treatment of the wounded when they were brought to the rear lines.[120] Sherman, not guessing why Johnston remained on his front, sent his trains to Kinston to get supplies which would be needed in case he had to fight the next day.[121]

The fighting on March 20, although of a relatively minor nature, did encompass a heated afternoon duel between Howard and Hoke. Between noon and sunset the Federals made repeated attacks on Hoke's division. Holding an important position in this Confederate line was the North Carolina brigade of Junior Reserves who in General Hoke's words: "repulsed every charge that was made upon them with very meagre and rapidly thrown up breastworks."[122] Major Walter Clark, the seventeen year old commander of the brigade's skirmish line which twice turned back the enemy, saw the afternoon's affair "as a regular Indian fight . . . behind trees."[123] The skirmishers to the right and left of Clark gave ground but not once did these North Carolina youths fall back.

Far from the line of fire, in fact safely situated "in the rear of the reserves," one could find General Sherman and his staff. When not receiving messages and sending orders, Sherman nervously paced back and forth under the shade of some large trees.[124] The cigar in his mouth was more often out than burning. Once he stopped an officer, who was smoking, and asked for a light. The officer obliged by handing him his own smoke. As the General lit his cigar, he seemed to be oblivious of those around him. His mind was on the noise of battle. Suddenly he turned, dropped the officer's cigar on the ground, and walked off puffing

119. Johnston, *Narrative*, p. 389. Johnston did not show sound military judgment in remaining on the field after both wings of Sherman's army had united. His explanation for remaining—to remove the wounded—was a humane policy but scarcely defensible from a military standpoint since he was "jeopardizing" one of the few remaining Confederate armies "for the sake of a few hundred wounded." Luvaas, "Bentonville," unpublished article in the possession of Jay Luvaas, Duke University, p. 31.
120. *OR*, XLVII, Pt. II, Ser. I, 1444.   121. *Ibid.*, p. 919.
122. Brooks and Lefler, *Clark Papers*, I, 53.   123. *Ibid.*, p. 136.
124. Howe, *Marching With Sherman*, p. 284.

his own. The startled soldier looked at him a moment, then laughed, picked up the cigar and continued his smoke.[125]

Even though he was intent on every detail of battle, Sherman was not disposed to ride forward and view firsthand the tide of events. This characteristic of the General disturbed Major Hitchcock no end. He was by now convinced that the safest position in the army was the one he now held, a place on Sherman's staff.[126] As commander of a large army Sherman's place was not on the front line, as the Major seemed to think, but in the rear where he could conduct the over-all operation of battle.

On March 21, there was heavy skirmishing along the entire Confederate front. Stewart and Taliaferro's skirmishers pushed forward far enough to learn that Sherman had drawn back his left and entrenched it also.[127] Detachments fom Walthall's and Bate's divisions drove the Federals from the vicinity of the Cole farm house and burned all buildings to prevent their further use by enemy sharpshooters.[128] But the most important development of the day was an impromptu dash on Johnston's extreme left flank by General Mower's First Division of the Seventeenth Corps, in position on the Federal right. Around four o'clock Mower put his command in motion along a road to his right which he understood crossed Mill Creek by a ford and would enable him to flank Johnston. After crossing a very bad swamp, Mower struck and easily pushed back the thin line of dimounted cavalry which joined Johnston's left on this part of the field. He rapidly approached the road and bridge across Mill Creek, Johnston's sole line of retreat.[129]

General Hampton was the first to report the Federal move to Johnston. General Johnston at once ordered Hardee to unite Taliaferro's division and a small detachment of infantry reserves, both of which were moving to the left at the time, and to oppose Mower. The Federal advance, however, was so sudden that the union could not be accomplished. Fortunately for the Confederates, General Hampton, while leading a cavalry reserve to meet Mower, saw A. Cumming's brigade of Stevenson's division, under command of Colonel R. J. Henderson, moving to the left and directed it toward the scene of action. Hardee, who had brought up a few members of the Eighth Texas cavalry, ordered Henderson to strike

125. Grigsby, *Smoked Yank,* p. 237.   126. Howe, *Marching With Sherman,* p. 284.
127. *OR,* XLVII, Pt. I, Ser. I, 1057.   128. *Ibid.,* p. 1092.
129. *Ibid.,* p. 391.

Mower in the front. The Eighth Texas whose ranks had been thinned by two days' fighting and was now commanded by "a mere boy," Captain "Doc" Mathews, hit the Federal left flank. Hampton, coming up on the other side with Young's brigade of cavalry, commanded by Colonel Gilbert J. Wright, charged Mower's right flank. Wheeler, at a considerable distance from this point, assailed the rear of the Federal column in flank with a part of Brigadier General W. Allen's brigade of Alabamians.[130]

Mower's movement had been made without authority of or consultation with any of his superior officers. General Howard, upon learning of Mower's movement, ordered Blair to support him and directed Logan to make a strong demonstration along his front,[131] but when Sherman learned of Mower's movements, he immediately ordered him to return to his original position. The General feared that a Confederate concentration might cut Mower off from the rest of the Seventeenth Corps.[132] This move was characteristic of Sherman who never had the "moral courage to order his whole army into an engagement."[133]

The simultaneous attacks upon a numerically stronger Federal column had been skillfully and bravely executed, and it is only natural that the Confederates, after such display of valor, should be slow to admit that Mower retired under orders.

In the gallant charge of the Texas cavalry General Hardee's sixteen-year-old son, Willie, fell mortally wounded. Only a few hours before the fight Hardee had reluctantly given his son permission to join the Texans. The news of Willie's death was sent through the Federal lines to General Howard who had once been the young boy's tutor and Sunday school teacher. For Willie's sake and in response to a letter from the youth's sister, Howard went out of his way to protect friends and relatives of the Hardee's in North Carolina.[134]

During the night of March 21, all of the Confederate wounded that could bear transportation were removed, and Johnston, learning that Schofield had reached Goldsboro, ordered his army to cross Mill Creek by the bridge at Bentonville and retreat on Smithfield.[135] The extreme darkness of the night and the heavy woods caused the Confederate troops

130. *Ibid.*, p. 1057; Johnston, *Narrative*, p. 391; Blackburn, "Reminiscences," *Southwestern Hist. Quar.*, XXII, 169.

131. *OR*, XLVII, Pt. I, Ser. I, 207.   132. *Ibid.*, p. 27.

133. McCartney, *Grant and His Generals*, p. 295.

134. Howard, *Autobiography*, II, 151.   135. *OR*, XLVII, Pt. I, Ser. I, 1057.

to move very slowly. At sunrise the rear of Johnston's army was still in Bentonville. General Wheeler, covering the retreat, found it necessary to dismount most of his men in order to check the Federals sent in pursuit.[136] Wheeler attempted to burn the bridge at Mill Creek, but Colonel R. F. Catterson, Second Brigade, First Division, Fifteenth Corps, pursuing him very closely, managed to extinguish the flames and save the bridge.[137] By ten o'clock Wheeler had fallen back to Hannah's Creek,[138] where it crossed the Smithfield road. Here a lively skirmish took place in which three Federal color bearers fell within fifty feet of Wheeler's line.[139] At this point the pursuit of Johnston was stopped by orders of General Logan. The Federal troops were directed to return to Mill Creek.[140]

General Johnston's strategy at Bentonville was bold and skillfully executed, but he failed in his primary objective to overwhelm Sherman's left wing. One important object, however, was gained. Confidence was restored to the Confederate troops.[141] To many of them Sherman had come out "second best" in this struggle.[142] Prior to the battle the morale of Johnston's men had been very low. They had not been paid for quite some time, and the prospects of their getting paid in the near future were very dim.[143] Furthermore, the defeats which parts of the Confederate army had suffered in Tennessee and at Wilmington and Kinston had caused them to lose confidence in themselves. The Army of Tennessee especially redeemed itself. Johnston wrote Lee on March 23: "Troops of Tennessee Army have fully disproved slanders that have been published against them."[144] The battle, however, did not restore confidence to all of Johnston's troops. Some went straight home from the battlefield and were never heard of again.[145] Others probably went into Bladen, Bruns-

---

136. *Ibid.*, p. 1131.

137. *Ibid.*, p. 259. According to T. F. Upson, One Hundredth Indiana, there was another bridge crossing Mill Creek at this point, one made of rosin and capable of holding up men. In this journal Upson entered: "We saw a curious sight at Mill Creek. There was a great pile of rosin—I cannot tell how much—[and] we set it on fire. It melted and ran out over the water; the rain finally put out the fire and there was a bridge of rosin from shore to shore. Some of our boys crossed it." Winther, Upson Diary, p. 160.

138. Wheeler said he skirmished with the Federals at Black Creek, but evidently he was mistaken because the Federal pursuit was stopped at Hannah's Creek which was east of Black Creek.

139. *OR*, XLVII, Pt. I, Ser. I, 1132. 140. *Ibid.*, p. 236.

141. *Ibid.*, p. 1057; Johnston, *Narrative.* p. 389. 142. Smith, *Smith Letters*, p. 172.

143. *OR*, XLVII, Pt. II, Ser. I, 1373-74. 144. *Ibid.*, pp. 1453-54.

145. Ford and Ford, *Life in the Confed. Army*, p. 59.

wick, and Columbus counties and joined the band of Confederate deserters which was raiding the countryside in that region.[146]

General Sherman claimed victory at Bentonville on the grounds that
he was in possession of the battlefield when the fighting ceased, and that
Johnston had failed in his attempt to crush the Federal left wing.[147]
Still the General had little of which to boast. His force was more than
twice the size of his opponents. Yet on March 19, the Federals tottered
on the brink of a resounding defeat. Sherman's conduct at Bentonville
bears out the truth in General Howard's statement: "Strategy was his
strongest point. Take him in battle and he did not seem to me to be
the equal of Thomas or Grant."[148]

From Savannah to Fayetteville Sherman had moved his corps in
flawless fashion, but from this latter place to Goldsboro his operations
were definitely characterized by carelessness in the management of a
large army. From Fayetteville he had written: "I will see that this army
marches . . . to Goldsborough in compact form."[149] But this resolve was
soon forgotten and when Johnston made his bold gamble, the Federal
columns were strung out over a considerable distance. This is all the
more significant when one considers the fact that Sherman supposed the
Confederate forces to be stronger than either one of his wings alone.[150]
Neither would he give credence to the reports that the enemy was concentrating on his front.[151] In the General's defense, however, it can be
said that a combination of adverse weather, topography, and poor roads in
part explain why the divisions were so far apart.

On the field of battle Sherman erred on two occasions. First, he failed
to follow up Mower's break through of Johnston's flank on March 21.
Secondly, he did not pursue the Confederate forces after the battle.
Sherman readily admitted he was wrong in halting Mower's charge.
Concerning this movement he said: "I think I made a mistake there, and
should rapidly have followed Mower's lead with the whole of the right
wing, which would have brought on a general battle, and it could not
have resulted otherwise than successfully to us, by reason of our vastly
superior numbers. . . ."[152] Sherman lacked that element of "confident

---

146. OR, XLVII, Pt. III, Ser. I, 14.   147. Ibid., XLVII, Pt. I, Ser. I, 27.
148. Fletcher, Sherman, p. 292.   149. OR, XLVII, Pt. II, Ser. I, 803.
150. See above p. 148.   151. Ibid., pp. 160-61.
152. Sherman, Memoirs, II, 304. Sherman made a mistake in not crushing Johnston
after Mower's breakthrough. "But this opportunity was not actually as golden as even
Sherman believed. Mower had actually retreated before receiving Sherman's orders, and if

boldness or audacity" necessary to all great field commanders. It is possible that the awareness of his own impulsive nature made him unduly cautious when under great responsibilities or emergencies.[153]

The General's explanation to Grant as to why he pushed on to Goldsboro rather than after Johnston leaves something to be desired.[154] In this communication he does not claim that his men were short of food or ammunition, "the only adequate excuse" for halting. He seemed to consider shoes, which were noticeably absent among the men, his most essential need. But the scarcity of footwear did not warrant a delay at this time. The Confederate soldiers were also without shoes.[155]

Sherman, who took his campaigns in stages with a pause to wash and "fix up a little," felt his men deserved a rest. For several weeks he had "constantly held out to the officers and men to bear patiently the want of clothing and other necessaries, for at Goldsborough awaited . . . [them] everything."[156] This promise he did not wish to break. He was a very popular general with the soldiers and desired to remain so.[157]

By going into camp at Goldsboro, Sherman knew that it would give Johnston time to lick his wounds, but he assumed that his adversary would remain inactive. This assumption proved correct but under sound military judgment Sherman had no right to count on it. Two days after the battle General McLaws was writing to his wife that Johnston would soon be in a position to chase General Sherman out of the state.[158]

The *Official Records* show the total Federal losses at Bentonville in killed, wounded, captured and missing as 1,527.[159] The Confederate losses are listed as 2,606.[160] These figures are not completely reliable because there are wide discrepancies in all of the Federal and Confederate tabulations. For instance, General Howard reported that the right wing alone took 1,287 Confederate prisoners.[161] Yet Confederate returns show Johnston's total loss in captured and missing as only 673.[162]

---

he had been permitted to advance a second time he would have found the Confederates heavily reinforced on his front." Luvaas, "Bentonville," p. 33.

153. Schofield, *Forty-six Years*, p. 341.

154. *OR*, XLVII, Pt. I, Ser. I, 950.

155. Although Sherman did not claim a shortage of food, he did tell Grant that he planned to pick up rations in Goldsboro. *Ibid.;* Burne, *Lee, Grant and Sherman*, p. 179.

156. *OR*, XLVII, Pt. II, Ser. I, 950, 970.

157. Burne, *Lee, Grant and Sherman*, p. 179.

158. L. McLaws to wife, Mar. 23, 1865, McLaws Papers, SHC, U.N.C.

159. *OR*, XLVII, Pt. I, Ser. I, 76.　　　　160. *Ibid.*, p. 1060.

161. *Ibid.*, p. 27.　　　　162. *Ibid.*, p. 1060.

Most of the Federal wounded were gathered in a building near the battlefield. Colonel Hamilton, Ninth Ohio Cavalry, gives an interesting description of this makeshift hospital:

A dozen surgeons and attendants in their shirt sleeves stood at rude benches cutting off arms and legs and throwing them out of the windows, where they lay scattered on the grass. The legs of infantrymen could be distinguished from those of the cavalry by the size of their calves, as the march of 1,000 miles had increased the size of the one and diminished the size of the other.[163]

Sherman directed General Howard and the cavalry to remain at Bentonville through March 22 in order to bury the dead and remove the wounded.[164] He himself rode to Cox's Bridge, where he met General Terry.

On March 23, the two Generals rode into Goldsboro. There they found General Schofield, thus effecting a junction of all three armies, as originally planned. Colonel S. D. Pool, Confederate commander at Goldsboro, had evacuated the town at 4:00 P.M.[165] on March 21, amidst the confusion of an excited citizenry and burning cotton.[166] He had been able to offer little resistance to Schofield. The unpleasant task of surrendering the city fell to Major James Privett.[167]

The left wing came in during March 23-24, and the right wing followed on the 24th, on which day the cavalry moved to Mount Olive and General Terry back to Faison.

163. Hamilton, *Recollections*, p. 194.
164. *OR*, XLVII, Pt. I, Ser. I, 28.
165. *Ibid.*, XLVII, Pt. II, Ser. I, 941, 1453.
166. R. P. Howell Memoirs (1854-1872), MS, SHC, U.N.C.; *New Bern N.C. Times*, Mar. 24, 1865.
167. *Goldsboro News-Argus*, Oct. 4, 1947.

CHAPTER XII

"Luxuriating in the . . . Spring Weather"

SHERMAN'S ARMY as it approached Goldsboro presented a comical picture. The soldiers trudged along in company with pets acquired along the line of march. It was not an unusual sight to see a squirrel perched on a knapsack, a coon on a string, or a fighting cock in hand. Many of the men, mounted on mules or horses, generally of the plug variety, had little to occupy their attention, while others on foot were busy tending to the large number of sheep, cattle, and hogs that were distinctive to this fighting force. In every column was at least one wagon loaded with geese, turkeys, and chickens, all of which were adding their say to the occasion.[1]

At Goldsboro Sherman held a review for the benefit of Generals Schofield, Terry, Cox, and other newly arrived officers. "Laughing and cursing, the men made clumsy attempts to close files that had been open for months." An Indiana soldier recorded the event in his diary as follows:

We marched in platoons, and I doubt if at any time the troops of the rebel army were more ragged than we. Probably one man in a dozen had a full suit of clothes, but even this suit was patched or full of holes. . . . Many were bareheaded or had a handkerchief tied around their head. Many had on hats they had found in the houses along the line of march, an old worn out affair in every instance—tall crushed silk hats, some revolutionary styles, many without tops, caps so holely that the hair was sticking out, brimless hats, brimless caps, hats mostly brim. Many men had no coats or wore buttonless blouses, and being without shirts their naked chests protruded. Many a coat had no sleeves, or one only, the sleeves having been used to patch the seat or knees of the trousers. . . . Generally both legs of the trousers were off nearly to the knees, though now and then a man more fortunate had only

1. Hatcher, *Four Weeks,* pp. 21-22; Conyngham, *Sherman's March,* p. 314.

one leg exposed. Socks had disappeared weeks before, and many a shoeless patriot . . . kept step with a half-shod comrade. But the men who had cut off the tails of their dress coats "to stop a hole to keep the wind away," though bronzed and weather-beaten, marched by General Sherman with heads up. . . .[2]

As the troops swung past, General Blair remarked: "See those poor fellows with bare legs." To this remark Sherman replied: "Splendid legs! Splendid legs! I would give both of mine for any one of them."[3] The review, nevertheless, turned out to be a failure, and after two regiments had passed, Sherman halted it.

The Negroes of Goldsboro when they saw these ragged soldiers with their faces begrimed by the soot of burning pine forest were heard to remark that "fer a fac" they were whiter than the soldiers.[4]

The contrast in personal appearance between Schofield's and Sherman's men was quite in evidence to all that saw them together. Sherman's unkempt veterans were not indisposed to chaff their newly uniformed comrades from the coast. The heroes of the "march to the sea" called them "bandbox soldiers."[5]

The final arrival of the Federal armies in Goldsboro was in one sense welcomed by the local citizens.[6] For weeks they had been living in frightful expectation of the day when the men in blue would appear.[7] Now the suspense was over and they turned out in large numbers to view the enemy. Joining them on the streets were throngs of Negroes who sang for General Sherman's benefit a little ditty that went like this:

> Brave Sherman, sent by God's decree
> Has led the Yankee's through the South
> And set four million "niggers" free.[8]

Very few of Goldsboro's residents had fled the city, but among those doing so was John Spelman, editor of the *Goldsboro State Journal*. It is probable, however, that he saved his skin by running. One Northern writer had termed him a "little, dirty, nasty, howling, snarling, hypocritical, demagogical secesh" who had done his best to involve the country in a fratricidal war.[9]

2. Merrill, *70 Ind.*, pp. 260-61; Lewis, Sherman, p. 516.
3. Force, "Marching," p. 10.   4. Bryant, *3 Wis.*, p. 327.
5. Merrill, *70 Ind.*, p. 261; Cox, *Reminiscences*, I, 447.
6. *New Bern N.C. Times.*, Mar. 4, 1865.
7. Elizabeth Collier Diary, Mar. 11, 1865, SHC, U.N.C.
8. Boise, *33 Mass.*, p. 118.   9. *New Bern N.C. Times*, Mar. 28, 1865.

At Goldsboro General Sherman found neither the railroad from New Bern nor the one from Wilmington fully repaired and no supplies awaiting him.[10] In an angry mood he wrote his Quartermaster General, L. C. Easton:

I have made junction of my armies at Goldsborough a few days later than I appointed, but I find neither railroad completed, nor have I a word or sign from you or General Beckwith of the vast store of supplies I hoped to meet here or hear of. We have sent wagons to Kinston in hopes to get something there, but at all events I should know what has been done and what is being done. I have constantly held out to the officers and men to bear patiently the want of clothing and other necessaries, for at Goldsborough awaited us everything. If you can expedite the movement of stores from the sea to the army, do so, and don't stand on expenses.[11]

For Colonel W. W. Wright of the Railroad Department Sherman also had some suggestions:

Colonel W. W. Wright, of the railroad department, will use extraordinary means, night and day, to complete the two railroads from Goldsborough back to Wilmington and Morehead City, and to equip them to capacity of 300 tons per day of freight. He may pay any price for labor, call for details of soldiers, and draw rolling stock from Savannah and Charleston, or any point within his command, and all commanding officers and quartermasters will give preference to the shipment of such stock over that of any other work whatever not involving life.[12]

Generals Logan and Blair wanted the chief quartermaster and commissary changed on the grounds of "utter incompetency and inefficiency."[13] Sherman did not side with Logan and Blair on this question. He stated that they knew nothing "of the difficulties arising from mud banks, storms at sea, difficulties of navigation, etc."[14]

Although provisions for the army had not arrived from the coast, Sherman decided to change the foraging system. All foragers were

---

10. The absence of supplies made Sherman's decision not to pursue Johnston look very bad. As previously pointed out, this move was based in part on his desire to replenish his quartermaster stores. See above p. 184.

11. *OR*, XLVII, Pt. II, Ser. I, 970.

12. *Ibid.*, XLVII, Pt. III, Ser. I, 7. Sherman must have forgotten that he had written Terry on March 12, that if the railroads were completed to Goldsboro by April 10, it would be soon enough. *Ibid.*, XLVII, Pt. II, Ser. I, 803. In his *Memoirs* General Sherman praises the work of Colonel Wright. Sherman, *Memoirs*, II, 306.

13. *OR*, XLVII, Pt. III, Ser. I, 28.

14. *Ibid.*, p. 173.

ordered dismounted and placed in the ranks. Their horses and mules were turned over to the quartermaster corps.[15] This meant quite a few animals. "About half of this army are mounted," wrote a Federal soldier before this order went into effect. "It rather don't care to do much more walking. Nearly everyone has his own coach, cab, buggy, cart or wagon, drawn by horses or mules—blind or lame—colts or old worn out horses or mules . . . General Sherman could now advertise a livery stable extensive enough to supply the whole country, provided they were not choice as to rigs."[16]

Nevertheless, the "corn-crib" and "fodder-stack" commandoes could look back upon a plentiful harvest between Fayetteville and Goldsboro. The countryside had supplied them with more forage, in some instances, than they could carry away. Meat and meal had been found in abundance. So skilfully had the "bummers" covered this region that the rooster no longer crowed in the morning because he no longed existed. Had the rooster escaped with his life there would have been no fence rail for him to stand on. Such was the opinion of a newspaper correspondent.[17]

As vital as the forager had been to the success of the campaign, General Morgan regretted that he had to exclude him from praise and credit. He wrote:

I regret that I have to except anyone from praise and credit, but I have some men in my command . . . who have mistaken the name and meaning of the term foragers, and have become under that name highwaymen, with all of their cruelty and ferocity and none of their courage; their victims are usually old men, women, and children, and Negroes whom they rob and maltreat without mercy, firing dwellings and outhouses even when filled with grain that the army needs, and sometimes endangering the trains by the universal firing of fences. These men are a disgrace to the name of soldier and the country. I desire to place upon record my detestation and abhorrence of their acts.[18]

The restrictive order on foraging curbed considerably the activities of the undisciplined, mounted "bummer." As late as March 28, however, Brigadier General John M. Oliver was disturbed over the large number of men in the Fifteenth Corps still possessing mounts. He reported to his superior:

15. *Ibid.*, XLVII, Pt. I, Ser. I, 424, 972.   16. Hatcher, *Four Weeks*, pp. 67-68.
17. *Ibid.*, p. 36.   18. *OR*, XLVII, Pt. I, Ser. I, 487.

I should respectfully call the attention of the general commanding to the fact that there are still a large number of mounted men from this corps; they are stripping the people of everything that can sustain life. I saw families of women, children, and Negroes who had absolutely nothing to eat, and their houses and quarters stripped of everything—cooking utensils, bedding, crockery, etc. Some rascals are beginning to set fire to the deserted houses of those who have fled to Goldsborough—also burning fences.[19]

Sherman's arrival had been announced by the columns of smoke which rose from burning farm houses on the south side of the Neuse.[20] Elizabeth Collier, an eighteen-year-old girl of Everettsville, entered in her diary:

On Monday morning, the 20th, the first foraging party made their appearance at Everettsville. We were of course all very much alarmed. They asked for flour and seeing that we were disposed not to give it, made a rush in the house and took it himself—the cowardly creature even pointed his gun at us—helpless women. Looking out, we soon found that poor little Everettsville was filled with Yankees and that they were plundering the houses. After a while we succeeded in getting a "safe guard" and for a week we got along comparatively well. But in the meantime everything outdoors was destroyed—all provisions taken—fences knocked down—horses, cows, carriages, and buggies stolen, and everything else the witches could lay their hands on—even to the servants clothes.[21]

The small town of Pikeville to the north of Goldsboro fared much the same as Everettsville at the hands of the Federal foragers. The tavern and inn were both destroyed and much damage was done to the property of Sarah Pike, widow of the Nathan Pike for whom the town was named, as well as to the property of others.[22]

Around Faison, where General Terry had his camp, Sherman's "bummers" managed to make an unwelcome appearance. In general, though, Terry kept good order in the vicinity. His troops were well behaved and he himself mingled freely with the local people. His considerations went so far as to have one of the Federal bands play "Dixie" at an afternoon concert.[23]

In the face of the outrageous conduct of the "bummers," a few rural souls managed to retain a sense of humor. At "Ravenswood," a planta-

19. *Ibid.*, XLVII, Pt. III, Ser. I, 46.   20. Spencer, *Ninety Days*, p. 94.
21. Collier Diary, Apr. 20, 1865, SHC, U.N.C.
22. *Goldsboro News-Argus*, Oct. 4, 1947.
23. *Raleigh News and Observer*, Mar. 11, 1923.

tion south of Goldsboro, the lady of the house burst into laughter when a soldier appeared dressed in her nephew's best suit of clothes. The resemblance between the rightful owner and wearer of the suit was so striking it was amusing to her.[24]

Within Goldsboro itself the "bummers" had little chance to pillage and destroy, as they had done in the surrounding countryside, because Schofield had occupied the town two days before they arrived and had guards stationed to prevent outrages.[25] The Federal officers did take forcible occupancy of the town's best homes, and the Wayne Female College was turned into a hospital.[26] But beyond the loss of fences and outhouses, torn down for fire wood and depredations on poultry yards and smoke houses, this Wayne County town suffered little at the hands of the occupying forces.[27]

In return the local inhabitants were generally "pleasant" to the Federal soldiers. Sergeant Theodore Upson found "them very poor as a general thing but very kind and hospitable with none of the treachery found in other places."[28] Still, the people of Goldsboro, according to H. M. Dewey of that town, were of the unanimous voice that the number of gentlemen in Sherman's army was exceedingly small.[29]

With no supplies awaiting them at Goldsboro, the first few days in camp were "far from days of feasting" for Sherman's weary troops. For many of them it was not until March 27 that a full commissary ration was issued, but in this ration were two luxuries—pickles and soap. The latter was much needed by the men to rid themselves of the "tenants that had lodgings inside their flannels." Brooks with plenty of water were in great demand.[30]

The absence of regular government rations had in no way affected the health of these men. The Georgia and Carolinas campaigns are the war's best examples of the virtues of living off the land. The effective work of the foragers had provided the army with a balanced diet of vegetables and meat.[31] The average percentage of sick for this army of 65,000 was only a little over 2 per cent, much less than the average for

24. R. P. Howell Memoirs (1854-1872), MS, SHC, U.N.C.
25. Spencer, *Ninety Days,* p. 94.   26. *Goldsboro News-Argus,* Oct. 4, 1947.
27. *Raleigh Conservative,* Mar. 27, 1865.   28. Winther, *Upson Diary,* p. 162.
29. H. M. Dewey to Cornelia P. Spencer, Mar. 5, 1865, D. L. Swain Papers, SHC, U.N.C.
30. Bryant, *3 Wis.,* p. 327; Underwood, *33 Mass.,* p. 286.
31. Adams, *Doctors in Blue,* pp. 211-12.

men in garrison.[32] Sherman maintained he did not hear a sneeze or cough for three months.[33]

As soon as supplies started rolling into Goldsboro, the different camps took on a regular routine of military life. Orders were out for all men to wash their hands and faces every day, comb and brush their beards, and keep their hair cut short.[34] In the mild spring weather daily drills were held. There were dress parades and inspections.[35] Chaplains once again held regular church services.[36] The different camps, for the most part located in the abundant pine forests of the region, were "sanitary and comfortable." All rubbish was hauled off and the areas were swept regularly with pine boughs. A hospital steward of the Fifty-seventh Illinois wrote home that his camp was "as neat as a parlor."[37] The men built tables and shelves and other minor conveniences for their tents to add to the comforts of camp life.[38]

Morale was high among both the officers and men, and the arrival of the first mail in two months helped keep spirits on a high level.[39] In two days alone 514 bags of mail arrived in New Bern for Sherman's army.[40] The General realized the importance of this mail as a morale factor. He remarked to an aide that commissary stores "were good for his boys' stomachs" but that mail "was good for the boys' minds as well as stomachs."[41]

During these days of rest the soldiers amused themselves in different ways. Passes were freely issued to those desiring a visit with buddies in other commands. But a general scarcity of money and the size of Goldsboro put a serious cramp in any plans for revelry. From General Sherman down to the lowest private all were "dead broke." No paymaster had awaited the army at Goldsboro and none was expected.[42] Things were so tight for Sherman that he wired Halleck for $40.00. Many of

32. *MR*, I, 322. At Goldsboro the majority of the sick were kept under canvas in the open country. The others were placed in private homes in the town. *Ibid.*, p. 322.
33. Howe, *Home Letters of Sherman*, p. 339.
34. *OR*, XLVII, Pt. III, Ser. I, 10.
35. Bircher, *Drummer-boy's Diary*, p. 176.
36. Smith, *Christian Commission*, p. 391.
37. J. M. Stetson to mother, Apr. 2, 1865, Stetson Papers, MS Div. Duke Univ. Lib.; Boyle, *111 Penn.*, p. 294.
38. Underwood, *33 Mass.*, p. 286; Quint. *2 Mass.*, p. 275.
39. Gage. *12 Ind.*, p. 299.
40. *N.Y. Herald*, Apr. 1, 1865.
41. *Ibid.*, Mar. 31, 1865.
42. Wright, *6 Ia.*, pp. 441, 444; C. S. Brown to "his folks and anyone else," n.d., Brown Papers, MS Div., Duke Univ. Lib.

the soldiers, in an effort to alleviate their financial straits, went into Goldsboro loaded down with tobacco, cigars, stationery, and canned milk. From every street corner and crossing they vigorously peddled their merchandise as though their livelihood depended upon the success of a sale.[43]

Goldsboro was entirely too small to hold much interest for the Federal soldiers. A trooper of the One Hundred and Third Illinois wrote in his diary that the "town don't amount to anything."[44] Lieutenant Charles Brown called it "a little 7 x 9 sort of a hole about as large as Bentonville was once. . . ." In the Lieutenant's opinion Fayetteville was a "gal durned" handsome town which completely knocked "the socks all off from it [Goldsboro]."[45]

Not all of the men were disturbed over the absence of a paymaster and the shortcomings of Goldsboro. Many could be found in attendance at religious services while others contented themselves around camp "luxuriating in the delicious spring weather," as one New Jersey soldier put it.[46] At the Rouse plantation the men of the Hundredth Indiana passed time by shooting alligators in the plantation mill pond.[47]

"All Fool's Day" was observed in the camp of the Fifty-fifth Illinois and every man who did not stay close to his quarters was sooner or later the butt of some ridiculous joke. Officers and men alike entered into the frolic. All discipline was abandoned on this occasion. The postmaster pulled the biggest prank of the day when he prepared a number of "blank" letters and then shouted mail call. The soldiers, momentarily forgetting the day, rushed forward. Back in their quarters they opened the letters only to learn of their deception.[48]

Chaplain Hight thought that quite a moral reformation took hold of the army at Goldsboro. He was encouraged over the large number of men converted to the different religious faiths,[49] but out of an army of over eighty thousand men many remained untouched by this spiritual revival. More than one soldier got into serious trouble. One of the new recruits who joined Sherman at Goldsboro was executed for the murder of an old man.[50] A New York cavalryman died before a firing squad for the crime of rape. On this occasion the condemned man's division had

43. Hatcher, Four Weeks, p. 158.   44. Orendorff, 103 Ill., p. 203.
45. Brown to "his folks and anyone else," n.d., Brown Papers, MS Div., Duke Univ. Lib.
46. Drake, 9 N.J., p. 364.   47. Winther, Upson Diary, pp. 161-62.
48. Crooker, 55 Ill., p. 429.   49. Stormont, Hight Diary, p. 512.
50. Hamilton, Recollections, pp. 200-1.

to watch the gruesome details of the excution. As the band played the "Dead March," the prisoner was led to his station in front of a freshly dug grave. Immediately to the rear was his pine coffin—after the execution the division was required to march past the grave.[51]

By March 25, repairs on the railroad from New Bern were finished, and the first train from the coast arrived in Goldsboro.[52] This completed the task Sherman set out to do upon leaving Savannah. His army was united at Goldsboro with those of Schofield and Terry. Large supply bases on the North Carolina coast were available by rail, and the countryside from Savannah to Goldsboro, for an average breadth of forty miles, had been laid waste. Writing in December, 1865, Sherman had this to say about his Carolinas campaign: ". . . no one ever has and may not agree with me as to the very great importance of the march north from Savannah. The march to the sea seems to have captivated everybody, whereas it was child's play compared with the other."[53]

The General now decided it was time to discuss with Grant the plans for a junction of their armies around Richmond. Sherman was a national hero as a result of his successful and self-devised campaigns in Georgia and the Carolinas and as yet the climactic battle of the war had not been fought. Sherman still hoped to share with Grant the glory of capturing Richmond. All the while his army was pushing through the Carolina swamps, Sherman had his eyes focused on the capital of the Confederacy where Grant and Lee were stalemated. He was almost obsessed with the idea of being present at Lee's surrender, but now he was acutely aware that Grant no longer needed his help in dealing with the depleted Confederate forces. So the primary purpose of a talk with the Commanding General was that of persuading him not to make a move until the armies at Goldsboro could cooperate.[54] This intense desire on Sherman's part to march into Virginia was also the general sentiment of the army, as shown by the soldier who one day called out to Sherman, "Uncle Billy, I guess Grant's waiting for us in Richmond."[55]

Late in the day of March 25, Sherman boarded a train for City Point, Virginia, Grant's headquarters. General Schofield was to be in command of the army during his absence.[56] In a jesting mood before departure, Sherman told friends that he planned to see Grant in order to

51. Bircher, *Drummer-Boy's Diary*, pp. 176-80.
52. *OR*, XLVII, Pt. I, Ser. I, 28.
53. Thorndike, *Sherman Letters*, p. 260.
54. Grant, *Memoirs*, II, 430.
55. Oakey, "Marching," p. 671.
56. *OR*, XLVII, Pt. I, Ser. I, 28.

"stir him up" for he had been behind fortifications so long "that he had got fossilized."[57]

Sherman reached New Bern during the evening. His arrival having been expected by the military officials of the town, a band was ready to serenade him as he ate supper at the Gaston House. A *New York Herald* reporter stated that as Sherman walked down the streets, the "soldiers rushed around him as though they were going to tear him to pieces and all the while calling on him for a speech." The General obliged them with a few remarks: "I'm going up to see Grant for five minutes and have it all chalked out for me and then come back and pitch in. I only want to see him for five minutes and won't be gone but two or three days."[58] Early the next morning Sherman continued on to Morehead City where he boarded the steamer, *Russia,* which landed him at City Point on the afternoon of March 27.

Sherman found General Grant, with his family and staff, occupying an attractive group of cottages on the banks of the James River. After a visit of an hour or so, Grant remarked to Sherman that President Lincoln was then on board the steamer, *River Queen,* tied up at the wharf, and suggested that they call upon him. Late in the afternoon of March 27, Sherman had his first of two talks with Lincoln. The other occurred around noon on the 28th, and both were held on board the *River Queen.* At one of these conferences Vice-Admiral David D. Porter was also present.[59]

Sherman and Lincoln dominated the conversation on both occasions, discussing steps necessary to terminate the war. The President feared most of all that Lee would escape Richmond, join Johnston and move south. After General Grant and Sherman put his mind at ease on this point, the conversation seems to have turned to a discussion of peace terms.[60] Lincoln intimated that he would be pleased if Jefferson Davis escaped the country. He added that he contemplated no revenge and no harsh measures for the South. President Lincoln left with Sherman the general impression that his primary concern was to reunite the country as quickly as possible and with as little hardship as possible.[61] At no time during either meeting, however, did Lincoln "name any special

57. Gray, *Gray and Ropes Letters,* p. 465.
58. *N.Y. Herald,* Mar. 31, 1865.
59. Sherman, *Memoirs,* II, 324-28.
60. Porter, *Incidents,* p. 313.
61. Sherman, *Memoirs,* II, 326-27.

terms of surrender" or issue any definite instructions for Sherman to follow in negotiating a peace.[62]

While not in conference with the President, Sherman was unleashing his forceful personality on Grant, imploring him to delay any major move against Lee until "he [Sherman] could come up and make a sure thing of it."[63] Grant had already issued orders for such a movement to commence on March 29, at least two weeks prior to Sherman's planned departure from Goldsboro.[64] Much to Sherman's dismay his superior was not disposed to change his plans. For two and a half months, while Sherman's army was wasted as a fighting force in the Carolina swamps, Grant had spent many anxious moments before Petersburg. He had felt that Lee at any moment would attempt an escape, and he would have the horror of awaking from his slumbers to learn that the Confederates had gone.[65] Now the Army of the Potomac was ready to commence a spring campaign against Lee to end this nightmare, and Sherman's Westerners were not needed for the job. Thus a two week's delay was out of the question. Grant had another reason for not desiring Sherman's assistance. He was very anxious to have the Eastern armies vanquish their old enemies who had so long and so gallantly repelled all attempts to subdue or drive them from their capital. He told Lincoln:

If the Western armies should be even upon the field, operating against Richmond and Lee, the credit would be given to them for the capture, by politicians and non-combatants from the section of country which those troops hailed from. It might lead to disagreeable bickerings between members of Congress of the East and those of the West in some of their debates. Western members might be throwing it up to the members of the East that in the suppression of the rebellion they were not able to capture an army, or to accomplish much in the way of contributing toward that end, but had to wait until the Western armies had conquered all the territory south and west of them, and then come on to help them capture the only army they had been engaged with.[66]

62. Sherman, "Surrender of Johnston," *Hist. Mag.*, XV, 333-34. General Schofield was of the opinion that at City Point Sherman's mind was so occupied with the matter of taking part in the capture of Lee's army that terms of surrender could have been only casually mentioned, if at all. Schofield, *Forty-six Years*, p. 348. Admiral Porter, on the other hand, in his account of the meeting between Sherman and Lincoln stated that the President outlined for the General the terms to offer Johnston when he should surrender. Sherman, *Memoirs*, II, 328-31. Porter's narrative is unreliable. It is "vague, rambling, and at times approaching incoherence." Naroll, "Peace-Fiasco," *JSH*, XX, 472-75.

63. Grant, *Memoirs*, II, 430.   64. *Ibid.*, p. 434.
65. *Ibid.*, p. 424.   66. *Ibid.*, p. 460.

At City Point Sherman also approached Grant on the matter of having Lieutenant General Phillip Sheridan's cavalry join him in the Carolinas. At Grant's request Sheridan called on Sherman, but he was loath to do so, fearing that "Sherman's zeal and power of emphasis" might persuade the Commanding General to order him south. The strong-willed Irishman was violently opposed to operating with the western armies against Johnston and then returning to Richmond with them, thus giving rise to the charge that the Army of the Potomac was not equal to the "task of defeating Lee." Again Sherman was rebuffed. His efficacy had failed him. At his meeting with Sheridan, the cavalryman emphatically objected to any plan of marching into North Carolina. But Sherman was in earnest and early the next morning he roused Sheridan out of bed with the same proposition, only to learn that a night's rest had done nothing to alter the Irishman's ideas.[67]

Grant ordered Sheridan to move south only in case the operations against Lee, commencing on March 29, were a failure. In private, he assured his cavalry commander that he fully intended to close the war with this move, and the cavalryman would have to go no farther.[68]

Before leaving City Point Sherman arranged with Grant for certain changes in the organization of his army and the date and destination of his next move. The date agreed upon was April 10, and the destination was still the Army of the Potomac around Richmond, but Sherman's sole chance of joining the fight in Virginia hinged on the improbability that Grant's move against Lee would fail. By March 30, Sherman was in Goldsboro, busily addressing himself to the task of the reorganization of his army and the replenishment of stores.

The reorganization of the fighting force was necessary for its better administration. The changes amounted to constituting the left wing a distinct army, carrying the title of the Army of Georgia, under the command of General Slocum. His two corps were commanded by Generals Davis and Mower. The center already constituted the Army of Ohio under Schofield. This included the Twenty-third Corps under General Cox and the divisions under General Terry which were permanently organized as the Tenth Corps. The right wing retained the organization it had as the Army of Tennessee.[69] With this reorganization the commanders of the three wings had the power to relieve Sherman

67. Sheridan, *Memoirs*, II, 127-33.   68. Grant, *Memoirs*, II, 437-38.
69. *OR*, XLVII, Pt. I, Ser. I, 46-50.

of many of the details of administering the entire army.[70] The only change in corps commanders was the assignment of General Mower, whom Sherman considered "one of the boldest and best fighting generals in the entire army," to the Twentieth Corps to replace General Williams.[71]

The effective strength of Sherman's army on April 10 was 88,948 men. Of this total 80,968 were in the infantry, 2,443 in the artillery, and 5,537 in the cavalry.[72] Among this number were a large number of new recruits who had been induced to sign up because of the high bounty being offered and the belief that the war was almost over.[73]

By the time of Sherman's return from City Point both railroads from the coast had been repaired and stores were arriving regularly from Morehead City and Wilmington. The problem of supplying almost ninety thousand soldiers with food, clothing, and war materials was no easy matter, and it contained many headaches for the supply officers. The Railroad Department made a mistake in sending locomotives and cars of the five-foot gauge which were useless on the four-foot, eight-and-a-half-inch gauge track in use on these roads. Thus the rolling stock at Colonel Wright's disposal was very limited.[74] The country, though, was so level that a single locomotive could pull twenty-five and thirty cars to a train, instead of only ten as was the case in Tennessee and upper Georgia.[75] To facilitate the matters of supply, Kinston was made a secondary base. Steamboats carried stores from Beaufort, Morehead City, and New Bern to Kinston; and from there, army trains hauled the supplies to Goldsboro. On several occasions these supplies moving up the Neuse did not reach their destination. Colonel J. N. Whitford of the Sixty-seventh North Carolina infantry reported that on April 5, detachments of his command burned the steamer, *Mystic,* near Maple Cypress and destroyed a transport loaded with commissary stores near Cowpen Landing. Two days later four privates of Whitford's regiment— George Hill, Turner May, William Salter, and R. Brewer—captured and destroyed the side-wheel steamer, *Minquas,* and two barges loaded with quartermasters and commissary stores. The captain and crew of the steamer escaped capture by jumping overboard and swimming ashore.[76]

By April 5, Sherman considered that sufficient progress had been made

70. Sherman, *Memoirs*, II, 333.
71. *Ibid.*, p. 332.
72. *Ibid.*, p. 334.
73. Hamilton, *Recollections*. pp. 200-1.
74. OR, XLVII, Pt. I, Ser. I, 29.
75. Sherman, *Memoirs*, II, 341.
76. OR, XLVII, Pt. I, Ser. I, 1134; *N.Y. Herald*, Apr. 13, 1865.

in supplying the army to issue Special Field Orders No. 48 prescribing the time and manner of the next march. The order reads:

The next grand objective is to place this army (with its full equipment) north of Roanoke River, facing west, with a base for supplies at Norfolk, and at Winton or Murfreesboro on the Chowan, and in full communication with the Army of the Potomac, about Petersburg; and also to do the enemy as much harm as possible en route. . . . Foraging and other details may continue as heretofore, only more caution and prudence should be observed; and foragers should not go in advance of the advance guard.[77]

But the plan was suddenly changed by the news of the fall of Richmond and Petersburg which reached Sherman at Goldsboro on April 6. The General fully realized that his opportunity to strike the Army of Northern Virginia was fast vanishing, but the possibility remained that Lee, with at least a fraction of his troops, would make junction with Johnston somewhere to the southwest. Thus Sherman changed Special Field Orders No. 48 and prepared to move directly on Raleigh as soon as he was ready. From a military standpoint the momentous events around Richmond justified immediate action by Sherman. He certainly had enough supplies at Goldsboro by this time to move. Yet he had no idea of putting his army in motion before April 10. One possible explanation for this delay rests on the fact that the date for the resumption of the march had been set for some time, and Sherman simply did not wish to change it. He had too long been acting on his own.[78] All the while details of Federal victories in Virginia came thick and fast, and on April 8, Sherman received a wire from Grant stating that the Confederate armies were the only strategic points at which to strike.[79] Sherman answered immediately that at daybreak on April 10 his army would move straight on Johnston, who was thought to be somewhere between Goldsboro and Raleigh, and that he would follow him wherever he retreated. Sherman, still hoping for that final crack at Lee, added in this wire to Grant that he thought it would be wise "to let Lee and Johnston come together, just as a billiard player would nurse the balls when he has them in a nice place."[80]

The news that Richmond had fallen was greeted in the different camps with ear splitting shouts and cheers. The soldiers forgot their disappointment at having no part in the victory. All day celebrations were in

77. Sherman, *Memoirs*, II, 341-42.
79. *OR*, XLVII, Pt. III, Ser. I, 100.
78. Burne, *Lee, Grant and Sherman*, p. 179.
80. *Ibid.*, p. 129.

order. Bands struck up tunes, hidden bottles were broken out, and canteens filled with powder were fired as salutes. There was no sleep in Goldsboro or neighboring territory that night.[81] Sergeant Rufus Meade could not "began to describe" the scene: "Such cheering, shouting, gun-firing, band playing, etc., I never heard before. Everybody was wild most."[82]

Orders of march for April 10 put General Slocum's left wing, supported by the Twenty-third Corps, on the two direct roads for Smithfield. The right wing was to make a circuit to the right by Pikeville and Whitley's Mill, with a division swinging round by Nahunta and Beulah. General Terry's and General Kilpatrick's troops were to move from their positions on the south side of the Neuse in the same general direction, by Cox's Bridge.[83] A small force was to be left at Goldsboro for garrison duty, and Schofield was ordered to detail a certain number of troops as railroad guards to protect the roads back to the coast.[84]

After the battle of Bentonville Johnston was uncertain whether Sherman's march to Virginia would be through Raleigh or by the more direct route through Weldon; consequently he located his army in and around Smithfield. From this small town northwest of Goldsboro, Johnston was in a position to place his army in front of Sherman on either one of the roads he chose to follow. Also, by doing this, Johnston made possible a junction with the Army of Northern Virginia should Lee abandon his intrenchments around Richmond in order to fall upon Sherman with the combined Confederate forces. The cavalry, at the same time, was placed in close observation of Sherman's army. Wheeler's division was encamped to the north and Butler's to the west of the Federal camps around Goldsboro.[85]

Johnston learned from Federal prisoners that Sherman planned to remain in his present camp for some time, to rest his troops and get supplies. This pause afforded him by Sherman proved very beneficial to Johnston. Besides providing an opportunity for the Quartermaster and Commissary corps to bring up supplies, it enabled several thousand troops

81. Stormont, *Hight Diary*, p. 507; Hatcher, *Four Weeks*, pp. 198-99; Capron, "Capron Diary," *Jour. of Ill. St. Hist. Soc.*, XII, 401.

82. Padgett, "Letters of a Federal Soldier," p. 75.

83. *OR*, XLVII, Pt. III, Ser. I, 123.

84. *Ibid.*, p. 129. The troops left in Goldsboro for garrison duty were of the Tenth Corps. *Ibid.*, p. 200.

85. Johnston, *Narrative*, p. 394. The Confederate cavalry had several skirmishes with Federal patrols operating from Sherman's bases in and around Goldsboro.

of the Army of Tennessee who were coming up from Georgia in independent detachments to rejoin their corps. Most of them had been united into one body at Augusta by Lieutenant General S. D. Lee and led to Smithfield. Upon arrival a great majority of them had no arms and by April 10, more than thirteen hundred were still without arms.[86] During this period of inaction Johnston had Lieutenant General T. H. Holmes confer with Lee on the subject of joining forces against Sherman.[87]

Johnston was also given time to reorganize his hodge-podge forces.[88] After the reorganization was completed a big review was held. Governor Vance of North Carolina and several ladies from Raleigh came out to view the troops who "once more . . . began to look like soldiers." Hoke's division of North Carolinians naturally received the loudest cheers from the women. Morale was high among the men.[89] Horse races were held every day in a field outside Smithfield. No thoroughbreds ran, but a considerable amount of Confederate money changed hands after every race.[90]

On April 5, rumors began to circulate around the Confederate camps that Richmond had fallen and with this disheartening news, spirits began to wane. "Heavens the gloom and how terrible our feelings" wrote a number of General Stewart's staff.[91] Desertions increased by leaps and bounds. General McLaws had to keep out two patrols every day arresting men absent from camp. In an effort to keep the soldiers close at hand as many as five divisional roll calls were held per day.[92]

Discouraging as the picture was, young Walter Clark of the North Carolina Junior Brigade could write his mother: "While I am able for service I intend to stand by the cause while a banner floats to tell where Freedom and freedom's sons still support her cause." His was the voice of that group willing to fight to the bitter end.[93]

Between April 5 and 9, Johnston received several dispatches on Lee's activities in Virginia, but for some unknown reason was not officially

86. Johnston, *Narrative*, pp. 394-95; *OR*, XLVII, Pt. III, Ser. I, 770.
87. Johnston, *Narrative*, p. 395.
88. *OR*, XLVII, Pt. I, Ser. I, 1061.
89. Ridley, *Battles*, p. 456; Thomas, "Last Battle," *So. Hist. Soc. Papers*, XXIX, 215-22. A young soldier of the Army of Tennessee thought the review "the saddest spectacle of his life." Ridley, *Battles*, p. 456.
90. Dickert, *Kershaws Brigade*, 1865, SHC, U.N.C., p. 526.
91. Ridley, *Battles*, p. 456.
92. McLaws Order Bk., 1865, SHC, U.N.C., p. 35.
93. Brooks and Lefler, *Clark Papers*, II, 139-40.

notified of Richmond's fall. He states: "There was nothing . . . to suggest the idea that General Lee had been 'driven' from the position held many months with so much skill and resolution." The last dispatch, one from the Secretary of War dated April 9, indicated, however, that Lee was encountering difficulties in attempting to move southward.[94]

Johnston, badly misinformed or uninformed, on the fighting in Virginia, did receive good intelligence on Sherman's activities. On April 9, General Hampton informed him that the country people living near the Federal camps reported the soldiers expected to move on Raleigh the next day. This report enabled Johnston to put his army in readiness to move at the first sign of Federal activity.

94. Johnston, *Narrative*, pp. 395-96; *OR*, XLVII, Pt. III, Ser. I, 755, 767.

CHAPTER XIII

Two Old Men and a White Flag

IN ACCORDANCE with General Sherman's orders the Federal troops broke camp early in the morning of April 10 and started their march on Raleigh. This movement was reported to Johnston who immediately put his army in motion for the same city. Hardee's corps, with Butler's cavalry as a rear guard, moved on the Raleigh road. Stewart's and Lee's corps, with Wheeler's cavalry in the rear, moved on the road which crossed the Neuse at Battle's Bridge.[1]

Federal progress on this date was slow. Most roads needed considerable corduroy and the Confederate cavalry in some areas put up "determined resistence."[2]

The heaviest fighting of the day fell on the First Division of the Twentieth Corps, which was the advance for General Mower's column. About a mile east of Moccasin Swamp on the "northerly road toward Smithfield" the First Division scouts encountered a strong Confederate force consisting of troops of the First South Carolina cavalry and possibly the Sixth North Carolina. General J. L. Selfridge, commanding the First Brigade of the First Division, immediately deployed the One Hundred and Twenty-third New York Regiment, Colonel James C. Rogers commanding, on the right of the road as skirmishers and supported it with the remainder of the brigade. Colonel Rogers advanced his command and slowly pushed the Confederates back. The latter, contesting every inch of the ground, showed a determination to hold Rogers at bay and prevent his gaining a position from which the Federal artillery could be made effective. After advancing approximately a mile, Rogers' troops reached Moccasin Creek. Behind the creek was a broad swamp which was almost impassable because of the depth of the water

1. Johnston, *Narrative*, p. 396.
2. *OR*, XLVII, Pt. I, Ser. I, 249.

and thick underbrush.[3] Also the bridges over the two unfordable channels into which the creek divided itself had been partially destroyed. The regiment was, nevertheless, ordered to cross the first channel upon the stringers of the bridge yet remaining and advance far enough to hold it while repairs were made.

Under heavy fire the One Hundred and Twenty-third crossed the channel on the stringers and, proceeding in waist-deep water, gained a position commanding the second bridge. When the first of the bridges had been repaired and the rest of the brigade had crossed, the New Yorkers gained the second. They withstood heavy fire until it too was in condition for the entire brigade to make a crossing. Once over the second channel, General Selfridge moved his command forward about a mile and a half, before General A. S. Williams, commanding the division, stopped the advance.

While the First Brigade skirmishers were advancing in the swamp, the One Hundred and Forty-third New York, General J. S. Robinson's brigade, had been sent a mile or so up the creek to attempt a crossing at a mill. This move was unnecessary for the Confederate forces at the mill retired before the regiment reached there.[4]

The Third Division of the Fourteenth Corps was the first unit of Sherman's army to enter Smithfield. The division had moved out of its camp on Moccasin Creek at 5:00 A.M. on April 11. After skirmishing with the Confederate cavalry all morning, it entered the town at noon.[5] Behind barricades in the streets of Smithfield the Confederates continued to fight stubbornly, but during the afternoon they were forced to retreat across the Neuse,[6] burning the bridge over the river at this point. This stopped the advance of the Fourteenth Corps for the day.[7]

The Twentieth Corps reached Smithfield at 2:00 P.M., its advance unit, the Thirty-third New Jersey, having met cavalry opposition at almost every swamp, bridge, and creek.[8] With the Thirty-third were two pieces of artillery[9] and a battalion of First Michigan engineers. The artillery was not used during the day, but the engineers performed one almost unbelievable feat. General Geary reported that at Borden's Creek

---

3. A short distance up the creek the Confederates had cut a dam. This added much to the depth of the water in the swamp. *Ibid.*, p. 627.
4. *Ibid.*, pp. 603, 614, 626-27.   5. *Ibid.*, p. 116.
6. Nichols, *Great March*, p. 291; Underwood, *33 Mass.*, p. 289.
7. *OR*, XLVII, Pt. I, Ser. I, 30.   8. *Ibid.*, p. 736.
9. *Ibid.*, p. 855.

the sixty-five-foot bridge had been destroyed but that two companies of his pioneers rebuilt it in seventeen minutes.[10]

A few Confederate prisoners were taken in the fighting around Smithfield. One of them, upon being asked by General Slocum what kind of man Hampton was, replied: "A sort of dandy gentleman, one of those fellows from West Point."[11] This hit General Slocum as a joke, he being one of that stripe himself. The General informed his prisoner that "some of the West Pointers did not know enough to straddle a horse."[12]

Federal troops burned little in the town of Smithfield other than the wooden stocks near the jail which a member of General Sherman's staff called "that comfortable institution for the improvement of criminals."[13] Escaping the torch but thoroughly rifled were the Masonic Lodge, Odd Fellow Hall, churches, and courthouse. At the courthouse the contents of all shelves were dumped on the floor and soon the archives of Johnston County lay "in confusion amongst the dirt."[14]

Major Nichols still looking for the supposedly strong Union sentiment in North Carolina referred to the inhabitants of Smithfield as intelligent and professing a sort of halfway Unionism in that they wanted the war to cease. He thought he found a few citizens who were "undemonstrative Union Men." As for the ladies, he said they were about equally divided in their sentiment, but all were anxious for the return of peace. He pointed out that when a woman had a lover or near relative in the Confederate army her sympathy was naturally with the Confederate cause.[15]

Near Pikeville on April 11, a very minor skirmish took place which certainly has little, if any, military significance but is interesting because of the two reports turned in to General Logan by S. C. Rogers, medical officer of the Thirtieth Iowa. Rogers was in charge of a party of twenty-three hospital attendants and convalescents who were on their way from Goldsboro to rejoin their commands in the Fifteenth Corps. This party was attacked by a force of "bushwhackers," as Rogers called them. Since only nine of the Federals were armed, they all fled into the woods. Four days later, having seen only one of the twenty-three, Rogers reported to Logan: "I have been informed by a soldier who was in the vicinity at the time of the attack (which was about 4:00 P.M.) that just before dark he

10. *Ibid.*, p. 700; Boyle, *111 Penn.*, p. 296.
11. General Hampton had never attended West Point and had no previous military training before he became a cavalry leader.
12. Eaton, "Diary of an Officer," p. 251.   13. Howe, *Marching With Sherman*, p. 296.
14. Stormont, *Hight Diary*, p. 514.   15. Nichols, *Great March*, p. 292.

heard a volley of fifteen or twenty guns. I fear they have all been shot."
Of course, this report brought about an investigation which ended on
April 25, with Rogers' letter to Logan informing him that since his last
report he had seen most of the men with him on the day of the attack and
that all had escaped except four who were captured but who escaped the
first night.[16]

The Seventeenth Corps moved into camp at Pine Level on April 11.
From this place General Howard sent a dispatch to Sherman at Smithfield asking if his wishes in regard to the destruction of factories and
mills were the same as in previous campaigns. Sherman told him not to
destroy the Lowell Factory and added: "I will wait our reception at Raleigh to shape our general policy. You may instruct General Logan to
exact bonds that the factory shall not be used for the Confederacy. Of
course, the bond is not worth a cent, but if the factory owners do not
abide by the conditions they cannot expect any mercy the next time."[17]

From his headquarters at the home of one Whiteley, eight miles from
Smithfield, General Cox reported that the stragglers of the army had
become much worse than they were in the Atlanta campaign. Two of
the best residences along his line of march that day had been burned.
One was the home of one Atkinson where he had stopped at noon for
lunch. Hardly had the General finished his lunch before the torch was
applied to the house.[18]

General Terry moved his corps as far as Hannah's Creek on April 11.
There he received a message from Schofield stating that it was not necessary for him to press his march. Schofield did not want the Tenth Corps
near Smithfield before late the next afternoon because most of April 12,
he knew, would be taken up by Slocum's column in crossing the
Neuse.[19]

From one Moore's house near Middle Creek[20] Kilpatrick sent Sherman word that the Confederates had all retired on Raleigh and would
hardly make any stand east or south of it.[21] Upon receiving this report
Sherman ordered Kilpatrick to go as near Raleigh as possible. He wrote
his chief of cavalry: "I don't care about Raleigh now, but want to defeat

16. OR, XLVII, Pt. I, Ser. I, 269-70.
17. Ibid., XLVII, Pt. III, Ser. I, 165.
18. Ibid., XLVII, Pt. I, Ser. I, 936.
19. Ibid., p. 294; Ibid., XLVII, Pt. III, Ser. I, 174-75.
20. Sherman reprimanded Kilpatrick for giving his position as "Moore's on Middle
Creek," because no such place was shown on his map. Ibid., XLVII, Pt. III, Ser. I, 172.
21. Ibid., p. 171.

and destroy the Confederate army; therefore, you may run any risk. Of course, don't break the railroad except to the rear (west) of Johnston, as we want the rails up to Raleigh."[22] Sherman also told Schofield to go as far to the westward of Raleigh as he pleased towards Chapel Hill and Hillsboro.[23]

During the night General Sherman learned of Lee's surrender. At 5:00 A.M. he wired Grant: "I hardly know how to express my feelings, but you can imagine them. The terms you have given Lee are magnanimous and liberal. Should Johnston follow Lee's example I shall of course grant the same."[24] To his men Sherman announced: "Glory to God and to our Country, and all honor to our comrades in arms, toward whom we are marching. A little more labor, a little more toil on our part, the great race is won, and our Government stands regenerated after four long years of bloody war."[25] Horsemen took the news through drowsy camps, bellowing, "Lee's surrendered!" "Begod," cried an Irish private in the Eighty-fifth Illinois, "You're the man we have been lookin' for the last four years!"[26]

This news brought rampant joy to the Federal camps.[27] Bands played, guns were fired, and shouting voices filled the air. An officer of the Twenty-third Corps clapped his heels together and with a wild yell turned a complete somersault in the road.[28] Quite a celebration took place in the camp of the First Division of the Fifteenth Corps. Sergeant Theodore Upson entered in his diary:

We have recd. word that Lee and his Army have surrendered to General Grant. Our boys hardly believed it at first, but it is sure now as we have an order to that effect. Just as we were starting from Goldsboro I was ordered by Colonel Johnson to go to General Woods Hd Quarters and take charge of his Hd Quarter guards.

We had a great blow out at Hd Quarters last night. I was just fasting [posting] my guards when Gen Woods came out saying "Dismiss the guard, Sergeant, and come into my tent." I thought he was crazy or something, so asked for what reason. Said he, "Don't you know Lee has surrendered? No man shall stand guard at my Quarters tonight. Bring all the

22. *Ibid.*, p. 172.　　　　23. *Ibid.*, p. 173.
24. *Ibid.*, p. 177.　　　　25. *Ibid.*, p. 180.
26. Aten, *85 Ill.*, p. 303.

27. There were a few skeptics in the Federal army who would not believe the news at first. Orendorff, *103 Ill.*, p. 205.

28. Ricks, "Carrying the News," *Mil. Order of Loyal Legion, Ohio Commandery*, II 240.

guard here." I went and got all the guards and marched them up in front of the General's tent. By that time officers were coming from every direction. I paraded the guard. Gen. Woods said, "Have them stack arms and bring two of them into my tent."

He had a great big bowl setting on a camp table. Everybody was helping themselves out of it. The General handed me a tin cup. "Help yourself," said he. I dipped in, took a little drink, handed it to the other boys. Then a Darky came with a tin pail full of what I suppose was punch. We took it out to the rest of the guards who stood in line behind the stack of guns. Gen Woods came out, made a little speech telling us Richmond was ours, that Lee and his Army had surrendered, that it was the end of the War and that we should celebrate as we had never done before. I think most of our boys did celebrate but I was pretty careful. I never had drank liquor, and I did not know what it would do to me.

After a while a Band came. They played once or twice, drank some, played some more, then drank some more of that never ending supply of punch, then they played again but did not keep very good time. Some of them could not wait till they got through with a tune till they had to pledge Grant and his gallant Army, also Lee and his grand fighters. Some of them seemed to think perhaps that was going a little too far but it passed. The Band finally got so they were trying to play two or three tunes at once. Officers from all the Regiments in our Brigade were there and some from others. Col. Johnson came over from our Regt after a while. He saw me, took me by the arm and brought me to Gen Woods, intorduced me by a flattering speech. General Woods shook my hand and said he would pro- mote me, that I could consider myself a Lieut. After a little more talk from Col Johnson he made me a Captain, and I might have got higher than that if the General had not noticed the Band was not playing. Going out to see about it, he found the members seated on the ground or anything else they could find, several on the big bass drum. Then he realized that they were tired, and he would relieve them. He got the big drum, other officers took the various horns and started on a tour through the camps—every fellow blowing his horn to suit himself and the jolly old General pounding the bass drum for all it was worth. Of course we all followed and some sang, or tried to sing, but when "Johnny Comes Marching Home Again" and "John Browns Body" or "Hail Columbia" and the "Star Spangled Banner" are all sung together they get mixed so I don't think the singing was a grand success from an artistic stand point at least. But it answered the purpose and let out a lot of pent up exuberant feeling that had to have an outlet. Away along in the wee small hours the parade broke up and a day or two later the General addressed me as Sergeant same as ever. But one thing is sure: Lee has surrendered and Richmon[d] is ours.[29]

In the Confederate camps the news of Lee's surrender was at first met with skepticism.[30] The parolees from the Army of Northern Virginia who brought this news were called liars and deserters.[31] Some were put under guard until their stories could be verified.[32] General Hampton called the surrender news "a rumor he did not believe," and announced he would lead the corps westward across the Mississippi.[33] To the boys in Johnston's army, such as Lieutenant Bromfield Ridley, the rumors of Lee's surrender meant little. An entry in Ridley's journal shows what occupied his thoughts at the time: "Camped three miles west of Raleigh, on Hillsboro Road. . . . As we passed the female seminary in Raleigh the beautiful school girls greeted us warmly. Each one had a pitcher of water and goblet. We drank, took their addresses and had a big time."[34]

After the battle of Bentonville in answer to the question—What did he think Johnston would do next?—General Sherman gave the rather witty reply: "Johnston and I are not on speaking terms."[35] Had this same question been asked the General on the morning of April 12, he could have answered it without the wit and more directly because he regarded the war as over. He knew well General Johnston had no army with which to oppose his. Only two questions remained—would Johnston surrender at Raleigh,[36] or would he allow his army to disperse into guerrilla bands?[37] Sherman was aware that he could not hope to catch Johnston. The Confederate General, having the railroad to lighten his supply trains, could retreat faster than he could pursue. The rains had also set in, making the resort to corduroy absolutely necessary to pass even

---

29. Whitner, *Upson Diary*, pp. 164-66.

30. Henry, *Confederacy*, p. 467. Johnston received the news of Lee's surrender at 1:00 A.M. on April 11, while encamped at Battle's Bridge. He kept the news a secret. Johnston, *Narrative*, p. 396.

31. Wellman, *Giant in Gray*, p. 180.

32. Mullen, "Last Days," *So. Hist. Soc. Papers*, XVIII, 105.

33. Hough, "Last Days," *Stories of the Confed.*, p. 306.

34. Ridley, *Battles*, p. 457.

35. Howe, *Marching With Sherman*, p. 295.

36. Johnston planned neither to defend Raleigh nor to surrender his army there but to continue his retreat and to have words with President Jefferson Davis. R. H. Battle to Cornelia P. Spencer, Feb. 26, 1866, D. L. Swain Papers, SHC, U.N.C.; *OR*, XLVII, Pt. III, Ser. I, pp. 787-88. Sometimes during April 11, Johnston gave evidence that he was ready to end all bloodshed by suspending orders for the execution of condemned prisoners. *Ibid.*, p. 790.

37. Sherman, *Memoirs*, II, 344.

ambulances.[38] Thus the small Confederate force could escape, disperse, and assemble again at some place agreed upon and consequently might prolong the war indefinitely.

Sherman now had no option but "to push Joe Johnston to the death."[39] He issued orders for his corps commanders to leave their supply trains well to the rear and proceed rapidly, but with due caution, on Raleigh. Slocum's column he designated as the column of direction. It was to move directly on the capital city.[40]

On April 12, the soldiers in Sherman's army were in a hilarious mood, even as the march went forward. They sang, they shouted, and they fired muskets in the air. Chaplain J. J. Hight, who had been unsuccessful in his efforts to hold a church service in honor of Richmond's fall, gave up all thought of doing anything religious on this date.[41] Toward this army was coming a Confederate locomotive drawing one passenger car, inside of which were peace commissioners. From the cowcatcher of the engine waved a white flag.[42]

April 8, David Lowry Swain, ex-Governor of North Carolina and at the time President of the University at Chapel Hill, wrote W. A. Graham, also an ex-Governor, suggesting they meet with Governor Vance in Raleigh on Monday, April 10, and discuss "the state of public affairs."[43] Having only recently discussed this topic with Vance, Graham did not think it necessary, perhaps not advisable, to accompany Swain to Raleigh; but he suggested that Swain stop by his home at Hillsboro on the way to Raleigh to discuss the best mode of effecting their common purpose— peace.[44] Swain spent April 9 with Graham, and a course of action was agreed upon which the next day was presented to Governor Vance.

The university president suggested to the governor that he convene the legislature and have it pass resolutions expressing a desire to stop the war and invite the concurrence of the other states. This body should elect commissioners to treat with the United States government and report to a convention which would be called. If, in the meantime, Sherman advanced upon Raleigh, the governor should send a commission to him to ask for a suspension of hostilities until final action of the state could be

---

38. *OR*, XLVII, Pt. I, Ser. I, 30.   39. *Ibid.*, XLVII, Pt. III, Ser. I, 150.
40. *Ibid.*, pp. 163-64.   41. Stormont, *Hight Diary*, p. 510.
42. White cloth was an extremely scarce item at this time. It took much effort on the part of young Dallas T. Ward, conductor on this special train, to secure a piece one yard wide, out of which the truce flag was fashioned. Ward, *Flag of Truce*, p. 10.
43. Spencer, *Ninety Days*, p. 136.   44. *Ibid.*, p. 140.

ascertained.[45] Vance agreed to the latter part of this plan on the condition that General Johnston's approval be obtained; but before he put the plan into effect he wished to have another interview with Graham.

Vance consulted Johnston "as to what is best for me to do." Johnston frankly advised Vance to remain in Raleigh, to communicate with Sherman, and if the General would agree to treat him "with respect" to stay and do the best he could.[46]

The Governor wired Graham on April 11 to join him that night in Raleigh since the city "will not hold longer than tomorrow."[47] At three o'clock on the morning of April 12, Graham arrived in Raleigh, and after an early breakfast Vance, Swain, and Graham repaired to the Capitol, where the following letter to Sherman was composed over Vance's signature:

Understanding that your army is advancing on this capital, I have to request, under proper safe-conduct, a personal interview, at such time as may be agreeable to you, for the purpose of conferring upon the subject of a suspension of hostilities, with view to further communications with the authorities of the United States, touching the final termination of the existing War. If you concur in the propriety of such a proceeding I shall be obliged by an early reply.[48]

The Governor then appointed Graham and Swain commissioners to visit General Sherman and to deliver to him this letter.

In the meantime, Johnston, with Hardee's, Stewart's, and Lee's corps, had reached Raleigh. There Johnston received a telegram dated Greensboro, April 11, 4:30 P.M., in which President Davis directed him to leave the troops under General Hardee's command and to report to him.[49] Thus it was General Hardee who gave the necessary permit for the commissioners to proceed. Armed with this permit and the letter from Vance, the two commissioners boarded their special train at 10:30 A.M., April 12. They were accompanied by Dr. Edward Warren, Surgeon General of the

45. *Ibid.*, p. 142.

46. Z. B. Vance to Cornelia P. Spencer, Feb. 17, 1866, D. L. Swain Papers, SHC, U.N.C.; Dowd, *Vance*, p. 483.

47. Z. B. Vance to W. A. Graham, Apr. 11, 1865, typed copy in possession of J. G. DeR. Hamilton. SHC, U.N.C.

48. *OR*, XLVII, Pt. III, Ser. I, 178. Twenty-five years later Vance thought his letter not only requested an interview with Sherman but also asked that the city and state records be spared and added that Swain and Graham were authorized to treat with him on these matters. Dowd, *Vance*, p. 483.

49. *OR*, XLVII, Pt. III, Ser. I, 788; Johnston, *Narrative* p. 396.

State, Colonel James G. Burr, an officer of the State Guards, and Major John Devereaux of Vance's staff. On the streets of Raleigh army officers were heard to say that "such cowardly traitors ought to be hanged."[50] The two old men were not to be intimidated, however, and shortly after ten o'clock started their journey.

A short distance out of Raleigh the special train reached the Confederate lines, held by General Hampton. The commissioners asked to see the General and to him they showed Vance's letter to Sherman and Hardee's safe conduct permit. Hampton expressed doubts of the propriety or expediency of the mission they had undertaken, but he at once prepared and sent by courier a dispatch to Sherman, together with a note from Graham and Swain, asking the time and place a conference might be held.[51]

The train then moved slowly on, but it had gone hardly two miles when a courier from Hampton rode up, stopped the train, and informed the commissioners that General Hampton had just received a dispatch withdrawing the safe conduct Hardee had given them and ordered the party to return to Raleigh.[52] The commissioners directed the courier to tell Hampton such an order ought to be given by him in person or in writing. In a short while Hampton rode up to the train, which the commissioners had stopped until they should hear from him. He read a second dispatch he had sent Sherman, saying: "Since my dispatch of half an hour ago, circumstances have occurred which induce me to give you no further trouble in relation to the mission of ex-Governors Graham and Swain. These gentlemen will return with the flag of truce to Raleigh."[53] Hampton also read them a dispatch which he had sent Kilpatrick requesting the Federal cavalry leader to allow the train to return to Raleigh.[54]

Hampton left the commissioners and returned to his command only to learn that a portion of his troops, he being one of the number, had

50. Lewis, *Sherman*, p. 530.

51. J. Devereux to D. L. Swain, July 7, 1866, W. Clark Papers, MS Div., N.C. Dept. of Arch. and Hist.; D. L. Swain to Sherman, Apr. 12, 1865, typed copy in possession of J. G. DeR. Hamilton, SHC, U.N.C.; Spencer, *Ninety Days*, p. 147.

52. *OR*, XLVII, Pt. III, Ser. I, 791. It was Johnston's Adjutant General, Archer Anderson, who sent Hampton the wire to stop the commission. The initiative for this move was his own, not Johnston's.

53. Spencer, *Ninety Days*, p. 148. I have been unable to locate this dispatch in the *Official Records*. Major Devereux gives a slightly different account of this incident. J. Devereux to D. L. Swain, W. Clark Papers, MS Div., N.C. Dept. of Arch. and Hist.

54. *OR*, XLVII, Pt. III, Ser. I, 187.

been cut off from Raleigh by Kilpatrick's cavalry which had been pressing him hard all day. Hampton was unable to break out of the trap
until after dark. He proceeded to Raleigh during the night.[55]

The peace commissioners' train was able to move only a mile or two
in the direction of Raleigh before it was stopped by the Federal cavalry.[56]
The commissioners, after being ordered "to come out of that coach," were
informed that they must proceed to the headquarters of Kilpatrick, a mile
or so away.[57] But no sooner had the party alighted from the train than
the cavalrymen "piled down on them like wild Indians."[58] In short order
all but Dr. Warren were relieved of their valuables. The prudent
Surgeon escaped robbery by staying "very near" one of the Federal
officers.[59]

General Kilpatrick, his manner a "happy compound of braggart and
brute," told the commissioners that they should not have crossed his
skirmish line while a fight was in progress but "as . . . [they] had started
to see General Sherman, see him . . . [they] should. . . ." The party was
ordered first to a farm house a mile or two behind the skirmish line.
While walking to the rear, the delegation met several cavalry regiments
whose soldiers took great delight in subjecting them to jibes and jeers.
The special target or butt of these jests were ex-Governors Swain and
Graham dressed in their long tailed coats and beaver hats. For Colonel
Burr the experience "was irritating almost beyond endurance." Late in
the afternoon Kilpatrick sent his carriage after the commissioners. The
second visit to the General's headquarters this day proved to be a rather
pleasant experience for the group. Kilpatrick, no longer pressed by
Hampton, was in a jovial mood—so much so that he had his band play
"Dixie." He told the commissioners that they might proceed with their
trip as soon as the engine was fired.[60]

While the commissioners were conferring with Kilpatrick, young
Dallas T. Ward, conductor on the train, was having his troubles. He
relates:

55. *Ibid.,* p. 186; Committee, *92 Ill.,* pp. 235-38.
56. A Soldier of the Thirty-third Massachusetts remarked, that Kilpatrick captured
"a load of ex-governors." Underwood, *33 Mass.,* p. 290.
57. J. G. Burr to D. L. Swain, June 18, 1866, W. Clark Papers, MS Div., N.C. Dept. of
Arch. and Hist.
58. Ward, *Flag of Truce,* p. 12.   59. Warren, *Doctor's Experiences,* p. 335.
60. J. Devereux to D. L. Swain, July 7, 1866, W. Clark Papers, MS Div., N.C. Dept. of
Arch. and Hist.; J. G. Burr to D. L. Swain, June 18, 1866, *ibid.;* Warren, *Doctor's Experiences,* p. 339.

At first I resisted the insults thrust upon me. However, a loaded musket pointed in my face, with the threat to blow my brains out, brought me quickly into submission. They robbed me of twenty-two hundred dollars in Confederate money, also of watch and everything of value on the car. They then enjoyed making sport of me and calling me little Johnnie rebel. I wasn't even permitted to speak to my engineer, Mr. Faison. They took the throttle lever off, put the fire out in the engine and placed a strong guard over us.[61]

Ward, too, was taken before Kilpatrick for questioning. Kilpatrick, on this occasion, had left his headquarters and was in the woods directing the fighting. Ward said he answered the General's questions as courteously and briefly as possible, but with bullets whizzing through the pines he was not altogether comfortable. To him Kilpatrick seemed angry and greatly excited, cursing at his men to go do this and that.[62] The General's use of profanity was known even among the Confederate troops. Colonel J. F. Waring of the Jeff Davis Legion, entered in his diary: "It is 'By God' and 'God-damn' all the time" with Kilpatrick.[63]

When Ward returned to the train he found the commissioners there and the Federal soldiers rebuilding the fire in the engine. This was, of course, done at Kilpatrick's orders.[64]

With about thirty or forty soldiers on top of the coach, the train started out for Gulley's, Sherman's headquarters.[65] Along the way it passed through open columns of thousands of Federal troops who were wildly cheering the news of Lee's surrender and also the arrival of the peace commission which they supposed was authorizd to treat for the surrender of Johnston's army.

General Sherman, attended by his aides, met the commission at the station at Gulley's and conducted them to his tent. So it was that the old men arrived at their destination. Captured by Hampton, rescued by Kilpatrick, they stood before Sherman, as he observed, "dreadfully excited" by their experiences.[66]

The commissioners presented Vance's letter and were gratified to find

61. Ward, *Flag of Truce*, pp. 12-13.
62. *Ibid.*, p. 13.
63. Waring Diary, Apr. 13, 1865, SHC, U.N.C.
64. Ward, *Flag of Truce*, p. 13.
65. Gulley's is present day Clayton. Dr. Warren, in recalling his experiences on April 12, thought that Kilpatrick sent the party to Sherman's headquarters, not by the special train, but by a railroad hand car propelled by two Negroes. He is the only one of the group, however, that mentions the hand car. Warren, *Doctor's Experiences*, p. 339.
66. Sherman, *Memoirs*, II, 345.

Sherman ready to make "an amicable and generous arrangement with the State Government."[67] The General was desirous that Governor Vance and other state officials remain in Raleigh and keep the government functioning. In recognizing the existing state government, Sherman acted on his own initiative, and not upon specific instructions from Lincoln.[68] This action was in complete accord with Sherman's pledge to the people of the South, that once they forgot the war they could count on him as the staunchest of friends.

Sherman answered the governor's letter as follows:

I have the honor to acknowledge the receipt of your communication of this date, and inclose you a safeguard for yourself and any members of the State government that choose to remain in Raleigh. I would gladly have enabled you to meet me here, but some interruption occurred to the train by orders of General Johnston, after it had passed within the lines of my cavalry advance, but as it came out of Raleigh in good faith, it shall return in good faith, and will in no measure, be claimed by us. I doubt if hostilities can be suspended as between the army of the Confederate Government and the one I command, but I will aid you all in my power to contribute to the end you aim to reach, the termination of the existing war.[69]

With this letter went an enclosure which ordered the Federal troops to "respect and protect" the governor of North Carolina and other state officials, as well as the mayor and civil authorities of Raleigh, provided no hostile act was committed against the invading army between Gulley's and Raleigh.[70]

The commissioners had hoped to return to Raleigh on the afternoon of April 12, but because of the various delays and impediments they had met with, this was impossible. Although General Sherman promised that their detention would be as brief as possible, it soon became obvious that he intended for them to spend the night at his headquarters. After a fine supper and a band serenade, the commissioners retired. General Sherman shared his tent with Graham, and Major Henry Hitchcock,

67. Spencer, *Ninety Days*, p. 151.

68. Sherman states that President Lincoln authorized him to deal with Governor Vance, and to avoid anarchy he, President Lincoln, would recognize the existing state government until Congress could provide another. Sherman, *Memoirs*, II, 327. This is certainly more than Sherman remembered of the City Point conference shortly after it occurred. See below pp. 242-43.

69. Sherman to D. L. Swain, Apr. 12, 1865, Swain Papers, SHC, U.N.C.; *OR*, XLVII, Pt. III, Ser. I, 178.

70. *OR*, XLVII, Pt. III, Ser. I, 178.

whose mother had been a schoolmate of Swain's, turned his tent over to the ex-Governor.[71] Swain, before retiring, spent several hours in conversation with General Blair who had been a student at the University in 1838.[72] The other members of the party were, in like manner, treated by the General and his staff with "the most considerate and gentleman-like hospitality." This courteous manner on the part of Federals was totally unexpected by Colonel Burr. He was amazed that Sherman's only show of temper came when someone mentioned the burning of Columbia—which was quickly charged to Hampton. Burr had to admit that however much Sherman might be condemned for his actions it could not be denied that he was a person "of decided abilities." Sherman forcibly impressed Burr "as a man of quick perception, resolute will and prompt action, a rough, unpolished man, who thought for himself and could not brook opposition to his opinions."[73]

In the meantime, Vance was anxiously waiting in Raleigh. Since the commissioners had left well before noon, he expected their return by 4:00 P.M. at the latest. "It was extremely important that they should return by that time," he later said, "for the city of Raleigh was to be completely uncovered that night and the remaining of the Governor and all State officers in the discharge of their duties depended on the reply which was expected from General Sherman."[74] Late in the day Wheeler informed Vance that the commissioners had been captured. No longer expecting their prompt return, he accordingly wrote Sherman a letter, saying that Mayor William H. Harrison had been authorized to surrender the city and requesting that the charitable institutions, the Capitol, and the museum be spared from destruction.[75] Vance lingered in Raleigh until midnight; then, unwilling to trust himself to Sherman's hands without terms so long as eight thousand of General Hoke's North Carolina troops remained under arms, he mounted his horse and rode out to Hoke's camp, about eight miles west of the city.[76] In his

71. Howe, *Marching With Sherman*, p. 297.

72. Lewis, *Sherman*, p. 531.

73. J. G. Burr to D. L. Swain, June 18, 1866, W. Clark Papers, MS Div., N.C. Dept. of Arch. and Hist.

74. Dowd, *Vance*, p. 484.

75. Z. B. Vance to Sherman, Apr. 12, 1865, typed copy in possession of J. G. DeR Hamilton, SHC, U.N.C.

76. Dowd, *Vance*, p. 485; Z. B. Vance to Cornelia P. Spencer, Feb. 17, 1866, D. L. Swain Papers, SHC, U.N.C. In neither Georgia nor South Carolina had the governor of the state fallen into Sherman's hands. Vance apparently had no desire to be the first to try "this interesting experiment." Yates, "Vance and the End of the War," p. 330.

flight the governor was accompanied by two volunteer aides. He later wrote Cornelia Spencer: "Many of my staff officers basely deserted me at the last. . . . I rode out of Raleigh at midnight without a single officer of all my staff with me! Not one. I shall hit the deserters some day, hard."[77]

When Vance instructed Harrison to surrender the city, he was apparently unaware that the mayor already had plans to do just that. It was on the day that Samuel Mordecai "lay a corpse" in his house, either April 10 or 11, that Bartholomew F. Moore, distinguished jurist of Raleigh, first addressed Kenneth Rayner, well-known political figure in the state, on the subject of turning the city over to Sherman. In Sam Mordecai's funeral procession these two men lingered in the extreme rear and finally stepped out of the line so they might consult privately on matters pertaining to the capital city's protection. Later in the day Rayner got Harrison's concurrence on the formation of a mixed commission of city officials and private citizens to go out and meet the Federal army. So on the night of April 12, the mayor, although sick in bed, planned to arise before day and go forth in search of Sherman. Now he had the governor's official sanction for the move.[78]

The night of April 12 found the Fourteenth Corps encamped at Gulley's and the Twentieth Corps was nearby at Swift Creek.[79] Both corps of General Howard's Army of Tennessee went into camp at Pineville.[80]

The Twenty-third Corps covered eighteen miles on April 12 and encamped a mile south of Middle Creek near the Elevation-Raleigh road.[81] In accordance with orders General Cox was not moving his troops on the most direct road to Raleigh. He seemed to resent this order and entered in his journal: "Instead of being in the center of the whole Army, where we belong, we are on the left, and Slocum in the center."[82] Cox thought the outrages committed by the stragglers of his army were more than ever reprehensible since the news of Lee's surrender

77. Z. B. Vance to Cornelia P. Spencer, Feb. 17, 1866, D. L. Swain Papers, SHC, U.N.C.

78. B. F. Moore to K. Rayner, May 10, 1867, B. F. Moore—J. T. Gatling Papers, SHC, U.N.C.; K. Rayner to B. F. Moore, May 13, 1867, *ibid.*

79. *OR,* XLVII, Pt. I, Ser. I, 116, 120, 786.

80. *Ibid.,* p. 210.

81. *Ibid.,* XLVII, Pt. III, Ser. I, 187.

82. *Ibid.,* XLVII, Pt. I, Ser. I, 937. Sherman had ordered a more "southerly" course for his infantry columns in order to prevent, if possible, a Confederate retreat to the South. Sherman, *Memoirs,* II, 344.

had brought the prospect of an early termination of the war. As a result he issued on April 12, the following order:

Since we have left Goldsborough there has been a constant succession of house burning in the rear of this command. . . . Division Commanders will take the most vigorous measures to put a stop to these outrages, whether committed by men of this command or by stragglers from other corps. Any one found firing a dwelling house, or any building in close proximity to one, should be summarily shot. A sentinel may be left by the advance division at each inhabited house along the road, to be relieved in succession from the other divisions as they come up, those left by the rear division reporting to the train guard and rejoining after the next halt.[83]

General Schofield had hoped the Tenth Corps would reach the Elevation-Raleigh road on the night of April 12 and encamp some four miles south of the Twenty-third Corps. However, Terry reported entrenched Confederates on his front and thus was unable to reach the Raleigh road.[84]

At sunrise on April 13, the commissioners began their return trip to Raleigh. They intended to meet Governor Vance, consult with him and return to General Sherman with Vance's answer before the Federal troops should enter the city.[85] Five miles from Raleigh their train was stopped by General Kilpatrick who informed the commissioners they might proceed under the flag of truce, but issued the warning that "we will give you hell" if any resistance is met in Raleigh.[86] Within a mile of the capital flames could be seen rising from the railway station, which had first been plundered and then set on fire by General Wheeler's troops who were evacuating the city at the time.[87] General Hardee had led all but Wheeler's cavalry out the day before.[88] The commissioners found Raleigh nearly deserted. Scarcely a person was to be seen on the streets. All shops were closed, the governor and state officials gone. At the Capitol they found only a faithful Negro servant who had been entrusted

83. OR, XLVII, Pt. II, Ser. I, 188-89.

84. Ibid., pp. 187-88.

85. Spencer, Ninety Days, p. 157; Yates, "Vance and End of the War," p. 330. Sherman had given Kilpatrick permission to enter Raleigh the night of the 12th if he so desired. OR, XLVII, Pt. III, Ser. I, 186-87.

86. Ward, Flag of Truce, p. 15.

87. Spencer, Ninety Days, p. 157; R. H. Battle to Cornelia P. Spencer, Feb. 26, 1866, D. L. Swain Papers, SHC, U.N.C.; OR, XLVII, Pt. I, Ser. I, 1132.

88. Stewart's and Lee's corps, with Butler's cavalry as a rear guard, moved on the Hillsboro road. Hardee marched his troops on that road through Chapel Hill. Johnston, Narrative, p. 400.

by Governor Vance with the keys to the building.[89] The interior of the Capitol presented a scene of disorder. Bound legislative documents and maps lay strewn about the floor of the library. The museum rooms were in an even worse plight. The glass of the cases had been broken, and many of the specimens of natural history had been taken. The geological collections had been broken and scattered. The floor of the assembly chamber was sprinkled with scraps of writing paper and ink stands. On a shelf behind the speaker's desk was a marble bust, on the base of which in relief were the words "John C. Calhoun." Poised on its crown was an inverted inkstand, the contents of which had streamed down over the face. Under the name, in pencil, was written this explanatory clause, "Yes, father of Secessionism."[90] After a hasty consultation, the commissioners decided that Swain should remain at the Capitol until the Federal army entered the city and Graham should make his way, as well as he could, to Hillsboro where it was supposed the governor had stopped.[91] Thus Raleigh, without defenders and without a government, awaited the invaders.

The city presented less external appearance of terror and confusion than might have been supposed. Most of the citizens had decided it would be best to remain quietly at home with their families.[92] Some were nursing the Confederate wounded from the battles of Averasboro and Bentonville who filled many private residences, the unfinished building for Peace Institute, and the basement of the First Baptist Church.[93] For those remaining at home many anxious moments were spent awaiting the arrival of the Federal army. General Jacob D. Cox, in his *Reminiscences,* tells of going to "one of the more comfortable homes in town" where he found a household of women and children collected in the shutter drawn parlors of the house. They had been in these rooms since midnight of Wednesday, having not dared to sleep or even open a window.[94]

That Sherman would arrive in Raleigh in the course of his march had been anticipated since the day he entered the state.[95] The local

89. Spencer, *Ninety Days,* pp. 157-60.   90. Mowris, *117 N.Y.,* pp. 210-11.

91. Sherman had given the commissioners permission to proceed to Hillsboro in the train after their interview with Vance. *OR,* XLVII, Pt. III, Ser. I, 179; Spencer, *Ninety Days,* p. 154.

92. R. H. Battle to Cornelia P. Spencer, Feb. 6, 1866, D. L. Swain Papers, SHC, U.N.C.

93. *Raleigh News and Observer,* Apr. 7, 1935.   94. Cox, *Reminiscences,* II, 464.

95. R. H. Battle to Cornelia P. Spencer, Feb. 26, 1860, D. L. Swain Papers, SHC, U.N.C.; Spencer, *Ninety Days,* p. 145.

papers had kept the citizens posted on the progress of his march. This fact plus wild stories of Federal atrocities circulated by Wheeler's men were not very comforting thoughts for the local inhabitants.[96] Following the general practice of those Carolinians caught in Sherman's path, the citizens of Raleigh hid their possessions in an effort to save them. Former Governor Charles Manly placed a portion of his possessions in a heavy wooden box and buried it three miles from the city. "It was a terrible job," he declared. "I laid on the ground perfectly exhausted before I could gain strength to mount my horse."[97] Soon after the Federal occupation of Fayetteville, Vance began the transfer of state records and huge military stores he had accumulated. To Graham, Greensboro, and Salisbury were transferred 40,000 blankets, overcoats, and clothes; English cloth for about 100,000 uniforms; shoes, and leather for 10,000 other pairs; 150,000 pounds of bacon; 40,000 bushels of corn; 6,000 scythe blades; and large quantities of cotton cloth, yarns, cotton cards, and imported medical stores.[98] The last train out of Raleigh with supplies, records, and state officials aboard left the depot shortly before 9:00 P.M. on April 12.[99]

"God save us from the retreating friend and advancing foe," wrote Bartholomew F. Moore.[100] This line by Moore expressed the feelings of the citizens who feared the arrival in the city of both Confederate and Federal troops. Charles Manly voiced this fear in two letters to David L. Swain. On March 29, he wrote: "The enemy as well as our own stragglers and deserters search every house and cottage and Negroes cabins and take everything they find. . . . Between the two fires desolation, plunder, and actual starvation await us."[101] April 8, he wrote again: "I don't know what to do. I think it pretty certain that Johnston and Sherman will both pass over this place. Utter and universal devastation and ruin will follow inevitably. There is no difference in the armies as to making a clean sweep wherever they go of provisions, stock and everything dead or alive. . . . Marauding parties and stragglers on horseback

96. Boies, *33 Mass.*, p. 126.
97. C. Manly to D. L. Swain, Apr. 8, 1865, Swain Papers, SHC, U.N.C.
98. Z. B. Vance to Cornelia P. Spencer, Feb. 17, 1866, D. L. Swain Papers, SHC, U.N.C. For further evidence of the bountiful supply of foodstuffs in and near Raleigh at this time see Margaret Devereux, *Plantation Sketches*, p. 150; *OR*, XLVII, Pt. III, Ser. I, 198; Committee, *92 Ill.*, p. 240; O. P. Hargis, Reminiscences, 1861-1865, MS, SHC, U.N.C.
99. R. H. Battle to Cornelia P. Spencer, Feb. 26, 1865, D. L. Swain Papers, SHC, U.N.C.
100. B. F. Moore to D. L. Swain, Apr. 9, 1865, Swain Papers, SHC, UN.C.
101. C. Manly to D. L. Swain, Mar. 29, 1865, Swain Papers, SHC, U.N.C.

go to my plantation and break open my corn crib and dairy and take what they please. Pigs and poultry stand no chance."[102]   A few stores were broken into by Wheeler's men and disorder marked their conduct in the suburbs and about the depot where the commissary stores were kept.[103]   The weathercock atop Christ Church was probably the first and only chicken Wheeler's troops saw which they could not reach.[104]   But there was no universal destruction of property as Manly and Moore had feared.

April 13 had dawned under threatening skies. By the time the mayor and his party set out to meet the Federal advance rain was falling in torrents. A mile outside of Raleigh this peace delegation was stopped by Kilpatrick.[105]   At Mayor Harrison's request Kenneth Rayner made a short speech formally surrendering the city to the cavalry commander and asking his "forebearance and protection of private persons and private property. . . ." Two years later Rayner had these modest words to say about his part in saving Raleigh from Columbia's fate: "But for me there would have been no formal surrender of the town at all. The people are indebted to me for having houses over their heads. The germ of all these movements and operations, toward the protection of our people was . . . on the day of Mr. Mordecai's funeral."[106]

From the Capitol Swain watched General Kilpatrick ride into the city at the head of his division.[107]   With banners and guidons unfurled and a band playing, the Federal cavalry rode up Fayetteville Street. When the advance was within one hundred yards of the "old New-Berne bank," a resounding "God damn 'em," accompanied by five shots scattered the troops.[108]   A rash young Texan of Wheeler's command by the name of Walsh, who had suspended his retreat in order to plunder, had emptied his revolver at the approaching Federals. Walsh, after firing the shots, wheeled, put spurs to his black mare and galloped up Morgan Street, closely pursued by twelve Federal horsemen. Turning a corner his

102. C. Manly to D. L. Swain, Apr. 8, 1865, D. L. Swain Papers, SHC, U.N.C.

103. R. H. Battle to Cornelia P. Spencer, Feb. 26, 1865, D. L. Swain Papers, SHC, U.N.C. They were supposed to be held accountable for any misdemeanors committed in the city. *OR*, XLVII, Pt. III, Ser. I, 795.

104. Devereux, *Plantation Sketches*, p. 150.

105. Unidentified newspapers clipping, NCC, U.N.C.

106. K. Rayner to B. F. Moore, May 13, 1867, B. F. Moore—J. T. Gatling Papers, SHC, U.N.C.

107. Kilpatrick had requested that he be allowed to take Raleigh. *OR*, XLVII, Pt. III, Ser. I, 186.

108. *Raleigh News and Observer*, July 3, 1927.

horse fell. He remounted but was soon overtaken and brought back to General Kilpatrick, who ordered his immediate execution. The young Confederate soldier pleaded in vain for five minutes' respite in order to write his wife.[109] The General assured Swain that he did not hold the act against Raleigh or the Confederate army; so there was no act of reprisal.[110]

After chopping down the flag pole on the Capitol grounds and raising the United States flag over the Capitol dome, Kilpatrick pushed forward in pursuit of Wheeler who was retreating toward Chapel Hill. He left behind one regiment to act as guards for the city until the main body of troops arrived.[111]

At approximately 7:30 A.M., General Sherman, traveling with the Fourteenth Corps, reached Raleigh and immediately set up headquarters in the Governor's mansion, which Major Nichols called "A musty old brick building . . . in derision called the 'Palace.'" It had been "skinned" of its furniture and consequently was almost uninhabitable.[112] From the "Palace" Sherman wired Grant of his entry into Raleigh and of his intention next to move on Asheboro and Salisbury or Charlotte. In his wire he again expressed the hope that Sheridan would join him with his cavalry.[113] This request for cavalry was not phrased in the boastful manner of five days previous when he had promised Sheridan, in return for his services, "a free gift of all the blooded stock of North Carolina, including Wade Hampton, whose pedigree and stud are of high repute."[114] Sherman wanted additional cavalry to check Johnston, who by this time had moved his small army westward as far as Haw River.[115] Once his adversary was checked, Sherman could march rapidly on Asheboro and Charlotte, thus blocking any move Johnston might make along the railroad to the south and west. The base for this operation was to be Raleigh. Accordingly he sent a dispatch to Colonel W. W. Wright of the Railroad Department urging him to push repairs on the railroad up to Gulley's and Raleigh.[116] Sherman was preparing not only

109. Spencer, *Ninety Days*, pp. 160-62; Ashe, *Hist. of N.C.*, II, 999-1000. In all probability persons other than Walsh fired upon the Federal advance because Kilpatrick reported to Sherman that his "staff was fired upon from the state-house yard and corners of the street." *OR*, XLVIII, Pt. III, Ser. I, 197.

110. Olds, "Surrender," *Orphans' Friend and Masonic Jour.*, L, 8.

111. Pepper, *Recollections*, p. 386; *Raleigh News and Observer*, Feb. 25, 1934.

112. Nichols, *Great March*, pp. 296-97.   113. *OR*, XLVII, Pt. III, Ser. I, 191.

114. *Ibid.*, p. 129.   115. Johnston, *Narrative*, p. 401.

116. *OR*, XLVII, Pt. III, Ser. I, 191.

for the dreaded possibility that Johnston would continue his retreat westward but also for the desired possibility that peace would soon be in the offing. In the hope of "an early reconciliation" he issued orders prohibiting the destruction of public or private property. The peoples along the line of march were "to be dealt with kindly," especially the poorer classes.[117] Foraging was still restricted to the brigade and regimental level. Any minor party found foraging was to be arrested and sent to headquarters under guard.[118] Such orders were not new with Sherman. Since leaving Savannah his "bummers" had been supposedly operating under instructions which forbade them to pillage and required them to confine their foraging to the limits of supplies and other articles necessary for the troops. But these regulations, as previously shown, were difficult to enforce, and the Carolinas had suffered accordingly. Near Smithfield a soldier of the One Hundred and Third Illinois wrote a letter in which he said: "Several of them [Confederate newspapers] assert that our treatment of the citizens is good. Don't believe a word of it, though I wish it were so."[119] Albion W. Tourgee, One Hundred and Fifth Ohio, believed that the blame for the lawless conduct of "bummers" rested squarely on General Sherman. The General, he said, laid down regulations, but did not enforce them. "By seeming to forbid, and failing to prevent, he left the blame to fall upon the men. . . . As a consequence, the opprobrium falls upon the soldiers, instead of resting where it ought, upon the General."[120] Only time would tell whether these last orders would be strictly enforced. Complete discipline for an army the size of Sherman's was, of course, out of the question.

General Sherman regretted Vance's departure from the city, and desired his return as speedily as possible.[121] He therefore wrote him a letter inviting his return and enclosed[122] a safe-conduct through his lines for him and any members of the state or city government.[123] This letter and safe-conduct he placed in the hands of Graham for delivery to Governor Vance. Graham had been unable to leave Raleigh, as planned, because of skirmishing on the outskirts of the city.[124]

117. *Ibid.*, pp. 208-9. 118. *Ibid.*, pp. 192-93.
119. Orendorff, *103 Ill.*, p. 199. 120. Tourgee, *105 Ohio*, p. 366.
121. Sherman to W. A. Graham, Apr. 13, 1865, typed copy in possession of J. G. DeR. Hamilton, SHC, U.N.C.
122. Spencer, *Ninety Days*, p. 163.
123. Sherman to Union officers, Apr. 13, 1865, typed copy in possession of J. G. DeR. Hamilton, SHC, U.N.C.
124. J. G. Burr to D. L. Swain, Jan. 18, 1866, Swain Papers, SHC, U.N.C.

Throughout the day of the 13th the soldiers of Sherman's army approached Raleigh in a happy and festive mood. The comforting thought of Lee's surrender lingered in their minds. Comforting also was the knowledge that Johnston had evacuated Raleigh, and Governor Vance had sent a delegation to Sherman asking for his protection for the city. General Cox noticed that his men, as they neared their camp outside of Raleigh, were apt to get a great deal of pleasure out of the mere "trifling" incidents of the day. Alongside the road stood a giant tree and perched upon a dead limb high above the foliage was a mocking bird pouring forth "the most wonderful melodies." The marching soldiers stopped their talk, listened intently and craned their necks to glimpse the music maker. This disposition to notice the fortuitous things was taken as a good omen by the officers and men. They sensed it as an omen of coming peace.[125]

The Fourteenth Corps went into camp near the Insane Asylum on the outskirts of Raleigh.[126] Brigadier General C. C. Walcott's division was detached and given the duty of garrisoning the city. He immediately posted guards at public buildings and other points and had patrols marching through the streets.[127] The Twentieth Corps reached Raleigh during the afternoon and went into camp on the south side of the city.[128] The day's march had been short but very unpleasant because of the intense heat. Numerous men collapsed with sunstrokes.[129]

General Logan moved his corps across the Neuse at Hinton's Bridge and encamped ten miles east of Raleigh.[130] His "bummers" must have sensed the forthcoming order restricting their foraging activities,[131] because during the day a large number were found "dead drunk by the roadside."[132] April 13, they feared, would be their last fling.

The Seventeenth Corps reached the east bank of the Neuse at Battle's Bridge.[133] The Tenth Corps encamped near Swift Creek on this date.[134]

125. Cox, *Reminiscences*, II, 461-62.
126. *OR*, XLVII, Pt. I, Ser. I, 117.
127. Nichols, *Great March*, p. 299.
128. *OR*, XLVII, Pt. I, Ser. I, 139, 604.
129. Bryant, *3 Wis.*, p. 329.
130. General Logan reported that the bridge was saved by a charge of the Twenty-ninth Missouri upon a detachment of Confederate cavalry that was trying to destroy the bridge. *OR*, XLVII, Pt. I, Ser. I, 210. I can find no reference to any Confederate cavalry operating in this area at the time. It is possible, but not probable, that these cavalry troops belonged to General L. S. Baker's command moving from Weldon toward Raleigh. Mullen, "Last Days," p. 103.
131. *OR*, XLVII, Pt. III, Ser. I, 192-93.
132. Orendorff, *103 Ill.*, p. 205.
133. *OR*, XLVII, Pt. III, Ser. I, 195; *Ibid.*, XLVII, Pt. I, Ser. I, 210.
134. *Ibid.*, XLVII, Pt. I, Ser. I, 924.

Two miles west of Raleigh on the Hillsboro road, Kilpatrick encountered Wheeler's rear guard, and was driven back a short distance.[135] At Morrisville, ten miles farther west, he again met Wheeler and a sharp skirmish followed, which nightfall ended. Kilpatrick encamped at Morrisville, and Wheeler retired two miles beyond the town on the road to Chapel Hill. Having captured during the day three engine-less trains loaded with Confederate supplies, Kilpatrick awaited word from General Sherman as to what should be done with them.[136] Late in the afternoon the commanding general wired that he was sending a locomotive to bring the captured cars back to Raleigh. He also informed the weary Kilpatrick that he could rest his command, but that he should be prepared for battle in a few days in case Johnston did not "disperse his army."[137]

135. O. P. Hargis Reminiscences, 1861-1865, MS, SHC, U.N.C.
136. *OR*, XLVII, Pt. I, Ser. I, 1132; Committee, 92 *Ill.*, p. 240; *OR*, XLVII, Pt. III, Ser. I, 197-98.
137. *OR*, XLVII, Pt. III, Ser. I, 198.

CHAPTER XIV

Bennett's Farmhouse

HOPING TO FORGET the rigors of war, Sherman went visiting on the morning of April 14. In company with a member of his staff the General paid a call on Thomas Bragg, former governor of the state and brother to General Braxton Bragg, Sherman's intimate prewar friend. After inquiring from Thomas Bragg the welfare of his brother and allaying his host's anxieties about the fate of Raleigh, Sherman terminated his visit.[1]

On the way back to his headquarters he was stopped by one of Kilpatrick's couriers who had just ridden in from Morrisville. The breathless rider dismounted and handed Sherman a brief note stating that Kilpatrick was in possession of a letter from General Johnston addressed to the commanding general and delivered under a flag truce. These few lines conveyed to Sherman the certainty that Johnston's message embodied more than routine military matters. He felt it was the preliminary to surrender.[2] Elated with the thought, he ordered the message sent to him at Raleigh and later in the day he received the following letter from Johnston dated April 14:

The results of the recent campaign in Virginia have changed the relative military condition of the belligerents. I am, therefore, induced to address you in this form the inquiry whether, to stop the further effusion of blood and devastation of property, you are willing to make a temporary suspension of active operations, and to communicate to Lieutenant-General Grant, commanding the armies of the United States, the request that he will take like action in regard to other armies, the object being to permit the civil authorities to enter into the needful arrangements to terminate the existing war.[3]

1. Hitchcock, "Sherman," *Mil. Order of Loyal Legion, Mo. Commandery,* I, 425. *Raleigh News and Observer,* July 7, 1940.
2. Hitchcock, "Sherman," p. 425.
3. Sherman, *Memoirs,* II, 346-47.

General Johnston, as previously stated, had received at Raleigh a telegram directing him to leave his troops under General Hardee's command and report immediately to President Davis at Greensboro. Johnston arrived in Greensboro around 8:00 A.M. on April 12. There he was met by General Beauregard who accompanied him to Davis' office. In later years, Johnston had the following to say about this first meeting with the President:

We had supposed that we were to be questioned concerning the military resources of our department in connection with the question of continuing or terminating the war. But the President's object seemed to be to give, not to obtain information; for, addressing the party, he said that in two or three weeks he would have a large army in the field. . . . Neither opinions nor information was asked, and the conference terminated.[4]

During the afternoon Major General John C. Breckinridge arrived in Greensboro with the official announcement that the Army of Northern Virginia had capitulated. The news of this disaster fully convinced Johnston that the Confederacy was doomed. His small army, its ranks growing thinner by the day, was no match for Sherman. Young Bromfield Ridley of the Army of Tennessee noted in his diary: "Desertions every night is frightful. . . . Our army is getting demoralized. A band of marauding soldiers visited our camp and coolly helped themselves to some leather and other goods that we had quietly secured from the Quartermaster Department."[5] Against this small force the Federal authorities could have marshalled troops outnumbering Johnston twelve or fifteen to one. Johnston knew that with such odds against him and "without means of procuring ammunition or repairing arms, without money or credit to provide food" it would be impossible to continue the war "except as robbers." The consequence of prolonging the struggle, Johnston felt, "would only have been the destruction or disposition of . . . [the South's] bravest men and great suffering of women and children by the desolation and ruin inevitable from marching of 200,000 men through the country."[6]

In Johnston's opinion President Davis had only one governmental power left, that of terminating the war, and he thought this power should be exercised immediately.[7] In a later conference with the President,

4. Johnston, *Narrative*, p. 397.
6. *OR*, XLVII, Pt. III, Ser. I, 872.
5. Ridley, *Battles*, pp. 458-59.
7. Johnston, *Narrative*, pp. 397-98.

Johnston was able to get Davis, after much discussion, to authorize him to send Sherman the communication of April 14 asking for a suspension of hostilities.[8]

This dispatch, sent to General Hampton near Hillsboro for delivery to Sherman, reached the cavalry commander's headquarters late that night. Hampton was not informed of the contents of the dispatch. The only instructions he received were to have it carried at once to the Federal lines by a member of his staff So the General awoke Captain Lowndes and entrusted the dispatch to him. The Captain delivered the communication to Kilpatrick in person, at Morrisville. Since the note had to be forwarded to Sherman in Raleigh, Lowndes was asked by Kilpatrick to remain as his guest, awaiting a reply to the letter. Most of the time was spent in amicable conversation between Lowndes and the Federal officers. But, as time wore on, the talk turned to military matters, and the conversation became rather heated. Kilpatrick's implication that the surprise attack on his camp the previous month would have resulted differently had notice been given nettled the Confederate officer into challenging Kilpatrick to a cavalry duel with Hampton. Lowndes was positive Kilpatrick with fifteen hundred men would be bested by Hampton with only one thousand men, both groups armed with sabers alone.[9]

Sherman wasted very little time in aswering Johnston. He sent the following letter to Kilpatrick for delivery to the Confederate General:

I have this moment received your communication of this date. I am fully empowered to arrange with you any terms for the suspension of further hostilities between the armies commanded by you and those commanded by myself, and will be willing to confer with you to that end. I will limit the advance of my main column, to-morrow, to Morrisville, and the cavalry to the university, and expect that you will also maintain the present position of your forces until each has notice of a failure to agree. That a basis of action may be had, I undertake to abide by the same terms and conditions as were made by Generals Grant and Lee at Appomattox Court-House, on the 9th instant, relative to our two armies; and, furthermore, to obtain from General Grant an order to suspend the movements of any troops from the direction of Virginia. General Stoneman is under my command, and my order will suspend any devastation or destruction contemplated by him. I will add that I really desire to save the people of North Carolina the damage they would

8. See above p. 226.
9. Wells, *Hampton and His Cavalry*, pp. 423-24.

sustain by the march of this army through the central or western parts of the State.[10]

Later in the day Sherman addressed a short note to his cavalry chief informing him that Johnston's dispatch was "the beginning of the end," and consequently to rush his answer at once to the Confederate lines. Pending a reply from Johnston, Kilpatrick was ordered to halt his advance at Chapel Hill "or to a point abreast of it on the railroad."[11]

In accordance with these instructions, Kilpatrick informed Hampton of the disposition of his troops but, filled with misgivings about the feasibility of a truce, ignored Sherman's desire for an early answer to this dispatch and rode off in the direction of Durham's Station. The responsibility for forwarding the message was thus left to his staff officers who were in no hurry to act. As a result, Sherman's urgent communication was not handed to Hampton until sundown of April 15.[12] Johnston received the message on the morning of the 16th and rushed to Greensboro with it but Davis had "quitted the town" and was on his way to Charlotte.[13]

Sherman became annoyed at the delay and sent Major James C. McCoy of his staff and C. G. Eddy, telegraph operator to Morrisville to expedite matters by opening telegraphic communications with headquarters at Raleigh. From Morrisville, Eddy wired that Kilpatrick "had left."[14] Sherman wired back immediately to stay with General Kilpatrick until Johnston's answer was received.[15] To facilitate the move to Durham's Station, location of Kilpatrick's headquarters, a locomotive engine was sent to Morrisville. Major McCoy, fearing torpedoes along the track, put several empty cars ahead of the engine to explode them. The precaution was unnecessary but it made the trip much easier on the Major and his operator. At Durham's Station communication with Raleigh was established.[16] During the day McCoy received Sherman's permission to open Johnston's letter and communicate its contents by wire to Raleigh. Before nightfall the Major was able to telegraph his anxious commander Johnston's proposal that they meet in conference the next day at a point on the Hillsboro road equidistant between Durham's Station and Hillsboro.[17] Upon receiving this wire, Sherman

10. OR, XLVII, Pt. III, Ser. I, 207.   11. Ibid., p. 215.
12. Ibid., p. 233.   13. Johnston, Narrative, p. 401.
14. OR, XLVII, Pt. III, Ser. I, 222.   15. Ibid.
16. Ibid., pp. 229-30; Cox, "Convention," Scribners, XXVIII, 492.
17. OR, XLVII, Pt. III, Ser. I, 234.

suspended for the time being Special Field Orders No 55.[18]   He also
wired Kilpatrick to expect him at Durham's Station the next morning
and to have a "good company" of cavalry ready to act as escort.[19]

Meanwhile Kilpatrick had been sending Sherman dispatches stating
that Johnston could not be trusted and would "escape" if the opportunity
presented itself.   "I have no confidence in the word of a rebel, no matter
what his position.   He is but a traitor at best."[20]   Sherman replied that
Jeff Davis had more lives than a cat and could not be trusted but that
Johnston was in earnest.   "I have faith in General Johnston's personal
sincerity and do not believe he would use subterfuge to cover his movements."   Sherman also reminded Kilpatrick that Johnston could not stop
the movements of his troops until he received his letter of April 14, which
he understood was delayed an entire day by Kilpatrick's adjutants not
sending it forward.[21]

On April 15, Sherman had written Grant and Stanton, enclosing
copies of his correspondence with Johnston.   He assured them that he
would offer the same terms that Grant had given Lee, and he also informed his superiors that he had invited Governor Vance to return to
Raleigh with the civil officials of that state.   He added that in conversation with some of North Carolina's leading citizens he had learned that
they felt the war was over "and that the States of the South must resume
their allegiance, subject to the constitution and laws of Congress, and
that the military power of the South must submit to national arms."
Sherman felt that once the South accepted these resolutions all the details
of peace would be "easy of arrangement."[22]   He did not envisage the
infliction of severe penalities upon the people of the South once they
renewed their fidelity to the Union.

Rumors were afloat in Federal camps on April 15 that Sherman and
Johnston were to meet.   With no confirmation of the rumor, however,
the "day wore wearily on."[23]   By the evening of April 16, suspense
gripped the being of every soldier.   They asked one another: "How long
does it take a rebel General to surrender?"[24]   There was a great quest for
news.   The officers and men of the different commands began to circulate
about the different headquarters, hoping to learn some information.   Before the morning of April 17, "an all prevailing thirst" for the alcoholic

18. *Ibid.*, p. 231.   19. *Ibid.*, p. 235.
20. *Ibid.*, pp. 224, 234.   21. *Ibid.*, pp. 215, 243.
22. *Ibid.*, p. 221.   23. Gage, *12 Ind.*, p. 306.
24. Mowris, *117 N.Y.*, p. 212.

beverages enveloped the soldiers. "Men who rarely took it took it that night, and men who were in the habit of taking it, took a great deal."[25]

On Monday morning, April 17, as Sherman prepared to board a special train for Durham's Station, the telegraph operator at the depot rushed up to him and said that at that instant he was receiving a coded message from Morehead City which he thought Sherman should see. The General held the train for almost thirty minutes while the message was decoded and written out. It was the announcement of Lincoln's assassination.[26] Fearing the effect this news would have on his troops, Sherman swore the operator to secrecy before commencing his trip.[27] Around eleven o'clock the train—composed of an engine of the Raleigh and Gaston line and two cars—pulled into Durham's Station.[28] There the General and his staff were met by Kilpatrick who escorted them to his flag draped headquarters in the home of a Dr. Blackwell. At 11:20 the party set out to meet Johnston. In the lead was a soldier with a white flag. He was followed by a small platoon of cavalry. Next came the official party of Sherman and Kilpatrick with their respective staffs. Bringing up the rear was Colonel Kerwin, Thirteenth Pennsylvania cavalry, with the remainder of the escort.[29]

From the west a party of gray clad cavalrymen were slowly approaching. In the advance was General Hampton's orderly, Wade H. Manning, glumly carrying a flag of truce. To his rear were Generals Johnston and Hampton with a few members of their respective staffs. The Fifth South Carolina cavalry was the acting escort.[30]

The Federal party had ridden approximately five miles when in the distance was seen a white flag. Soon the two flag bearers met, and word was passed back to Sherman that Johnston was near at hand. Sherman then rode forward and for the first time met in person the Confederate General who had been his chief opponent for many months and for whose military ability he had great respect. In personal appearances the two officers were in marked contrast. General Johnston, his graying beard and mustache well-groomed, was neatly dressed in his gray uniform, coat

25. Underwood, *33 Mass.,* p. 291.
26. *OR,* XLVII, Pt. III, Ser. I, 220-24.
27. Sherman, *Memoirs,* II, 347-48.
28. On the way to Durham's Station Sherman discovered a newspaper reporter on the train and had him put off. Hatcher, *Four Weeks,* p. 285.
29. Pepper, *Recollections,* p. 408.
30. Brooks, *Butler and His Cavalry,* p. 288.

buttoned to his chin. He carried his slight frame with full military bearing. The younger and taller Sherman with his unruly red hair, shaggy beard, and untidy dress resembled more the private soldier than the conquering general. After shaking hands and introducing their respective aides, Sherman asked if there was a place nearby where they might talk in private. Johnston replied that he had passed a small farmhouse a short distance back.[31] Side by side the two Generals rode to the small log home of Daniel Bennett.[32]

The two officers dismounted in the road, turned their mounts over to orderlies and walked toward the house. They were met at the door by Lucy Bennett. They requested and received her permission to use the house, and Lucy with her four children retired to one of the two outhouses in the yard.[33]

This historic homestead, although not pretentious in any respect, was sturdy, sufficient, and scrupulously neat.[34] Its log exterior, shingled roof, and massive stone chimney provided comfort for the Bennett household. The interior consisted of a single downstairs room approximately 18 by 18 feet and an attic over it, which was adjoined to the main floor by some form of stairway, most probably a crude ladder. Among the pieces of furniture in the home were a bed, desk, wing table, candle table, and chairs. It is probable one officer sat by the candle table near the center of the room while the other sat at the leaf table toward the west side.[35]

When the officers closed the door to the Bennett home behind them, there were no witnesses to their conference. Both Sherman in his *Memoirs* and Johnston in his *Narrative* give substantially the same account of what occurred. Only on minor points is there a variance in their stories. Sherman stated that when he showed Johnston the telegram announcing Lincoln's assassination, the Confederate General broke out in large beads of perspiration and expressed the hope that Sherman did not suspect the Confederate government as originator of the plot.[36] Johnston, on the other hand, mentions no show of emotion on his part other than his expression that Lincoln's death "was the greatest possible

---

31. Sherman, *Memoirs*, II, 348.
32. Wellman, "Bennett Home," Newspaper clipping, 1953, NCC, U.N.C.
33. *Ibid.*
34. Hatcher, *Four Weeks*, p. 330.
35. Everett, "War Ended West of Durham," *Uplift*, XXVII, 11.
36. Sherman, *Memoirs*, II, 349.

calamity to the South."[37]   That the Confederates could be suspected of such a crime never entered his mind.[38]

After a discussion of the effect this tragedy would have on the country at large and on the armies, Sherman, according to Johnston's version, expressed "with an air and manner carrying conviction of sincerity, an earnest wish to avert from the Southern people the devastation inevitable from war."[39]   He then offered to Johnston the same terms Grant had given Lee at Appomattox. Evidently Sherman had overlooked the clause in Johnston's dispatch of April 14, stating the object of the meeting to be a cessation of hostilities "to permit the Civil Authorities to enter into needful arrangements to terminate the existing war."[40]   When Johnston reminded Sherman of this fact, the latter was quick to point out that the government of the United States did not recognize the existence of Confederate States and consequently he would not transmit any correspondence orginating with the civil authorities.

At this point Johnston shrewdly pointed out that his position was different from that of Lee. The capitulation of the Army of Northern Virginia was unavoidable, but his army was four days march in advance of Sherman. Then, instead of a partial suspension of hostilities Johnston suggested they "arrange terms of a permanent peace" which would embody the surrender of all the Southern armies still in the field.[41] Johnston had resumed his military duties in February with full consciousness that the South could have no other object in continuing the war than to obtain fair terms of peace.[42]   By offering to surrender all Confederate troops still under arms he was now making his bid for this one hope left to the Confederacy—generous terms of surrender. This line of reasoning appealed to Sherman immensely. As his able biographer, Lloyd Lewis, states, the possibility of unifying his wartorn country with one stroke of the pen "kindled in Sherman's mind like a fire on the altar. It radiated to the very core of his religious belief in unity—one act of sweeping harmony."[43]   With emotion he addressed Johnston, stating "that to put an end to further devastation and bloodshed, and restore the Union, and with it the prosperity of the country were to him objects of ambition."[44]

37. Johnston, *Narrative,* p. 402.
38. Johnston, "Negotiations," *No. Amer. Rev.,* CXLIII, 188.
39. *Ibid.*   40. See above p. 226.
41. Johnston, "Negotiations," p. 188-89.   42. *Ibid.,* p. 183.
43. Lewis, *Sherman,* p. 535.   44. Johnston, *Narrative,* p. 403.

Accompanying this strong desire for unity was the ever-present fear that Johnston would not disband his army but would allow it to disintegrate into guerrilla bands.[45] Sherman bore the major responsibility for this army still being an active fighting force. He had allowed Hood to escape at Atlanta and Hardee at Savannah. Neither had he destroyed Johnston at Bentonville, and on this date, April 17, the Confederate army was still a great distance away. These facts along with the desire for union weighed strong in Sherman's mind while he talked of peace.

As the afternoon wore on, the two Generals discussed terms that might be granted the seceded states upon their submission to Federal authority. Sherman informed Johnston of his talks with Lincoln at City Point and his agreement with the President's conviction that the restoration of the Union was the object of the war. Much of the time was spent in debate over the disposition of President Davis and his cabinet members under a general amnesty clause. Johnston wanted Davis and his cabinet explicitly included in the amnesty. No decision was reached on this latter matter by midafternoon. So it was decided to meet again the next morning at the same place.[46]

Outside it was a lovely spring day and the soldiers in blue and gray were mingling freely. Groups of men could be seen under the great white oak in the front yard, at the well, or around the shed to the side. Most of the talk centered on past military experiences. Often the conversation was heated, but much of it was completely amiable. Colonel Waring of Hampton's staff stated that he was treated civilly by all the Federals he met.[47] He, in turn, must have treated them likewise for the Northern Captain, George W. Pepper, said the Colonel was a wide awake and "withy little officer who put aside hostility and reserve and partook of the courtesies and conference."[48] One Federal soldier considered the occasion like a meeting of old friends, but this did not hold true for the blue clad soldier who offered to hold Munce Buford's horse. For his efforts he was informed that no damned Yankee would hold his horse. Buford later informed his friend, Lowndes, that he considered all Yankees "horse thiefs." Another blue coat was rebuffed when he offered

45. *Report of the Joint Committee on the Conduct of the War*, p. 15.
46. Johnston, *Narrative*, p. 403; Sherman, *Memoirs*, II, 350. The fate of Jefferson Davis was the only point on which Lincoln had given anything like specific instructions to Sherman at City Point.
47. Waring Diary, Apr. 17, 1865, SHC, U.N.C.
48. Pepper, *Recollections*, p. 409.

Wade Manning a cup of hot coffee. This bit of courtesy brought forth from the Southerner the curt suggestion his host drink from the cup first.[49]

Around two figures, in particular, most attention centered—the heavily bearded Hampton "stretched in an indifferent manner" upon an old work bench beside the house and the red-sideburned Kilpatrick standing nearby. These two were incapable of friendly conversation. At times the Confederate General looked savage enough to eat "little Kil." The two taunted each other about past military encounters and future policies in case the war continued. Hampton made it clear to all about him that had he the responsibility for writing the terms of an armistice, they never would be written.[50]

When Johnston and Sherman emerged from the house, all eyes turned in their direction for some word of greeting, but none was forthcoming. Johnston lifted his hat to the Federal soldiers gathered in the yard and then mounted his horse and rode off in the direction of Hillsboro. Sherman's usually expressive face showed no emotion. Preying on his mind was Lincoln's assassination and the fear that the news would leak out before he could return to his headquarters.

That night in Raleigh Sherman announced through Special Field Orders No. 56 the news of Lincoln's death, but in this announcement he stated his conviction that "the great mass of the Confederate army would scorn to sanction such acts."[51] Before having the order published and distributed, he drew up special instructions for General Cox, whose troops were garrisoning the city. Sherman feared that should the news become known at that moment it would occasion serious disorders among the soldiers. Hence, before releasing his announcement, Sherman had Cox carry out certain precautions for safeguarding the city. These precautionary measures included a strengthened garrison and strong guard at the edge of the city on all roads leading to the different camps. All soldiers off duty were sent immediately to their commands until the first excitement passed. Cox was "to allow no one to visit the city or wander about it, and to keep all under strict military surveillance."[52]

The startling proclamation that Lincoln was dead brought varied

49. Brooks, *Butler, and His Cavalry*, p. 288.
50. Nichols, *Great March*, p. 311; Conyngham, *Sherman's March*, pp. 364-65; Pepper, *Recollections*, pp. 409-11.
51. Sherman, *Memoirs*, II, 351.
52. Cox, *Reminiscences*, II, 465.

reactions from the Federal troops. Fortunately, accompanying Special Field Order No. 56 was the announcement of the first day's truce talk between Sherman and Johnston. This helped turn the thoughts of soldiers from vengeance to peace. The men of this inclination either sat around their campfires in silence[53] or occasionally expressed opinions to the effect "that if it had been Andy Johnson and Stanton, it would not have been much of a calamity."[54] To many of the soldiers, though, "Father Abraham" was no unmeaning term.[55] Beyond the light of the campfire vengeful and vituperative oaths could be heard. Regiments talked of inscribing "Lincoln's Avengers" on their banners.[56] A soldier of the One Hundred and Third Illinois wrote in his diary: "We hope Johnston will not surrender. God pity this country if he retreats or fights us."[57] Captain Theodore F. Upson noted that his men were "fearfully angry," and he was afraid of what they might do.[58]

That night a small portion of Logan's troops, along with stragglers from other commands, started a march on Raleigh. This group, with torches in hand, was met on the edge of town by General Logan, who had been informed of their approach. He dispersed the mob by threatening to shoot any man not returning immediately to his camp.[59]

The inhabitants of Raleigh were very much alarmed over the news that Lincoln had been assassinated. Rumors that the army intended to sack the city immediately began to circulate. These unverified stories were abetted by threatening talk of guards on duty in the city. Sheriff High heard several of them threaten to burn the Capitol. A Federal captain who was quartered at the K. P. Battle home suggested that all the vessels in the house be filled with water to fight a possible fire, and to remove all clothes from the dwelling for safety's sake.[60] None of these threats materialized, but a large portion of Raleigh's population sat up the entire night expecting any moment the appearance of an angry mob. Federal cavalry patrolled the streets that night and for once the sound of Northern hoofbeats was a welcome relief. The long vigil, though, did not pass without some extremely anxious moments. Around 9:00 P.M. the fire alarm sounded and to the southeast was seen the red

53. *Ibid.*, p. 466; Schurz, *Reminiscences*, III, 112; Howard, *Autobiography*, II, 157.
54. Bryant, *3 Wis.*, p. 174.   55. Aten, *58 Ill.*, p. 304.
56. Stormont, *Hight Diary*, p. 523.   57. Orendorff, *103 Ill.*, p. 208.
58. Winther, *Upson Diary*, p. 166.
59. *Ibid.*, p. 167; Dawson, *Logan*, p. 96; Bryant, *3 Wis.*, p. 330; *City of Raleigh*, p. 64.
60. Battle, *Memoires*, p. 195.

glow of a fire. At the scene of the blaze the local residents were happy to find only an old deserted workshop in flames, and upon investigation it was learned that the fire had started accidentally.[61]

During the evening of April 17 and the morning of the 18th, Sherman talked with Generals Schofield, Slocum, Howard, Logan, and Blair, and without exception they urged him to make terms with Johnston. They expressed dread at the thought of another long march. Johnston could be defeated they were positive, but forcing him to do battle was another matter.[62]

From Hampton's headquarters in the home of Dr. Dickerson, two miles east of Hillsboro, Johnston wired Breckinridge to join him at once. He hoped that General Breckinridge's close association with President Davis, as Secretary of War, would enable him to influence the President favorably on any terms that might be agreed upon the next day. Breckinridge, in company with Postmaster General John H. Reagan, arrived at Hampton's headquarters shortly before daybreak on April 18. Johnston immediately informed them of his conference with Sherman, and repeated as best he could the terms they had agreed upon. Reagan suggested that the terms be put in writing to facilitate discussion at the next meeting. Before this could be done Johnston and Breckinridge had to depart for the Bennett house. They left behind instructions that the paper including a general amnesty clause protecting Davis and his cabinet members be forwarded there immediately.[63]

Relieved that no violence had occurred during the night, Sherman, on the morning of April 18, boarded his special train for Durham's Station. There Kilpatrick again conducted him to his headquarters. On this occasion the band of the Third Kentucky serenaded the General while the horses were being saddled. As the party rode out in the direction of Hillsboro, the men, sensing the importance of the occasion, lined the roadside to view their commanding general, who without belt, sabre, or pistol, and attired in his usual untidy manner, was astride a white charger. "An old, low crowned, round topped, faded black felt hat sat clapped close on his head" and his unbuttoned coat flapped in the breeze. The vain Kilpatrick presented an entirely different appearance. He could not

61. *City of Raleigh,* pp. 63-64; *Raleigh News and Observer,* Apr. 13, 1930.

62. Sherman, *Memoirs,* II, 351. General Schurz voiced objection to the terms on the grounds that the military could not decide civil policy. Schurz, *Reminiscences,* III, 754.

63. Johnston, "Negotiations," pp. 188-89; Boynton, *Sherman's Raid,* pp. 244-58; *OR,* XLVII, Pt. III, Ser. I, 806; Everett, "War Ended West of Durham," p. 10.

resist the opportunity to bedeck himself in all his finery. Belted, sashed, and sabred he rode next to his chief.[64]

Sherman reached the Bennett home around noon but General Johnston had not arrived. It was not long before a courier appeared with the word that the Confederate General was on his way. When Johnston arrived and the conference commenced, it was on the same cordial level of the previous day. After assuring Sherman he had the authority to surrender all the Confederate armies in the field, Johnston approached his companion on the topic of political rights for his soldiers after the surrender. He pointed out that the officers and men were greatly perturbed over this matter. Sherman pointed out that Lincoln's Amnesty Proclamation of 1863 granted an absolute pardon to all officers and men below the rank of colonel who would lay down their arms and take an oath of allegiance to the Federal government. He further showed that the amnesty clause in Grant's terms to Lee fully pardoned "all" officers, including General Lee. As Sherman understood this, it meant a full restoration to the Confederate soldiers of their rights of citizenship. This still did not satisfy Johnston and he suggested to Sherman that General Breckinridge be allowed to join the conference. Knowing Breckinridge's legal and political background, Johnston thought the Kentuckian might help them iron out the details of the surrender, especially the points pertaining to the political status of the South. Sherman at first objected on the grounds that Breckinridge was a civil official of the Confederacy but consented when Johnston assured him his appearance would be solely as a major general in the army of the Confederate States, not as Secretary of War.[65]

Soon after Breckinridge entered the room Sherman stepped to the door and called for his saddlebags. The soldiers in the yard, as they watched the orderly take the bags to the door, thought this was a request for pen and paper. An agreement must be near at hand, they reasoned.[66] They were mistaken. It so happened Sherman was thirsty and desired a drink of whiskey. The sight of the whiskey bottle brought a sparkle to Breckinridge's eyes. It was like manna from heaven for this gentleman from Kentucky who had been without his daily toddy for quite some time. After pouring himself a healthy drink, Breckinridge addressed Sherman in a most eloquent and persuasive manner for some six or eight

64. Pepper, *Recollections*, p. 414.   65. Sherman, *Memoirs*, II, 352.
66. Pepper, *Recollections*, p. 416.

minutes, quoting "law of war, laws governing rebellion and laws of nation" with such force and elegance that Sherman pushed his chair back and exclaimed: "See here, Gentlemen, who is doing this surrendering anyway? If this thing goes on, you'll have me sending an apology to Jeff Davis."[67]

When Breckinridge sat down, Johnston who had been sitting by a window intently watching the soldiers plucking leaves and flowers for souvenirs,[68] addressed Sherman on the possibility of an amnesty which would specifically include Davis, but Sherman turned a deaf ear to him. Sherman could have been thinking of President Lincoln's intimation given at City Point, that it might be wise if Davis "escaped the country."[69]

The talks were still in progress when a courier arrived from Hillsboro with Reagan's memorandum on the previous day's meeting.[70] Johnston and Breckinridge examined the paper and after a short consultation between themselves turned the memo over to Sherman. He read the terms Reagan had proposed but announced they were too general and verbose to be acceptable.[71] Sherman then sat down and began to write very rapidly. Only once did he arise from the table. On this occasion he slowly walked over to his saddle bags and withdrew the whiskey bottle. Breckinridge prepared himself for another stiff drink by throwing away his chew of tobacco. But General Sherman, with his mind upon the terms he was writing, poured only himself a drink. To the Kentuckian this was inexcusable. General Sherman was "a hog. Yes, sir, a hog!" Breckinridge exclaimed afterwards.[72] In a short while Sherman handed to Johnston the following paper, stating he was willing to submit it to President Johnson:

1. The contending armies now in the field to maintain the status quo until notice is given by the commanding general of any one to its opponent, and reasonable time—say, forty-eight hours—allowed.

2. The Confederate armies now in existence to be disbanded and conducted to their several State capitals, there to disposit their arms and public property in the State Arsenal; and each officer and man to execute and file an agreement to cease from acts of war, and to abide the action of the State and Federal authority. The number of arms and munitions of war to be reported

67. Wise, *End of an Era*, pp. 449-53; Horn, *Army of Tenn.*, p. 427; "A Little Whiskey," Newspaper clipping, 1926, NCC, U.N.C.

68. Pepper, *Recollections*, p. 419.   69. Sherman, *Memoirs*, II, 326-27, 353.

70. *OR*, XLVII, Pt. III, 806-7.   71. Sherman, *Memoirs*, II, 353.

72. Wise, *End of an Era*, p. 453.

to the Chief of Ordnance at Washington City, subject to the future action of the Congress of the United States, and, in the mean time, to be used solely to maintain peace and order within the borders of the States respectively.

3. The recognition, by the Executive of the United States, of the several State governments, on their officers and Legislatures taking the oaths prescribed by the Constitution of the United States, and, where conflicting State governments have resulted from the war, the legitimacy of all shall be submitted to the Supreme Court of the United States.

4. The reestablishment of all the Federal Courts in the several States, with powers as defined by the Constitution of the United States, and of the States respectively.

5. The people and inhabitants of all the States to be guaranteed, so far as the Executive can, their political rights and franchises, as well as their rights of person and property, as defined by the Constitution of the United States and of the States respectively.

6. The Executive authority of the Government of the United States not to disturb any of the people by reason of the late war, so long as they live in peace and quiet, abstain from acts of armed hostility, and obey the laws in existence at the place of their residence.

7. In general terms—the war to cease; a general amnesty, so far as the Executive of the United States can command, on condition of the disbandment of the Confederate armies, the distribution of the arms, and the resumption of peaceful pursuits by the officers and men hitherto composing said armies.

Not being fully empowered by our respective authorities to fulfill these terms, we individually and officially pledge ourselves to promptly obtain the necessary authority, and to carry out the above programme.[73]

A careful scrutiny of these terms showed Johnston that they differed very little from the Reagan memorandum,[74] and as soon as the necessary copies of the agreement were made, both parties signed them. Then the two officers parted. Sherman left with complete faith that Johnston would honor the truce, and Johnston with the hope that Davis would approve his work.

Sherman in later years stated emphatically that neither Breckinridge nor Johnston wrote one word of the paper. It was his own composition, he maintained.[75] Johnston supports this claim by admitting that Sher-

73. *OR,* XLVII, Pt. III, Ser. I, 243-44.

74. The Confederate Postmaster General had embodied in his draft a long preamble and an amnesty clause without exception.

75. Sherman, *Memoirs,* II, 353; Sherman, "Surrender," *Hist. Mag.,* XV, 333-34. Warren, whose home was General Blair's headquarters while in Raleigh, recalling this

man wrote the draft so rapidly that, at the time, it caused him to think the General had come to the meeting prepared on what terms he would offer.[76]

Sherman had now kept his oftmade promise to befriend the people of the South once they laid down their arms. Through the Carolinas he had reiterated this statement and at Bennett's farmhouse he had proved his words. A defeated foe could ask for little more than Sherman's terms contained: orderly disbandment of the Confederate army; recognition of existing state governments "by the Executive of the United States"; the re-establishment of Federal courts; the guarantee of political, property, and personal rights "as defined by the Consitution of the United States and of the States respectively" freedom from molestation due to participation in the war; adjudication by the United States Supreme Court of the legitimacy of rival state governments, where they existed; and, lastly, for a general amnesty "so far as the Executive can command." These terms restored to the South a large measure of its "status quo" antebellum.[77]

Sherman's actions were primarily motivated by his controlling passion to reunite the Union and at the same time aid the South. Influencing him to a small extent, it seems, was the cold fact that a truce whether lasting or not would at least temporarily stop Johnston's retreat westward and also gain time for the completion of repairs on the railroad to Raleigh.[78]

Sherman did not compose the terms which touched on political questions without certain precedents to follow. His City Point conference with Lincoln, without question, influenced his thinking, but it in no way provided him with specific instructions to follow. Both the voice and pen at Bennett's farmhouse belonged to Sherman.

Lloyd Lewis takes a contradictory view on this point. In his work, *Sherman, The Fighting Prophet,* Lewis marshalled a tremendous amount of evidence to show that General Sherman was following Lincoln's program. Supporting this thesis, and, accepting the evidence compiled by Lewis, are such notable historians as Ellis Merton Coulter, James

---

experience twenty years later, said that one night prior to April 17 Blair came into his room and asked him to write down what was dictated since he, the General, was very tired. Blair then proceeded to outline some very generous terms for North Carolina's readmittance to the Union. This bit of correspondence, so Warren maintains, was shown to Sherman and received his unofficial approval. On the basis of this account it may be assumed that when Sherman talked with Johnston on April 17, he had already given thought to specific terms of surrender. Warren, *Doctor's Experiences,* pp. 345-48.

76. Johnston, *Narrative,* p. 405. 77. See above pp. 239-40.
78. Sherman, *Memoirs,* II, 353.

Garfield Randall, Henry Steele Commanger. Refuting this idea is the scholarly article, "Lincoln and Sherman Peace Fiasco—Another Fable?" by Raoul S. Naroll. In his paper Naroll shows conclusively that "(1) Sherman's terms were inconsistent with Lincoln's known views, as already outlined; (2) the evidence cited in support of Lewis' argument . . . is unreliable and misleading; and (3) Lewis' thesis is as inconsistent with statements Sherman made before he met Johnston, and while Lincoln was still living, as it is with those made after."[79]

Sherman's concessions to Johnston "went far beyond anything" President Lincoln had offered even when the bargaining position of the South was stronger. Lincoln hardly would have authorized terms that "in effect guaranteed property in slaves";[80] that made possible the payment of the Confederate war debt;[81] that recognized existing insurgent state governments;[82] and that might well have "put in question the legitimacy of all Union state governments where rival insurgent state governments existed."[83]

Five distinct times during April and May, 1865, Sherman made it clear that he had entered into negotiations with Johnston completely uninstructed by Lincoln or anyone else.[84] One of these occasions was his official report of the Carolina's campaign. In this document he stated that up to his meeting with the Confederate General, he had received not one word of "instruction, advice, or counsel as to the 'plan or policy' of government, looking to restoration of peace. . . ."[85]

Sherman never tried to justify his peace terms on the allegation that Lincoln had dictated them. He maintained this position even after his

79. Naroll, "Peace—Fiasco," pp. 459-83.

80. *Ibid.*, p. 464. There was no mention of slavery in the agreement as both commanders considered the institution dead. *OR*, XLVII, Pt. III, Ser. I, 266. The property guarantees of the terms, however, might have been applied to slaves. Reagan saw this and wrote Davis that the convention left the question of slavery "subject to the Constitution and laws of the United States and of the several states just as it was before the war." *Ibid.*, pp. 824.

81. Here again a vital question was not considered in the convention. The skilled legal mind of Reagan was quick to see that through this omission Davis could "endeavor to secure provisions for the auditing of the debt of the Confederacy, and for its payment in common with the war debt of the United States." *Ibid.*, pp. 825-26.

82. See above p. 240.

83. Naroll, "Peace-Fiasco," p. 470. By recognizing existing Confederate state governments, Sherman not only put in question the legality of the Union state governments in Louisiana, Arkansas, Tennessee, and Virginia, but also the governments of Missouri, Kentucky, and West Virginia.

84. *OR*, XLVII, Pt. III, Ser. I, 177, 221, 234-35; *Sherman's Official Account*, pp. 164-65.

85. *OR*, XLVII, Pt. I, Ser. I, 33.

terms had been rejected in Washington and he himself had been severely ridiculed for his actions. As late as April, 1869, he was writing in the *New York Tribune*: "I repeat that according to my memory, Mr. Lincoln did not expressly name any specific terms of surrender, but he was in a kindly and gentle frame of mind that would have induced him to approve fully what I had done."[86] To explain this seeming contradiction of his thesis, Lewis maintained that Sherman deliberately suppressed the truth in order to protect the martyrdom of the dead President.[87] But this line of reasoning does not hold up under the consideration that on two occasions before Sherman talked with Johnston and before he knew of Lincoln's death, he made it clear he had received no instructions from Lincoln.[88]

In the light of the evidence disproving the contention that Sherman operated under instructions from the President, it can be safely concluded that he acted foremost in accordance with the dictates of his own conscience. The generosity of his terms to Johnston were in complete harmony with his design for reconstruction in the South.

Sherman assumed that his peace terms would be acceptable to the administration. Had not his letters to the Mayor of Atlanta and to "N.W." of Savannah been widely published? In neither case was he reprimanded by the civil authorities in Washington. In both of these letters, as previously stated, Sherman had expressed the view that when the people of the South ceased fighting and submitted to the authority of the United States "the war was over as to them," and when their newly elected members were seated in Congress, the states would become as much a part of the Union as New York and Ohio.[89] Strengthening Sherman's conjecture that his terms would be satisfactory in the nation's capital was the news that President Lincoln had assented to the calling of the Virginia legislature in Richmond. Sherman learned this information through unofficial sources on April 18, and was in possession of this knowledge when talking with Johnston. Two days later in a New York newspaper he read a copy of the official order calling the legislature to meet. What he did not know at the time of his talks with Johnston was that Lincoln on April 12, had rescinded this order. Neither had Sherman been shown Lincoln's instructions to Grant of March 3, 1865,

86. Sherman, "Sherman Letter," *Hist. Mag.* XV, 333-34.
87. Lewis, *Sherman*, pp. 568-69.
88. *OR*, XLVII, Pt. III, Ser. I, 177, 221.
89. See above pp. 20-21, 29-30.

in which the President had directed Grant to have no conference with Lee except on matters pertaining to the military and "not to decide, discuss, or confer upon any political questions."[90]

The evening of April 18, Sherman sat down at his desk to write letters to Grant and Halleck containing the momentous events of the day. Sherman was satisfied that in his dealing with Johnston he had acted "honestly and conscientiously, without assuming more authority than he had good reason to believe had been granted to him."[91] He urged speedy action on the agreement as it was "important to get the Confederate armies to their homes. . . ."[92] But Sherman, neither politician nor lawyer, was unaware of the full political and legal implications of his concessions. In a letter to his wife this night, the General expressed relief that the "cruel war" was over and soon he could come home to her for at least a month.[93]

On April 19, Sherman wired Federal authorities in Morehead City to prepare a "fleet-steamer" to carry a messenger to Washington. Shortly afterwards he dispatched by rail for the coast Major Henry Hitchcock of his staff. The Major carried with him letters to Halleck and Grant and copies of the Sherman-Johnston agreement of the previous day. Hitchcock was also instructed by his commander to return to Raleigh "with all expedition."[94] Later in the day Sherman published orders to his troops informing them of the armistice and signifying that a line passing "through Tyrrell's Mount, Chapel University, Durham's Station, and West Point on the Neuse River" would separate the two armies.[95]

In the meantime Johnston had dispatched to Davis at Charlotte a copy of the agreement of April 18. Johnston returned to Greensboro, arriving there on the morning of April 19.

90. Sherman, *Memoirs,* II, 364-67.
91. Naroll, "Peace—Fiasco," p. 478.
92. *OR,* XLVII, Pt. III, Ser. I, 243-44.
93. Howe, *Home Letters of Sherman,* pp. 344-45.
94. Sherman, *Memoirs,* II, 354. By this time both Grant and Stanton should have suspected that Sherman intended to include civil matters in his terms with Johnston. In his letters, dated April 15, Sherman stated that he had invited Governor Vance and other state officials to return to Raleigh. As these dispatches were sent part of the way by wire, they should have reached Washington long before Hitchcock arrived with the terms of the Convention of April 18. However, there seems to have been no answer to these dispatches. Cox, "Convention," p. 493.
95. *OR,* XLVII, Pt. III, Ser. I, 250.

CHAPTER XV

"Beautiful Raleigh, City of Oaks"

FOR SEVERAL DAYS all was well for Sherman. Confident the terms agreed to on April 18 would be approved in Washington, he sent Johnston a newspaper telling of General Weitzel's authorization to convene the Virginia state legislature.[1] The lawyers might have to define what was meant by the "guarantee of rights of persons and property" but nothing else would be confusing, he thought. Neither did Sherman envisage a Negro problem. He expressed to Johnston his conviction that if the South would "simply and publicly declare . . . that slavery is dead," an era of peace and prosperity would soon erase from the South the ravages of war. The Negroes, he thought, should remain in the South for the primary purpose of furnishing an abundance of cheap labor which would be greatly needed in rebuilding the land.[2] He did not believe that the Negro was intelligent enough to fill the political offices of the states. "For some time the marching of the state Governments," he wrote his brother, John, "must be controlled by the same class of whites as went into the rebellion against us."[3] Sherman was positive that if the Negro was enfranchised it would produce a "new war . . . more bloody and destructive than the last."[4]

While the negotiations at Bennett's farmhouse were in progress, two Federal cavalry corps, one under Major General James H. Wilson in Georgia and the other under Major General George Stoneman in western North Carolina, were devastating the land. To halt as quickly as possible these operations, Sherman used Johnston's telegraph lines to communicate with these generals. In doing this, he sent to the Confederate General messages in Federal cipher, the contents of which had been made known to Johnston. Johnston, in turn, was to transmit the messages to

1. *OR*, XLVII, Pt. III, Ser. I, 257.　　2. *Ibid.*, p. 266.
3. Thorndike, *Sherman Letters*, p. 254.　　4. *OR*, XLVII, Pt. III, Ser. I, 411.

Wilson and Stoneman. Sherman felt that in halting Wilson and Stoneman without direct communication with either, he had "almost exceeded the hands of prudence," but had done so on his absolute faith in Johnston's personal character.[5]

At Raleigh, Sherman received a number of requests for favors from citizens throughout the state. He must have been amused by a communication he received from W. H. Pleasants, Mayor of Louisburg. The Mayor formally surrendered the town to Federal authorities and requested a guard for the town under the authority and laws of the Constitution of the United States. Sherman told the Mayor not to worry—a guard for the town was unnecessary for he had no intention to move any part of his army through the place.[6]

S. L. Fremont of Wilmington, superintendent of Wilmington and Weldon Railroad, asked Sherman's protection for himself and his family on the grounds of their friendship, dating back to service in the army together. This railroad official pointed out that he was not engaged in arms against the flag of the United States and, until North Carolina seceded from the Union, he was a strong "Union man."[7] This was the wrong approach to Sherman's sympathies. The General informed this friend "of other and better days" just what he thought of submissive Southerners who professed Union sentiments. Said he:

> Had the Northern men residing at the South spoken out manfully and truly at the outset the active secessionists could not have carried the masses of men they did. . . . I do have a feeling allied to abhorrence toward Northern men resident South, for their silence or acquiescence was one of the causes of the war assuming the magnitude it did. . . . The result is nearly accomplished, and is what you might have foreseen, and in a measure prevented—desolation from the Ohio to the Gulf and mourning in every household. I am not made of stone, and cannot help indulging in a feeling toward Union men South, who failed at the proper time to meet a storm and check it before it gained full headway.

Sherman, it will be remembered, was in Louisiana in 1861 and gave up security, happiness, and close personal ties to fight for the preservation of the Union. Consequently, he was in a position to tell Fremont that for men of his stripe, he had "not a particle of sympathy."[8]

5. Ibid., p. 286; Johnston, Narrative, p. 409.
6. OR, XLVII, Pt. III, Ser. I, 225.
7. S. L. Fremont to Sherman, Feb. 20, 1865, Sherman Papers, MS Div., L.C.
8. OR, XLVII, Pt. III, Ser. I, 273.

Raleigh, unmarred by the ravages of war, made an impression on the General and his soldiers. The men, with but few exceptions, acclaimed the city's lovely trees, stately public buildings, fine residences, wide streets, and well-kept lawns. To the members of the Eighty-sixth Illinois, "Raleigh was the handsomest city in famous Dixie, it being neat and clean and its situation grand. . . ."[9] Captain G. W. Pepper, a war correspondent, was most lavish in extolling the city. He wrote:

The attractions of this handsome capital are extensively and favorably known. . . . The wide and commodious streets are shaded by rows of elms. The magnificent dwellings in and around the city, with their ample yards and gardens, adorned with choicest flowers and shrubbery, give the city a most attractive appearance. Perhaps there is no town of the same population in the South that affords so many evidences of wealth, elegance and social refinement. . . . Beautiful Raleigh! It was laid out in the good old English Southern manner. The spacious Fayetteville street is lined with stores so solid and elegant that they would not look out of place in New York, whose stores are palaces. The suburbs of the place abound in elegant mansions, gardens, and ornamental trees. . . . The Baptist denomination have the finest religious edifice in the State. . . . There are many public buildings in Raleigh. Among them are the Capitol, the Asylums, and the Episcopal Seminary. The Lunatic Asylum is a glorious structure. . . . The Deaf, Dumb, and Blind Asylum is large, tasteful, and commodious. . . . The Capitol is a substantial building.[10]

The beauty Pepper described inspired the poetic genius of one New Yorker. In verse he described the capital city as follows:

> Beautiful Raleigh, city of Oaks,
> City of Hills, also thy name
> How like a Fairey Queen thy looks
> Or diamond set in diadem.

And for eight more stanzas the author proclaimed the many charms of this place.[11]

A Massachusetts soldier grudgingly admitted that Raleigh was pretty but, with seeming pleasure, he listed in his diary the principal places worthy of note as "Frog Level," "Vinegar Hill," and "Devils Half Acre." "Vinegar Hill," he understood, derived its name from the people of most sour countenance who lived upon it.[12]

9. Kinnear, *86 Ill.*, p. 110.
11. *Raleigh Daily Standard*, Apr. 28, 1865.
10. Pepper, *Recollections*, pp. 387-89.
12. Boise, *33 Mass.*, p. 123.

There was very little open hostility between the soldiers and the citizens of Raleigh. The men in blue seemed to have made a conscientious effort to conciliate rather than antagonize the inhabitants. The friendly intercourse between soldier and civilian was evidenced when Colonel Poe, Sherman's chief engineer, made his carriage and a ten-man cavalry escort available to ex-Governor Charles Manly, who wished to dig up a box of valuables he feared the soldiers would find.[13] The editor of the *Raleigh Daily Standard* was impressed "by the gentlemanly bearing of the officers and men. From General Sherman to the humblest private, we have witnessed nothing but what has been proper and courteous."[14] Sherman in turn observed that Raleigh was "full of fine people who were secesh but now are willing to encourage the visits of handsome men."[15] General Howard was treated with such cordiality in the R. S. Tucker home that he acquired a great fondness for his young host and hostess.[16] Sherman himself made calls on several of the city's better-known residents. The day following his visit with former United States Secretary of the Navy, George E. Badger, a member of his staff was seen at a corps review in the company of Mrs. Badger and her two daughters.[17] It was an everyday occurrence to see a Federal officer out strolling with one of the "pretty" young ladies of Raleigh. In most cases, though, a local beauty would accept the favors of only one officer and in return restrict her attention to him alone, completely ignoring all other military personnel.[18] But there were those who were haughty and defiant to all the men in blue. Such an attitude led one Federal officer to remark to a young lady: "Is there no such thing as conquering the Southern woman? What makes you ladies behave so absurdly silly?" Without hesitation the young lady replied: "I don't know unless its from a sincere desire to render ourselves suitable companions for you gentlemen of the U. S. Army." For a rejoinder all the officer could say was: "This is certainly the most God-forsaken place on earth." To this, his sharp-tongued companion retorted: "Yes, the devil took possession of it last month and

13. C. Manly to C. P. Spencer, Apr. 25, 1866, D. L. Swain Papers, SHC, U.N.C.
14. Unidentified newspaper clipping, NCC, U.N.C.; *Raleigh Daily Standard,* Apr. 17, 1865.
15. Howe, *Home Letters of Sherman,* p. 347.
16. Howard, *Autobiography,* II, 159.
17. Howe, *Marching With Sherman,* p. 298.
18. Ellen Mordecai to Emma Mordecai, Raleigh 1865. Copy in Mordecai Diary, SHC, U.N.C.; *Raleigh News and Observer,* Aug. 20, 1939, quoting *Old Guard,* May, 1866.

has never let go his hold on it for an instant since you have been here."[19]

All the while Sherman was in Raleigh many of the paroled veterans of Lee's army were passing through the city. Some liked to stop and rest on the Capitol grounds, where they mingled freely and cordially with the Federal troops.[20] Many of these parolees were given rides on the Federal supply trains going to Goldsboro in the direction of their homes. No guards were placed by the Federal officers because a mutual feeling of friendliness had arisen almost at once between these former enemies. Sleeping accommodations and rations were shared alike.[21]

Raleigh was fortunate in that there was no interval between the departure of the Confederates and the arrival of the Federals for the "bummers" to ply their thievery within the town. The guards who had been immediately posted at most homes had very little trouble protecting property. "Discipline was now so good that the men didn't know themselves and took out their mischief in frightening Negroes."[22] Nevertheless, there were several instances of pillaging and plundering within the city. The home of General W. R. Cox, of Lee's army, was thoroughly ransacked before a guard could be secured. When one did arrive, he refused to make the soldiers return their loot, stating: "I wasn't sent to [make] anybody put down what they got but to keep them from getting things after I have arrived."[23] When this guard marched off with his command, the pillagers returned. Charles Manly also lost property as a result of the Federal occupation.[24]

Following the general policy applied in other Southern towns, the offices of ardent Confederate newspapers were destroyed. Thus the printing establishments of the *Confederate* and the *Conservative* were promptly wrecked. The *Daily Progress* was allowed to continue publication until an article appeared in its columns reflecting upon General

19. *Raleigh News and Observer*, Aug. 20, 1939, quoting *Old Guard*, May, 1866. A correspondent for the *North Carolina Times*, reported that in Raleigh could be heard much "outspoken secessionism and treason, especially among the females. Rebellious songs and tunes greet one's ears from every open parlor window and every mansion is hermetically sealed when our troops pass by." *New Bern N.C. Times*, Apr. 25, 1865.

20. Wright, *6 Ia.*, p. 451. This assemblage of potential voters presented to the politically minded Carl Schurz a golden opportunity for a speech; on one occasion he addressed these men on matters of politics. *Ibid.*

21. Jackson, *Colonel's Diary*, p. 208.

22. Lewis, *Sherman*, p. 534.

23. Battle, *Memoires*, p. 193.

24. C. Manly to D. L. Swain, May 16, 1865, W. Clark Papers, MS Div., N.C. Dept. of Arch. and Hist.

Sherman's order allowing private property to be taken for army purposes without compensation.[25]

Soon after Sherman's entry into Raleigh, W. W. Holden, through his paper, *The Daily Standard,* began to campaign successfully for the resumption of normal business.[26] The Exchange Hotel reopened but in the words of a reporter for the *New York Times,* it furnished "poor lodgings and poorer meals at four dollars per day." Still hanging in the office was a placard from the war days informing the reader that board might be paid with either ten pounds of bacon or ten pounds of lard.[27] Many Raleigh merchants, after reopening their doors, made transactions only in barter.[28] A few new businesses were established during these troubled times. A. D. and V. C. Royster, by acquiring a German sutler's franchise for a $500 note, opened The Royster Candy Company.[29]

The rural population of Wake and adjoining counties where Federal troops were encamped did not fare as well as the citizens of Raleigh. George W. Mordecai wrote David L. Swain that farms in Wake, Orange, and Granville Counties were "completely dispoiled of everything in the shape of provisions and forage." In addition many houses were either burned or torn down.[30] At Charles Manly's plantation three miles from Raleigh, the devastation was "thorough and unsparing." Manly listed as lost all weather boarding, flooring, windows, and furniture in his dwelling houses. Barns, sheds, and cotton houses were stripped of siding; fences were burned; gear was broken up. All hogs and poultry were either driven off or killed. Medicine, "excellent brandy," whiskey, wine, and two hundred gallons of vinegar were taken. Federal wagon trains came out every day until 150 barrels of corn, 15,000 pounds of fodder, 12,000 pounds of hay, and a few bushels of peas and wheat were hauled off.[31]

The Negroes suffered a fate similar to that of their masters. Their "deliberes" usually greeted them with "durn your black skin, give me the watch in your pocket."[32] Jonathan Worth told a Northern writer how the Negroes on his plantation were particularly mistreated by the

25. Spencer, *Ninety Days,* pp. 247-48.   26. *Raleigh Daily Standard,* Apr. 20, 1865.
27. *N.Y. Times,* May 2, 1865.
28. Yates, "Vance and the End of the War," p. 331.
29. Newspaper clipping, 1927, NCC, U.N.C.
30. G. W. Mordecai to D. L. Swain, May 15, 1865, W. Clark Papers, MS Div., N.C. Dept. of Arch. and Hist.
31. C. Manly to D. L. Swain, May 16, 1865, W. Clark Papers, MS Div., N.C. Dept. of Arch. and Hist.
32. Battle, "Sherman's Entry," Newspaper clipping, n.d., NCC, U.N.C.

"bummers." In one instance an axe was held over a Negro's head to make him disclose the hiding place of some bacon. On another occasion, a new dress was stolen from an aged and blind Negro woman.[33] At Manly's plantation the seventy Negroes were "thoroughly plundered of their provisions and clothing."[34]

General Howard was so disturbed by reports that many of the country folk had been stripped of their stock and provisions, that he issued orders that no more animals or subsistence stores were to be taken without specific orders from either the division or corps commanders. He pointed out that a majority of the animals were worthless to the army but invaluable to the farmer in planting his next crop. To enforce this order, guards were made available to those in the country living not more than five miles from any one of the camps of the Army of Tennessee. These guards were instructed to arrest all men out of camp without authority.[35] Almost immediately the different camps were overrun with citizens and parolled Confederate soldiers seeking horses and mules. In most cases spare animals and large quantities of rations were given to them.[36] The more destitute of the civilian and military population were allowed to draw rations from the Federal commissary.[37]

Sometimes foraging operations were not carried on in as thorough a manner as the commissary officers had ordered. An infantry column, advancing to the assistance of a group of foragers, completely forgot the purpose of its mission and stopped to enjoy the hospitality of a small town along its line of march. While there, all, from the major to the ambulance driver, proceeded to get drunk off apple-jack. "But the boys claimed it was persimmon beer that threw down the chaplain."[38] Lieutenant Charles S. Brown, on a foraging detail near Haywood in Chatham County, was interested primarily in the pretty girls of the vicinity. "I

33. Trowbridge, *South*, pp. 581-82.

34. C. Manly to D. L. Swain, May 16, 1865, W. Clark Papers, MS Div., N.C. Dept. of Arch. and Hist.

35. *OR*, XLVII, Pt. III, Ser. I, 251. General Baird in hopes of curbing the lawlessness among his men asked permission to change the site of his camp from Collins Crossroads to more open country where numerous exercises and drills could be held. He asserted that much of the "straggling into the country" could be prevented by keeping the men occupied. In addition Baird wanted to move his camp in order "to relieve the poor inhabitants, who have been stripped of almost everything they possessed." *Ibid.*, p. 260.

36. Hinkley, *3 Wis.*, p. 176.

37. *Raleigh Daily Standard*, May 4, 1865; Yates, "Vance and the End of the War," p. 351.

38. Belknap, "Recollections," *War of the Sixties*, pp. 350-51.

found some of the prettiest girls there I have seen in the South. I would have some fun with the four Misses Bryant and others."[39] Rufus Meade, commissary sergeant for the Fifth Connecticut, stopped at a small cabin near Raleigh and instead of acquiring forage gave the occupants food. The man of the house, so he himself said, was a cousin of Andrew Johnson, "but what a contrast" to the President he was, thought Meade. "This man cannot read, had five little children and scarcely a thing to eat, lives in a house about 15 feet square with only one room and the roof more like a sieve than a covering. . . . I gave them some coffee, etc. so we did what we could for them and think we'll tell Andrew about it when we see him."[40]

The official curtailment of all foraging activities left the soldiers to subsist primarily on government-furnished rations of hard bread and salt pork. Such food soon became distasteful to men accustomed to living off the fat of the land. A group of enterprising troopers from the Fifty-fifth Illinois decided to improve the unhappy situation. A squad of men from the regiment visited a plantation near their camp and "persuaded" the planter to sell them very cheap a wagon load of his miscellaneous provisions. So there would be no question as to the legality of the transaction, the planter was "permitted to transport" the provisions to the camp in his own wagons but he was "mildly enjoined" to tell impertinent inquisitors that the provisions were fully paid for.[41]

Raleigh presented little in the way of entertainment for the Federal soldiers. There was nothing for them to do except make themselves as comfortable as possible. A few of the men who had not drawn clothing issues in Goldsboro were given new uniforms and the recently issued "pup" tents were again erected, giving the camps a more uniform appearance.[42]

The daily routine of camp life, in contrast to the hardships of the march, did not agree with the men. There was an unusual amount of sickness. A soldier of the One Hundred and Seventeenth New York thought it was the "want of military excitement and rising temperatures" that brought on the "intermittent and typhoid fevers" so prevalent among

39. C. S. Brown to Etta (Brown?), Apr. 26, 1865, Brown Papers, MS Div., Duke Univ. Lib.

40. Padgett, "Letters of a Federal Soldier," pp. 79-80.

41. Crooker, 55 Ill., p. 431.

42. Bryant, 3 Wis., p. 329. The smaller pup tent which would accommodate two men replaced the cumbersome Sibley tent in which from twenty to twenty-two soldiers slept.

the troops.[43] With an increasing sick call each day the medical corps found it necessary to take over operation of the large Confederate hospital on the eastern outskirts of the city.[44]

Before moving in, the authorities thought it best to change the names of the different wards since each ward bore the name of a Confederate general. Other than this minor change and the placing of the Confederate wounded in "consecutive wards," the occupation by the Federals of the several hospital buildings was without incident.[45] One policy, unfortunately adopted by the new occupants, caused much resentment among the citizens of Raleigh. Near the hospital was a Confederate burying ground which the Federals wished to use as a cemetery for their own dead. Hence the youth of Raleigh were forced to move the Confederate dead to a lot in another part of the city.[46]

A good many soldiers with time on their hands attended a religious revival conducted by three Protestant chaplains. The grounds were arranged "in old camp meeting style." This called for placing logs at regular distances across which boards were laid for seats. A platform was constructed for the chaplains, and at the four corners of the grounds elevated fire stands were erected. Pine knots burning on these tall lamp poles gave off ample light. There were from twelve to fifteen "inquirers" every night, and on the evening the Lord's Supper was observed fifteen soldiers were baptised.[47]

The regimental bands helped break the monotony of camp life. The work of the Thirty-third Massachusetts was especially well received by both the civilian and military population of Raleigh.[48] The praise heaped upon this fine musical body was appreciated by its members, but more pleasing to them were the mint juleps and milk punch served on their rounds.[49]

One of the favorite pastimes of the soldiers was to gather on the grounds of the Insane Asylum and listen to one of the inmates, Rainy by name, sing and tell stories. Several hundred would gather at one time to

43. Mowris, *117 N.Y.*, p. 214.
44. Bradley, "First N.C. Soldier," *N.C. Regiments,* V, 577.
45. Mowris, *117 N.Y.*, p. 214.
46. Fisher, "Confed. Cemetery," Newspaper clipping, 1927, NCC, U.N.C. The burying plot was given by Mrs. Henry Mordecai for the purpose of establishing a Confederate cemetery. *Ibid.*
47. Merrill, *70 Ind.*, pp. 267-68.
48. Howe, *Marching With Sherman,* p. 300.
49. Underwood, *33 Mass.*, p. 292.

hear Rainy, who occupied a cell overlooking the yard, play his violin, sing "rebel songs" and tell "stories to perfection." Professing to be a strong Union man, he aroused the sympathies of the soldiers to such an extent that on one occasion they attempted to storm the building and effect his release.[50]

General Sherman took time one day to visit the Asylum. In reply to one of the inmates, who asked Sherman to secure his release, the General suggested he put his faith in God. The old man replied that he believed "in a sort of Divine Providence; but when it comes to the question of power it strikes me that . . . you have a damn sight more power than anybody I know."[51]

General Slocum became interested in the school for the blind, deaf, and dumb in the city. He was present once at the exercises put on by the pupils and was so impressed by what he saw that he informed the officials in charge that he would supply all the institutions of the city with an abundance of supplies from the army commissary.[52]

Besides visiting the public institutions within the city, the soldiers liked to saunter through the legislative halls of the state to see how they compared with the Capitols of Mississippi, Tennessee, Georgia, and South Carolina. They considered themselves, from experience, authorities on the subject.[53] The building evidently met with their approval for they used its halls as a meeting place for veteran's associations. The Society of the Army of Tennessee was organized in Raleigh.[54] The Ohio troops also met in the Capitol to select a candidate for governor of the state. According to Colonel Oscar L. Jackson of the Sixty-third Ohio, the meeting was a "big gizzle," proving only that every brigadier general from Ohio considered himself a candidate.[55]

The only duty demanded of the soldiers was attendance at the military reviews. Sherman reviewed his entire army corps while in Raleigh. These occasions were very imposing. As far as the eye could reach it was a sea of bayonets.[56] To the citizens of Raleigh who watched the troops march past Sherman's reviewing stand, a sense of futility in prolonging the war must have seemed obvious. General Slocum overheard a young lady

50. Merrill, 70 Ind., pp. 269-70.   51. Nichols, Great March, p. 289.
52. Wright, 6 Ia., p. 451.
53. New Bern N.C. Times, Apr. 25, 1865; Howe, Marching With Sherman, p. 298.
54. Lewis, Sherman, p. 550.
55. Raleigh Daily Standard, Apr. 18, 20, 1865; Jackson, Colonel's Diary, p. 207.
56. New Bern N.C. Times, Apr. 25, 1865.

standing in the company of an officer remark tearfully: "It's all over with us. . . . A few days ago I saw General Johnston's army, ragged and starved. . . ."[57]

One of the sharpest outfits to parade was the Third Division of the Tenth Corps, composed entirely of Negro troops. General Slocum thought "they were well drilled. Dressed in new and handsome uniforms and with their bright bayonets gleaming in the sun, they made a splendid appearance."[58]   Even a member of Hampton's cavalry, viewing the parade in disguise, had to admit the troops looked good.[59]

The dignity of the spectacle was sometimes broken by the behavior of an unruly horse. A colonel of the Fifteenth Corps was mortified when, just as he gave Sherman a salute, his horse "did some of the finest kicking that ever was seen."[60]

Approximately thirty miles west of Raleigh at the small university town of Chapel Hill, a division of Kilpatrick's cavalry was encamped. The cavalrymen, with the exception of their commanding general, whiled away their time in much the same manner as the troops in Raleigh.

57. Schafer, "Schurz Letters," *Pub. of St. Hist. Soc. of Wis.*, p. 333.
58. Slocum, "Final Operations," *B and L*, IV, 754.
59. Waring Diary, Apr. 22, 1865, SHC, U.N.C.
60. Orendorff, *103 Ill.*, p. 206; Wills, *Wills Diary*, p. 369.

CHAPTER XVI

The General and a Lady

At MORRISVILLE, where the Federal cavalry had halted on the afternoon of April 13, the road divided. The left fork led to Chapel Hill and the right to Hillsboro. General Kilpatrick, with Jordan's brigade, had followed Hampton in the direction of Hillsboro on April 14, while General Atkins, with his brigade, had skirmished Wheeler, who fell back on Chapel Hill.[1] On the afternoon of the 14th the leading detachments of Wheeler's cavalry entered Chapel Hill.[2] Among the first to arrive was a detail of fifteen men under the command of Lieutenant McBurnay Broyles, Fifth Tennessee cavalry. Lieutenant Broyles had orders to report to President Swain[3] and offer the services of his detail for the protection of the University buildings and grounds. Learning that President Swain was in Raleigh, Broyles reported to Professor Charles Phillips, stating that he was ready to guard the University buildings and obey any other instructions the Professor might have. Broyles' detail had been formed at the suggestion of James P. Coffin, a graduate of the University of North Carolina, class of 1859, and at the time a member of Hume's division, Wheeler's corps. After the skirmish at Morrisville the previous day, Coffin went to his commanding officer in person and asked him to send a special detail to Chapel Hill to protect the University campus from injury. Coffin, knowing the character of some of his fellow soldiers and especially that group known as "Wheeler's men," thought only a special guard could protect his alma mater from pillage. General Wheeler ap-

1. *OR*, XLVII, Pt. I, Ser. I, 148; Committee, *92 Ill.*, p. 240.
2. Cheatham's corps had passed through Chapel Hill on April 13. *OR*, XLVII, Pt. I, Ser. I, 148.
3. Swain returned from Raleigh on April 14, but evidently he had not reached home
3. Swain returned from Raleigh on April 14, but evidently he had not reached home when Broyles asked for him. Cornelia P. Spencer, Notebook, May 4, 1865, SHC, U.N.C.

proved the suggestion and told Coffin to select the detail and give what instructions he thought necessary.[4]

Later in the day General Wheeler rode into town.[5] Immediately after establishing his headquarters at the home of Kenneth Waite, on Franklin Street, he broke out his maps and spread them upon the floor. Passers-by could see the General and his young aide, Captain De Rossett, down on their knees studying the maps. Having heard only rumors of Lee's surrender, Wheeler was attempting to trace the line of retreat of the Army of Northern Virginia.[6] Could Lee escape Grant and join forces with Johnston? The question weighed on Wheeler's mind as he knelt on the floor of the Waite home, but more pressing to him at the moment was the question of making a stand at Chapel Hill. His map showed Atkins' brigade still more than a day's march away. Thus he could delay until morning a decision on whether to give battle or continue his retreat. To be safe, orders were issued for the men to dig in, and strong pickets were ordered out on all roads.[7]

The morning of April 15 was cloudy and overcast. Early in the day a heavy rain storm broke, causing the streams to flood. Under these conditions, General Atkins was reluctant to order his brigade out of camp. Around noon, however, orders were received from General Kilpatrick to "go ahead." With much effort, Atkins was able to move his command as far as New Hope Creek, some eight miles east of Chapel Hill. Here a halt was called because the Confederate cavalry had, the previous day, destroyed the bridge over this swollen stream and placed a few pieces of artillery[8] and a small detachment of men on the opposite bank. General Atkins decided that the least costly method of attaining the opposite bank was to cross as many men as possible upstream and thus direct the Confederate artillery fire from the few remaining stringers of the bridge. With artillery removed, the remainder of his attacking force could cross on these stringers. Approximately one hundred men were dismounted and armed with newly issued seven-shot Spencer carbines. Firing these rapid-shot rifles as they crossed, the detachment gained and held the

4. Coffin, "Chapel Hill," *N.C. Univ. Mag.,* XVIII, 273.
5. *OR,* XLVII, Pt. I, Ser. I, 1132.
6. Coffin, "Chapel Hill," p. 274.
7. Spencer, Notebook, May 4, 1865, SHC, U.N.C.
8. Hamilton, "In at the Death," *Mil. Order of the Loyal Legion, Ohio Commandery,* VI, 288-89. W. D. Hamilton, Ninth Ohio cavalry, is the only writer to mention the use of artillery by the Confederates.

opposite bank. By nightfall a new bridge had been constructed, but the heavy rains continued, washing away the bridge during the night. The next morning Atkins received orders to press on to Chapel Hill. After the bridge was rebuilt, the command moved out.[9]

Wheeler, in the meantime, had decided to evacuate the town without a fight. Around two o'clock Sunday afternoon, April 16, he called in his pickets and withdrew his small force.[10] In charge of the rear guard, with orders to clear the town of stragglers, was young James Coffin. He had protected his alma mater from depredations for two days and was now to see that his good work would not be undone by a few stragglers, remaining behind to pillage.[11]

April 16, Easter Sunday, was a beautiful day in Chapel Hill. The sun was shining brightly and the air was redolent with spring. Hearts were heavy, however, as the troopers in gray rode by. Anxiety was written on all faces. No one knew what the next few hours would hold since the town was at the complete mercy of the advancing foe. A Sabbath stillness and silence ensued. The stillness was broken occasionally by one who wished to speculate on the forthcoming events.[12]

Most of the people remained at home and awaited events with a quiet resignation. The University campus was empty. Classes had previously been suspended, and the students who were not residents of Chapel Hill had gone home.[13] In Chapel Hill all valuables had been hidden. Professor Charles Phillips hid the family silver in a horseradish bed; Dr. Mallet put his treasures in a well, and Judge W. H. Battle buried a silver service under a maple tree in the woods near his home, only to forget which one. Professor Phillips and his father, assuming there was little interest among the Federal troops in astronomy, used the University telescope as a hiding place for their watches.[14]

Late in the afternoon President Swain, accompanied by one or two faculty members and several of the principal citizens of the town, was seen with a white handkerchief tied to a pole proceeding first down the Durham and then down the Raleigh road. Thus for the second

9. Spencer, *Ninety Days,* p. 169; Committee, *92 Ill.,* p. 241.
10. Spencer, Notebook, May 4, 1865, SHC, U.N.C.
11. Coffin, "Chapel Hill," p. 274.
12. Spencer, *Ninety Days,* p. 170.
13. Battle, *Univ. of N.C.,* I, 743.
14. Lucy P. Russell, "Memories," Newspaper clippings, 1935, NCC, U.N.C. Battle, *Memories,* p. 199. A bank cashier is supposed to have hidden $30,000 in one of the stone walls surrounding the campus.

time in a matter of days, Swain with a flag of truce, had ventured forth
to meet the enemy. On this occasion his mission was unsuccessful. After
several fruitless trips down each road, the banner was furled and the
people of the village repaired to their respective homes to await the
Federals.[15] It was around sunset when Captain J. M. Schermerhorn,
Ninety-second Illinois, quietly rode into Chapel Hill at the head of
twelve blue-clad cavalrymen.[16]

A sigh of relief went up from the townspeople when the Captain
informed President Swain that he had orders to protect[17] the University.
Following a hasty and fruitless search for Confederate stragglers, the
Captain withdrew his small force from the town.

The next morning General Smith D. Atkins' brigade of Kilpatrick's
cavalry entered Chapel Hill and took possession of the town. Guards
were immediately placed at every home.[18] The greater portion of the
troops went into camp on "the sloping fields north of town, from the
Tenney plantation westward for about a mile."[19] The University buildings were used as quarters for both the officers and their mounts. The
stabling of horses in the library[20] led some Federal officers to remark that
General Atkins' officers were mounted on the best educated horses in
the world.[21] Evidence of this equestrian occupation was still visible in
October, 1865, when the University again opened its doors to students.
Young Peter Mitchel Wilson of Warrenton noted that "the alcoves of
the college library were filled with straw bedding and stable litter left
by the detachment of Federal cavalry recently departed, which converted
the alcoves into stables for their horses. In ultra Roman histories we had
read of the horse that was made a consul. But never before, surely,

15. Spencer, "Old Times," *N.C. Univ. Mag.*, VII, 215. There is another version of
the attempted surrender of Chapel Hill to the Federal forces. Colonel J. L. Cilley of
Atkins command told the daughter of Professor Charles Phillips that he and his command
were startled, as they approached Chapel Hill, by Professor Phillips who stepped out from
beside the road and said: "Halt." Phillips informed the officer that he was surrendering
the town in the absence of President Swain. Russell, "Memories," Newspaper clipping,
1935, NCC, U.N.C. This account does not seem reliable because Captain Schermerhorn,
not Cilly, led the first detachment in on April 16. The Colonel could have been in the
lead the next day when the main body of troops entered, but if this were the case, Lucy P.
Russell, author of the account, was mistaken in stating that Swain was out of town.

16. Committee, *92 Ill.*, p. 241.

17. *OR*, XLVII, Pt. III, Ser. I, 215.

18. Cornelia P. Spencer, Diary, Apr. 17, 1865, SHC, U.N.C.

19. Henderson, *Campus of the Univ.*, p. 184.

20. The college library of 1865 is the present Carolina Playmaker Theatre.

21. This anecdote is tradition around Chapel Hill.

had a horse been a student."[22] These mounts were exposed not only to the intellectual pursuits of the college boy but also to other phases of University life. One inhabitant of Chapel Hill reported seeing horses looking out of the windows of Old West building;[23] and South building, as late as 1874, was still defiled by the "ordure of cattle and horses."[24] And W. H. Battle, in a speech delivered in June, 1865, said that South building: "has lately sheltered cavalry of the conquering Union army in the great Civil War."[25]

Nevertheless, with the exception of the grounds which were used as pasture for the cavalry mounts, the University campus suffered very little at the hands of the invader. President Swain estimated the damage at not over $100.[26] In February, 1874, the Board of Trustees, meeting in Raleigh, appointed a three-man committee to visit Chapel Hill and "report the condition of the property and funds of the University." This group made its report on April 9, 1874. It found the University property in very bad condition but attributed it to neglect and the weather. Nowhere in the report was there mention of any damage that might have been sustained during the Federal occupation.[27]

Neither did the town itself suffer much property damage. Some families were inconvenienced by the quartering of officers in the home, but even this was not the general practice. The guards, belonging to Ninth Michigan, did an excellent job of protecting property. According to Cornelia Spencer they deserved "especial mention as being a decent set of men . . . who behaved with civility and propriety."[28] Many of the officers and men visited the families of Chapel Hill and "were extremely courteous and were treated with courtesy." Others spent considerable time playing with the local children. Even the privates, who spent most of their hours lounging around, "appeared in all respects like other human beings" for they behaved and spoke well.[29]

Colonel W. D. Hamilton, Tenth Ohio, soon after his arrival

22. Wilson, *Southern Exposure*, p. 40.
23. Henderson, *Campus of the Univ.*, p. 184.
24. Minutes of Executive Committee of the Board of Trustees of the Univ. of N.C., Apr. 9, 1874, SHC, U.N.C.
25. Wheeler, *Memories of N.C.*, p. 351.
26. Weeks, "Univ. of N.C.," *So. Hist. Soc. Papers*, XXIV, 31.
27. Minutes of Executive Committee of the Board of Trustees of the Univ. of N.C., Apr. 9, 1874, SHC, U.N.C.
28. Spencer, *Ninety Days*, p. 172.
29. Spencer, Notebook, May 4, 1865, SHC, U.N.C.

in Chapel Hill, was invited to the home of Professor Fordyce M. Hubbard where he had "the pleasure of meeting two very charming ladies in the person of his [Hubbard's] wife and daughter." The dinner was frugal, but the white bread brought forth compliments from the guest. Upon learning that a barrel of flour cost $1,000 and that the hostess had scraped the bottom of the barrel for the baking, Hamilton doubly appreciated his dinner invitation. A few days later he was happy to have the opportunity to send Mrs. Hubbard a barrel of flour as a gift. This kindness brought from the daughter "a beautiful specimen of the fragrant magnolia in full bloom" and an invitation to meet some young people of the town at the home of another faculty member.[30]

The household of Professor Charles Phillips became quite fond of the guard at their home, a young Michigan soldier named Tenny. This fondness was not dampened even when "Rosebud," the cow, had to be dislodged from her stall to make room for Tenny's big roan, "Bob." Young Tenny spent much of his time either nursing the sick grandmother in the home or taking Lucy and Mary Phillips to ride on "Bob."[31]

General Atkins found it imperative that he forage liberally off the country until the railroad from Goldsboro to Raleigh could be repaired and supplies brought up for the army. Consequently the residents out from Chapel Hill suffered.

Conditions became so bad that on April 19, President Swain addressed a letter to Sherman stating:

GENERAL. . . . On my return to this village on Saturday morning, fifteenth instant, I found that General Wheeler, with his division of cavalry, had been encamped here for two days. He resumed his march on Sunday morning, leaving the country denuded to a considerable extent of forage, and taking with him a number of horses and mules. General Atkins arrived with his Brigade on Monday morning, and it is in camp here now. I have had several interviews with General Atkins, and have pleasure in stating that he manifests a disposition to execute his orders with as much forbearance as he deems compatible with a proper discharge of his duty. Nevertheless, many worthy families have been stripped by his soldiers of the necessary means of subsistence. A Baptist clergyman—a most estimable citizen, and the most extensive farmer within a circle of three miles—is almost entirely destitute of provision for man and beast; and with a family of more than fifty persons (white and colored), has not a single horse or mule. Other instances, not less

30. Hamilton, "In at the Death," pp. 291-92.
31. Russell, "Memories," Newspaper clipping, 1935, NCC, U.N.C.

striking, exist, of families in less affluent circumstances; but I refer particularly to Mr. Purefoy, because he has been my near neighbor for about thirty years, and I hold him in the highest estimation. He, like many others, is not merely without the present means of subsistence, but unless his horses and mules are restored or replaced, can make no provision for the future. The delay of a few days even may render it impossible to plant corn within the proper time.

I am satisfied from the impression made upon me in our recent interview, that, personally, you have no disposition to add to the unavoidable horrors of war, by availing yourself of the utmost license which writers on the subject deem admissible, but that, on the contrary, you would prefer to treat the peaceful tillers of the soil with no unnecessary harshness. I venture to hope, therefore, that the present state of negotiations between the contending armies will enable you to relax the severity of the orders under which General Atkins is acting, and I am satisfied that if you shall feel yourself justified by the course of events in doing so, an intimation of your purpose will be welcome intelligence to him.[32]

On April 22, Sherman sat down and penned Swain an answer:

Yours of April nineteenth was laid before me yesterday, and I am pleased that you recognize in General Atkins a fair representative of our army.

The moment war ceases, and I think that time is at hand, all seizures of horses and private property will cease on our part. And it may be that we will be able to spare some animals for the use of the farmers of your neighborhood. There now exists a species of truce, but we must stand prepared for action; but I believe that in a very few days a definite and general peace will be arranged, when I will make orders that will be in accordance with the new state of affairs.

I do believe that I fairly represent the feelings of my countrymen—that we prefer peace to war; but, if war is forced upon us, we must meet it; but, if peace be possible, we will accept it, and be the friends of the farmers and working classes of North Carolina, as well as actual patrons of churches,

32. D. L. Swain to Sherman, Apr. 19, 1865, W. Clark Papers, MS Div., N.C. Dept. of Arch. and Hist. Even under these conditions, acts of kindness by the foragers was not unknown. One group of foragers rode several miles through a blinding rainstorm to fetch a midwife for a lady alone at her home and in labor. Feeling a special interest in the prospective birth, the foragers remained until the baby was born. The next morning one of the soldiers paced the floor with the child. To the infant he sang the following "lullaby" (Belknap, "Recollections," *War of the Sixties.*, p. 353):

I'm a raw recruit in a brand new suit
    Nine hundred dollars bounty;
And I've come from the Tar-heel town
    To fight for North Caroliny.

colleges, asylums, and all institutions of learning and charity. Accept the assurances of my respect and high esteem.[33]

Work on the railroad progressed rapidly, and when supplies became available at rail bases nearby, Atkins ordered his commissary officer to issue rations to all citizens both black and white who applied for them.[34] Earlier he had written Kilpatrick that it would be a pleasure for him to return to the citizens all the animals his command had taken, provided no campaign was in the offing. He thought this move would relieve much of the suffering in the community. Kilpatrick, however, answered that horses and mules could not be returned without dismounting men.[35]

The Federal occupation of Chapel Hill was uneventful until the news of Lincoln's assassination was learned. This announcement made the citizens very uneasy. They feared some form of retaliation might be taken by the troops. Many went to the Federal officers and inquired if the town was to be burned. Upon learning there was no danger of this, the townspeople became more cordial with the troopers.[36] Cornelia Spencer thought the announcement of the President's death put the local heads in the lions mouth "and it behooved . . . them to be careful."[37]

One of the most interesting incidents of the occupation of Chapel Hill by the Federal troops was General Atkins' courtship of "Ellie" Swain. During the period of tension, General Atkins decided to make a formal call upon President Swain.[38] He was warmly received by Swain. In the course of their conversation the host mentioned that he possessed Lord Cornwallis' order book and wondered if his military visitor would be interested in seeing it. When the General showed interest in seeing the old volume, Swain stepped into the adjoining room and asked his attractive young daughter, Eleanor, to go upstairs and get it. "The young lady did so, perhaps not unwilling to have a look at the Yankee General. She threw up her head and marched in with a great display of hauteur. An introduction was unavoidable. . . . They changed eyes at first sight."[39] Colonel Hamilton stated: "A feathered arrow from the

33. Sherman to D. L. Swain, Apr. 22, 1865, W. Clark Papers, MS Div., N.C. Dept. of Arch. and Hist.

34. Committee, 92 *Ill.*, p. 245.   35. *OR*, XLVII, Pt. III, Ser. I, 248.

36. Hamilton, "In at the Death," p. 205.

37. Spencer, "Old Times," p. 216.

38. Colonel W. D. Hamilton maintains that it was he who arranged for General Atkins to visit the Swain home and for the express purpose of meeting young Eleanor Swain. Hamilton, "In at the Death," pp. 291-93.

39. Spencer, "Old Times," p. 216.

ancient bow had pierced the heart the modern bullet had failed to reach."[40] A romance blossomed from this meeting. Each evening Atkins sent his regimental band to serenade his lady-love,[41] and when General Sherman sent President Swain a fine carriage horse, Atkins matched the gift by presenting the President's daughter a handsome riding horse.[42] Acceptance of these gifts by the Swains was unwise, as it was assumed by most Chapel Hillians that these steeds were spoils of war taken from Southern stables.[43] For retaining these favors the recipients were condemned by their neighbors and friends.

The General spent a goodly portion of his waking hours in the company of "Ellie" Swain. When they noticed that their daughter was not in a budding but a flowering romance, the President and his wife became greatly perturbed. Neither parent knew what their daughter would decide. They purposely refrained from asking her, perferring, the President said, not to know until after the General's departure.[44]

The romance brought repercussions outside of the Swain home. Both the Federal troops and local citizens became incensed over the affair. The soldiers knew something was wrong when their popular General stopped making them speeches. Before arriving in Chapel Hill, Atkins, a lawyer by profession, had always responded cheerfully to their calls for a speech. On one occasion the band of the Ninety-second Illinois decided to serenade the General. Not finding him at his headquarters, they proceeded to the most logical place of his whereabouts, the Swain home. Sure enough he was there. After serenading him with several selections, the members of the band called for a few words. Shortly Atkins appeared on the porch of the Swain residence and addressed the band as follows:

Soldiers, I am making a speech to a young lady here tonight, and I have no eloquence to waste—she requires it all. The War, as I told you it would, at Mount Olive, has played out, and in less than the ninety days I then named. I think speech making has played out also, except to the young ladies. You must go to your quarters.

This was one of the few unpopular talks Atkins ever made. The troopers sullenly returned to camp. The men, though, received some consolation

40. Hamilton, "In at the Death," p. 291.   41. Spencer, "Old Times," p. 217.
42. Chamberlain, *Old Days,* p. 95.
43. Spencer, Notebook, May 4, 1865, SHC, U.N.C.
44. *Ibid.*

from the fact that their General was cross to everyone those days, with the exception of "Ellie."[45]

The simple fact that Atkins was a Federal officer was reason enough for the locals to view this affair with complete disgust. One diarist wrote: "Who can sympathize with or even pity a young lady who willingly throws herself into the arms of a Yankee General, while his sword is yet reeking with the blood of its victims, her own relations or at least her own countrymen."[46] The fact that Atkins was handsome and well mannered could not outweight the realization that he was a brigade commander for the notorious Kilpatrick, who had boasted that his march through the South would be marked by "chimney stacks without houses."[47] In Chapel Hill, neighbor asked neighbor just how many of these homes had Atkins himself ordered burned. Rumors were soon afloat that Atkins' brigade was responsible for most of the depredations in Sampson County, and around Faison in Duplin County. Adding fuel in the flame were charges that Atkins cursed a lady in Chapel Hill and stole silver plates from the home of one Rebecca Jones of Hillsboro.[48]

In later years Swain had many talks with Atkins who convinced him that the stories of spoilations had no foundation. Atkins also had many long conversations with Cornelia Phillips Spencer. On one occasion he told her that "he would be willing to go into any house where he was quartered in North Carolina and be sure of receiving a courteous welcome. . . . He admitted many things about the army and some of the officers—but that himself and all the officers of his brigade (with one exception) did their best to prevent plundering and protect the people. . . . He admitted that there was little or no discipline in the army and said it was impossible to enforce it." After this talk Cornelia wrote Zebulon B. Vance that she was inclined to believe Atkins. But she could say little complimentary about the General. "Evidently" he was not a well-educated man. In addition, he "talked through his nose and was artificial

45. Committee, 92 *Ill.*, p. 246.
46. Henderson, *Campus of the Univ.*, p. 186, quoting from the "diary of a member of the class of 1865," in the possession of A. Henderson, Chapel Hill, N. C.
47. Committee, 92 *Ill.*, p. 211.
48. E. J. Hale to D. L. Swain, June 26, 1866, W. Clark Papers, MS Div., N.C. Dept. of Arch. and Hist. The charge of stealing silver was definitely proven to be groundless. Dr. Pride Jones, son of Rebecca Jones, authorized John W. Graham of Hillsboro to state for him: "No silver was taken the night General Atkins stayed at the house of his mother, Mrs. Rebecca Jones." The silver was stolen by Negro servants. J. W. Graham to D. L. Swain, June 11, 1866, W. Clark Papers, MS Div., N.C. Dept. of Arch. and Hist.

in manner." Even after acknowledging that he had "sense and smartness," she qualified these virtues as being "Yankee like."[49]

While the troops were encamped in Chapel Hill, one could only speculate as to the outcome of this romance. Eleanor's parents certainly did not know, having refrained from questioning her on the subject. It was not until after General Atkins' departure on May 3 that the long awaited announcement came. In a short note addressed to her parents "Miss Ellie" stated that she intended to marry General Atkins. She reminded her parents that she was twenty-one years old and capable of judging for herself. In the face of the furor caused by her decision, the strong-willed Eleanor wrote a friend that "but one voice can prevent this affair, and that is higher than man."[50] God did not see fit to intervene and the couple was married August 23, 1865. It was a victory for "true love," wrote Cornelia Spencer.[51]

Surely Atkins, as he led his troops out of Chapel Hill on April 3, felt that war is not altogether hell.

49. C. P. Spencer to Z. B. Vance, n.d., Vance Papers, MS Div., N.C. Dept. of Arch. and Hist.

50. Chamberlain, *Old Days*, p. 95.

51. Spencer, Notebook, Aug. 23-25, 1865, SHC, U.N.C.

CHAPTER XVII

From Glory to Disrepute

SHERMAN'S CONFIDENCE that the war was over and peace and quiet were in the offing was given a rude jolt on April 23. On this date he read in the New York newspapers for the first time that Federal authorities had rescinded the order permitting the Virginia legislature to convene. This startling news along with the intense feeling in the North over Lincoln's murder, described also in the newspapers, prompted Sherman to write Johnston that their efforts to recognize existing state governments "might now be thwarted."[1] Major Hitchcock's return from Washington would tell whether his consternation was well founded. On the evening of the 23rd the Major wired from Morehead City that he would arrive in Raleigh the next morning. No mention was made of the message he carried. At 6:00 A.M. on the morning of April 24, Hitchcock arrived in Raleigh in company with General Grant.[2] Sherman was greatly surprised and totally unprepared to greet his commanding officer. In fact he was still in his night clothes.[3]

As soon as the two Generals were alone, Grant informed Sherman that his terms with Johnston had been disapproved and that Sherman was authorized to offer only the terms given at Appomattox to Lee. For the first time Sherman saw a copy of Lincoln's famous telegram of March 4, 1865, to Grant instructing the latter in his negotiations with Lee not "to decide, discuss, or confer upon any political question."[4]

Grant had arrived in Raleigh purposely unannounced. He hoped his presence would be unnoticed by Sherman's troops who might suspect that the motive of his visit was to supercede Sherman in command. Grant had neither the heart nor the desire to tell his close friend of this order nor of the one directing the Federal troops in the South not to obey

1. *OR*, XLVII, Pt. III, Ser. I, 287.   2. Sherman, *Memoirs*, II, 358-59.
3. Howe, *Marching With Sherman*, p. 308.   4. Sherman, *Memoirs*, II, 358-60.

Sherman's orders. Thus he deliberately withheld the information from his host.[5] Neither did he give Sherman the details of the hastily assembled cabinet meeting of the night of April 21. At that meeting Stanton had stampeded the members into a unanimous disapproval of Sherman's memorandum. The frantic Secretary of War expressed the belief that Sherman, at the head of his victorious army, actually had designs upon the government. Grant, silent during the Secretary's emotional outburst and denunciation of Sherman, felt his friend had acted unwisely by embodying civil matters in a military truce, but he would not accept the charge that Sherman had designs on the government.[6] He had been present at City Point where Lincoln and Sherman had agreed that a hasty restoration of the South to its proper place in the Union was best for the nation as a whole. Grant was certain that Sherman had acted with absolute sincerity in his benevolent attitude toward the South.

The New York newspapers of the previous day had prepared Sherman for the possibility that the agreement would be disapproved, and with little show of emotion he addressed two notes to Johnston. In the first he informed the Confederate General that the suspension of hostilities would cease forty-eight hours after the note reached his lines. This was in accordance with the first article of their agreement of April 18. In the second dispatch, penned shortly after the first, Sherman informed Johnston that he was empowered to offer only the terms Grant gave Lee at Appomattox.[7] This dispatch was rushed to Kilpatrick at Durham's Station for immediate delivery to the Confederate lines.[8] Later in the day Sherman issued orders for all commands to be ready to move within forty-eight hours.[9]

While awaiting a reply from Johnston, Sherman addressed a short note to Stanton admitting his folly in embracing civil matters in a military convention, but he was quick to point out that he still believed the

5. Grant, *Memoirs*, II, 516-17; *OR*, XLVII, Pt. III, Ser. I, 321; Sherman, *Memoirs*, II, 359.

6. Welles, *Welles Diary*, II, 294-98; Sherman, *Memoirs*, II, 360. Stanton wrote of Sherman's terms: "I am beyond measure at the terms. . . . They are inadmissible. There should now be literally no terms granted. We should not only brand leading rebels with infamy, but the whole rebellion should bear the badge of the penitentiary." Commager, *Documents of Amer. Hist.*, I, 447.

7. *OR*, XLVII, Pt. III, Ser. I, 293-94.

8. *Ibid.*, p. 298.

9. Sherman, *Memoirs*, II, 358. This order came as a bitter disappointment to the soldiers who had hoped their next march would be home. Nevertheless, they knew "orders were orders" and had to be obeyed. Committee, *92 Ill.*, p. 247.

Federal authorities were making a mistake in not approving the agreement.[10] Although General Grant was staying at his headquarters, Sherman also wrote him an official letter in which he restated his strong conviction that the use of existing state governments was the best possible method to get the "desired result," namely, complete submission of the South to the authority of the United States government.[11]

On the afternoon of April 24, Johnston, who had been in Greensboro since the meeting at Bennett's farmhouse, received a wire from President Davis, then in Charlotte, approving the terms of April 18.[12] Before Johnston could communicate this news to Sherman he received the latter's two dispatches. The contents of these communications were wired immediately to Charlotte, and on the morning of April 25, Davis' reply was in Johnston's hands. The President ordered the disbanding of the infantry to meet again at some appointed location. As for the cavalry and all soldiers who could be mounted, Johnston was ordered to organize this conglomeration into an escort for the President in his flight through the South. Johnston, more convinced than ever that it would be a great crime to prolong the war, "deliberately disobeyed these orders." Instead of joining Davis, he suggested to Sherman that they meet again to discuss terms of surrender.[13] Sherman answered that he would meet Johnston at Bennett's at noon on April 26.[14]

The armistice had created a hopeless disciplinary problem in the Confederate army. General Johnston estimated that, between April 19 and 24, over four thousand from the infantry and artillery deserted and almost as many from the cavalry.[15] A Northern newspaper correspondent was near the truth when he expressed the opinion that if the terms were not agreed upon soon, Sherman would have to lend Johnston some men to surrender.[16] Although its authenticity is highly doubtful, the following letter conveys the feeling prevalent among many of the Confederate troops at this time:

> deer sister Lizzy: i hev conkluded that the dam fulishness uv tryin to lick shurmin had better be stoped. we hav bin gettin nuthin but hell and lots uv it ever since we saw the dam yankys and i am tirde uv it. shurmin has a lots

10. Sherman, *Memoirs*, II, 362.   11. *Ibid.*, pp. 360-62.
12. *OR*, XLVII, Pt. III, Ser. I, 821-34.
13. Johnston, *Narrative*, pp. 441-42; *OR*, XLVII, Pt. III, Ser. I, 303.
14. *OR*, XLVII, Pt. III, Ser. I, 304.   15. Johnston, *Narrative*, p. 410.
16. *New Bern N.C. Times*, Apr. 25, 1865.

of pemps that don't care a dam what they doo, and its no use trying to whip em. if we don't git hell when shurmin starts again i miss my gess. if i cood get home ide tri dam hard to git thare. my old horse is plaid out or ide trie to go now. maibee ile start to nite fur ime dam tire duv this war fur nuthin. if the dam yankees haven't got thair yit its a dam wunder. thair thicker an lise on a hen and a dam site ornraier. your brother jim.[17]

General Baird reported to Sherman that large numbers of Johnston's men, passing into this line on their way home, reported that no objections were made by the Confederate officers to their leaving.[18] Colonel Wright of Hampton's cavalry allowed his men to desert so they might avoid the humility of surrender.[19] But there was absolutely no surrender in Hampton. The popular cavalry leader rallied his men by personal appearances. To help his troops divert their minds from home, he approved of camp tournaments such as the one held by Waring's brigade on April 22, and witnessed by females from "far and near."[20] For many of Hampton's staff, as well as the General himself, the truce was a "bitter pill."[21] The army could revive again and the South "yet be free" they felt sure.[22]

Sherman once more went to Durham's Station by rail. There he was met by Kilpatrick and escorted to the place of meeting. After the usual salutations, Sherman and Johnston retired to the one downstairs room of the Bennett house. They were inside "a long time" before Sherman called Schofield, who had accompanied him. Schofield was informed by his commander that they had been unable to reach an agreement. Johnston objected to the terms being based solely on those given to Lee by Grant on April 9. He pointed out that the disbanding of Lee's army at Appomattox, without sufficient provisions for subsistence or arms for protection and no transportation to their homes, had turned the parolees into a band of robbers.[23] Sherman on the other hand felt that any terms not based on Lee's terms of the 9th would be disapproved in Washington. Schofield solved this dilemma by pointing out that he would be departmental commander after Sherman's departure and could then take care of any difficulties that might arise with the disbanding of the army. This solution to their problem suited both generals. So Schofield with

17. Welch, *Surgeon's Letters*, p. 121.
18. A. Baird to Sherman, Apr. 24, 1865, Sherman Papers, MS Div., L.C.
19. Waring Diary, Apr. 26, 1865, SHC, U.N.C.
20. *Ibid.*, Apr. 22, 1865.   21. *Ibid.*, Apr. 21, 1865.
22. *Ibid.*, Apr. 19, 1865.   23. *OR*, XLVII, Pt. III, Ser. I, 304.

pen in hand sat down and wrote the Military Convention of April 26,[24] which was agreed to by Johnston "without difficulty"[25] and Sherman, "without hesitation."[26] By the terms of this short agreement, Johnston's army was to be mustered at Greensboro where ordnance supplies were to be deposited and men paroled to their homes.[27]

Still in the company of Johnston, Schofield sketched a series of six supplemental terms in which he assured Johnston that transportation would be provided for the majority of the troops on their way home. He also agreed that each Confederate brigade or group could keep one-seventh of their arms until they reached their respective state capitals. Both officers and enlisted men were to be allowed retention of their private property and horses.[28] This agreement was dated April 26, and was signed by Johnston and Schofield, not Sherman. The next day, Sherman instructed Schofield to facilitate in any way he could the return of the Confederate soldiers to their homes. He was ordered to furnish this disbanded army with enough rations for ten days.[29] In carrying out these instructions, Schofield was able to furnish the Confederate troops 250,000 rations and wagons to haul them. These rations in a large measure kept the Confederate soldiers from subsisting on the already depleted countryside, as they returned to their homes.[30]

After leaving Bennett's farmhouse, Johnston announced the termination of hostilities in two dispatches, one to the governors of the states, the other to the Confederate army.[31]

Early in the evening of the 26th, Sherman reached Raleigh. He proceeded directly to his headquarters in the governor's mansion. Outside a band was serenading the large crowd of officers standing on the front patio, but Sherman was in no mood to stop and mingle with this group. He hastily entered the house for he wished to show Grant the terms he had in his pocket.[32] Upon Sherman's request the General wrote his approval on the terms. Grant remarked that the only change he would have made would have been to put Sherman's name before Johnston's. The next morning with the original of this agreement in his possession, Grant departed for New Bern.[33]

24. Schofield, *Forty-six Years*, pp. 351-52.   25. Johnston, *Narrative*, p. 412.
26. Sherman, *Memoirs*, II, 362.   27. *OR*, XLVII, Pt. III, Ser. I, 313.
28. *Ibid.*, p. 482.   29. *Ibid.*, p. 320.
30. Schofield, *Forty-six Years*, p. 352.   Johnston, *Narrative*, p. 418.
31. Johnston, *Narrative*, p. 415.
32. Howe, *Marching With Sherman*, p. 316.
33. Sherman, *Memoirs*, II, 363.

News of the final surrender did not bring the "exciting freshness" that accompanied the first announcement of the previous week.[34] There was no triumphant show put on by the victorious troops of Sherman's army.[35] The absence of boasting did not mean that the news was accepted without celebration. Fire works blazed in the streets of Raleigh; torchlight processions were numerous; bands played and everyone sang and cheered.[36] In fact the celebration continued for a couple of days. When the *Raleigh Standard* went to press on Friday, April 28, rockets were still going off, bands still playing and the soldiers yet rejoicing over the thought of peace.[37] Julian W. Hinkley of the Third Wisconsin exclaimed: "Just think of it! I can hardly realize it. No more skirmishing, no more digging trenches and building breastworks, no more whistling bullets, rattling grapeshot, or screaming shells, no more friends and comrades to be killed or wounded."[38] In contrast to Hinkley was a young soldier of the One Hundred and Third Illinois, who was positive that civil life would go "sorely against the grain," at least for a time. For him the soldier's way was much the best. He dreaded being a civilian again, trying to be sharp and trying to make money.[39] From Chapel Hill and members of the Ninety-second Illinois came the most common reaction to peace. These Illinois cavalrymen certainly were not afraid of civilian life as was the Illinois infantryman; nor did they look upon peace merely as no more bullets and no more screaming shells. To them peace meant mustering out and discharge from the army. These two facts occupied their minds. Just why were they not being discharged as were some infantry regiments, they asked.[40]

Rebuffed in his efforts to befriend the South politically, Sherman did what he could to alleviate the economic distresses in the region around Raleigh. Army commanders were ordered to "loan" the inhabitants at once all the captured horses, mules, wagons, and vehicles that could be spared from immediate use. Generals were encouraged to issue provisions, animals and any public supplies that could be spared "to relieve present wants and to encourage the inhabitants to renew their peaceful pursuits and to restore the relations of friendship among our fellow-

34. Underwood, *33 Mass.*, p. 293.   35. Aten, *85 Ill.*, p. 307.
36. Underwood, *33 Mass.*, p. 293.   37. *Raleigh Daily Standard,* Apr. 28, 1865.
38. Hinkly, *3 Wis.*, pp. 173-75.   39. Orendorff, *103 Ill.*, p. 206.
40. Committee, *92 Ill.*, p. 247.

citizens and countrymen." Foraging was to cease and all provisions acquired were to be paid for on the spot.[41]

To Johnston, Sherman expressed the hope that the animals "loaned" the farmers would be enough to insure a crop. In closing, he repeated the familiar promise: "Now that the war is over, I am willing to risk my person and reputation as heretofore to heal the wounds made by the past war. . . ."[42] He went on to say that he thought his feeling was shared by his army and that of Johnston's also. In his reply, Johnston informed Sherman that in all of their interviews he had been impressed by his sincere desire "to heal the wounds made by the [past] war." The most amazing line in this letter was the usually impassive Johnston's confession that the misfortune of his life was that of having had to encounter Sherman in the field.[43]

Having placed upon Schofield the responsibility of carrying out the surrender terms, Sherman prepared to leave for Savannah, Georgia. There he planned a short conference with General Wilson. Then it would be a quick return to his troops at Richmond.

His plans for departure were temporarily interrupted with the arrival in Raleigh of the New York newspapers of April 24. As he read the *New York Times,* his face became flushed and his anger began to rise. Prominent in the paper's columns, banded in heavy mourning for Lincoln, was an official War Department bulletin published over Stanton's signature.[44] This bulletin implied that Sherman had deliberately disobeyed Lincoln's order of March 3, directing Grant to discuss only military matters with Lee, an order Sherman was completely ignorant of until Grant's arrival in Raleigh. More besmirching of Sherman, yet more absurd, was Stanton's implication that the General, for "bankers gold," might allow Davis to escape.[45] On April 21, Halleck had wired Stanton that Davis was fleeing south with a large amount of specie, hoping to make terms with Sherman or some Southern official for the continuance of his flight to Mexico or Europe.[46] This news, coupled with the knowledge of Sherman's order of April 18 to Stoneman to join him near Raleigh,[47] caused the jumpy Secretary to reason that Sherman was deliberately allowing Davis to escape.

41. *OR*, XLVII, Pt. III, Ser. I, 322.   42. *Ibid.,* p. 320.
43. *Ibid.,* pp. 336-37.   44. *N.Y. Times,* Apr. 24, 1865.
45. Sherman, *Memoirs,* II, 365.   46. *OR,* XLVII, Pt. III, Ser. I, 277.
47. *Ibid.,* p. 249. Stoneman never received the order. He and his staff had already departed for Knoxville while the cavalry raided to the southwest.

Sherman's order to Stoneman was issued in complete indifference to Davis' flight. He merely hoped, in accordance with the truce of April 18, to halt Stoneman's devastation of the western part of the state.[48] Had Stanton known the intent of Sherman's order it is doubtful he would have accepted it. He had deliberately deleted the following sentence from Halleck's wire of April 21: "Would it not be well to put Sherman and all other commanding generals on their guard in this respect."[49] The deletion of this line made it look as though Halleck also suspicioned Sherman's motives. In view of the fact that Davis left Greensboro for Charlotte on April 16 and that Sherman did not wire Stoneman until the evening of the 18th, Stanton's accusation seems all the more ridiculous.

Following these implications was a copy of the memorandum of April 18 and Stanton's nine reasons for its rejection. Among the reasons listed were: "It was a practical acknowledgement of the rebel government"; it "placed the arms and munitions of war in the hands of rebels at their respective capitals. . . ."; it would enable the re-establishment of slavery through the restoration "of rebel authority in their respective states"; it would furnish grounds of responsibility by the Federal government to pay "the rebel debt"; it put in dispute the existence of local state governments and the new state government of West Virginia; it practically abolished the confiscation laws; it gave terms that Lincoln would have rejected; and, "it formed no basis of true and lasting peace."[50] Stanton's legal mind had caught the loopholes in Sherman's peace terms, but the implication that Sherman might be part of a conspiracy to allow Davis to escape was the product of a disturbed state of mind.

The publication of this bulletin made Sherman see red. Reacting as if he were a caged lion, Sherman, before members of his staff, lashed out at Stanton as a "mean, scheming, vindictive politician who made it his business to rob military men of their credit earned by exposing their lives in the service of their country. He berated the people who blamed him for what he had done as a mass of fools, not worth fighting for, who did not know when a thing was well done. He railed at the press . . . which had become the engine of vilification. . . ."[51]

---

48. On April 18, Stoneman was in Statesville, approximately seventy-five miles southwest of Greensboro. Had Stanton bothered to examine a map he would have seen that in order to reach Raleigh, Stoneman would have moved along the railroad upon which Davis was fleeing.

49. *OR*, XLVII, Pt. III, Ser. I, 277.

50. *N.Y. Times*, Apr. 24, 1865.

51. Schurz, *Reminiscences*, III, 116-18.

Considering the bulletin "a personal and official insult," Sherman gave vent to his feeling in a lengthy letter to Grant. In closing this letter the General took a direct dig at Stanton when he stated:

It is true that non-combatants, men who sleep in comfort and security while we watch on the distant lines, are better able to judge than we poor soldiers, who rarely see a newspaper, hardly hear from our families, or stop long enough to draw our pay. I envy not the task of "reconstruction," and am delighted that the Secretary of War has relieved me of it.[52]

The official announcement of Sherman's actions at Bennett's farmhouse brought forth a storm of criticism from the press of the country. One could read in the *New York Herald* that Sherman's "splendid military career" was at an end, that he would retire under a cloud having fatally blundered, for, "with a few unlucky strokes of his pen," he had "blurred all the triumphs of his sword."[53] The *Chicago Tribune* informed its readers that Sherman had been "completely over-reached and outwitted by Joe Johnston."[54] His actions could be accounted for only "on the hypothesis of stark insanity." An American diplomat, quoted in the *New York Times,* opinioned that the General's brain had been "seriously affected." He now had "White House on the Brain."[55] The periodicals joined the daily press in the condemnation of Sherman. H. M. Alden, editor of *Harper's Weekly,* declared: "General Sherman could not have surprised his country more if he had surrendered his army to Johnston. . . ." Alden admitted that the best of soldiers might be the worst of statesmen, but it was lamentable that the truth had to be illustrated by one whom the people so revered.[56]

From Ohio, however, came a loud voice in defense of her native son. The *Cincinnati Commercial,* in a series of four editorials entitled "A Word for Sherman," defended the General's actions of April 18. The editor pointed out that "Lee only proposed to surrender the army then in the field under his immediate command. Johnston proposed to disband all the armies in the Confederacy. Lee did not propose to put an end to the war. Johnston did. Lee asked and obtained terms for every soldier and officer embraced in his surrender, for he comprised no others. Johnston asked for terms for every officer and soldier, and for every citizen and rebel embraced in his surrender, for he comprised every one of them.

---

52. Sherman, *Memoirs,* II, 365-67. 53. *N.Y. Herald,* Apr. 24, 1865.
54. Lewis, *Sherman,* p. 553. 55. *N.Y. Times,* Apr. 26, 1865.
56. Alden, "Sherman," *Harpers Weekly,* IX, 274.

If it was proper for Lee to ask for terms for his soldiers, it was quite as proper for Johnston to ask for terms for all the rebels, armed and unarmed, soldiers and civilians, for he surrendered them all."[57]

As the papers filled their columns with charges of insanity, stupidity, and disloyalty on the part of Sherman, the men of his army became incensed at what they read. Soldiers, with officer's permission, took delight in burning all the New York newspapers they could find.[58] Theodore F. Upson warned the gentlemen of the press that they "had better look a leedle [little] out or they would have General Sherman's army to reckon with," for, said he, the soldiers did not propose to have their popular commander slandered.[59] A private from the Midwest entered in his diary: "I won't believe he has made a mistake until I know all about it. It can't be. ... I'd rather fight under him than Grant and if he were Mahomet we'd be devoted Mussulmen."[60] General Schofield, in a letter dated Raleigh, June 7, 1865, reasserted this faith in Sherman as expressed by Upson and the above mentioned private. He wrote his commanding officer as follows: "I believe you have the earnest sympathy and support of every officer and man in this army as well as those under your immediate command."[61]

Many personal letters written to Sherman after the publication of Stanton's bulletin helped strengthen him in his conviction that he had acted wisely in his first negotiations with Johnston. His close friend of West Point days, Stewart Van Vliet, thought time would prove his classmate's course to have been the best.[62] S. P. Sawyer of Joliet, Illinois, was "sorely grieved and pained" to learn that the just, humane, and magnanimous terms given a fallen foe had been rejected.[63] From the nation's capital, H. S. Fitch could not resist the impulse "to salute" the General. After reading the conditions proposed by Sherman on April 18, Fitch's admiration for him became "as light, irrepressible." To Fitch there was statesmanship in every paragraph of the terms and, as if to extract a leaf from Sherman's book of thoughts, he expressed the opinion that the people of the South as disfranchised citizens would "work more injury to

57. *Criticism on Surrender*, p. 10., quoting the *Cincinnati Commercial*, April [?], 1865.
58. Slocum, "Final Operations," p. 757.
59. Winther, *Upson Diary*, p. 167.
60. Lewis, *Sherman*, p. 564.
61. J. M. Schofield to Sherman, June 6, 1865, Sherman Papers, MS Div., L.C.
62. S. Van Vliet to Sherman, Apr. 27, 1865, Sherman Papers, MS Div., L.C.
63. S. P. Sawyer, to Sherman, Apr. 25, 1865, Sherman Papers, MS Div., L.C.

American society" than they ever injected upon the Federal government as insurgents.[64] And from Georgia came a letter in which the writer expressed the belief that Sherman's "great instincts of humanity" as exemplified in his first convention with Johnston had won for him the hearts of six million Southerners.[65]

Bitter at Northern politicians and the press, Sherman now considered as his best friends the defeated Confederates and the soldiers of his own army. In a letter to Chief Justice Chase, Sherman voiced a strong feeling for the people of the South. He told the Judge that in case of war against a foreign foe he "would not hesitate" to mingle with the Southerners and lead them in battle.[66] In the same temper he wrote his wife, Ellen: "The mass of the people south will never trouble us again. They have suffered terribly, and I now feel disposed to befriend them—of course not the leaders and lawyers, but the armies who have fought and manifested their sincerity though misled by risking their persons."[67]

On April 28, Sherman summoned to his headquarters in the governor's mansion all corps and army commanders. He explained to them their duties after his departure. The necessary orders were completed and on April 29, Sherman departed by rail for Wilmington. He could leave Raleigh knowing he had honestly endeavored to shorten the road to reunion. If the terms first offered Johnston had been accepted, the Southern people would have resumed the place they held in the Union in 1860, and the evils of congressional reconstruction might have been forestalled.

Inscribed on a statue of General Sherman in Washington is the following line: "The legitimate object of war is a more perfect peace." This phrase was the key to the General's thoughts and actions during the war.[68] In his judgment "a more perfect peace" was a more strongly unified country, not a humbled and subjugated South.

* * * * * * * *

During reconstruction, Sherman was often asked by the veterans of his army if he did not think that all their labors were in vain since the South had not resumed its proper place in the Union. In a speech de-

64. H. S. Fitch to Sherman, Apr. 23, 1865, Sherman Papers, MS Div., L.C.
65. M. B. Hodgson (?) to Sherman, May 1, 1865, Sherman Papers, MS Div., L.C.
66. *OR*, XLVII, Pt. III, Ser. I, 411.
67. Howe, *Home Letters of Sherman*, p. 350.
68. Liddell Hart, *Sherman*, p. 425.

livered before the Society of the Army of Tennessee in November, 1867, Sherman answered this question. He told his audience that when his soldiers laid down their arms "not an armed rebel remained to question the national authority, and if perfect subordination and tranquility have not resulted, we must look for the cause in the nature of things or in the civil administration of government." He went on to say that the North had helped fasten slavery on the South and had shared in the profits of cotton and slavery and consequently "should be charitable and liberal in the final distribution of natural penalities to the South." In conclusion he stated: "If our friends at the South will heartily and cheerfully join with us in this future career, I, for one, would welcome them back, our equals but not our superiors and then lend them a helping hand."[69]

Throughout the period of reconstruction Sherman remained a bitter critic of the Radical Republican Party. He considered Washington "corrupt as Hell" and avoided "it as a pest house."[70] He saw no need for military governments because "the South . . . broken and ruined . . . appeals to . . . pity. To ride the people down with persecutions and military exactions would be like slashing away at the crew of a sinking ship."[71] He was certain that the South wanted peace, and once declared that the country might look for "outbreaks in Ohio quicker than in Georgia and Mississippi."[72] He was a strong advocate of white supremacy, and declared that: "the white men of this country . . . control it, and the Negro, in mass, . . . occupy a subordinate place as a race."[73]

Nor did Sherman ignore his personal friends in the South who turned to him for help. Professor David French Boyd, Sherman's former colleague at the Louisiana Academy, wrote him from New Orleans on September 22, 1865: "There is no help in ourselves—to our conquerors we must look for aid and comfort; and to no one more than yourself does the South rely. You were mainly instrumental in our discomfiture; yet the very liberal terms you proposed to grant us thro' Joe Johnston and your course since have led the people of the South to expect more from you than any of the high northern officials."[74] Whenever possible,

69. *Report of the Proceedings of the Soc. of the Army of Tenn.*, Nov. 13-14, pp. 22-23.
70. Howe, *Home Letters of Sherman*, p. 352.
71. *OR*, XLVII, Ser. I, Pt. III, 345.
72. Thorndike, *Sherman Letters*, p. 256.
73. *Ibid.*, p. 263.
74. D. F. Boyd to Sherman, Sept. 22, 1865, Sherman Papers, MS Div., L.C.

Sherman aided those who asked for his assistance. He was instrumental in having restored to Thomas O. Moore, former governor of Louisiana, a plantation which had been confiscated[75] and to Braxton Bragg he offered his services in any capacity that "could aid him."[76] To Dr. S. A. Smith, a Louisiana acquaintance, Sherman gave information on the proper procedure for the removal of disabilities placed upon him by the United States government.[77]

After the war Sherman made several trips through the South, each of which was a pleasant experience. He was gratified to learn that he was not unpopular with most Southerners. Even in Mississippi where "chimney stacks and broken railroads" were grim reminders of a previous visit, Sherman was received "in the most friendly spirit."[78] His trip of 1869 was "in every sense agreeable." Said Sherman: "I never received more marked attention by all classses and not a word or look reached me that was not most respectful and gratifying."[79]

In retrospect, Sherman considered the march north from Savannah "by far the most important in conception and execution of any act of . . . his life."[80] He placed particular importance on his operations in the Carolinas because, as he states it: "I honestly believe that the grand march of the western army . . . from Savannah to Raleigh was an important factor in the final result, the overwhelming victory at Appomattox, and the glorious triumph of the Union cause."[81] This statement by Sherman raises the question as to whether the devastation wrought in the Carolinas by his army had a direct and immediate bearing on the end of the war.

75. Sherman, *Memoirs*, I, 165.

76. Sherman to B. Bragg, Jan. 28, 1867, Sherman Papers, MS Div., L.C.

77. S. A. Smith to Sherman, Aug. 25, 1865, Sherman Papers, MS Div., L.C.

78. Thorndike, *Sherman Letters*, p. 287.

79. *Ibid.*, pp. 327-28. With the publication of his *Memoirs* in 1875, Sherman's name became an anathema in the South. His frank account of the Federal operations in the Confederacy reminded most Southerners of the horrors of the late war. In the grasp of radical reconstruction, it was impossible for the people of the South to read the book as Sherman intended—a lesson in obedience to the United States Constitution. Lewis, *Sherman*, p. 619.

80. Howe, *Home Letters of Sherman*, p. 340.

81. Sherman, "Strategy," *B and L*, IV, 257. In this article Sherman refers to the "march to the sea" along with the Carolinas campaign as having a direct bearing on Lee's defeat. Various studies by authorities on the Georgia campaign, however, fully support the present author's conclusion concerning the effect of Sherman's Carolinas operations on the final defeat of the Army of Northern Virginia. See Ballard, *Genius of Lincoln*, p. 223; Schofield, *Forty-six Years*, pp. 341-53; Burne, *Lee, Grant, Sherman*, pp. 198-201; Hay, *Hood*, p. 198; Ropes, "Sherman," p. 149; Palfrey, "Sherman's Plans," p. 523.

Sherman's movements through South and North Carolina were bold, imaginative strokes, masterfully executed. One historian has rightly characterized the Carolinas campaign as "a triumph of physical endurance and mechanical skill on the part of the army and of inflexible resolution in the general. . . ."[82] Sherman was absolutely sincere in his conviction that total war was the most effective means at hand to shorten the conflict; yet, this method of warfare, as applied in the Carolinas, had little appreciable effect on the Confederate collapse. It was the practical annihilation of Hood's army in Tennessee that paved the way for Appomattox.[83]

Sherman disrupted much of the rail communications in the two Carolinas, as well as destroying large quantities of the South's dwindling supplies, but Lee's army was not short of rations because of Sherman's march. The Confederate plight at Richmond was due largely to a breakdown in the transportation system in Virginia. Cavalry raids to Lee's rear in late 1864 and early 1865 had destroyed much in the way of railroad installations. The rolling stock, especially engines, was in a bad state of deterioration, and disastrous floods had ruined the Danville-Greensboro line. Up to the day of Lee's capitulation special depots, in Virginia and North Carolina, were filled with ample provisions earmarked for the Army of Northern Virginia. Had transportation been available during the later months of the war, Lee's men would not have had to subsist on meager provisions. The chief of the Confederate commissary reported in February, 1865, that it was even possible to draw a surplus for the Richmond and Petersburg depots "whenever transportation could be procured."[84]

The Federal march north from Savannah brought home to the people of the Carolinas the stern realities of war. The use of a military force against the civilian population and economic resources unquestionably helped to undermine the morale of the South, producing a "defeatest psychology" both on the home front and on the battlefield.[85] Lee's

82. Sheppard, *Civil War*, p. 133.

83. General Schofield, although a great admirer of Sherman's generalship, goes so far as to say that militarily the Carolinas march ranks only as an auxiliary to the more important operations of Grant and Thomas. In one sense he thought it was no more than a grand raid. Schofield, *Forty-six Years*, pp. 347-48.

84. St. John, "Resources of the Confed.," *So. Hist. Soc. Papers*, III, 97-103; Turner, "Va. Central Railroad," *JSH*, XII, 532; Johnston, *Narrative*, p. 410; Burne, *Lee, Grant, Sherman*, p. 200.

85. Owsley, "Defeatism," *NCHR*, III, 446-48.

ranks were thinned daily by the desertions of soldiers going home to protect their families in the line of Sherman's march. In this respect the Carolinas campaign had an indirect effect on Grant's operations in Virginia. In applying total war to the people of the South, Sherman inflicted wounds which would remain open for generations to come. The hatred for the North instilled in the hearts of many Southerners by Sherman's operations lengthened the South's road to reunion and in so doing partially undid Sherman's major purpose in taking up arms, that of preserving the Union.[86]

General Sherman's military stature rests not upon the effect his campaign in the Carolinas had upon Lee's defeat but upon his refusal to be bound by orthodox strategy and stubborn military tradition which called for him to defeat or destroy the enemy's main army before striking at the "state sheltered behind it."[87] To have seen and grasped the importance of such a move has given Sherman a ranking position among the country's great military leaders. As a strategist he was far ahead of his time. Some present day writers see in the flexibility of Sherman's operations a similarity to modern panzer tactics[88] and in his destruction of the South's economic resources a picture of strategic bombing.[89]

For a true insight into Sherman's character one must balance the man in wartime against the man in peacetime, otherwise the picture is distorted. Though pitiless in campaign and intemperate in language, Sherman was not a cruel individual with the instincts of a barbarian. "He had a big heart, filled with a great deal of kindness for his fellow man. To him, war must be fought effectively or not at all. An enemy in war, in peace a friend."[90]

86. Walters, "Total War," pp. 479-80.
87. Sheppard, *Civil War*, p. 136.
88. Liddell Hart, *Strategy*, p. 152.
89. Fellers, *Wings for Peace*, pp. 139-41.
90. Coulter, "Sherman and the South," p. 54.

Bibliography

PRIMARY SOURCES

MANUSCRIPTS

Edward Porter Alexander Papers, 1820-1925. 3,500 items including 30 volumes. Southern Historical Collection, University of North Carolina.

Mrs. W. K. Bachman Letters, March 27, 1865. Typed copy of original telling of the Federal occupation of Columbia, South Carolina. South Caroliniana Library, University of South Carolina.

Ulysses Robert Brooks Papers, 1861 (1902-1908) 1911. 86 items. Many letters of General Matthew C. Butler. They contain his Civil War reminiscences and were used by Brooks in his articles, many of which appear in the collection as clippings. Manuscript Division, Duke University Library.

Charles S. Brown Papers, 1846-1865. 30 items. Lieutenant Brown, Twenty-first Michigan, wrote clever, informative letters. Manuscript Division, Duke University Library.

Walter Clark Papers, 1783-1920. 8,000 items. This collection is very informative on the Graham-Swain mission to General Sherman as well as the North Carolina Junior Reserves of which Clark was a member. Manuscript Division, North Carolina Department of Archives and History.

Washington Sanford Chaffin Papers, 1841-1900. 158 items and 23 volumes. Personal correspondence, sermon notes, diaries, and bills of Chaffin, a North Carolina Methodist minister and circuit rider. Manuscript Division, Duke University Library.

Elizabeth Collier Diary, 1862-1865. Civil War diary of Elizabeth Collier, an eighteen year old girl, who lived at Everittsville, a village near Goldsboro, North Carolina. Southern Historical Collection, University of North Carolina.

John Hamilton Cornish Diary, 1833-1877. 35 volumes. Diary of an Episcopal minister in Charleston, South Carolina. Entries for 1846 contain several references to Sherman. Southern Historical Collection, University of North Carolina.

Henry William DeSaussure Papers, 1800-1916. 118 items including the Wilmot G. DeSaussure diary. Various members of the DeSaussure family are represented in the collection. Civil War letters are concerned mostly with family and personal matters. Manuscript Division, Duke University Library.

William Alexander Graham Papers, 1750-1927. 14,614 items, including 7 volumes. As Confederate Senator, Graham corresponded on both civil and military matters. Southern Historical Collection, University of North Carolina.

William Alexander Graham Papers, 1827-1877. No. of items not yet compiled. Typed copies from originals in several depositories, compiled and edited for projected publication by Joseph Gregoire deRouhlac Hamilton. In possession of Joseph Gregoire deRouhlac Hamilton, Southern Historical Collection, University of North Carolina.

Mrs. Hiram Gray Papers, 1858-1865. 4 items. Mrs. Gray was in Cheraw, South Carolina, when Sherman occupied the town. Manuscript Division, Duke University Library.

O. P. Hargis Reminiscences, no date. Unpublished Civil War reminiscences (1861-1865) of Hargis, a member of Wheeler's cavalry. On 1 reel of microfilm in Southern Historical Collection, University of North Carolina.

Robert Phillip Howell Memoirs, no date. Unpublished memoirs (1854-1872) of Howell, a native of Wayne County, North Carolina, and soldier in the Confederate army. Southern Historical Collection, University of North Carolina.

Charles Colcock Jones, Jr., Papers, 1861-(1872-1890) 1893. 153 items, including 61 volumes. The correspondence of Jones, a Georgian in Johnston's army, contains a lengthy letter from General Joseph Wheeler describing Confederate cavalry operations from Savannah, Georgia to Columbia, South Carolina. Manuscript Division, Duke University Library.

Emma Florence LeConte Diary, 1864-1865. 1 volume. Civil War diary of a young girl living at Columbia, South Carolina. Southern Historical Collection, University of North Carolina.

Mrs. J. Hardy Lee Letter, no date. Letter describing the burning of Columbia, South Carolina. Southern Historical Collection, University of North Carolina.

Lafayette McLaws Papers, 1836-1897. 800 items, including a small volume of war orders, 1865. General McLaws' papers are especially rich for the Civil War period. Southern Historical Collection. University of North Carolina.

Fritz William McMaster Papers, 1865. Letters from a South Carolina soldier

BIBLIOGRAPHY

in Lee's army around Richmond. South Caroliniana Library, University of South Carolina.

William Porcher Miles Papers, 1782-1907. 3,263 items. The Civil War correspondence of Miles, a member of the Confederate Congress, covers every phase of the conflict. Southern Historical Collection, University of North Carolina.

Bartholomew Figures Moore—John T. Gatling Papers, 1753-1934. 12,038 items, including 14 volumes. Collection consists chiefly of professional and business papers of the law firms of Moore-Gatling. Also to be found is the personal correspondence of the Moore and Gatling families relating to the Civil War in North Carolina. Southern Historical Collection, University of North Carolina.

Emma Mordecai Diary, 1864-1865. 1 volume. Civil War diary, interspersed with newspaper clippings, of Emma Mordecai, Rosewood, near Richmond, Virginia. Southern Historical Collection, University of North Carolina.

William P. Palmer Papers, 1861-1865; 1868. Miscellaneous Confederate papers relating to war activities, especially in Georgia, also in Tennessee, South Carolina, Virginia and North Carolina. On 2 reels of microfilm in Southern Historical Collection, University of North Carolina.

Charles Stevens Powell Reminiscences, 1916. Unpublished Civil War Reminiscences (1864-1865) of a soldier in Johnston's army. North Carolina Collection, University of North Carolina.

William Tecumseh Sherman Papers, 1837-1891. 88 volumes. One volume contains copies of letters and reminiscences of California, Louisiana and Missouri, 1846-1861, written at a later date. Manuscript Division, Library of Congress.

William Tecumseh Sherman Papers, 1864-1888, 10 items. In one letter, 1888, Sherman stoutly defends his war policy toward the South. Manuscript Division, Duke University Library.

Cornelia Phillips Spencer Papers, 1830-1930. 1,900 items, 75 volumes including a notebook and diary, and 20 volumes of typed copies of selected letters and writings. Of particular interest is the light thrown on Sherman's activities in North Carolina. Southern Historical Collection, University of North Carolina.

Madame S. Sosnowski Reminiscences, no date. Madame Sosnowski, a teacher at Barhamville College, two miles north of Columbia, recalls the burning of Columbia by the Federal army. South Caroliniana Library, University of South Carolina.

Joseph Stetson Papers, 1865. 3 items. These letters of Stetson, a Federal soldier stationed at Goldsboro, North Carolina, tell of Johnston's surrender and Lincoln's assassination. Manuscript Division, Duke University Library.

David Lowry Swain Papers, 1704-(1835-1868) 1896. 1,200 items. The Swain papers for 1865-1866 furnish much valuable information on the last months of the Civil War in North Carolina. Southern Historical Collection, University of North Carolina.

Alexander Ross Taylor Letter, January 22, 1865. An anonymous letter to Colonel Taylor, South Carolina militia, threatening dire consequences for him if he tried to arrest militia members who failed to assemble, as ordered. South Caroliniana Library, University of South Carolina.

Daniel M. Tedder Memoirs, 1864-1865. Unpublished Civil War memoirs (1861-1865) of Tedder. Southern Historical Collection, University of North Carolina.

Daniel Heyward Trezevant Papers, 1796-1873. One volume in this collection contains copies of letters, reminiscences and other materials on the burning of Columbia, South Carolina. South Caroliniana Library, University of South Carolina.

University of North Carolina Archives, 1792—. Minutes of the Board and Executive Committee of the Board of Trustees, University of North Carolina, 1868-1883. Minutes contain a report on the condition of University property after the Federal departure. Southern Historical Collection, University of North Carolina.

Zebulon Baird Vance Papers, 1827-1903. 18 volumes of mounted papers and 6 manuscript boxes. Volumes I-VII cover chiefly Vance's political career as "war governor" of North Carolina, 1862-1865. Manuscript Division, North Carolina Department of Archives and History.

Zebulon Baird Vance Letter Book, 1863-1865. Official letter book of Governor Vance of North Carolina. Manuscript Division, North Carolina Department of Archives and History.

Joseph Fred Waring Diary, 1864-1865. 1 volume. Civil War diary of Colonel Waring. Southern Historical Collection, University of North Carolina.

Samuel Hoey Walkup Diary, 1862-1865. 2 volumes. Civil War diary of Colonel Walkup. Southern Historical Collection, University of North Carolina.

Isabella Ann (Roberts) Woodruff Papers, 1857-1869. 277 items. These letters of a school teacher give many details of the period during and after Sherman's march through South Carolina. Manuscript Division, Duke University Library.

Letter of Nellie Worth, March 21, 1865. Letter describing the work of

Sherman's "bummers." Typed copy of original in North Carolina Collection, University of North Carolina.

OFFICIAL DOCUMENTS

Atlas to Accompany the Official Records of the Union and Confederate Armies. 2 vols. Washington: Government Printing Office, 1891-1895.
Congressional Globe. 39 Congress, 1865-1866.
Congressional Record. 48 Congress, 1884-1885.
Destruction of Property in Columbia, S. C. by Sherman's Army—Speech of Honorable Cole L. Blease. A Senator from the State of South Carolina—Delivered in the Senate May 15, 1930. Relative to the Destruction of Property in Columbia, S. C., by Sherman's Army. Washington: Government Printing Office, 1930.
Keim, DeBenneville Randolph. *Sherman, A Memorial in Art, Oratory and Literature by the Society of the Army of Tennessee with Aid of the Congress of the United States of America.* Washington: Government Printing Office, 1904.
The Medical and Surgical History of the War of the Rebellion 1861-1865. 3 vols. Washington: Government Printing Office, 1875.
Official Records of the Union and Confederate Navies in the War of Rebellion. 30 vols. Washington: Government Printing Office, 1880-1919.
Report of the Joint Committee on the Conduct of the War. Sherman-Johnston. Washington: Government Printing Office, 1865.
Senate Executive Document No. 36, 48 Cong. 2 Sess. Washington: Government Printing Office, 1885.
Sherman, William Tecumseh. *General Sherman's Official Accounts of His Great March Through Georgia and the Carolinas.* New York: Bunce and Huntington, 1865.
Supplemental Report of the Joint Committee on the Conduct of the War. 2 vols. Washington: Government Printing Office, 1866.
The War of the Rebellion: A Compilation of the Official Records of the Union and Confederate Armies. 128 vols. Washington: Government Printing Office, 1880-1901.

REGIMENTAL HISTORIES

Ambrose, Daniel Leib. *History of the Seventh Regiment, Illinois Volunteer Infantry from Its Muster into the United States Service, April 25, 1861 to Its Final Muster Out, July 9, 1865.* Springfield: Illinois Journal Company, 1868.
Aten, Henry J. *History of the Eighty-fifth Regiment, Illinois Volunteer Infantry.* Hiawatha: Regimental Association, 1901.

Boies, Andrew J. *Record of the Thirty-third Massachusetts Volunteer Infantry from August 1862-August 1865.* Fitchburg: Sentinel Printing Company, 1880.

Boyle, John Richard. *Soldiers True, The Story of the One Hundred and Eleventh Regiment Pennsylvania Veteran Volunteers and of Its Campaigns in the War for the Union.* New York: Eaton and Morris, 1903.

Bryant, Edwin Eustace. *History of the Third Regiment of Wisconsin Veteran Volunteer Infantry 1861-1865.* Madison: Veterans Association of the Regiment, 1891.

Calkins, William Wirt. *The History of the One Hundred and Fourth Regiment of Illinois Volunteer Infantry. War of the Great Rebellion 1862-1865.* Chicago: Donahue and Henneberry, 1895.

Chamberlin, William Henry. *History of the Eighty-first Regiment Ohio Infantry Volunteers During the War of Rebellion.* Cincinnati: Gazette Steam Printing House, 1865.

Crooker, Lucien B. and others. *The Story of the Fifty-fifth Regiment Illinois Volunteer Infantry in the Civil War.* Clinton: W. J. Coulter, 1887.

Deckert, D. Augustua. *History of Kershaw's Brigade, with Complete Roll of Companies, Biographical Sketches, Incidents, Anecdotes, etc.* Newberry: Elbert H. Aull Company, 1899.

Drake, James Madison. *The History of the Ninth New Jersey Veteran Volunteers. A Record of Its Service from September 13, 1861 to July 12, 1865.* Elizabeth: Journal Printing House, 1889.

Fleharty, Stephen F. *Our Regiment. A History of the One Hundred and Second Illinois Infantry Volunteers with Sketches of the Atlanta Campaign. The Georgia Raid, and the Campaign of the Carolinas.* Chicago: Brewster and Hanscom, 1865.

Gage, Moses D. *From Vicksburg to Raleigh; Or, a Complete History of the Twelfth Regiment Indiana Volunteer Infantry, and the Compaigns of Grant and Sherman, with an Outline of the Great Rebellion.* Chicago: Clarke and Company, 1865.

Hinkley, Julian Wisner. *A Narrative of Service with the Third Wisconsin Infantry.* Madison: Wisconsin Historical Commission, 1912.

Hinman, Wilbur F. *The Story of the Sherman Brigade.* Privately printed, 1897.

Hurst, Samuel H. *Journal-History of the Seventy-third Ohio Volunteer Infantry.* Chillicothe: 1866.

Kinnear, John R. *History of the Eighty-sixth Regiment Illinois Volunteer Infantry During Its Term of Service.* Chicago: Tribune Company's Book and Job Printing Office, 1866.

Merrill, Samuel. *The Seventieth Indiana Volunteer Infantry in the War of Rebellion.* Indianapolis: The Bowen-Merrill Company, 1900.

Mowris, James A. *A History of the One Hundred and Seventeenth Regiment, New York Volunteers, From the Date of its Organization, August, 1862, Till That of Its Muster Out, June, 1865.* Hartford: Case, Lockwood and Company, 1866.

Osborn, Hartwell, and others. *Trials and Triumphs. The Record of the Fifty-fifth Ohio Volunteer Infantry.* Chicago: A. C. McClurg, 1904.

Palmer, Abraham John. *History of the Forty-eighth Regiment New York State Volunteers in the War for Union 1861-1865.* New York: Charles T. Dillingham, 1885.

Quint, Alonzo Hall. *The Record of the Second Massachusetts Infantry 1861-1865.* Boston: James P. Walker, 1867.

Regimental Committee, *Ninety-second Illinois Volunteers.* Freeport: Journal Steam Publishing House and Book Bindery, 1875.

Sherlock, Eli J. *Memorabilia of the Marches and Battles in which the One Hundreth Regiment of Indiana Infantry Volunteers Took an Active Part.* Kansas City: Gerard-Wood Printing Company, 1896.

Story of the Fifty-fifth Regiment Illinois Volunteer Infantry in the Civil War 1861-1865. Clinton: W. J. Coulter, 1887.

Tourgée, Albion Winegar. *The Story of a Thousand. Being a History of the Service of the One Hundred and Fifth Ohio Volunteer Infantry, in the War of Union from August 21, 1862 to June 6, 1865.* Buffalo: S. McGerald and Company, 1896.

Underwood, Adin Ballou. *The Three Years Service of the Thirty-third Massachusetts Infantry Regiment, 1862-1865.* Boston: A. Williams and Company, 1881.

Wright, Henry H. *A History of the Sixth Iowa Infantry.* Iowa City: State Historical Society, 1923.

NEWSPAPERS AND PERIODICALS

Augusta Southern Presbyterian, 1865.
Camden Journal and Confederate, 1865.
Charleston Daily Courier, 1864-1865.
Columbia Phoenix, 1865.
Fayetteville Observer, 1864-1865.
Harpers New Monthly Magazine, XXIX-XXXIII, 1864-1866.
Hillsboro Recorder, 1865.
The Nation, I-IV, 1865-1867.
New Bern North Carolina Times, 1865.
New York Herald, 1865.

New York Times, 1865.
Raleigh Conservative, 1865.
Raleigh Daily Standard, 1865.
Raleigh North Carolina Standard, 1865.
Sumter Banner of Freedom, 1865.
Wilmington Daily North Carolinian, 1865.
Wilmington Herald of the Union, 1865.

DIARIES AND CORRESPONDENCE

Bircher, William. *A Drummer Boy's Diary: Comprising Four Years of Service with the Second Regiment Minnesota Veteran Volunteers.* St. Paul: St. Paul Book and Stationery Company, 1889.

Brooks, Aubrey Lee and Hugh Talmadge Lefler (eds.). *The Papers of Walter Clark.* 2 vols. Chapel Hill: The University of North Carolina Press, 1948.

"The Burning of Columbia," Extract from a circular letter addressed to the "Congregation de Paris" by the Monastere de Sainte—Ursule de Valle Crucis," *South Carolina Women in the Confederacy*, ed. Mrs. Thomas Taylor (Columbia: The State Company, 1903), pp. 288-98.

Burton, Elijah P. *Diary of E. P. Burton, Surgeon Seventh Regiment Illinois, Third Brigade, Second Division, Sixteenth Army Corps.* 2 vols. Des Moines: The Historical Records Survey, 1939.

Capron, Thaddeus Hurlburt. "War Diary of Thaddeus H. Capron 1861-1865," *Journal of the Illinois State Historical Society*, XII (October, 1919), 330-407.

Childs, Arney Robinson (ed.). *The Private Journal of Henry William Ravenel 1859-1887.* Columbia: University of South Carolina Press, 1947.

Chisolm, A. R. "Beauregard's and Hampton's Orders on Evacuating Columbia—Letter from Colonel A. R. Chisolm," *Southern Historical Society Papers*, VII (May, 1879), 249-50.

Coffin, James Park. "Chapel Hill at the Close of Civil War—Letter from James P. Coffin to R. H. Battle," *North Carolina University Magazine*, XVIII (June, 1901), 270-75.

Connolly, James Austin. "Major James Austin Connolly's Letters to His Wife, 1862-1865," *Transactions of the Illinois State Historical Society*, publication No. 35. (Springfield: Illinois State Historical Library, 1928), pp. 215-438.

Eaton, Clement (ed.). "Diary of an Officer in Sherman's Army Marching Through the Carolinas," *The Journal of Southern History*, IX (May, 1943), 238-54.

Farwell, Sewell S. "Letter of Major S. S. Farwell to His Home Paper from the

Field," *The Annals of Iowa, A Historical Quarterly*, XV (July, 1925), 61-66.

Franklin, John Hope (ed.). *The Diary of James T. Ayers*. Springfield: Illinois State Historical Society, 1947.

Gray, John Chipman and John Codman Ropes. *War Letters 1862-1865 of John Chipman Gray and John Codman Ropes*. New York: Houghton Mifflin Company, 1927.

Hamilton, Joseph Gregoire deRoulhac (ed.). *The Correspondence of Jonathan Worth*. 2 vols. Raleigh: Edwards and Broughton, 1909.

――――. *The Papers of Thomas Ruffin*. 4 vols. Raleigh: Edwards and Broughton, 1920.

Hampton, Wade, "Letter from General Hampton on the Burning of Columbia," *Southern Historical Society Papers*, VII (March, 1879), 156-58.

Howe, Mark Antony DeWolfe (ed.). *Home Letters of General Sherman*. New York: Charles Scribner's Sons, 1909.

――――. *Marching With Sherman. Passages from the Letters and Campaign Diaries of Henry Hitchcock, Major and Assistant Adjutant General of the Volunteers November 1864-May 1865*. New Haven: Yale University Press, 1927.

Jackson, Oscar Lawrence. *The Colonel's Diary. Journals Kept Before and During the Civil War by the Late Colonel Oscar L. Jackson Sometime Commander of the Sixty-third Regiment Ohio Volunteer Infantry*. Sherron: 1922.

Jervey, Susan Ravenel and Charlotte St. John Ravenel. *Two Diaries from Middle St. Johns: Berkley South Carolina, February-May, 1865*. Pinopolis: St. Johns Hunt Club, 1921.

LeConte, Joseph. *Ware Sherman. A Journal of Three Months Experience in the Last Days of the Confederacy*. Berkeley: University of California Press, 1937.

Magrath, Andrew Gordon to Peoples of South Carolina, February 27, 1865. Circular in South Caroliniana Library, University of South Carolina.

Martin, Isabella D. and Myrta Lockett Avery (eds.). *A Diary from Dixie as Written by Mary Boykin Chesnut*. New York: Peter Smith, 1929.

Morse, Charles Fessenden. *Letters Written During the Civil War*. Boston: Privately Printed, 1898.

Orendorff, H. H., and others (eds.). *Reminiscences of the Civil War from Diaries of Members of the One Hundred and Third Illinois Volunteer Infantry*. Chicago: J. F. Learning and Company, 1905.

Padgett, James A. (ed.). "With Sherman Through Georgia and the Carolinas: Letters of a Federal Soldier," *The Georgia Historical Quarterly*, XXXIII (March, 1949), 49-81.

St. John, Isaac Munroe. "Resources of the Confederacy in 1865—Letter of I. M. St. John, Commissary General," *Southern Historical Society Papers,* III (March, 1877), 97-103.

Schafer, Joseph (ed.). "Intimate Letters of Carl Schurz 1841-1869," *Publications of the State Historical Society of Wisconsin.* Madison: State Historical Society of Wisconsin, 1928.

Sherman, William Tecumseh. "The Surrender of General Johnston. Letter from General Sherman," *The Historical Magazine and Notes and Queries Concerning the Antiques, History and Biography of America,* XV (May, 1869), 333-34.

————. "True Copy of a Letter Written by General Sherman in 1864," *The Historical Magazine and Notes and Queries Concerning the Antiques, History and Biography of America,* XXI (February, 1872), 113.

————. "Unpublished Letter of General Sherman," *North American Review,* CLII (March, 1891), 372-74.

Smith, Daniel E. Huger, and others (eds.). *Mason Smith Family Letters 1860-1865.* Columbia: University of South Carolina Press, 1950.

Stormont, Gilbert R. (ed.). *History of the Fifty-eight Regiment of Indiana Volunteer Infantry. Its Organization, Campaigns and Battles from 1861-1865. From the Manuscript Prepared by the Late Chaplain John J. Hight During His Service with the Regiment in the Field.* Princeton: Press of the Clarion, 1895.

Thorndike, Rachel Sherman (ed.). *The Sherman Letters, Correspondence Between General and Senator Sherman from 1837 to 1891.* New York: Charles Scribner's Sons, 1894.

Volwiler, Albert Tangeman (ed.). "Letters from a Civil War Officer," *Mississippi Valley Historical Review,* XIV (March, 1928), 508-29.

Wagstaff, Henry McGilbert (ed.). *The James A. Graham Papers 1861-1884.* (Volume XX, Robert Digges Wimberly Connor [ed.]. *James Sprunt Historical Studies.*) Chapel Hill: The University of North Carolina Press, 1928.

Welch, Spencer Glasgow. *A Confederate Surgeon's Letters to His Wife.* New York: Neale Publishing Company, 1911.

Wells, Gideon, *Diary of Gideon Wells, Secretary of the Navy Under Lincoln and Johnson.* 3 vols. New York: Houghton-Mifflin Company, 1911.

Wills, Charles Wright. *Army Life of an Illinois Soldier. Letters and Diary of the Late Charles W. Wills.* Washington: Globe Printing Company, 1906.

Winther, Oscar Osburn (ed.). *With Sherman to the Sea. The Civil War*

Letters, Diaries, and Reminiscences of Theodore F. Upson. Baton Rouge: Louisiana State University Press, 1934.

MEMOIRS, REMINISCENCES, AND RECOLLECTIONS

Aldrick, A. P. "The Oakes," *Our Women in the War. The Lives They Lived; the Deaths They Died. From the Weekly News and Courier, Charleston, S. C.,* ed. *Francis Warrington Dawson* (Charleston: News and Courier Book Presses, 1885), pp. 192-211.

Arbuckle, John C. *Civil War Experiences of a Foot-Soldier Who Marched with Sherman.* Columbus: 1930.

Battle, Kemp Plummer. *Memories of an Old-Time Tar Heel.* Chapel Hill: The University of North Carolina Press, 1945.

Baum, J. Croll. "An Incident of the Burning of Columbia, S. C.," *Magazine of American History with Notes and Queries,* XIV (December, 1885), 619-20.

Belknap, Charles Eugene. "Recollections of a Bummer," *The War of the Sixties,* ed. Edward Ridgeway Hutchins (New York: Neale Publishing Company, 1912), pp. 345-55.

Blackburn, J. P. K. "Reminiscences of the Terry Rangers," *The Southwestern Historical Quarterly,* XXII (July, October, 1918), 38-79, 143-79.

Bradley, George S. *The Star Corps: or, Notes of an Army Chaplain During Sherman's Famous March to the Sea.* Milwaukee: Jermain and Brightman, 1865.

Bryce, Campbell. *The Personal Experiences of Mrs. Campbell Bryce During the Burning of Columbia, South Carolina by General W. T. Sherman's Army, February 17, 1865.* Philadelphia: Lippincott Press, 1899.

Byers, Samuel Hawken Marshall. "Some Personal Recollections of General Sherman," *McClure's Magazine,* III (August, 1894), 212-224.

———. *With Fire and Sword.* New York: Neale Publishing Company, 1911.

Carroll, Lilla. "Recollections of a School Girl," *Stories of the Confederacy,* ed. Ulysses Robert Brooks (Columbia: The State Company, 1912), pp. 22-28.

Clark, Walter Augustus. *Under the Stars and Bars or Memories of Four Years Service with the Oglethorpes of Augusta, Georgia.* Augusta: Chronicle Printing Company, 1900.

Commager, Henry Steele (ed.). *The Blue and the Gray. The Story of the Civil War as Told by Participants.* 2 vols. New York: Bobbs-Merrill, 1950.

Conyngham, David Power. *Sherman's March Through the South with Sketches and Incidents of the Campaign.* New York: Sheldon and Company, 1865.

Cox, Jacob Dolson. *Military Reminiscences of the Civil War.* 2 vols. New York: Charles Scribner's Sons, 1900.

Crittenden, Mrs. S. A. "The Sack of Columbia," *South Carolina Women of the Confederacy,* ed. Mrs. Thomas Taylor (Columbia: The State Company, 1903), pp. 328-34.

Devereux, Margaret. *Plantation Sketches.* Cambridge: The Riverside Press, 1906.

Eisenchiml, Etto, and Ralph Newman (eds.). *The American Iliad, The Epic Story of the Civil War as Narrated by Eyewitnesses.* Indianapolis: Bobbs-Merrill, 1947.

Fletcher, William Andrew. *Rebel Private, Front and Rear.* Austin: University of Texas Press, 1954.

"Fighting Fair Women," *Our Women in the War. The Lives They Lived; the Deaths They Died. From the Weekly News and Courier, Charleston, S. C.,* ed. Francis Warrington Dawson (Charleston: News and Courier Book Press, 1885), pp. 326-31.

Ford, Arthur Peronneau, and Marion Johnstone Ford. *Life in the Confederate Army.* New York: Neale Publishing Company, 1905.

Foster, Mrs. J. H. "When Sherman Passed through Lancaster," *South Carolina Women of the Confederacy,* ed. Mrs. Thomas Taylor (Columbia: The State Company, 1903), pp. 344-51.

Grant, Ulysses Simpson. *Personal Memoirs of U. S. Grant.* 2 vols. New York: Charles L. Webster, 1886.

Garber, Michael C. "Reminiscences of the Burning of Columbia, South Carolina," *Indiana Magazine of History,* XI (December, 1915), 285-300.

Gibbes, James Guiguard. *Who Burnt Columbia?* Newberry: Elbert H. Aull Company, 1902.

Grigsby, Melvin. *The Smoked Yank.* Sioux Falls: Bell Publishing Company, 1888.

Hamilton, William Douglas. *Recollections of a Cavalryman of the Civil War after Fifty Years.* Columbia: F. J. Heer Printing Company, 1915.

Hedley, Fenwick Y. *Marching Through Georgia. Pen-Pictures of Every-Day Life in General Sherman's Army from the Beginning of the Atlanta Campaign Until the Close of the War.* Chicago: M. A. Donahue and Company, 1884.

Hitchcock, Henry. "General W. T. Sherman," *War Papers and Personal Reminiscences, 1861-1865. Read before the Commandery of the State Missouri Military Order of the Loyal Legion of the United States,* I (St. Louis: Becktold and Company, 1892), 416-29. 1 vol.

Hood, H. J. B. "Sherman in Orangeburg," *Our Women in the War. The Lives They Lived; the Deaths They Died. From the Weekly News and*

Courier, Charleston, S. C., ed. Francis Warrington Dawson (Charleston: News and Courier Book Presses, 1885), pp. 153-60.

Hood, John Bell. *Advance and Retreat. Personal Experiences in the United States and Confederate Armies.* New Orleans: Hood Orphan Memorial Fund, 1880.

Howard, Oliver Otis. *Autobiography of Oliver Otis Howard, Major General United States Army.* 2 vols. New York: Baker and Taylor Company, 1907.

Johnston, Joseph Eggleston. "My Negotiations with General Sherman," *North American Review,* CXLIII (August, 1886), 182-97.

——. *Narrative of Military Operations, Directed, During the Late War Between the States, by Joseph E. Johnston, General, C. S. A.* New York: D. Appleton and Company, 1874.

King, Charles. "A Boy's Recollections of our Great Generals," *War Papers Read before the Commandery of the State of Wisconsin, Military Order of the Loyal Legion of the United States,* III (Milwaukee: Published by the Commandery, 1891-1903), 125-39. 3 vols.

Kyle, Anne K. "Incidents of Hospital Life," *War Days in Fayetteville, North Carolina* (Fayetteville: Judge Printing Company, 1910), pp. 35-45.

Law, Agnes. "Incidents on the Burning of Columbia," *Southern Historical Society Papers,* XII (May, 1884), 233-34.

Leaphart, Mary Janney. "Experiences During the Civil War," *South Carolina Women in the Confederacy,* ed. Mrs. Thomas Taylor (Columbia: The State Company, 1903), pp. 247-50.

Lord, William Wilberforce, Jr. "In the Path of Sherman," *Harpers Magazine,* CXX (February, 1910), 438-46.

Maclean, Clara Dargan. "Return of a Refugee," *Southern Historical Papers,* XIII (January-December, 1885), 502-15.

——. "The Last Raid," *Southern Historical Society Papers,* XIII (January-December, 1885), 466-76.

McGill, Samuel D. *Narrative of Reminiscences in Williamsburg County.* Columbia: The Bryan Company, 1897.

Nichols, George Ward. *The Story of the Great March From the Diary of a Staff Officer.* New York: Harper and Brothers, 1865.

Pepper, George Whitefield. *Personal Recollections of Sherman's Campaigns in Georgia and the Carolinas.* Zanesville: Hugh Dunne, 1866.

Pike, James. *The Scout and Ranger: Being the Personal Adventures of Corporal Pike of the Fourth Ohio Cavalry.* Cincinnati: J. R. Hawley and Company, 1865.

Poppenheim, Mrs. C. P. "Experiences with Sherman at Liberty Hill," *South*

Carolina Women in the Confederacy, ed. Mrs. Thomas Taylor (Columbia: The State Company, 1903), pp. 254-61.

Porter, David Dixon. *Incidents and Anecdotes of the Civil War.* New York: D. Appleton and Company, 1886.

Porter, Anthony Toomer. *The History of a Work of Faith and Love in Charleston, South Carolina, Which Grew out of the Calamities of the Late Civil War, and Is a Record of God's Wonderful Providence.* New York: D. Appleton and Company, 1881.

Pringle, Elizabeth Waties Allston. *The Chronicles of Chicora Wood.* New York: Charles Scribner's Sons, 1922.

Ravenel, Harriott. "When Columbia Burned," *South Carolina Women in the Confederacy,* ed. Mrs. Thomas Taylor (Columbia: The State Company, 1903), pp. 319-28.

Ridley, Bromfield Lewis. *Battles and Sketches of the Army of Tennessee.* Mexico: Missouri Printing and Publishing Company, 1906.

Salley, Alexander Samuel (ed.). *Sack and Destruction of the City of Columbia, South Carolina. By William Gilmore Simms.* Atlanta: Oglethorpe University Press, 1937.

Savage, James W. "The Loyal Element of North Carolina During the War," *Civil War Sketches and Incidents. Papers Read by Companions of the Commandery of the State of Nebraska Military Order of the Loyal Legion of the United States,* I (St. Louis: Published by the Commandery, 1902), 1-15. 1 vol.

Schofield, John McAllister. *Forty-six Years in the Army.* New York: The Century Company, 1897.

Schurz, Carl. *The Reminiscences of Carl Schurz with a Sketch of His Life and Public Services from 1869 to 1906 by Frederick Bancroft and William A. Dunning.* 3 vols. New York: The McClure Company, 1908.

Scott, Edwin J. *Random Recollections of a Long Life.* Columbia: Charles A Calvo, 1884.

Shanks, William Franklin Gore. "Recollections of General Sherman," *Harpers New Monthly Magazine,* XXX (April, 1865), 640-46.

Sherman, William Tecumseh. *Memoirs of General W. T. Sherman.* 2 vols. New York: D. Appleton and Company, 1875.

Sheridan, Philip Henry. *Personal Memoirs of P. H. Sheridan.* New York: Charles L. Webster, 1886.

Slocum, Henry Warner, and others. "In Commemoration of General William Tecumseh Sherman," *Personal Recollections of the War of Rebellion. Addresses Delivered before the New York Commandery of the Loyal Legion of the United States,* II (New York: G. P. Putnam's Sons, 1891-1912), 30-63. 4 vols.

Sosnowski, Madame S. "The Burning of Columbia," *South Carolina Women of the Confederacy,* ed. Mrs. Thomas Taylor (Columbia: The State Company, 1903), pp. 261-72.

Spencer, Cornelia Phillips. "Old Times in Chapel Hill," *North Carolina University Magazine,* VII (May, 1888), 214-21.

Stinson, Eliza Tillinghast. "How the Arsenal Was Taken," *Our Women in The War. The Lives They Lived; the Deaths They Died. From the Weekly News and Courier, Charleston, S. C.,* ed. Francis Warrington Dawson (Charleston: News and Courier Book Presses, 1885), pp. 22-30.

———. "Taking of the Arsenal," *War Days in Fayetteville, North Carolina* (Fayetteville: Judge Printing Company, 1910), pp. 7-27.

Trezevant, Daniel Heyward. *The Burning of Columbia, South Carolina. A Review of Northern Assertions and Southern Facts.* Columbia: South Carolinian Power Press, 1866.

Trowbridge, John Townsend. *The South: A Tour of Its Battlefields and Ruined Cities. A Journey Through the Desolated States, and Talks with the People.* Hartford: L. Stebbins, 1866.

Warren, Edward. *A Doctor's Experiences in Three Continents.* Baltimore, Cushing and Baily, 1885.

Wheeler, John Hill. *Reminiscences and Memoirs of North Carolina and Eminent North Carolinians.* Columbus: Columbus Printing Work, 1884.

Williams, James Franklin. *Old and New Columbia.* Columbia: Epworth Orphanage Press, 1929.

Wilson, Peter Mitchell. *Southern Exposure.* Chapel Hill: The University of North Carolina Press, 1927.

Wise, John Sergeant. *End of an Era.* New York: Houghton, Mifflin and Company, 1899.

Worth, Josephine Bryan. "Sherman's Raid," *War Days in Fayetteville, North Carolina* (Fayetteville: Judge Printing Company, 1910), pp. 46-56.

Wright, Mrs. D. Giraud. *A Southern Girl in '61—The War-time Memories of a Confederate Senator's Daughter.* New York: Doubleday, Page and Company, 1905.

SECONDARY SOURCES

MILITARY HISTORIES

Allen, W. G. "About the Fight at Fayetteville, N. C." *Confederate Veteran,* XIX (September, 1911), 433-34.

Anderson, Mrs. John Huske. "Confederate Arsenal at Fayetteville, N. C.," *Confederate Veteran,* XXXVI (June, 1928), 222-23, 238.

————. "Memorial on the Battlefield of Bentonville," *Confederate Veteran*, XXXV (October, 1927), 367.

Atkins, Smith Dykins. "With Sherman's Cavalry," *Military Essays and Recollections. Read Before the Commandery of the State of Illinois, Military Order of the Loyal Legion of the United States*, II (Chicago: A. C. McClurg and Company, 1891-1907), 383-98. 4 vols.

Barnwell, Robert Woodward. "Bentonville—The Last Battle of Johnston and Sherman," *Proceedings of the South Carolina Historical Association*, XIII (Annual, 1943), 42-54.

Barrett, John Gilchrist. "General William T. Sherman's Military Operations in North Carolina, March 4, 1865—March 25, 1865." Unpublished Master's thesis, University of North Carolina, 1949.

Belknap, Charles Eugene. "Bentonville: What A Bummer Knows About It," *War Papers Read before the Military Order of the Loyal Legion of the United States, Commandery of the District of Columbia*, War Paper No. 12 (Washington: Published by the Commandery, 1893), pp. 1-10.

Bennett, Sam. "Another Brief Account," *Confederate Veteran*, XIX (September, 1911), 434.

Bradley, Robert H. "First North Carolina Soldier Who Died," *Histories of the Several Regiments and Battalions from North Carolina in the Great War 1861-1865, Written by Members of the Respective Commands*, ed. Walter Clark, V (Goldsboro: Nash Brothers, 1901), 577-79. 5 vols.

Broadfoot, Charles W. "Seventieth Regiment," *Histories of the Several Regiments and Battalions from North Carolina in the Great War 1861-1865, Written by Members of the Respective Commands*, ed. Walter Clark, IV (Goldsboro; Nash Brothers, 1901), 9-23. 5 vols.

Butler, Matthew Calbraith. "The Curtain Falls—Butler Surrenders His Cavalry," *Butler and His Cavalry in the War of Secession, 1861-1865*, ed. Ulysses Robert Brooks (Columbia: The State Company, 1909), pp. 465-77.

————. "General Kilpatrick's Narrow Escape," *Butler and His Cavalry in the War of Secession, 1861-1865*, ed. Ulysses Robert Brooks (Columbia: The State Company, 1909), pp. 443-47.

Carlin, William P. "The Battle of Bentonville," *Sketches of War History of 1861-1865. Papers Read before the Ohio Commandery of the Military Order of the Loyal Legion of the United States*, III (Cincinnati: Robert Clarke and Company, 1888-1908), 231-51. 6 vols.

Cauthen, Charles Edward. *South Carolina Goes to War, 1860-65* (Volume XXXII, Fletcher Melvin Green and others [eds.], *The James Sprunt Hill Studies*). Chapel Hill: The University of North Carolina Press, 1950.

"The Charge on Kilpatrick's Camp," *Butler and His Cavalry in the War of*

Secession, 1861-1865, ed. Ulysses Robert Brooks (Columbia: The State Company, 1909), pp. 417-31.

Cox, Jacob Dolson. *The March to the Sea. Franklin and Nashville.* New York: Charles Scribner's Sons, 1882.

————. "Sherman-Johnston Convention," *Scribners,* XXVIII (October, 1900), 489-505.

Davidson, James Wood, "Who Burned Columbia? A Review of General Sherman's Version of the Affair," *Southern Historical Society Papers,* VII (April, 1879), 185-92.

Davis, Graham. "The Battle of Averasboro," *Southern Historical Society Papers,* VII (March, 1879), 125-26.

Dodson, William Carey. "Burning of the Broad River Bridge," *Confederate Veteran,* XVII (September, 1909), 462-65.

Dougall, Allan H. "Bentonville," *War Papers Read before the Indiana Commandery, Military Order of the Loyal Legion of the United States,* I (Indianapolis: Published by the Commandery, 1898), 212-19. 1 vol.

DuBose, John Witherspoon. "Fayetteville (N. C.) Road Fight," *Confederate Veteran,* XX (February, 1912), 84-86.

Dyer, John Percy. "Northern Relief for Savannah During Sherman's Occupation," *The Journal of Southern History,* XIX (November, 1953), 457-72.

Eddy, Thomas Mears. *The Patriotism of Illinois, A Record of the Civil and Military History of the State in the War of the Union.* 2 vols. Chicago: Clarke and Company, 1866.

Everett, R. O. "War Between the States Ended a Few Miles West of Durham," *The Uplift,* XXVII (June, 1939), 10-17.

Fellers, Bonner. *Wings for Peace.* Chicago: Henry Regney Company, 1953.

Fiebeger, Gustave Joseph. *Campaigns of the American Civil War.* West Point: U. S. Military Academy Printing Office, 1914.

Force, Manning Ferguson. "Marching Across Carolina," *Sketches of War History 1861-1865. Papers Read before the Ohio Commandery of the Loyal Legion of the United States,* I (Cincinnati: R. Clarke and Company, 1888-1908), 1-18. 6 vols.

Ford, Arthur Peronneau. "Last Battles of Hardee's Corps," *The Southern Bivouac,* I (July, 1885), 140-43.

Freeman, John C. "Address on the Civil and Military Career of General William Tecumseh Sherman," *War Papers Read before the Commandery of the State of Wisconsin, Military Order of the Loyal Legion of the United States,* III (Milwaukee: Burdick, Armitage, and Allen, 1903), 296-316. 3 vols.

Fuller, John Frederick Charles. *Decisive Battles of the U. S. A.* New York: Harper and Brothers, 1942.

Graham, William Alexander, Jr. "Adjutant-General's office—January 1, 1863 to the Surrender—The Breakup," *Histories of the Several Regiments and Battalions from North Carolina in the Great War 1861-1865, Written by Members of the Respective Commands,* ed. Walter Clark, V (Goldsboro: Nash Brothers, 1901), 51-65. 5 vols.

Grant, Ulysses Simpson. "Preparing for the Campaigns of '64," *Battles and Leaders of the Civil War,* eds. Robert Underwood Johnson and Clarence Clough Buel, IV (New York: The Century Company, 1888), 97-118. 4 vols.

Hale, Edward Jones, Jr. "Sherman's Bummers and Some of Their Work," *Southern Historical Society Papers,* XII (July-August-September, 1884), 427-28.

Hamilton, Posey. "The Effort to Capture Kilpatrick," *Confederate Veteran,* XXIX (September, 1921), 329.

Hamilton, William Douglas. "In at the Death or the Last Shot at the Confederacy," *Sketches of War History 1861-1865. Papers Read before the Ohio Commandery of the Loyal Legion of the United States,* VI (Cincinnati: R. Clarke and Company, 1908), 287-95. 6 vols.

Hampton, Wade. "Battle of Bentonville," *Battles and Leaders of the Civil War,* eds. Robert Underwood Johnson and Clarence Clough Buel, IV (New York: The Century Company, 1888), 700-5. 4 vols.

Hatcher, Edmund Neuson. *The Last Four Weeks of the War.* Columbus: Edmund N. Hatcher Publisher, 1891.

Hay, Thomas Robson. *Hood's Tennessee Campaign.* New York: W. Neale, 1928.

Henry, Robert Selph. *The Story of the Confederacy.* New York: The New Home Library, 1931.

Hill, James D. "The Burning of Columbia Reconsidered," *The South Atlantic Quarterly,* XXV (July, 1926), 269-82.

Horn, Stanley Fitzgerald. *The Army of Tennessee. A Military History.* New York: Bobbs-Merrill Company, 1941.

Hough, J. M. "Last Days of the Confederacy," *Stories of the Confederacy,* ed. Ulysses Robert Brooks (Columbia: The State Company, 1912), pp. 304-7.

Jones, Joseph A. "Fayetteville Road Fight," *Confederate Veteran,* XIX (September, 1911), 434.

Kennedy, Edward. "Scouting with Wheeler," *Confederate Veteran,* XXVI (August, 1918), 344.

Lamb, William. "Thirty-sixth Regiment," *Histories of the Several Regiments and Battalions from North Carolina in the Great War 1861-1865, Written by Members of the Respective Commands,* ed. Walter Clark, II (Goldsboro: Nash Brothers, 1901), 629-51. 5 vols.

Liddell Hart, Basil Henry. *Strategy, The Indirect Approach.* New York: Praeger, 1954.

Luvaas, Jay. "Bentonville—Johnston's Last Stand." Unpublished article in the possession of Jay Luvaas, Duke University.

Marcy, Henry O. "Sherman's Campaign in the Carolinas," *Civil War Papers Read before the Commandery of the State of Massachusetts, Military Order of the Loyal Legion of the United States,* II (Boston: Published by the Commandery, 1900), 331-38. 2 vols.

McClurg, Alexander C. "The Last Chance of the Confederacy," *The Atlantic Monthly,* L (September, 1882), 389-400.

Milling, Chapman J. "Ilium in Flames," *Confederate Veteran,* XXXVI (April-May-June, 1928), 135-38, 179-82, 212-16.

Morgan, D. B. "Incidents of the Fighting at Aiken, S. C.," *Confederate Veteran,* XXXII (August, 1924), 300-1.

Morris, John M. (ed.). *The Connecticut War Record.* 2 vols. New Haven: Peck, White and Peck, 1863-1865.

Mullen, James M. "Last Days of Johnston's Army," *Southern Historical Society Papers,* XVIII (January, 1890), 97-109.

Naroll, Raoul S. "Lincoln and the Sherman Peace Fiasco—Another Fable?" *Journal of Southern History,* XX (November, 1954), 459-83.

Northrup, Theodore F. "Other Side of the Fayetteville Road Fight," *Confederate Veteran,* XX (September, 1912), 423.

Nourse, Henry S. "The Burning of Columbia, S. C., February 17, 1865," *Operations on the Atlantic Coast, 1861-1865, Virginia 1862, 1864, Vicksburg* (Volume IX, 417-47, *Papers Read before the Military Historical Society of Massachusetts*). Boston: Military Historical Society of Massachusetts, 1912.

Oakey, Daniel. "Marching Through Georgia and the Carolinas," *Battles and Leaders of the Civil War,* eds. Robert Underwood Johnson and Clarence Clough Buel, IV (New York: The Century Company, 1888), 671-679. 4 vols.

Olds, Frederick A. "The Last Big Battle," *Confederate Veteran,* XXXVII (February, 1929), 50-51, 75.

———. "Story of the Surrender of Raleigh to the Federal Army," *The Orphans' Friend and Masonic Journal,* L (December, 1925), 7-8.

Overly, Milford. "The Burning of Columbia, S. C.," *Confederate Veteran,* XI (December, 1903), 550.

――――. "Sherman Helped Starve Union Prisoners," *Confederate Veteran*, XIV (November, 1906), 512.

Pfang, Harry W. "The Surrender Negotiations Between General Johnston and General Sherman," *Military Affairs*, XVI (Summer, 1952), 61-70.

Palfrey, John C. "General Sherman's Plans After the Fall of Atlanta," *The Mississippi Valley, Tennessee, Georgia, Alabama, 1861-1864* (Volume VIII, 493-527, *Papers Read before the Military Historical Society of Massachusetts*) Boston: Military Historical Society of Massachusetts, 1910.

Pickett, William D. "Why General Sherman's Name Is Detested," *Confederate Veteran*, XIV (September, 1906), 397-98.

Putney, Frank H. "Incidents of Sherman's March through the Carolinas," *War Papers Read before the Commandery of the State of Wisconsin, Military Order of the Loyal Legion of the United States*, III (Milwaukee: Burdick, Armitage, Allen, 1903), 381-87. 3 vols.

Ravenel, Samuel W. "Ask the Survivors of Bentonville," *Confederate Veteran*, XVIII (March, 1910), 124.

Reid, Whitelaw. *Ohio in the War, Her Statesmen, Generals and Soldiers.* 2 volumes. Columbus: Electric Publishing Company, 1893.

Ricks, Augustus J. "Carrying the News of Lee's Surrender to the Army of the Ohio," *Sketches of War History, 1861-1865. Papers Read before the Ohio Commandery of the Military Order of the Loyal Legion of the United States*, I (Cincinnati: R. Clarke and Company, 1888-1908), 234-46. 6 vols.

Rhodes, James Ford. "Who Burned Columbia?" *The American Historical Review*, VII (April, 1902), 485-93.

――――. "Sherman's March to the Sea," *The American Historical Review*, VI (April, 1901), 466-74.

Robertson, John. *Michigan in the War.* Lansing: W. S. George and Company, 1880.

Ropes, John Codman. "General Sherman," *Critical Sketches of Some of the Federal and Confederate Commanders*, ed. Theodore Frelinghuysen Dwight (Volume X, 125-52, *Papers Read before the Military Historical Society of Massachusetts*). Boston: Houghton, Mifflin and Company, 1895.

Sanders, Robert W. "The Battle of Bentonville," *Confederate Veteran*, XXXIV (August, 1926), 299-300.

Shand, Robert W. "Bridges in the Vicinity of Columbia," *Confederate Veteran*, XIX (February, 1911), 57.

Sheppard, Eric William. *The American Civil War 1864-65.* Aldershot: Gale and Polden, 1938.

Sherman, William Tecumseh. "The Grand Strategy of the Last Year of the War," *Battles and Leaders of the Civil War*, eds. Robert Underwood

Johnson and Clarence Clough Buel, IV (New York: The Century Company, 1888), 247-59. 4 vols.

Sill, Edward. "Who is Responsible for the Destruction of the City of Columbia, S. C. on the Night of 17 February, 1865," *Land We Love,* IV (March, 1868), 361-69.

Slocum, Henry Warner. "Final Operations of Sherman's Army," *Battles and Leaders of the Civil War,* eds. Robert Underwood Johnson and Clarence Clough Buel, IV (New York: The Century Company, 1888), 754-59. 4 vols.

——. "Sherman's March from Savannah to Bentonville," *Battles and Leaders of the Civil War,* eds. Robert Underwood Johnson and Clarence Clough Buel, IV (New York: The Century Company, 1888), 681-96. 4 vols.

Smith, Jessie S. "On the Battlefield of Averasboro, N. C.," *Confederate Veteran,* XXXIV (February, 1926), 48-49.

Spencer, Cornelia Phillips. *The Last Ninety Days of the War in North Carolina.* New York: Watchman Publishing Company, 1866.

Thomas L. P. "Their Last Battle," *Southern Historical Society Papers,* XXIX (January-December, 1901), 215-22.

Turner, Charles Wilson. "The Virginia Central Railroad at War, 1861-65," *The Journal of Southern History,* XII (November, 1946), 510-33.

Walters, John Bennett. "General William T. Sherman and Total War," *The Journal of Southern History,* XIV (November, 1948), 451-52.

——. "General William T. Sherman and Total War." Unpublished Ph.D. dissertation, Vanderbilt University, 1947.

Ward, Dallas T. *The Last Flag of Truce.* Franklinton: Privately printed, 1914.

Watkins, E. W. "Another Account," *Confederate Veteran,* XX (February, 1912), 84.

Weeks, Stephen Beauregard. "University of North Carolina in the Civil War," *Southern Historical Society Papers,* XXIV (January, 1896), 1-40.

Wells, Edward Laight. "A Morning Call on General Kilpatrick," *Southern Historical Society Papers,* XII (March, 1884), 123-30.

——. "Who Burnt Columbia?" *Southern Historical Society Papers,* X (March, 1882), 109-19.

"Where the War Between the States Ended," *The North Carolina Teacher,* I (November, 1924), 81-82.

"Who Burned Columbia?—General Sherman's Latest Story Examined," *Southern Historical Society Papers,* XIII (January-December, 1885), 448-53.

Witcher, J. C. "Shannon's Scouts—Kilpatrick," *Confederate Veteran,* XIV (November, 1906), 511-12.

GENERAL HISTORIES

Abbott, John Stevens Cabot. *The History of the Civil War in America.* 2 vols. Norwich: Henry Bill Publishing Company, 1873.

Ashe, Samuel A'Court. *History of North Carolina.* 2 vols. Volume I. Greensboro: Charles L. Van Noppen, 1908. Volume II. Raleigh: Edwards and Broughton Printing Company, 1925.

Connor, Robert Diggs Wimberly. *History of North Carolina.* 6 vols. New York: Lewis Publishing Company, 1919.

Guernsey, Alfred H., and Henry M. Alden (eds.). *Harper's Pictorial History of the Civil War.* 2 vols. Chicago: The Puritan Press Company, 1894.

Henderson, Archibald. *North Carolina. The Old North State and the New.* 5 vols. New York: Lewis Publishing Company, 1941.

Lossing, Benson John. *Pictorial History of the Civil War in the United States of America.* 3 vols. Hartford: Thomas Belknap, 1877.

Pollard, Edward Albert. *Southern History of the War.* New York: Charles B. Richardson, 1866.

Randall, James Garfield. *The Civil War and Reconstruction.* New York: D. C. Heath and Company, 1937.

Rhodes, James Ford. *History of the United States from the Compromise of 1850.* 8 vols. New York: The MacMillan Company, 1904.

Snowden, Yates (ed.). *History of South Carolina.* 5 vols. New York: Lewis Publishing Company, 1920.

Wallace, David Duncan. *The History of South Carolina,* 2 vols. New York: The American Society, 1934.

NEWSPAPERS, PERIODICALS, AND PERIODICAL ARTICLES

Boyd, David French. "General W. T. Sherman, His Early Life in the South and His Relations with Southern Men," *Confederate Veteran,* XVIII (September, 1910), 409-14.

Brown, John Mason. "Man and the Myth," *Saturday Review of Literature,* XXXVI (January 17, 1953), 25-28.

The Century Illustrated Monthly Magazine, I-V, 1881-1884.

Chapel Hill Weekly, 1935.

Charlotte Observer, 1927.

Coulter, Ellis Merton. "Sherman and the South," *North Carolina Historical Review,* VIII (January, 1931), 41-54.

Cunningham, S. A. "Major Boyd's Sketch of General Sherman," *Confederate Veteran,* XVIII (October, 1910), 453-54.

Fayetteville Observer, 1928-1939.

Goldsboro News-Argus, 1947.

Harpers New Monthly Magazine, XXIX-XXXIII, 1864-1866.

The Independent, L-LII, 1898-1900.

Indiana Magazine of History, 50 vols., 1905-1954.

Liddell Hart, Basil Henry. "The Psychology of a Commander. General R. E. Lee: His Latest Biography," Typed copy in the possession of Francis Butler Simkins, Longwood College.

Massey, Mary Elizabeth. "Southern Refugees in the Civil War," *North Carolina Historical Review,* XX (January-April, 1943), 1-21, 132-56.

The Nation, I-IV, 1865-1867.

Newspaper clippings. Over fifty thousand mounted items pertaining to North Caroliniana from about 1830 to the present. North Carolina Collection, University of North Carolina.

Owsley, Frank Lawrence. "Defeatism in the Confederacy," *North Carolina Historical Review,* III (July, 1926), 446-56.

The Palimpsest, 35 vols., 1920-1954.

Raleigh News and Observer, 1909-1943.

Ross, Earle Dudley. "Northern Sectionalism in the Civil War Era," *The Iowa Journal of History and Politics,* XXX (October, 1932), 454-512.

South Carolina Historical and Genealogical Magazine, 54 vols., 1900-1953.

The Southern Bivouac, I-V, 1883-1887.

Virginia Magazine of History and Biography, 55 vols., 1893-1947.

Wiley, Bell Irwin. "Billy Yank and the Black Folk," *Journal of Negro History,* XXXVI (January, 1951), 35-52.

———. "Billy Yank and the Brass," *Journal of Illinois State Historical Society,* XLIII (Winter, 1950), 249-64.

———. "Billy Yank Down South," *The Virginia Quarterly Review,* XXVI (Autumn,, 1950), 559-75.

Wisconsin Magazine of History, 36 vols., 1917-1953.

Woody, Robert Hilliard. "Some Aspects of the Economic Condition of South Carolina After the Civil War," *North Carolina Historical Review,* VII (July, 1930), 346-63.

Yates, Richard E. "Governor Vance and the End of the War in North Carolina," *North Carolina Historical Review,* XVIII (October, 1941), 315-38.

BIOGRAPHIES

Ballard, Colin Robert. *The Military Genius of Abraham Lincoln.* New York: The World Publishing Company, 1952.

Bowman, Samuel Millard and Richard Bache Irwin. *Sherman and His Compaigns, A Military Biography.* New York: Charles B. Richardson, 1865.

Boyd, James Penny. *The Life of General William T. Sherman.* Philadelphia: Publishers Union, 1891.

Brockett, Linus Pierpont. *Our Great Captains. Grant, Sherman, Thomas, Sheridan and Farragut.* New York: Charles B. Richardson, 1865.

Burne, Alfred Higgins. *Lee, Grant and Sherman. A Study in Leadership in the 1864-65 Campaign.* New York: Charles Scribner's Sons, 1939.

Chamberlain, Hope Summerell. *Old Days in Chapel Hill, Being the Life and Letters of Cornelia Phillips Spencer.* Chapel Hill: The University of North Carolina Press, 1926.

Dawson, George Francis. *Life and Services of General John A. Logan as Soldier and Statesman.* Chicago: Belford, Clarke and Company, 1887.

Dodson, William Carey. *Campaigns of Wheeler and His Cavalry 1862-1865 from Material Furnished by General Joseph Wheeler to Which Is Added His Concise and Graphic Account of the Santiago Campaign of 1898.* Atlanta: Hudgins Publishing Company, 1899.

Dowd, Clement. *Life of Zebulon B. Vance.* Charlotte: Observer Publishing and Printing House, 1897.

DuBose, John Witherspoon. *General Joseph Wheeler and the Army of Tennessee.* New York: Neale Publishing Company, 1912.

Dyer, John Percy. *"Fightin' Joe" Wheeler.* Baton Rouge: Louisiana State University Press, 1941.

Fleming, Walter Lynwood. *General W. T. Sherman as a College President.* Cleveland: Arthur H. Clark Company, 1912.

Force, Manning Ferguson. *General Sherman.* New York: D. Appleton and Company, 1899.

Fuller, John Frederick Charles. *The Generalship of Ulysses S. Grant.* London: Murray, 1929.

Garland, Hamlin. *Ulysses S. Grant, His Life and Character.* New York: Doubleday and McClure Company, 1889.

Headley, Joel Tyler. *Grant and Sherman; Their Campaigns and Generals.* New York: E. B. Treat and Company, 1865.

Johnson, Bradley Tyler. *A Memoir of the Life and Public Service of Joseph E. Johnston, Once Quartermaster General of the Army of the United States and a General in the Army of the Confederate States of America.* Baltimore: R. H. Woodward and Company, 1891.

Johnson, Willis Fletcher. *Life of William Tecumseh Sherman, Late Retired General, U. S. A.* Philadelphia: Edgewood Publishing Company, 1891.

Lewis, Lloyd. *Sherman, Fighting Prophet.* New York: Harcourt, Brace and Company, 1932.

Liddell Hart, Basil Henry. *Sherman, The Genius of the Civil War.* London, Ernest Benn, 1930.

———. *Sherman, Soldier, Realist, American.* New York: Dodd, Mead, and Company, 1929.

Fletcher, Thomas Clement (ed.). *Life and Reminiscences of General William T. Sherman by Distinguished Men of His Time.* Baltimore: R. H. Woodward Company, 1891.

Macartney, Clarence Edward. *Grant and His Generals.* New York: The McBride Company, 1953.

McCormick, Robert Rutherford. *Ulysses S. Grant, The Great Soldier of America.* D. Appleton-Century Company, 1934.

Miers, Earl Schenck. *The General Who Marched to Hell; William Tecumseh Sherman and His March to Fame and Infamy.* New York: Alfred Knopf, 1951.

Roman, Alfred. *The Military Operations of General Beauregard in the War Between the States 1861-65 Including a Brief Sketch and Narrative of Service in the War with Mexico.* New York: Harper and Brattens, 1884.

Russell, Phillips. *The Woman Who Rang the Bell, The Story of Cornelia Phillips Spencer.* Chapel Hill: The University of North Carolina Press, 1949.

Seitz, Don Carlos. *Braxton Bragg, General of the Confederacy.* Columbia: The State Company, 1924.

Senour, Fauntleroy. *Major General William T. Sherman and His Campaigns.* Chicago: Henry M. Sherwood, 1865.

Slocum, Charles Elihu. *Life and Services of Major-General Henry Warner Slocum, Officer in the United States Army.* Toledo: Slocum Publishing Company, 1913.

Wellman, Manly Wade. *Giant in Gray, A Biography of Wade Hampton of South Carolina.* New York: Charles Scribner's Sons, 1949.

Wells, Edward Laight. *Hampton and His Cavalry in '64.* Richmond: Johnson Publishing Company, 1899.

———. *Hampton and Reconstruction.* Columbia: The State Company, 1907.

MONOGRAPHS AND SPECIAL STUDIES

Adams, George Washington. *Doctors in Blue. The Medical History of the Union Army in the Civil War.* New York: Henry Shuman, 1952.

Anderson, Mrs. John Huske. *North Carolina Women of the Confederacy.* Fayetteville: Privately printed, 1926.

Andrews, Matthew Page. *The Women of the South in War Times.* Baltimore: The Norman, Remington Company, 1927.

Battle, Kemp Plummer. *History of the University of North Carolina.* 2 vols. Raleigh: Edwards and Broughton. 1907.

Black, Robert C. *The Railroads of the Confederacy.* Chapel Hill: The University of North Carolina Press, 1952.

Boddie, William Willis. *History of Williamsburg. Something About the People of Williamsburg County, S. C., from the First Settlement by Europeans about 1705 until 1923*. Columbia: The State Company, 1923.

Boyd, William Kenneth. *The Story of Durham—City of the New South*. Durham: Duke University Press, 1925.

Boynton, Henry Van Ness. *Sherman's Historical Raid. The Memoirs in the Light of the Record*. Cincinnati: Wilstach, Baldwin and Company, 1875.

Chamberlain, Hope Summerell. *History of Wake County North Carolina with Sketches of Those Who Have Most Influenced Its Development*. Raleigh: Edwards and Broughton, 1922.

Green, Edwin Luther. *A History of the University of South Carolina*. Columbia: The State Company, 1916.

Hay, Thomas Robson. "The Question of Arming the Slaves," *Mississippi Valley Historical Review,* VI (June, 1919), 34-74.

Henderson, Archibald, *The Campus of the First State University*. Chapel Hill: The University of North Carolina Press, 1949.

Hollis, Daniel Walker. *University of South Carolina—Vol. I—South Carolina College*. Columbia: University of South Carolina Press, 1951.

Kirkland, Thomas J. and Robert M. Kennedy. *Historic Camden*. Columbia: The State Company, 1926.

Link, Arthur Stanley. "A History of the Buildings at the University of North Carolina." Unpublished honors essay, University of North Carolina, 1941.

Moulton, Charles William. *The Review of General Sherman's Memoirs Examined Chiefly in the Light of its Own Evidence*. Cincinnati: Robert Clarke and Company, 1875.

Oates, John A. *The Story of Fayetteville and the Upper Cape Fear*. Charlotte: Dawd Press, 1950.

O'Neall, John Belton and John Abney Chapman. *The Annals of Newberry . in Two Parts*. Newberry: Aull and Hauseal, 1892.

Simkins, Francis Butler and James Welch Patton. *The Women of the Confederacy*. Richmond: Garrett and Massie, 1936.

Simkins, Francis Butler and Robert Hilliard Woody. *South Carolina During Reconstruction*. Chapel Hill: The University of North Carolina Press, 1932.

Smith, Edward Parmelee. *Incidents of the United States Christian Commission*. Philadelphia: J. B. Lippincott and Company, 1869.

Tatum, Georgia Lee. *Disloyalty in the Confederacy*. Chapel Hill: The University of North Carolina Press, 1934.

PAMPHLETS

Barnwell, Robert Woodward, Sr. *Sherman and Grant Contrasted.* n.p., n.p. n.d. South Caroliniana Library, University of South Carolina.

Boyd, David French. *General W. T. Sherman as a College President.* Baton Rouge, Ortlieb Printing House, 1910.

The Burning of Columbia—I. Letter of General Wade Hampton, June 24, 1873, With Appendix.—II. Report of Committee of Citizens, Ex-Chancellor J. P. Carroll, Chairman, May, 1866. Charleston: Evans, Walker and Cogswell Company, 1888.

A Checkered Life Being a Brief History of the Countess Pourtales, Formerly Miss Marie Boozer of Columbia, S. C., Her Birth, Early Life, Marriage, Adventures in New York and Europe, Separation from Her Husband, Marriage to an Irish Count, Off to China, Etc., Etc., Etc., by One Who Knows. Columbia: Daily Phoenix, 1878.

The City of Raleigh, Historical Sketches from Its Foundation, A Review of the City in All Its Varied Aspects—Commercial, Industrial, Statistical, Religious, Social, Etc. Raleigh: Edwards and Broughton, 1887.

Cook, Harvey Toliver. *Sherman's March Through South Carolina in 1865.* Greenville: n.p., 1938.

Criticisms on the Surrender of Johnston. n.p., n.p., n.d. North Carolina Collection, University of North Carolina.

Fleming Walter Lynwood. *W. T. Sherman as a History Teacher.* Baton Rouge: Ortlieb Printing House, 1910.

The Kid Soldiers of the Sixties. Reprinted from the Newberry Observer, 1915. n.p., n.p., 1916. Confederate States Pamphlets, Duke University Library.

Love, James Stanhope. *The Burning of Columbia, A Wonderful Story Wonderfully Written with a Sketch of My Life and Work and Other Items.* n.p., n.p., 1936. South Caroliniana Library, University of South Carolina.

McArthur, Henry Clay. *Capture and Destruction of Columbia, South Carolina, February 17, 1865.* Washington: n.p., 1911.

Official Report of the Historical Commission of the Grand Camp, Confederate Veterans, Department of Virginia. Nashville: Confederate Veteran, 1904.

Proceedings of the Stockholders of the Wilmington, Charlotte and Rutherford Railroad Company. Wilmington: William H. Bernard's Printing and Publishing House, 1866.

Report of the Proceedings of the Second Annual Meeting of the Society of the Army of Tennessee Held at St. Louis, Missouri, November 13-14, 1867. St. Louis: Missouri Democrat Book and Job Printing House, 1868.

Waddell, Alfred Moore. *The Last Year of the War in North Carolina, In-*

cluding Plymouth, Fort Fisher, and Bentonville. Richmond: William Ellis Jones, 1888.

Who Burnt Columbia?—Part 1st—Official Depositions of William Tecumseh Sherman, General of the Army of the United States, and General O. O. Howard, U. S. A., for the Defense; and Extracts from Some of the Depositions for the Claimants. Filed in Certain Claims V United States, Pending before the Mixed Commission on British and American Claims in Washington, D. C. Charleston: Walker, Evans and Cogswell, 1873.

BIBLIOGRAPHICAL AIDS

Bartlett, John Russell. *The Literature of the Rebellion. A Catalogue of Books and Pamphlets Relating to the Civil War in the United States and on Subjects Growing Out of that Event Together with Works on American Slavery, and Essays from Reviews and Magazines on the Same Subjects.* Boston: Draper and Holliday, 1866.

Bibliography of State Participation in the Civil War 1861-1865. Washington: Government Printing Office, 1913.

Catalogue of the Library of Brevet Lieutenant-Colonel John Page Nicholson Relating to the War of Rebellion 1861-1866. Philadelphia: Privately printed, 1914.

Coulter, Ellis Merton. *Travels in the Confederate States. A Bibliography.* Norman: University of Oklahoma Press, 1948.

Greogray, Winifred (ed.). *American Newspapers 1821-1936. A Union List of Files Available in the United States and Canada.* New York: The H. W. Wilson Company, 1937.

Ryan, Daniel J. *The Civil War Literature of Ohio. A Bibliography with Explanatory and Historical Notes.* Cleveland: The Burrows Brothers Company, 1911.

Index

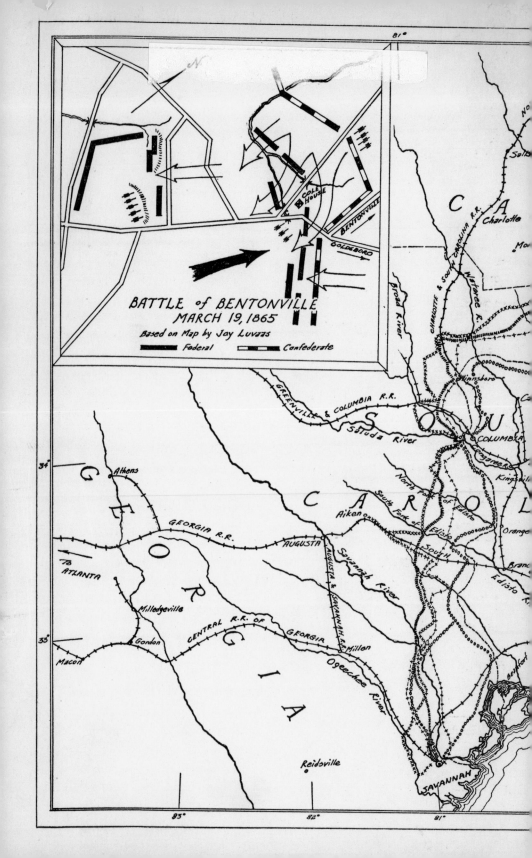

BATTLE of BENTONVILLE
MARCH 19, 1865
Based on Map by Jay Luvaas
━━━ Federal   ▭▭▭ Confederate